PREPARE!

A Weekly Worship Planbook for Pastors and Musicians

2011–2012

David L. Bone
and
Mary J. Scifres

Abingdon Press
Nashville

PREPARE! A WEEKLY WORSHIP PLANBOOK FOR PASTORS AND MUSICIANS 2011–2012

Copyright © 2011 by Abingdon Press

All rights reserved.
Worksheets in this book may be reproduced by local congregations, provided the following credit line and copyright notice appear on all copies:
"From *Prepare!* Copyright © 2011 by Abingdon Press. Used by permission."
No other part of this work may be reproduced or transmitted in any form or by any means, electronic or mechanical, including photocopying and recording, or by any information storage or retrieval system, except as may be expressly permitted by the 1976 Copyright Act or in writing from the publisher. Requests for permission should be addressed to Abingdon Press, P.O. Box 801, 201 Eighth Avenue South, Nashville, TN 37202-0801 or e-mailed to permissions@umpublishing.org.

This book is printed on acid-free paper.

ISBN 978-1-4267-1016-2

Scripture quotations in this publication are from the New Revised Standard Version of the Bible, copyright 1989, Division of Christian Education of the National Council of the Churches of Christ in the United States of America. Used by permission. All rights reserved.

11 12 13 14 15 16 17 18 19 20 — 10 9 8 7 6 5 4 3 2 1

MANUFACTURED IN THE UNITED STATES OF AMERICA

Do you have the book you need?

We want you to have the best planner, designed to meet your specific needs. How do you know if you have the right resource? Simply complete this one-question quiz:

Do you lead worship in a United Methodist congregation?

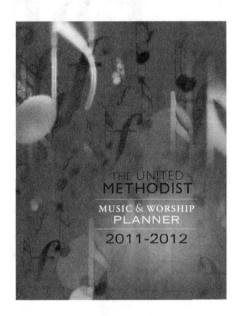

Yes.

Use *The United Methodist Music and Worship Planner 2011 – 2012*
(ISBN: 9781426710179)

No.

Use *Prepare! A Weekly Worship Planbook for Pastors and Musicians 2011 – 2012*
(ISBN: 9781426710162)

To order these resources, call Cokesbury Music Service toll-free at 1-877-877-8674, visit your local Cokesbury store, or shop online at www.cokesbury.com. Do you find yourself rushing at the last minute to order your new planner? Subscribe today and receive your new *The United Methodist Music and Worship Planner* or *Prepare!* automatically next year and every year. Call toll-free 1-800-672-1789 to request subscription.

 Abingdon Press

USING *PREPARE!*

Prepare! is designed to give you as many ideas as possible about a given worship service. Use it along with a worship plan notebook that you create, and a copy of your church's hymnal. Features of *Prepare!* include:

- New in 2011! The hymnal *Evangelical Lutheran Worship* has been added to *Prepare!* These hymns are noted with the prefix "EL."
- Each week, **Primary Hymns and Songs for the Day** are suggested first. These suggestions include various helps for singing the hymns. These hymns and songs have the closest relationship to the scriptures and are widely known.
- The suggestions for each week are chosen to suggest a wide variety of styles.
- Each item is referenced to scripture or occasion.
- At least one "Communion hymn" is recommended for the first Sunday of each month and liturgical season. Where space permits, Communion hymns appropriate to the lections are suggested on other Sundays as well.
- Opening (O) and Closing (C) hymns are suggested for each worship service.
- **Additional Hymn Suggestions** contain a notation as to the copyright status of the hymns. If a hymn is in the public domain, it is marked (PD). This means that you may legally copy this hymn without obtaining further permission. You may find this useful if a hymn is not in your hymnal. Please be advised: The (PD) mark only refers only the hymn that it follows, not all hymns in the listing. Many times an arrangement in one hymnal may be public domain but another arrangement of the same hymn tune in another hymnal may be copyrighted.
- Suggestions for "Visuals" are offered for each service. See the article "Visuals in Worship" (page 6) for discussion on these suggestions. "Visuals" are found under each week's **Other Suggestions** list. They have been compiled by the Reverend Ashley M. Calhoun, who is known for his inventive use of "found" items in creating visual worship settings. Worship committees and altar guilds can use these ideas to create unique worship centers and altar pieces.
- *Prepare!* also includes **Additional Contemporary Suggestions** for use in contemporary, blended, and emergent worship services. Several resources are referenced in this section. Music suggested includes praise choruses, global and ethnic music, folk music, and meditative music from traditions such as Taizé and Iona. Please note that contemporary songs may also be listed under **Hymn Suggestions**, **Vocal Solos**, or **Other Suggestions**. Find more information on page 7.

ONE WORD OF ADVICE: Be sure to consult all the suggestions regardless of the type of service you are planning. In the changing world of worship, no one style defines a song or a worship service. Many items appropriate for contemporary and emergent styles are listed under the **Additional Hymn Suggestions,** and many resources for traditional and blended services can be found in the **Additional Contemporary Suggestions** list. **Vocal Solos**, **Anthems**, and **Other Suggestions** may be appropriate for congregational use as well. Don't let the "category" here deter you from using any item that will enhance your worship service. Planners should consult all lists when choosing congregational music.

All the scriptures in the Revised Common Lectionary are listed for each day. From the Second Sunday After Pentecost to Christ the King Sunday, the lectionary includes two patterns of readings:

1) One pattern includes semicontinuous readings from the Hebrew Scriptures, Epistles, and Gospels. These readings are not necessarily related but allow for a sequential experience of the biblical narrative. This is the pattern used to determine which scripture texts are included in *Prepare!* It is the pattern followed by most users of the hymnals referenced.

2) In the second pattern, the Hebrew Scripture is chosen to relate to the Gospel passage. This pattern is used primarily in traditions where Communion is celebrated at every service of worship. These lections are noted at the beginning of the **Other Suggestions**. Some items are also referenced to these lections.

Worship planners may choose to follow the pattern that best serves the needs and traditions of their individual churches. Neither pattern is necessarily better than the other; they are simply different ways of offering Scriptures in the worship setting over a three-year cycle in the church.

When planning any worship service, it is always best to start with the scripture text and let it guide your thoughts and plans. If your church is not using the Revised Common Lectionary, but you know what the scripture will be for a service, look up that scripture in the **Index of Scriptures Referenced** on pages 134. Nonlectionary worship planners may wish to keep the three most recent volumes of *Prepare!* on hand.

As you read and study the scripture passages, read all of the suggested hymn texts. The hymns may remind you of anthems, solos, or keyboard selections. It is wise to mark your hymnal with the dates individual hymns are sung to avoid singing some too frequently. The **Hymn Resources** (see page 7) can enhance congregational singing but should be used sparingly.

Use a three-ring binder to organize your plans. For each service of worship, include a copy of one of the **Worship Planning Sheets** found on pages 138–140 (or design your own!), along with blank paper for listing further ideas. Do not simply "fill in the blanks" for each service, but use the planning sheets to guide your work.

If *Prepare!* is new to you, you will want to be aware of several other items. The **Vocal Solos** are taken from a group of eleven collections that range from contemporary settings of hymn texts and praise choruses to spirituals to well-known classics (see page 7). Augment these with resources from your own library.

The **Anthems** sections include new works as well as generally known works that are already in many church choral libraries. Your study of the scripture and hymn texts will lead you to anthems in your church library that are appropriate.

The **Other Suggestions** for each service are varied in their intent and function, including visual ideas, words for worship, and choral response ideas. Add to this list as you study the scripture and hymn texts.

Use the suggestions in *Prepare!* along with your own page of ideas to begin making decisions about worship. Will the choir sing a "Call to Worship"? Can a hymn verse serve as a prayer response? Can a particular anthem or vocal solo give direction to the sermon? What prayers will be used?

Once your decisions are made, complete the **Worship Planning Sheet**. Make a separate list of tasks related to that service. Planning worship is an awesome responsibility, but one that can be accomplished with an organized effort along with spiritual guidance.

PLANNING CORPORATE WORSHIP WITH A TEAM

Mary J. Scifres

Planning worship provides an important opportunity for church staff members to work together as a team. Such planning also provides an opportunity for worship committees to find an important aspect of their ministry. Unfortunately, our fast-paced society and the production focus in our current culture push far too many pastors into a solo effort in worship planning. We call this all-too-common worship planning model "The Lonesome Approach."

The Lonesome Approach—A Nonteam Model for Worship Planning

- Preaching pastor picks the scripture readings, prayers, hymns, and sermon title.
- Church secretary or pastor types and prints bulletins.
- Musician(s) pick up note in mailbox with hymn numbers for coming Sunday. If time permits, choir rehearses hymns during evening rehearsal along with anthem(s) and choral responses for Sunday.
- Preaching pastor writes sermon.
- Lay liturgist arrives early to review worship plans.
- Worship commences.

Is this how worship most often comes together in your church? If so, you may want to consider other models for planning worship. Although some find this "Lonesome Approach" convenient, worship planning with this approach is neither integrated into nor representative of the worshiping community. Within the book you hold in your hands, we hope that pastors, musicians, and worship leaders find encouragement and assistance for planning worship in cooperation with one another. Perhaps the "Lonesome Approach" will one day be the exception rather than the rule.

We suggest that pastors, musicians, and worship leaders consider a "**Team-based Approach**" to planning. First, gather a team: review the talents of your church for artists, visionaries, leaders, organizers, and workers. Choose team members, balancing gifts and talents, as well as time and commitment levels. Members of the worship planning team can expect to meet at least bi-annually. Some worship teams find weekly, monthly, or seasonal planning meetings helpful, but even two meetings a year can improve communication and coordination efforts immensely. Consider hiring worship consultants, such as Mary Scifres or Marcia McFee, to run planning retreats—a helpful gift to many worship-planning teams and pastors. Organizations such as The Fellowship of United Methodists in Music and Worship Arts often provide convocations and training events to assist worship leaders and teams in developing skills for planning worship as well.

Many models exist for the actual planning; one model is offered here. In order to use this model, the team needs several copies of *Prepare!* (particularly for use of scripture readings and hymn lists), a Bible, hymnals, and—for United Methodists—*The United Methodist Book of Worship.* Musicians may find it helpful to have copies of the music collections suggested in *Prepare!* as well as a single copy file of the anthem collection and praise song collection of your church. Distribute copies of the **Worship Planning Sheets** from pages 138–140 to each team member for each Sunday being discussed.

A Team-based Model for Worship Planning

1) Prior to meeting, pastor(s) prepares scripture and sermon themes; musicians prepare repertoire lists as well as special performance plans.
2) Team meets for a designated time period. (A retreat setting is particularly helpful, followed by monthly or weekly meetings.)
3) Open meeting with prayer and discussion of worship. Worship leaders may bring a diversity of views about the meaning and focus of worship, enhancing the process by expressing philosophies and values honestly.
4) Read or review scriptures, with emphasis on the pastor's primary focus.
5) The pastor(s) introduces and outlines sermon topics or emphases.
6) Discuss and outline seasonal needs.
7) Team chooses hymns, keeping in mind thematic and scriptural emphases; musical abilities, sermon topics, congregational hymn preferences, and plans to introduce new music.
8) Introduce and discuss special ideas or plans for specific worship services (e.g., Palm Sunday cantata, Christmas Eve candlelight service, Children's Sunday).
9) Choose spoken words (prayers, responsive readings, blessings). The entire team or part of the team may do this, depending on number of participants.
10) Choose vocal, choral, and keyboard music (entire team or part of team).
11) Review services for integration, unity, and diversity.
12) Address specific service logistics.
13) Close with worship, music, and prayer.

In any one of these steps, all members of the planning team may have valuable input. A pastor may have an idea for a choral anthem to enhance a sermon idea; a musician may have an insight into a sermon topic as it relates to the congregation. At any of these steps, all members of the team will find helpful suggestions in *Prepare!* Each week's entry provides the text of each scripture reading, season and liturgical color, suggestions of visual images for artists, hymn and music suggestions, liturgical suggestions, and other ideas that may spark interest in an innovative type of worship service.

When worship leaders, pastors, musicians, visual artists, and other worship leaders coordinate their work, they can educate one another about preparation timing and skills. Pastors need to know the time requirements for planning music. Choir directors can alert the pastor to the time needed to choose, obtain, and rehearse an anthem prior to a worship performance. Organists and pianists can communicate the time needed to choose, obtain, and rehearse instrumental music prior to use in worship. Likewise, organists, pianists, and choir directors need to advise the pastor of the time needed to prepare congregational music for use in worship. (Pastors often discover that both playing and singing improve greatly on hymns rehearsed a few weeks in advance!) Finally, the musicians can share with the pastor their visions for music ministry in worship.

Pastors, likewise, need to inform musicians of how they might interact not only in worship planning but also in worship leadership. Some pastors establish cues to alert musicians when light background music is needed during worship. A pastor can educate musicians about their roles as worship leaders. Additionally, the pastor can communicate with the musicians what her or his visions are for music ministry in worship.

These initial communications are essential when worship planners begin to work together and also as personnel changes affect the worship planning team. Constant communication and interaction in the creative and logistical planning processes of worship flow through the worship leaders into the congregation, with the unity of the worship leadership team strengthening the entire worshiping community.

Worship planning need not be a point of departure for worship staff. Rather, it can be a point of unity and team-building. The team that works together models corporate worship for the congregation. If we expect people to walk in the church doors on Sunday mornings from their many walks of life to have a corporate experience, we need to avoid individual approaches in planning worship and begin team planning. In so doing, we will find that the Holy Spirit has found a new freedom in which to work within the body of Christ.

VISUALS IN WORSHIP

Ashley M. Calhoun

The suggestions for visuals in this planner can help worship leaders use objects and images to increase the impact of the gospel on people who are increasingly visually oriented. These suggestions can be incorporated into many visual elements: hanging and processional banners, worship settings (whether on the altar, in the chancel, or in the narthex), worship folder covers, bulletin boards, screen visuals, and other graphic arts. The ideas can also suggest ways to use classical and contemporary works of art, sculpture, needlework, and photography in worship services.

With more churches incorporating screens and video walls into their worship spaces, there is a tremendous potential for the use of still or moving imagery. Also, interpretive movement and drama can be very strong in their visual impact.

The visual suggestions in *Prepare!* have several characteristics. The suggestions are meant not to give detailed plans but to spark your imagination and creativity. Some are drawn literally from the lessons; others are thematic. The suggestions are organized by reference to the lectionary passages:

O Old Testament reading
P Psalm reading or Canticle
E Epistle or New Testament reading
G Gospel reading

Chapter and verse numbers indicate actual phrases in the scripture passage that can serve as visual elements.

Themes such as "forgiveness," "love," and "rejoicing" encourage creative use of video and photographic images of people engaged in demonstrating those themes.

So much about worship is visual and intended to strengthen the proclamation of the gospel. The visual elements that fill the worship space send a message—positive or negative. The church year is a treasure trove of color, texture, symbolism, and visual imagery. Special Sundays and special days in cultural and denominational calendars also offer opportunities for visual expression. Evaluate the visual aspects of your worship services and find ways to enhance the worship experience with a more thoughtful use of visual elements.

RESOURCE KEY

B   Forbis, Wesley, ed. *The Baptist Hymnal.* Nashville: Convention Press, 1991.

C   Merrick, Daniel, and David Polk, ed. *Chalice Hymnal.* St. Louis: Chalice Press, 1996.

E   *The Hymnal 1982.* New York: The Church Hymnal Corporation, 1985.

EL   *Evangelical Lutheran Worship.* Minneapolis: Augsburg Fortress, 2006.

F   Bock, Fred, ed. *Hymns for the Family of God.* Nashville: Paragon Associates, Inc., 1976.

L   *Lutheran Book of Worship.* Minneapolis: Augsburg Publishing House, 1978.

N   Clyde, Arthur G., ed. *The New Century Hymnal.* Cleveland: The Pilgrim Press, 1995.

P   McKim, LindaJo, ed. *The Presbyterian Hymnal.* Louisville: Westminster/John Knox Press, 1990.

S   Hickman, Hoyt L., ed. *The Faith We Sing.* Nashville: Abingdon Press, 2000.

SF   *Sing the Faith.* Louisville, Westminster John Knox Press, 2003.

UM   Young, Carlton R., ed. *The United Methodist Hymnal.* Nashville: The United Methodist Publishing House, 1989.

VU   Ambrose, John E., ed. *Voices United.* Etobicoke, Ontario, Canada: The United Church Publishing House, 1996.

W   Batastini, Robert J., ed. *Worship.* Chicago: GIA Publications, Inc., 1986.

HYMN RESOURCES

S-1   Smith, Gary Alan, ed. *The United Methodist Hymnal: Music Supplement.* Nashville: Abingdon Press, 1991. Cokesbury Order #431476.

S-2   Bennett, Robert C., ed. *The United Methodist Hymnal: Music Supplement II.* Nashville: Abingdon Press, 1993. Cokesbury Order #430135.

H-3   Hopson, Hal H. *The Creative Church Musician Series.* Carol Stream, IL: Hope Publishing Co.

     Hbl—Vol. 1. *The Creative Use of Handbells in Worship* (1997). Cokesbury Order #921992.

     Chr—Vol. 2. *The Creative Use of Choirs in Worship* (1999). Cokesbury Order #732807.

     Desc—*The Creative Use of Descants in Worship* (1999). Cokesbury Order #732864.

     Org—*The Creative Use of the Organ in Worship* (1997). Cokesbury Order #323904.

VOCAL SOLOS RESOURCES

V-1   Kimbrough, Steven, ed. *Sweet Singer: Hymns of Charles Wesley.* Chapel Hill, NC: Hinshaw Music, 1987. Catalog #CV-1. Cokesbury Order #811712.

V-2   Handel, George Frideric. *Messiah.* Various editions available.

V-3   Inman, Bryce. *I Can Only Imagine: 25 Modern Praise Favorites.* Nashville: Word Music, 2002. Catalogue #080689-432286. *This resource is now out of print.*

V-4   Scott, K. Lee. *Sing a Song of Joy.* Minneapolis: Augsburg Fortress, 1989. Catalogue #11-8194 ISBN #0800647882 (Medium High Voice) ISBN #9780800647889 or

#0800652827 (Medium Low Voice) ISBN #9780800652821.

V-5   Courtney, Craig. *Music for the Master.* Beckenhorst VC1.; ISBN #748769970010.

V-6   Walters, Richard, arr. *Hymn Classics: Concert Arrangements of Traditional Hymns for Voice and Piano.* Hal Leonard Publishing, 1993. Catalogue #HL00747048. High Voice: Cokesbury Item #811290. Low Voice: Cokesbury Item #811233.

V-7   Johnson, Hall, arr. *Thirty (30) Spirituals.* New York: G. Schirmer, Inc., 1949. Catalogue #IL50328310.

V-8   Wilson, John F., Don Doig, and Jack Schrader, ed. *Everything for the Church Soloist.* Carol Stream, IL: Hope Publishing Co., 1980. Catalogue #804. Cokesbury Item #810103.

V-9   Scott, K. Lee. *Rejoice Now My Spirit: Vocal Solos for the Church Year.* Minneapolis: Augsburg Fortress, 1992. Catalogue #0800651081. Cokesbury Item #9780800651084.

V-10   Hayes, Mark et al. *From the Manger to the Cross—Seasonal Solos for Medium Voice.* Dayton: The Lorenz Corporation, 2006. Catalogue #30/2157L. Cokesbury Item #526369.

V-11   Pote, Allen. *A Song of Joy.* Carol Stream, IL: Hope Publishing, 2003. Catalogue #8135. Cokesbury Item #505068.

CONTEMPORARY RESOURCES

R   Webber, Robert et al., ed. *Renew! Songs & Hymns for Blended Worship.* Carol Stream, IL: Hope Publishing Co., 1995. Accompaniment edition: (#1998) #735812. Singers edition: (#1997) #735878.

SP   Various. *Songs for Praise and Worship PVG Edition.* Waco, TX: Word Music, 1992. Catalogue #080689-006395.

M1-M55   Barker, Ken, ed. *More Songs for Praise and Worship.* Waco, TX: Word Music, 2000. Choir/Worship Team Edition. Catalogue #0-80689-31317-2. Keyboard Edition. Catalogue #0-80689-39087-6. Piano/Guitar/Vocal Edition. Catalogue #0-80689-31018-8.

M56-M115   Baker, Ken, ed. *More Songs for Praise and Worship 2.* Waco, TX: Word Music, 2002. Choir/Worship Team Edition. Catalogue #0-80689-35117-4. Keyboard Edition. Catalogue #080689-41187-8. Piano/Guitar/Vocal Edition Catalogue #0-80689-31418-6).

M116-M168   Barker, Ken, ed. *More Songs for Praise and Worship 3.* Waco, TX: Word Music, 2005. Choir/Worship Team Edition. Catalogue #0-80689-36917-5. Keyboard Edition. Catalogue #0-80689-45187-4. Piano/Guitar/Vocal Edition. Catalogue #0-80689-31818-4).

M169-M219   Barker, Ken, ed. *More Songs for Praise and Worship 4.* Waco, TX: Word Music, 2006. Choir/Worship Team Edition. Catalogue #0-80689-41217-2. Keyboard Edition. Catalogue #0-80689-47287-9. Piano/Guitar/Vocal Edition. #0-80689-32018-7.

See also V-3 under "Vocal Solo Resources."

Exodus 12:1-14

[1] The LORD said to Moses and Aaron in the land of Egypt: [2] This month shall mark for you the beginning of months; it shall be the first month of the year for you. [3] Tell the whole congregation of Israel that on the tenth of this month they are to take a lamb for each family, a lamb for each household. [4] If a household is too small for a whole lamb, it shall join its closest neighbor in obtaining one; the lamb shall be divided in proportion to the number of people who eat of it. [5] Your lamb shall be without blemish, a year-old male; you may take it from the sheep or from the goats. [6] You shall keep it until the fourteenth day of this month; then the whole assembled congregation of Israel shall slaughter it at twilight. [7] They shall take some of the blood and put it on the two doorposts and the lintel of the houses in which they eat it. [8] They shall eat the lamb that same night; they shall eat it roasted over the fire with unleavened bread and bitter herbs. [9] Do not eat any of it raw or boiled in water, but roasted over the fire, with its head, legs, and inner organs. [10] You shall let none of it remain until the morning; anything that remains until the morning you shall burn. [11] This is how you shall eat it: your loins girded, your sandals on your feet, and your staff in your hand; and you shall eat it hurriedly. It is the passover of the LORD. [12] For I will pass through the land of Egypt that night, and I will strike down every firstborn in the land of Egypt, both human beings and animals; on all the gods of Egypt I will execute judgments: I am the LORD. [13] The blood shall be a sign for you on the houses where you live: when I see the blood, I will pass over you, and no plague shall destroy you when I strike the land of Egypt.

[14] This day shall be a day of remembrance for you. You shall celebrate it as a festival to the LORD; throughout your generations you shall observe it as a perpetual ordinance.

Psalm 149 (or Psalm 148)

[1] Praise the LORD! Sing to the LORD a new song, his praise in the assembly of the faithful. [2] Let Israel be glad in its Maker; let the children of Zion rejoice in their King. [3] Let them praise his name with dancing, making melody to him with tambourine and lyre. [4] For the LORD takes pleasure in his people; he adorns the humble with victory. [5] Let the faithful exult in glory; let them sing for joy on their couches. [6] Let the high praises of God be in their throats and two-edged swords in their hands, [7] to execute vengeance on the nations and punishment on the peoples, [8] to bind their kings with fetters and their nobles with chains of iron, [9] to execute on them the judgment decreed. This is glory for all his faithful ones. Praise the LORD!

Romans 13:8-14

[8] Owe no one anything, except to love one another; for the one who loves another has fulfilled the law. [9] The commandments, "You shall not commit adultery; You shall not murder; You shall not steal; You shall not covet"; and any other commandment, are summed up in this word, "Love your neighbor as yourself." [10] Love does no wrong to a neighbor; therefore, love is the fulfilling of the law.

[11] Besides this, you know what time it is, how it is now the moment for you to wake from sleep. For salvation is nearer to us now than when we became believers; [12] the night is far gone, the day is near. Let us then lay aside the works of darkness and put on the armor of light; [13] let us live honorably as in the day, not in reveling and drunkenness, not in debauchery and licentiousness, not in quarreling and jealousy. [14] Instead, put on the Lord Jesus Christ, and make no provision for the flesh, to gratify its desires.

Matthew 18:15-20

[15] "If another member of the church sins against you, go and point out the fault when the two of you are alone. If the member listens to you, you have regained that one.

[16] But if you are not listened to, take one or two others along with you, so that every word may be confirmed by the evidence of two or three witnesses. [17] If the member refuses to listen to them, tell it to the church; and if the offender refuses to listen even to the church, let such a one be to you as a Gentile and a tax collector. [18] Truly I tell you, whatever you bind on earth will be bound in heaven, and whatever you loose on earth will be loosed in heaven. [19] Again, truly I tell you, if two of you agree on earth about anything you ask, it will be done for you by my Father in heaven. [20] For where two or three are gathered in my name, I am there among them."

Primary Hymns and Songs for the Day

"We Are Called" (Rom) (O)
> EL720, S2172, SF2172

"Cantemos al Señor" ("Let's Sing unto the Lord")
(Exod, Pss)
> B38, C60, EL555, N39, R11, UM149
>> H-3   Chr-128; Org-129
>> S-2   #154. Performance note

"Wake, Awake, for Night Is Flying" (Rom)
> E61, EL436, L31, P17, UM720 (PD), VU711, W371
>> H-3   Chr-174, 203; Org-172

"Draw Us in the Spirit's Tether" (Rom, Matt, Communion)
> C392, EL470, N337, P504, UM632, VU479, W731
>> H-3   Chr-62
>> S-1   #337. Performance Note

"Bind Us Together" (Rom, Matt) (C)
> R292, S2226, SF2226, SP140

"Blest Be the Tie That Binds" (Matt) (C)
> B387, C433, EL656, F560, L370, N393, P438, UM557 (PD), VU602
>> H-3   Hbl-49; Chr-14; Desc-27; Org-25

Additional Hymn Suggestions

"Go Down, Moses" (Exod)
> C663, E648, N572, P334, UM448, W508

"God the Sculptor of the Mountains" (Exod)
> EL736, S2060, SF2060

"Lead On, O Cloud of Presence" (Exod)
> C633, S2234, SF2234, VU421

"Deep in the Shadows of the Past" (Exod)
> N320, P330, S2246

"All Creatures of Our God and King" (Pss) (O)
> B27, C22, E400, EL835, F347, L527, N17, P455, R47, UM62, VU217 (Fr.), W520

"I Want to Walk as a Child of the Light" (Rom)
> E490, EL815, R152, UM206, W510

"Awake, O Sleeper" (Rom)
> E547, EL452, UM551, VU566, W586

"Healer of Our Every Ill" (Rom)
> C506, EL612, S2213, SF2213, VU619

"In Remembrance of Me" (Rom, Communion)
> B365, C403, S2254

"Let Us Be Bread" (Rom, Communion)
> S2260, SF2260

"Love Divine, All Loves Excelling" (Rom, Matt)
> B208, C517, E657, EL631 (PD), L315, P376, N43, R196, UM384, VU333, W588

"Lord, I Want to Be a Christian" (Rom, Matt)
> B489, C589, F421, N454, P372 (PD), R145, UM402

"The Gift of Love" (Rom, Matt)
> B423, C526, EL644, P335, R155, UM408, VU372

"Where Charity and Love Prevail" (Rom, Matt)
> E581, EL359, L126, N396, UM549

"Help Us Accept Each Other" (Rom, Matt)
> C487, N388, P358, UM560, W656

"I Come with Joy" (Rom, Matt, Communion)
> B371, C420, E304, EL482, P607, R195, UM617, W726

"Forgive Our Sins as We Forgive" (Matt)
> E674, EL605, L307, P347, R184, UM390, W754

"Here Am I" (Matt)
> C654, S2178, SF2178

Additional Contemporary Suggestions

"El-Shaddai" (Exod)
> UM123, S-2 #54

"I Will Enter His Gates" (Exod, Pss)
> S2270, SF2270, SP168

"We Bring the Sacrifice of Praise" (Exod, Pss)
> R3, S2031, SF2031, SP1

"I Will Celebrate" (Pss)
> R77, M46, SP147

"Jesu, Jesu" (Rom)
> B501, C600, E602, EL708, N498, P367, R289, UM432, VU593, W431, S-1 #63 Vocal part

"Make Us One" (Rom)
> S2224, SF2224, SP137

"Make Me a Channel of Your Peace" (Rom, Matt)
> S2171, SF2171, VU684

"They'll Know We Are Christians" (Rom, Matt)
> C494, S2223, SF2223

"Dwell" (Matt)
> M154

Vocal Solos

"Sing a Song of Joy" (Pss)
V-4   p. 2
"I Will Sing of Thy Great Mercies" (Pss)
V-4   p. 43
"There's a Quiet Understanding" (Matt)
V-8   p. 2

Anthems

"Teach Us to Love" (Rom, Matt)
Mark Patterson; Choristers Guild CGA1183
Unison/two part with keyboard

"Be Our Light" (Rom)
Michael Wolnaikowski; Walton Music HL08501578
SATB with organ

Other Suggestions

Visuals:
O	Sin/salvation (black/gold), darkness/light, lamp, candles, Passover meal, lamb, blood, wine/bread
P	Dancing figures, tambourine, lyre
E	Paschal Lamb, portrait of Christ
E/G	Reconciliation, bridges, alarm clock
G	Worship, reconciliation, joined hands, four hands folded in prayer

Greeting: C279. Reach Out and Worship (Matt)
Prayer: UM412. Prayer of John Chrysostom (Matt)
Response: C523, EL642, R226, S2179, SF2179, W604. "Live in Charity" ("Ubi Caritas") (Rom)
Alternate Lessons: Eze 33:7-11; Ps 119:33-40 (*See page 3*)

Exodus 14:19-31

¹⁹ The angel of God who was going before the Israelite army moved and went behind them; and the pillar of cloud moved from in front of them and took its place behind them. ²⁰ It came between the army of Egypt and the army of Israel. And so the cloud was there with the darkness, and it lit up the night; one did not come near the other all night.

²¹ Then Moses stretched out his hand over the sea. The LORD drove the sea back by a strong east wind all night, and turned the sea into dry land; and the waters were divided. ²²The Israelites went into the sea on dry ground, the waters forming a wall for them on their right and on their left. ²³The Egyptians pursued, and went into the sea after them, all of Pharaoh's horses, chariots, and chariot drivers. ²⁴ At the morning watch the LORD in the pillar of fire and cloud looked down upon the Egyptian army, and threw the Egyptian army into panic. ²⁵ He clogged their chariot wheels so that they turned with difficulty. The Egyptians said, "Let us flee from the Israelites, for the LORD is fighting for them against Egypt."

²⁶ Then the LORD said to Moses, "Stretch out your hand over the sea, so that the water may come back upon the Egyptians, upon their chariots and chariot drivers." ²⁷ So Moses stretched out his hand over the sea, and at dawn the sea returned to its normal depth. As the Egyptians fled before it, the LORD tossed the Egyptians into the sea. ²⁸ The waters returned and covered the chariots and the chariot drivers, the entire army of Pharaoh that had followed them into the sea; not one of them remained. ²⁹ But the Israelites walked on dry ground through the sea, the waters forming a wall for them on their right and on their left.

³⁰ Thus the LORD saved Israel that day from the Egyptians; and Israel saw the Egyptians dead on the seashore. ³¹ Israel saw the great work that the LORD did against the Egyptians. So the people feared the Lord and believed in the LORD and in his servant Moses.

Exodus 15:1b-11, 20-21

¹ᵇ "I will sing to the LORD, for he has triumphed gloriously; horse and rider he has thrown into the sea. ² The LORD is my strength and my might, and he has become my salvation; this is my God, and I will praise him, my father's God, and I will exalt him. ³ The LORD is a warrior; the LORD is his name. ⁴ Pharaoh's chariots and his army he cast into the sea; his picked officers were sunk in the Red Sea. ⁵ The floods covered them; they went down into the depths like a stone. ⁶ Your right hand, O LORD, glorious in power—your right hand, O LORD, shattered the enemy. ⁷ In the greatness of your majesty you overthrew your adversaries; you sent out your fury, it consumed them like stubble. ⁸ At the blast of your nostrils the waters piled up, the floods stood up in a heap; the deeps congealed in the heart of the sea. ⁹ The enemy said, 'I will pursue, I will overtake, I will divide the spoil, my desire shall have its fill of them. I will draw my sword, my hand shall destroy them.' ¹⁰ You blew with your wind, the sea covered them; they sank like lead in the mighty waters. ¹¹ Who is like you, O LORD, among the gods? Who is like you, majestic in holiness, awesome in splendor, doing wonders?" . . .

²⁰ Then the prophet Miriam, Aaron's sister, took a tambourine in her hand; and all the women went out after her with tambourines and with dancing. ²¹ And Miriam sang to them:

"Sing to the LORD, for he has triumphed gloriously; horse and rider he has thrown into the sea."

Romans 14:1-12

¹ Welcome those who are weak in faith, but not for the purpose of quarreling over opinions. ² Some believe in eating anything, while the weak eat only vegetables. ³ Those who eat must not despise those who abstain, and those who abstain must not pass judgment on those who eat; for God has welcomed them. ⁴ Who are you to pass judgment on servants of another? It is before their own lord that they stand or fall. And they will be upheld, for the Lord is able to make them stand.

⁵ Some judge one day to be better than another, while others judge all days to be alike. Let all be fully convinced in their own minds. ⁶ Those who observe the day, observe it in honor of the Lord. Also those who eat, eat in honor of the Lord, since they give thanks to God; while those who abstain, abstain in honor of the Lord and give thanks to God.

⁷ We do not live to ourselves, and we do not die to ourselves. ⁸ If we live, we live to the Lord, and if we die, we die to the Lord; so then, whether we live or whether we die, we are the Lord's. ⁹ For to this end Christ died and lived again, so that he might be Lord of both the dead and the living.

¹⁰ Why do you pass judgment on your brother or sister? Or you, why do you despise your brother or sister? For we will all stand before the judgment seat of God. ¹¹ For it is written, "As I live, says the Lord, every knee shall bow to me, and every tongue shall give praise to God." ¹² So then, each of us will be accountable to God.

Matthew 18:21-35

²¹ Then Peter came and said to him, "Lord, if another member of the church sins against me, how often should I forgive? As many as seven times?" ²² Jesus said to him, "Not seven times, but, I tell you, seventy-seven times.

²³ "For this reason the kingdom of heaven may be compared to a king who wished to settle accounts with his slaves. ²⁴ When he began the reckoning, one who owed him ten thousand talents was brought to him; ²⁵ and, as he could not pay, his lord ordered him to be sold, together with his wife and children and all his possessions, and payment to be made. ²⁶ So the slave fell on his knees before him, saying, 'Have patience with me, and I will pay you everything.' ²⁷And out of pity for him, the lord of that slave released him and forgave him the debt. ²⁸ But that same slave, as he went out, came upon one of his fellow slaves who owed him a hundred denarii; and seizing him by the throat, he said, 'Pay what you owe.' ²⁹ Then his fellow slave fell down and pleaded with him, 'Have patience with me, and I will pay you.' ³⁰ But he refused; then he went and threw him into prison until he would pay the debt. ³¹ When his fellow slaves saw what had happened, they were greatly distressed, and they went and reported to their lord all that had taken place. ³² Then his lord summoned him and said to him, 'You wicked slave! I forgave you all that debt because you pleaded with me. ³³ Should you not have had mercy on your fellow slave, as I had mercy on you?' ³⁴ And in anger his lord handed him over to be tortured until he would pay his entire debt. ³⁵ So my heavenly Father will also do to every one of you, if you do not forgive your brother or sister from your heart."

Primary Hymns and Songs for the Day

"Lead On, O Cloud of Presence" (Exod) (O)
  C633, S2234, SF2234, VU421
      H-3   Hbl-74; Chr-123; Desc-64; Org-71
      S-1   #9-197. Various treatments
"Cantemos al Señor" ("Let's Sing unto the Lord")
  (Exod, Canticle)
  B38, C60, EL555, N39, R11, UM149
      H-3   Chr-128; Org-129
      S-2   #154. Performance note
"Pues Si Vivimos" ("When We Are Living") (Rom)
  C536, EL639, N499, P400, UM356, VU581
      S-1   #320. Orff instrument arrangement
      H-3   Chr-218; Org-155
"Forgive Our Sins as We Forgive" (Matt)
  E674, EL605, L307, P347, R184, UM390, W754
      H-3   Chr-68; Desc-28; Org-27
      S-1   #85. Choral harmonization
  VU364
"Freely, Freely" (Matt) (C)
  B273, R192, UM389
      S-1   #135. Vocal descant idea

Additional Hymn Suggestions

"Come, Ye Faithful, Raise the Strain" (Exod) (O)
  C215, E199, EL363, L132, N230, P115, UM315 (PD),
  VU165, W456
"Go Down, Moses" (Exod)
  C663, E648, N572, P334, UM448, W508
"Faith, While Trees Are Still in Blossom" (Exod)
  C535, UM508, VU643
"God the Sculptor of the Mountains" (Exod)
  EL736, S2060, SF2060
"Wade in the Water" (Exod, Baptism)
  C371, EL459 (PD), S2107, SF2107
"Spirit, Spirit of Gentleness" (Exod)
  C249, EL396, N286, P319, S2120, VU375 (Fr.)
"In the Midst of New Dimensions" (Exod)
  N391, S2238, SF2238
"Deep in the Shadows of the Past" (Exod)
  N320, P330, S2246
"At the Name of Jesus" (Rom)
  B198 (PD), E435, F351, L179, P148, R133, UM168, VU335,
  W499
"In Thee Is Gladness" (Rom)
  EL867, L552, UM169 (PD)
"There's a Wideness in God's Mercy" (Rom, Matt)
  B25, C73, E470, EL587/EL588, F115, L290, N23, P298,
  UM121, VU271, W595
"O How I Love Jesus" (Rom, Matt)
  B217, C99, F634, N52, UM170 (PD)
"Rise, Shine, You People" (Matt)
  EL665, L393, UM187
"Lord, I Want to Be a Christian" (Matt)
  B489, C589, F421, N454, P372 (PD), R145, UM402
"Help Us Accept Each Other" (Matt)
  C487, N388, P358, UM560, W656

"Come, Share the Lord" (Matt, Communion)
  C408, S2269, SF2269, VU469
"Lord, Speak to Me" (Rom) (C)
  B568, EL676, F625, L403, N531, P426, UM463 (PD), VU589

Additional Contemporary Suggestions

"How Majestic Is Your Name" (Exod)
  C63, R98, S2023, SF2023, SP14
"Majesty" (Exod, Rom)
  B215, R63, SP73, UM176
"My Life Is in You, Lord" (Exod, Rom)
  S2032, SF2032, SP204
"I Exalt You" (Exod, Rom)
  R44, SP18
"Shout to the North" (Exod, Pss)
  M99
"He Is Exalted" (Pss, Rom)
  R238, S2070, SF2070, SP66
"Jesus, Name Above All Names" (Rom)
  R26, S2071, SF2071, SP76
"Sanctuary" (Rom)
  M52, R185, S2164, SF2164
"Come, Now Is the Time to Worship" (Rom)
  M56; V-3 p. 114 Vocal Solo

Vocal Solos

"Oh, Freedom" (Exod)
V-7   p. 10
"My Father's Heart" (Rom)
V-3   p. 134

Anthems

"He Never Failed Me Yet" (Exod)
Ray, arr. Christopher; Hal Leonard 08745113
TTBB with piano

"In the Shadow of Your Wings" (Matt)
John Leavitt, GIA Publications G-3345
SATB with keyboard

Other Suggestions

Visuals:
  O   Symbols of hope: cloud, pillar of fire, rainbow, star
  P   Musical notes, sea, tambourine, dancing, Exod 15:21b
  E   Reconciliation, unity, clasped hands, Christ, scales of
      justice
  G   Reconciliation, forgiveness, embrace, no. 77, 70x7,
      scales of justice
Call to Worship: B38, C60, EL555, N39, R11, UM149, stanza 1.
  "Cantemos al Señor" ("Let's Sing unto the Lord") (Exod)
Canticle: UM135 (Exod) or UM167 (Rom)
Prayer: C332. God of Wondrous Darkness (Exod)
Scripture Response: B489, C589, F421, N454, P372 (PD), R145,
  UM402, stanza 2. "Lord, I Want to Be a Christian" (Matt)
Blessing: C436, UM666. "Shalom to You" (Exod, Matt)
Alternate Lessons: Gen 50:15-21; Ps 103:(1-7) 8-13 (*See page 3.*)

Exodus 16:2-15

[2] The whole congregation of the Israelites complained against Moses and Aaron in the wilderness. [3] The Israelites said to them, "If only we had died by the hand of the LORD in the land of Egypt, when we sat by the fleshpots and ate our fill of bread; for you have brought us out into this wilderness to kill this whole assembly with hunger."

[4] Then the LORD said to Moses, "I am going to rain bread from heaven for you, and each day the people shall go out and gather enough for that day. In that way I will test them, whether they will follow my instruction or not. [5] On the sixth day, when they prepare what they bring in, it will be twice as much as they gather on other days." [6] So Moses and Aaron said to all the Israelites, "In the evening you shall know that it was the LORD who brought you out of the land of Egypt, [7] and in the morning you shall see the glory of the LORD, because he has heard your complaining against the LORD. For what are we, that you complain against us?" [8] And Moses said, "When the LORD gives you meat to eat in the evening and your fill of bread in the morning, because the LORD has heard the complaining that you utter against him—what are we? Your complaining is not against us but against the LORD."

[9] Then Moses said to Aaron, "Say to the whole congregation of the Israelites, 'Draw near to the LORD, for he has heard your complaining.'" [10] And as Aaron spoke to the whole congregation of the Israelites, they looked toward the wilderness, and the glory of the LORD appeared in the cloud. [11] The LORD spoke to Moses and said, [12] "I have heard the complaining of the Israelites; say to them, 'At twilight you shall eat meat, and in the morning you shall have your fill of bread; then you shall know that I am the LORD your God.'"

[13] In the evening quails came up and covered the camp; and in the morning there was a layer of dew around the camp. [14] When the layer of dew lifted, there on the surface of the wilderness was a fine flaky substance, as fine as frost on the ground. [15] When the Israelites saw it, they said to one another, "What is it?" For they did not know what it was. Moses said to them, "It is the bread that the LORD has given you to eat."

Psalm 105:1-6, 37-45

[1] O give thanks to the LORD, call on his name, make known his deeds among the peoples. [2] Sing to him, sing praises to him; tell of all his wonderful works. [3] Glory in his holy name; let the hearts of those who seek the LORD rejoice. [4] Seek the LORD and his strength; seek his presence continually. [5] Remember the wonderful works he has done, his miracles, and the judgments he uttered, [6] O offspring of his servant Abraham, children of Jacob, his chosen ones. . . .

[37] Then he brought Israel out with silver and gold, and there was no one among their tribes who stumbled. [38] Egypt was glad when they departed, for dread of them had fallen upon it. [39] He spread a cloud for a covering, and fire to give light by night. [40] They asked, and he brought quails, and gave them food from heaven in abundance. [41] He opened the rock, and water gushed out; it flowed through the desert like a river. [42] For he remembered his holy promise, and Abraham, his servant. [43] So he brought his people out with joy, his chosen ones with singing. [44] He gave them the lands of the nations, and they took possession of the wealth of the peoples, [45] that they might keep his statutes and observe his laws. Praise the LORD!

Philippians 1:21-30

[21] For to me, living is Christ and dying is gain. [22] If I am to live in the flesh, that means fruitful labor for me; and I do not know which I prefer. [23] I am hard pressed between the two: my desire is to depart and be with Christ, for that is far better; [24] but to remain in the flesh is more necessary for you. [25] Since I am convinced of this, I know that I will remain and continue with all of you for your progress and joy in faith, [26] so that I may share abundantly in your boasting in Christ Jesus when I come to you again.

[27] Only, live your life in a manner worthy of the gospel of Christ, so that, whether I come and see you or am absent and hear about you, I will know that you are standing firm in one spirit, striving side by side with one mind for the faith of the gospel, [28] and are in no way intimidated by your opponents. For them this is evidence of their destruction, but of your salvation. And this is God's doing. [29] For he has graciously granted you the privilege not only of believing in Christ, but of suffering for him as well— [30] since you are having the same struggle that you saw I had and now hear that I still have.

Matthew 20:1-16

[1] "For the kingdom of heaven is like a landowner who went out early in the morning to hire laborers for his vineyard. [2] After agreeing with the laborers for the usual daily wage, he sent them into his vineyard. [3] When he went out about nine o'clock, he saw others standing idle in the marketplace; [4] and he said to them, 'You also go into the vineyard, and I will pay you whatever is right.' So they went. [5] When he went out again about noon and about three o'clock, he did the same. [6] And about five o'clock he went out and found others standing around; and he said to them, 'Why are you standing here idle all day?' [7] They said to him, 'Because no one has hired us.' He said to them, 'You also go into the vineyard.' [8] When evening came, the owner of the vineyard said to his manager, 'Call the laborers and give them their pay, beginning with the last and then going to the first.' [9] When those hired about five o'clock came, each of them received the usual daily wage. [10] Now when the first came, they thought they would receive more; but each of them also received the usual daily wage. [11] And when they received it, they grumbled against the landowner, [12] saying, 'These last worked only one hour, and you have made them equal to us who have borne the burden of the day and the scorching heat.' [13] But he replied to one of them, 'Friend, I am doing you no wrong; did you not agree with me for the usual daily wage? [14] Take what belongs to you and go; I choose to give to this last the same as I give to you. [15] Am I not allowed to do what I choose with what belongs to me? Or are you envious because I am generous?' [16] So the last will be first, and the first will be last."

Primary Hymns and Songs for the Day

"Guide Me, O Thou Great Jehovah" (Exod, Pss) (O)
 B56, C622, E690, EL618, F608, L343, N18/N19, P281,
 UM127 (PD), VU651 (Fr.)
"In the Midst of New Dimensions" (Exod)
 N391, S2238, SF2238
"Give Thanks" (Pss, Matt)
 C528, R266, S2036, SF2036, SP170
"Living for Jesus" (Phil)
 B282, C610, F462, S2149, SF2149
"All Who Love and Serve Your City" (Matt, Pss)
 C670, E570/E571, EL724, L436, P413, UM433, W621
  H-3   Chr-26, 65; Org-19
  S-1   #62. Descant
"Lift Every Voice and Sing" (Exod, Pss) (C)
 B627, C631, E599, EL841, L562, N593, P563, UM519, W641
  H-3   Chr-128

Additional Hymn Suggestions

"All My Hope Is Firmly Grounded" (Exod)
 C88, E665, EL757, N408, UM132, VU654/VU655
"O Food to Pilgrims Given" (Exod, Communion)
 E308/E309, L222, UM631
"Glorious Things of Thee Are Spoken" (Exod, Matt)
 B398, C709, E522/E523, EL647, F376, L358, N307, P446,
 UM731 (PD)
"All Who Hunger" (Exod, Matt)
 C419, EL461, S2126, SF2126, VU460
"Lead On, O Cloud of Presence" (Exod)
 C633, S2234, SF2234, VU421
"Come to the Table" (Exod, Communion)
 EL481, S2264, SF2264
"In Thee Is Gladness" (Phil)
 EL867, L552, UM169 (PD)
"Pues Si Vivimos" ("When We Are Living") (Phil)
 C536, EL639, N499, P400, UM356, VU581
"I'm Gonna Live So God Can Use Me" (Phil)
 C614, P369, S2153, VU575
"Live in Charity" ("Ubi Caritas") (Phil)
 C523, EL642, R226, S2179, SF2179, W604
"There's a Wideness in God's Mercy" (Matt)
 B25, C73, E470, EL587/EL588, F115, L290, N23, P298,
 UM121, VU271, W595
"Come, Ye Sinners, Poor and Needy" (Matt)
 B323 (PD), R141, UM340, W756
"O God of Every Nation" (Matt)
 C680, E607, EL713, L416, P289, UM435, VU677, W650
"By Gracious Powers" (Matt)
 E695/E696, EL626, N413, P342, UM517, W577
"Lord, Whose Love Through Humble Service" (Matt)
 C461, E610, EL712, R286, L423, UM581, W630
"Wounded World That Cries for Healing" (Matt)
 S2177, SF2177
"As We Gather at Your Table" (Matt, Communion)
 EL522, N332, S2268, SF2268, VU457
"God the Spirit, Guide and Guardian" (Exod) (C)
 C450, N355, P523, UM648, VU514

"Lord, Dismiss Us with Thy Blessing" (Exod) (C)
 C439, E344, EL545, F520, L259, N77, P538, UM671 (PD),
 VU425

Additional Contemporary Suggestions

"Let It Rise" (Exod)
 M4
"You Who Are Thirsty" (Exod, Communion)
 S2132, SP219
"Hungry" ("Falling on My Knees") (Exod)
 M155
"Someone Asked the Question" (Pss)
 N523, S2144
"My Life Is in You, Lord" (Phil)
 S2032, SF2032, SP204
"Sanctuary" (Phil)
 M52, R185, S2164, SF2164
"Make Us One" (Phil)
 S2224, SF2224, SP137
"Humble Thyself in the Sight of the Lord" (Matt)
 S2131, SF2131, R188, SP223
"Make Me a Servant" (Matt)
 S2176, SF2176, SP193

Vocal Solos

"Patiently Have I Waited for the Lord" (Exod, Matt)
V-4   p. 24
"If My People Will Pray" (Exod, Pss)
V-8   p. 66

Anthems

"All Who Hunger" (Exod)
Bob Moore; GIA Publications G-3859
SAT(B) with piano

"My Heart Is Longing" (Phil)
arr. Bradley Ellingboe; Kjos 9033
SATB with harp or piano and oboe or clarinet

Other Suggestions

Visuals:
  O   Bread, quails, hungry being fed
  P   Singing, praising, cloud, fire, bread, quails, rock/water
  E   People at work, service to God with people
     (bowl/pitcher/towel)
  G   Grapes, leaves, tools for work, clocks set at 6:00 a.m.,
     9:00 a.m., noon, 3:00 p.m., 6:00 p.m.
Call to Worship: B56, C622, E690, EL618, F608, L343, N18/N19,
 P281, UM127 (PD), VU651 (Fr.). "Guide Me, O Thou Great
 Jehovah." A selected stanza may be used each Sunday from
 today until Oct. 30, when the Hebrew Scripture tells of
 Israel's crossing the Jordan.
Prayer: UM409 (Matt) or C597 (Phil)
Scripture response: UM731, stanza 3. "Glorious Things of Thee
 Are Spoken" (Exod)
Alternate Lessons: Jonah 3:10–4:11; Ps 145:1-8 (*See page 3.*)

Exodus 17:1-7

[1] From the wilderness of Sin the whole congregation of the Israelites journeyed by stages, as the LORD commanded. They camped at Rephidim, but there was no water for the people to drink. [2] The people quarreled with Moses, and said, "Give us water to drink." Moses said to them, "Why do you quarrel with me? Why do you test the LORD?" [3] But the people thirsted there for water; and the people complained against Moses and said, "Why did you bring us out of Egypt, to kill us and our children and livestock with thirst?" [4] So Moses cried out to the LORD, "What shall I do with this people? They are almost ready to stone me." [5] The LORD said to Moses, "Go on ahead of the people, and take some of the elders of Israel with you; take in your hand the staff with which you struck the Nile, and go. [6] I will be standing there in front of you on the rock at Horeb. Strike the rock, and water will come out of it, so that the people may drink." Moses did so, in the sight of the elders of Israel. [7] He called the place Massah and Meribah, because the Israelites quarreled and tested the LORD, saying, "Is the LORD among us or not?"

Psalm 78:1-4, 12-16

[1] Give ear, O my people, to my teaching; incline your ears to the words of my mouth. [2] I will open my mouth in a parable; I will utter dark sayings from of old, [3] things that we have heard and known, that our ancestors have told us. [4] We will not hide them from their children; we will tell to the coming generation the glorious deeds of the LORD, and his might, and the wonders that he has done. . . .

[12] In the sight of their ancestors he worked marvels in the land of Egypt, in the fields of Zoan. [13] He divided the sea and let them pass through it, and made the waters stand like a heap. [14] In the daytime he led them with a cloud, and all night long with a fiery light. [15] He split rocks open in the wilderness, and gave them drink abundantly as from the deep. [16] He made streams come out of the rock, and caused waters to flow down like rivers.

Philippians 2:1-13

[1] If then there is any encouragement in Christ, any consolation from love, any sharing in the Spirit, any compassion and sympathy, [2] make my joy complete: be of the same mind, having the same love, being in full accord and of one mind. [3] Do nothing from selfish ambition or conceit, but in humility regard others as better than yourselves. [4] Let each of you look not to your own interests, but to the interests of others. [5] Let the same mind be in you that was in Christ Jesus, [6] who, though he was in the form of God, did not regard equality with God as something to be exploited, [7] but emptied himself, taking the form of a slave, being born in human likeness. And being found in human form, [8] he humbled himself and became obedient to the point of death—even death on a cross.

[9] Therefore God also highly exalted him and gave him the name that is above every name, [10] so that at the name of Jesus every knee should bend, in heaven and on earth and under the earth, [11] and every tongue should confess that Jesus Christ is Lord, to the glory of God the Father.

[12] Therefore, my beloved, just as you have always obeyed me, not only in my presence, but much more now in my absence, work out your own salvation with fear and trembling; [13] for it is God who is at work in you, enabling you both to will and to work for his good pleasure.

Matthew 21:23-32

[23] When he entered the temple, the chief priests and the elders of the people came to him as he was teaching, and said, "By what authority are you doing these things, and who gave you this authority?" [24] Jesus said to them, "I will also ask you one question; if you tell me the answer, then I will also tell you by what authority I do these things. [25] Did the baptism of John come from heaven, or was it of human origin?" And they argued with one another, "If we say, 'From heaven,' he will say to us, 'Why then did you not believe him?' [26] But if we say, 'Of human origin,' we are afraid of the crowd; for all regard John as a prophet." [27] So they answered Jesus, "We do not know." And he said to them, "'Neither will I tell you by what authority I am doing these things.

[28] "What do you think? A man had two sons; he went to the first and said, 'Son, go and work in the vineyard today.' [29] He answered, 'I will not'; but later he changed his mind and went. [30] The father went to the second and said the same; and he answered, 'I go, sir'; but he did not go. [31] Which of the two did the will of his father?" They said, "The first." Jesus said to them, "Truly I tell you, the tax collectors and the prostitutes are going into the kingdom of God ahead of you. [32] For John came to you in the way of righteousness and you did not believe him, but the tax collectors and the prostitutes believed him; and even after you saw it, you did not change your minds and believe him."

Primary Hymns and Songs for the Day

"All Praise to Thee, for Thou, O King Divine" (O) (Phil)
  B229, E477, UM166, VU327
       H-3   Hbl-58; Chr-65; Org-152
       S-1   #314-318. Various treatments

"Thou Didst Leave Thy Throne" (Phil)
  B121, F170, S2100, SF2100
       H-3   Chr-200

"O God, Our Help in Ages Past" (Exod)
  B74, C67, E680, EL632, F370, L320, N25, P210, UM117
  (PD), VU806, W579
       H-3   Hbl-87; Chr-60, 143; Desc-93; Org-132
       S-1   #293-296. Various treatments

"Trust and Obey" (Phil, Matt) (C)
  B447, C556, F454, UM467 (PD)
       H-3   Chr-202
       S-1   #336. Harmonization

Additional Hymn Suggestions

"All Hail the Power of Jesus' Name" (Phil, Matt) (O)
  B200/B201/B202, C91/C92, E450/E451, EL634,
  F325/F326/F327, L328/L329, N304, P142/P143, R45,
  UM154/UM155, VU334, W494

"Guide Me, O Thou Great Jehovah" (Exod)
  B56, C622, E690, EL618, F608, L343, N18/N19, P281,
  UM127 (PD), VU651 (Fr.)

"All My Hope Is Firmly Grounded" (Exod)
  C88, E665, EL757, N408, UM132, VU654/VU655

"Wellspring of Wisdom" (Exod)
  C596, UM506, VU287

"Come, Ye Sinners, Poor and Needy" (Exod, Matt)
  B323 (PD), R141, UM340, W756

"Glorious Things of Thee Are Spoken" (Exod, Matt)
  B398, C709, E522/E523, EL647, F376, L358, N307, P446,
  UM731 (PD)

"At the Name of Jesus" (Phil)
  B198 (PD), E435, F351, L179, P148, R133, UM168, VU335,
  W499

"What Wondrous Love Is This" (Phil)
  B143 (PD), C200, E439, EL666, F283, L385, N223, P85,
  R277, UM292, VU147 (Fr.), W600

"Creator of the Stars of Night" (Phil)
  C127, E60, EL245, L323, N111, P4, UM692 (PD), W368

"Woke Up This Morning" (Phil)
  C623, N85, S2082, SF2082

"Precious Name" (Phil) (C)
  B576, C625, UM536 (PD)

"Song of Hope" ("Canto de Esperanza") (Phil) (C)
  P432, S2186, VU424

"Lord of the Dance" (Matt)
  P302, UM261, VU352, W636

Additional Contemporary Suggestions

"Ancient of Days" (Exod, Pss, Phil)
  M1

"He Is Exalted" (Phil)
  R238, S2070, SF2070, SP66

"Majesty" (Phil)
  B215, R63, SP73, UM176

"He Is Lord" (Phil)
  B178, C117, F234, R29, SP122, UM177

"How Majestic Is Your Name" (Phil)
  C63, R98, S2023, SF2023, SP14

"Jesus, Name above All Names" (Phil)
  R26, S2071, SF2071, SP76

"Humble Thyself in the Sight of the Lord" (Phil)
  S2131, SF2131, R188, SP223

"Make Us One" (Phil)
  S2224, SF2224, SP137

"At the Name of Jesus" (Phil)
  R133/ R279, SP234

"Knowing You" ("All I Once Held Dear") (Phil, Matt)
  M30

"In the Secret" ("I Want to Know You") (Phil)
  M38; V-3 p. 36 Vocal Solo

"Come, Now Is the Time to Worship" (Phil) (O)
  M56

"Let It Be Said of Us" (Phil, Matt)
  M53

"Take My Life" (Phil, Matt)
  M91

"More Like You" (Phil, Matt)
  S2167, SF2167

"Seek Ye First" (Matt)
  B478, C354, E711, P333, UM405, SP182, VU356, W580

Vocal Solos

"This Is De Healin' Water" (Exod, Baptism)
V-7   p. 52

"My Father's Heart" (Phil)
V-3   p. 134

"Into My Heart" (Phil)
V-8   p. 121

Anthems

"Let This Mind Be in You" (Phil)
Austin Lovelace; Alfred 00-FEC08458
SATB with Organ

"Who Is This?" (Matt)
John Ferguson; Morningstar 50-6509
A cappella with viola

Other Suggestions

Visuals:
    O/P/G   Rock, flowing water, sand, staff, images of baptism
    E   Reminders of Crucifixion, Resurrection, Birth of
            Christ
    G   Vineyard, grapes, vine, leaves, "Reconsider Your Call"
Canticle: C96 or UM167 (See S-1, p. 381) (Phil)
Prayer: C541. "Draw Compassion from Us" (Phil)
Scripture Response: B398, C709, E522/E523, EL647, F376,
    L358, N307, P446, UM731, stanza 2. "Glorious Things of
    Thee Are Spoken" (Exod)
Alternate Lessons: Eze 18:1-4, 25-32; Ps 25:1-9 (*See page 3*).

Exodus 20:1-4, 7-9, 12-20

[1] Then God spoke all these words:

[2] I am the LORD your God, who brought you out of the land of Egypt, out of the house of slavery; [3] you shall have no other gods before me.

[4] You shall not make for yourself an idol, whether in the form of anything that is in heaven above, or that is on the earth beneath, or that is in the water under the earth.

[7] You shall not make wrongful use of the name of the LORD your God, for the LORD will not acquit anyone who misuses his name.

[8] Remember the sabbath day, and keep it holy. [9] Six days you shall labor and do all your work.

[12] Honor your father and your mother, so that your days may be long in the land that the LORD your God is giving you.

[13] You shall not murder.

[14] You shall not commit adultery.

[15] You shall not steal.

[16] You shall not bear false witness against your neighbor.

[17] You shall not covet your neighbor's house; you shall not covet your neighbor's wife, or male or female slave, or ox, or donkey, or anything that belongs to your neighbor.

[18] When all the people witnessed the thunder and lightning, the sound of the trumpet, and the mountain smoking, they were afraid and trembled and stood at a distance, [19] and said to Moses, "You speak to us, and we will listen; but do not let God speak to us, or we will die." [20] Moses said to the people, "Do not be afraid; for God has come only to test you and to put the fear of him upon you so that you do not sin."

Psalm 19

[1] The heavens are telling the glory of God; and the firmament proclaims his handiwork. [2] Day to day pours forth speech, and night to night declares knowledge. [3] There is no speech, nor are there words; their voice is not heard; [4] yet their voice goes out through all the earth, and their words to the end of the world. In the heavens he has set a tent for the sun, [5] which comes out like a bridegroom from his wedding canopy, and like a strong man runs its course with joy. [6] Its rising is from the end of the heavens, and its circuit to the end of them; and nothing is hid from its heat. [7] The law of the LORD is perfect, reviving the soul; the decrees of the LORD are sure, making wise the simple; [8] the precepts of the LORD are right, rejoicing the heart; the commandment of the LORD is clear, enlightening the eyes; [9] the fear of the LORD is pure, enduring forever; the ordinances of the LORD are true and righteous altogether. [10] More to be desired are they than gold, even much fine gold; sweeter also than honey, and drippings of the honeycomb. [11] Moreover by them is your servant warned; in keeping them there is great reward. [12] But who can detect their errors? Clear me from hidden faults. [13] Keep back your servant also from the insolent; do not let them have dominion over me. Then I shall be blameless, and innocent of great transgression. [14] Let the words of my mouth and the meditation of my heart be acceptable to you, O LORD, my rock and my redeemer.

Philippians 3:4b-14

[4b] If anyone else has reason to be confident in the flesh, I have more: [5] circumcised on the eighth day, a member of the people of Israel, of the tribe of Benjamin, a Hebrew born of Hebrews; as to the law, a Pharisee; [6] as to zeal, a persecutor of the church; as to righteousness under the law, blameless.

[7] Yet whatever gains I had, these I have come to regard as loss because of Christ. [8] More than that, I regard everything as loss because of the surpassing value of knowing Christ Jesus my Lord. For his sake I have suffered the loss of all things, and I regard them as rubbish, in order that I may gain Christ [9] and be found in him, not having a righteousness of my own that comes from the law, but one that comes through faith in Christ, the righteousness from God based on faith. [10] I want to know Christ and the power of his resurrection and the sharing of his sufferings by becoming like him in his death, [11] if somehow I may attain the resurrection from the dead.

[12] Not that I have already obtained this or have already reached the goal; but I press on to make it my own, because Christ Jesus has made me his own. [13] Beloved, I do not consider that I have made it my own; but this one thing I do: forgetting what lies behind and straining forward to what lies ahead, [14] I press on toward the goal for the prize of the heavenly call of God in Christ Jesus.

Matthew 21:33-46

[33] "Listen to another parable. There was a landowner who planted a vineyard, put a fence around it, dug a wine press in it, and built a watchtower. Then he leased it to tenants and went to another country. [34] When the harvest time had come, he sent his slaves to the tenants to collect his produce. [35] But the tenants seized his slaves and beat one, killed another, and stoned another. [36] Again he sent other slaves, more than the first; and they treated them in the same way. [37] Finally he sent his son to them, saying, 'They will respect my son.' [38] But when the tenants saw the son, they said to themselves, 'This is the heir; come, let us kill him and get his inheritance.' [39] So they seized him, threw him out of the vineyard, and killed him. [40] Now when the owner of the vineyard comes, what will he do to those tenants?" [41] They said to him, "He will put those wretches to a miserable death, and lease the vineyard to other tenants who will give him the produce at the harvest time."

[42] Jesus said to them, "Have you never read in the scriptures: 'The stone that the builders rejected has become the cornerstone; this was the Lord's doing, and it is amazing in our eyes'? [43] Therefore I tell you, the kingdom of God will be taken away from you and given to a people that produces the fruits of the kingdom. [44] The one who falls on this stone will be broken to pieces; and it will crush anyone on whom it falls."

[45] When the chief priests and the Pharisees heard his parables, they realized that he was speaking about them. [46] They wanted to arrest him, but they feared the crowds, because they regarded him as a prophet.

Primary Hymns and Songs for the Day

"Christ Is Made the Sure Foundation" (Matt) (O)
    C275, E518, EL645, P416, UM559 (PD), VU325, W617
        H-3   Chr-49; Desc-103; Org-180
        S-1   #346. Descant
    F557, N400, P417
        H-3   Chr-30, 48, 62; Desc-89; Org-121
        S-1   #280. Descant and harmonization
    B356 (PD), L367
"God of Wonders" (Pss)
    M80; V-3 p. 184 Vocal Solo
"My Hope Is Built" (Phil, Matt)
    B406, C537, EL596, F92, L293, N368, P379, UM368 (PD)
        H-3   Chr-191
        S-2   #171-172. Trumpet and vocal descants
    L294 (PD)
        H-3   Chr-63; Desc-74; Org-89
"One Bread, One Body" (World Communion)
    C393, EL496, UM620, VU467
        H-3   Chr-156
"The Church's One Foundation" (Phil, Matt, Communion) (C)
    B350, C272, E525, EL654, F547, L369, N386, P442, UM545
    (PD) and UM 546, VU332 (Fr.)
        C272   Descant
        H-3   Hbl-94; Chr-180; Desc-16; Org-9
        S-1   #25-26. Descant and harmonization

Additional Hymn Suggestions

"Every Time I Feel the Spirit" (Exod) (O)
    C592, N282, P315, UM404
"Forgive Our Sins as We Forgive" (Exod)
    E674, EL605, L307, P347, R184, UM390, VU364, W754
"Jesus Calls Us" (Exod, Phil)
    B293, C337, EL696, F399, L494, N172, UM398 (PD), VU562
"How Firm a Foundation" (Exod, Matt)
    B338, C618, E636, EL796, F32, L507, N407, P361, UM529
    (PD), VU660, W585
"Spirit, Spirit of Gentleness" (Exod)
    C249, EL396, N286, P319, S2120, VU375 (Fr.)
"Cantemos al Señor" ("Let's Sing unto the Lord") (Pss)
    B38, C60, EL555, N39, R11, UM149
"Let Us with a Joyful Mind" (Pss)
    E389, L521, P244, N16, S2012, SF2012, VU234
"Jesus, the Very Thought of Thee" (Phil)
    B225, C102, E642, EL754, F465, L316, N507, P310, UM175
    (PD)
"When I Survey the Wondrous Cross" (Phil)
    B144, C195, EL803, F258, N224, P101, R236, UM298 (PD)
"When I Survey the Wondrous Cross" (Phil)
    E474, L482, P100, UM299 (PD), VU149 (Fr.), W433
"And Can It Be that I Should Gain" (Phil)
    B147, F260, R193, UM363 (PD)
"All Who Love and Serve Your City" (Matt)
    C670, E570/E571, EL724, L436, P413, UM433, W621
"We Are God's People" (Matt, World Communion)
    B383, F546, S2220, SF2220
"God Made from One Blood" (World Communion)
    C500, N427, S2170, SF2170, VU554

"In Unity We Lift Our Song" (World Communion)
    S2221, SF2221

Additional Contemporary Suggestions

"Awesome God" (Pss)
    R245, S2040, SF2040, SP11
"All Heaven Declares" (Pss)
    R163, M58
"The Heavens Shall Declare" (Pss)
    M111
"Guide My Feet" (Phil)
    N497, P354, S2208
"He Who Began a Good Work in You" (Phil)
    S2163, SF2163, SP180, R134
"In the Secret" ("I Want to Know You") (Phil)
    M38; V-3 p. 36 Vocal Solo
"The Wonderful Cross" (Phil)
    M76
"Come to the Table" (Phil, Communion)
    EL481, S2264, SF2264
"Grace Alone" (Phil, Matt)
    M100, S2162, SF2162
"Make Us One" (World Communion)
    S2224, SF2224, SP137

Vocal Solos

"The Heavens Declare His Glory" (Pss)
    V-8   p. 248
"The Body of the Lord" (World Communion)
    V-8   p. 344

Anthems

"Christ Is Made the Sure Foundation" (Matt)
Purcell/ arr. Rutter; Hinshaw HMC1796
SATB with organ; opt. congregation

"Face to Face" (Communion)
Mark Burrows; Abingdon 0687075629
SATB with keyboard

Other Suggestions

Visuals:
    O   Clay tablets, Ten Commandments, lightening, trumpet,
           mountain
    P   Tent, wedding canopy, planets/stars/space, gold, rock,
           honey/comb
    E   "Yet," rubbish, portrait of Christ, resurrection, crown of
           laurel leaves, trophy
    G   Vineyard, wine press, building cornerstone, fruit
    World Communion: flags, costumes, artifacts of nations,
                         unity, breads of the world, globe
Call to Worship: B76, C119, E56, EL257, F169, L34, N116, P9,
    UM211, VU1, W357, stanza 3. "O Come, O Come,
    Emmanuel" (Exod)
World Communion Resources Include: C394, C481, F549,
    UM556, UM564, N786, and N853.
Alternate Lessons: Isa 5:1-7; Ps 80:7-15 (*See page 3*)

Exodus 32:1-14

[1] When the people saw that Moses delayed to come down from the mountain, the people gathered around Aaron, and said to him, "Come, make gods for us, who shall go before us; as for this Moses, the man who brought us up out of the land of Egypt, we do not know what has become of him." [2] Aaron said to them, "Take off the gold rings that are on the ears of your wives, your sons, and your daughters, and bring them to me." [3] So all the people took off the gold rings from their ears, and brought them to Aaron. [4] He took the gold from them, formed it in a mold, and cast an image of a calf; and they said, "These are your gods, O Israel, who brought you up out of the land of Egypt!" [5] When Aaron saw this, he built an altar before it; and Aaron made proclamation and said, "Tomorrow shall be a festival to the LORD." [6] They rose early the next day, and offered burnt offerings and brought sacrifices of well-being; and the people sat down to eat and drink, and rose up to revel.

[7] The LORD said to Moses, "Go down at once! Your people, whom you brought up out of the land of Egypt, have acted perversely; [8] they have been quick to turn aside from the way that I commanded them; they have cast for themselves an image of a calf, and have worshiped it and sacrificed to it, and said, 'These are your gods, O Israel, who brought you up out of the land of Egypt!' " [9] The LORD said to Moses, "I have seen this people, how stiff-necked they are. [10] Now let me alone, so that my wrath may burn hot against them and I may consume them; and of you I will make a great nation."

[11] But Moses implored the LORD his God, and said, "O LORD, why does your wrath burn hot against your people, whom you brought out of the land of Egypt with great power and with a mighty hand? [12] Why should the Egyptians say, 'It was with evil intent that he brought them out to kill them in the mountains, and to consume them from the face of the earth'? Turn from your fierce wrath; change your mind and do not bring disaster on your people. [13] Remember Abraham, Isaac, and Israel, your servants, how you swore to them by your own self, saying to them, 'I will multiply your descendants like the stars of heaven, and all this land that I have promised I will give to your descendants, and they shall inherit it forever.' " [14] And the LORD changed his mind about the disaster that he planned to bring on his people.

Psalm 106:1-6, 19-23

[1] Praise the LORD! O give thanks to the LORD, for he is good; for his steadfast love endures forever. [2] Who can utter the mighty doings of the LORD, or declare all his praise? [3] Happy are those who observe justice, who do righteousness at all times. [4] Remember me, O LORD when you show favor to your people; help me when you deliver them; [5] that I may see the prosperity of your chosen ones, that I may rejoice in the gladness of your nation, that I may glory in your heritage. [6] Both we and our ancestors have sinned; we have committed iniquity, have done wickedly.

[19] They made a calf at Horeb and worshiped a cast image. [20] They exchanged the glory of God for the image of an ox that eats grass. [21] They forgot God, their Savior, who had done great things in Egypt, [22] wondrous works in the land of Ham, and awesome deeds by the Red Sea. [23] Therefore he said he would destroy them—had not Moses, his chosen one, stood in the breach before him, to turn away his wrath from destroying them.

Philippians 4:1-9

[1] Therefore, my brothers and sisters, whom I love and long for, my joy and crown, stand firm in the Lord in this way, my beloved.

[2] I urge Euodia and I urge Syntyche to be of the same mind in the Lord. [3] Yes, and I ask you also, my loyal companion, help these women, for they have struggled beside me in the work of the gospel, together with Clement and the rest of my co-workers, whose names are in the book of life.

[4] Rejoice in the Lord always; again I will say, Rejoice. [5] Let your gentleness be known to everyone. The Lord is near. [6] Do not worry about anything, but in everything by prayer and supplication with thanksgiving let your requests be made known to God. [7] And the peace of God, which surpasses all understanding, will guard your hearts and your minds in Christ Jesus.

[8] Finally, beloved, whatever is true, whatever is honorable, whatever is just, whatever is pure, whatever is pleasing, whatever is commendable, if there is any excellence and if there is anything worthy of praise, think about these things. [9] Keep on doing the things that you have learned and received and heard and seen in me, and the God of peace will be with you.

Matthew 22:1-14

[1] Once more Jesus spoke to them in parables, saying: [2] "The kingdom of heaven may be compared to a king who gave a wedding banquet for his son. [3] He sent his slaves to call those who had been invited to the wedding banquet, but they would not come. [4] Again he sent other slaves, saying, 'Tell those who have been invited: Look, I have prepared my dinner, my oxen and my fat calves have been slaughtered, and everything is ready; come to the wedding banquet.' [5] But they made light of it and went away, one to his farm, another to his business, [6] while the rest seized his slaves, mistreated them, and killed them. [7] The king was enraged. He sent his troops, destroyed those murderers, and burned their city. [8] Then he said to his slaves, 'The wedding is ready, but those invited were not worthy. [9] Go therefore into the main streets, and invite everyone you find to the wedding banquet.' [10] Those slaves went out into the streets and gathered all whom they found, both good and bad; so the wedding hall was filled with guests.

[11] "But when the king came in to see the guests, he noticed a man there who was not wearing a wedding robe, [12] and he said to him, 'Friend, how did you get in here without a wedding robe?' And he was speechless. [13] Then the king said to the attendants, 'Bind him hand and foot, and throw him into the outer darkness, where there will be weeping and gnashing of teeth.' [14] For many are called, but few are chosen."

Primary Hymns and Songs for the Day

"Rejoice, Ye Pure in Heart" (Phil) (O)
    B39, C15, E556, EL873, F394, N55, P145, UM160 (PD)
        H-3   Hbl-17, 90; Chr-166; Desc-73; Org-85
        S-1   #228. Descant
    E557, EL874, N71, P146, UM161
        H-3   Chr-166; Desc-102
"Forever" (Pss)
    M68
"Where Cross the Crowded Ways of Life" (C) (Matt)
    C665, E609, EL719, F665, L429, N543, P408, UM427 (PD),
    VU681
        H-3   Chr-178, 180; Org-44
        S-1   #141-3 Various treatments
"Rejoice, the Lord Is King" (Phil) (C)
    B197, C699, F374, N303, P155, UM715 (PD), VU213, W493
        H-3   Hbl-8, 53, 90; Chr-37; Desc-27; Org-24
        S-1   #78-80. Various treatments
    E481, UM716
        S-1   #147. Arrangement for two trumpets
    EL430 (PD), L171

Additional Hymn Suggestions

"God Created Heaven and Earth" (Exod)
    EL738, N33, P290, UM151, VU251
"For the Healing of the Nations" (Exod)
    C668, N576, UM428, VU678, W643
"Spirit, Spirit of Gentleness" (Exod)
    C249, EL396, N286, P319, S2120, VU375 (Fr.)
"Now Thank We All Our God" (Exod, Pss)
    B638, C715, E396 or 397, EL839 or 840, F525, L533 or
    L534, N419, P555, UM102 (PD), VU236 (Fr.), W560
"There's a Wideness in God's Mercy" (Exod, Matt)
    B25, C73, E470, EL587/EL588, F115, L290, N23, P298,
    UM121, VU271, W595
"Jesus Calls Us" (Exod, Matt)
    B293, C337, EL696, F399, L494, N172, UM398 (PD), VU562
"Take Time to Be Holy" (Phil)
    B446, C572, F457, UM395 (PD), VU672
"What a Friend We Have in Jesus" (Phil)
    B182, C585, EL742, F466, L439, N506, P403, UM526 (PD),
    VU661
"Lord of All Hopefulness" (Phil, Matt)
    E482, EL765, L469, R174, S2197, SF2197, W568
"Come and Find the Quiet Center" (Phil)
    C575, S2128, SF2128, VU374
"My Life Flows On" (Phil)
    C619, EL763, N476, S2212, SF2212, VU716
"Come, Ye Sinners, Poor and Needy" (Matt)
    B323 (PD), R141, UM340, W756
"O Jesus, I Have Promised" (Matt)
    B276, C612, E655, EL810, F402, L503, N493, P388, UM396
    (PD)
"Softly and Tenderly Jesus Is Calling" (Matt)
    B312, C340, EL608 (PD), F432, N449, R147, UM348
"Deck Thyself, My Soul, with Gladness" (Matt, Communion)
    E339, EL488/EL489, L224, P506, UM612 (PD), VU463

"Together We Serve" (Matt)
    S2175, SF2175
"As We Gather at Your Table" (Matt, Communion)
    EL522, N332, S2268, SF2268, VU457
"Go Forth for God" (Phil) (C)
    E347, R291, UM670, VU418

Additional Contemporary Suggestions

"God Is So Good" (Pss)
    B23, S2056, SF2056
"Give Thanks" (Pss)
    C528, R266, S2036, SF2036, SP170
"In the Lord I'll Be Ever Thankful" (Pss)
    S2195, SF2195
"I Will Enter His Gates" (Phil)
    S2270, SF2270, SP168
"I've Got Peace Like a River" (Phil)
    B418, C530, N478, P368, S2145, VU577
"Give Peace" ("Da Pacem Cordium") (Phil)
    S2156, SF2156
"Lord, Listen to Your Children Praying" (Phil)
    C305, S2193, SF2193, VU400
"Jesus, We Are Here" ("Yesu Tawa Pano") (Phil)
    EL529, S2273, SF2273
"Let the Peace of God Reign" (Phil)
    M87

Vocal Solo

"Stan'in' In De Need of Prayer" (Exod)
V-7   p. 40
"A Song of Trust" (Phil)
V-4   p. 20

Anthems

"Rejoice in the Lord Always" (Phil)
George Rathbone; Novello 15652
SATB with organ

"God Is So Good" (Pss)
arr. John D. Horman; Abingdon 0687044073
Two-part treble with keyboard

Other Suggestions

Visuals:
    O/P   Gold, jewelry, golden calf, hands folded/lifted in
               prayer
    E   Praying hands, "Rejoice in the Lord always,"
               "Again I say, Rejoice"
    G   Wedding garments, other wedding items (invita-
               tions, rings, flowers)
Call to Prayer: EL538, S2157, SF2157, W561. "Come and Fill Our
    Hearts" (Phil)
Prayer: C547, UM329, UM392, or UM459 (Phil)
Response: S2195, SF2195. "In the Lord I'll Be Ever Thankful" (Pss)
Blessing: Philippians 4:8-9
Response: C444, UM668. "Let Us Now Depart in Your Peace"
    (Phil)
Alternate Lessons: Isa 25:1-9; Ps 23 (*See page 3*)

Exodus 33:12-23

[12] Moses said to the LORD, "See, you have said to me, 'Bring up this people'; but you have not let me know whom you will send with me. Yet you have said, 'I know you by name, and you have also found favor in my sight.' [13] Now if I have found favor in your sight, show me your ways, so that I may know you and find favor in your sight. Consider too that this nation is your people." [14] He said, "My presence will go with you, and I will give you rest." [15] And he said to him, "If your presence will not go, do not carry us up from here. [16] For how shall it be known that I have found favor in your sight, I and your people, unless you go with us? In this way, we shall be distinct, I and your people, from every people on the face of the earth."

[17] The LORD said to Moses, "I will do the very thing that you have asked; for you have found favor in my sight, and I know you by name." [18] Moses said, "Show me your glory, I pray." [19] And he said, "I will make all my goodness pass before you, and will proclaim before you the name, 'The LORD'; and I will be gracious to whom I will be gracious, and will show mercy on whom I will show mercy. [20] But," he said, "you cannot see my face; for no one shall see me and live." [21] And the LORD continued, "See, there is a place by me where you shall stand on the rock; [22] and while my glory passes by I will put you in a cleft of the rock, and I will cover you with my hand until I have passed by; [23] then I will take away my hand, and you shall see my back; but my face shall not be seen."

Psalm 99

[1] The LORD is king; let the peoples tremble! He sits enthroned upon the cherubim; let the earth quake! [2] The LORD is great in Zion; he is exalted over all the peoples. [3] Let them praise your great and awesome name. Holy is he! [4] Mighty King, lover of justice, you have established equity; you have executed justice and righteousness in Jacob. [5] Extol the LORD our God; worship at his footstool. Holy is he! [6] Moses and Aaron were among his priests, Samuel also was among those who called on his name. They cried to the LORD, and he answered them. [7] He spoke to them in the pillar of cloud; they kept his decrees, and the statutes that he gave them. [8] O LORD our God, you answered them; you were a forgiving God to them, but an avenger of their wrongdoings. [9] Extol the LORD our God, and worship at his holy mountain; for the LORD our God is holy.

1 Thessalonians 1:1-10

[1] Paul, Silvanus, and Timothy,

To the church of the Thessalonians in God the Father and the Lord Jesus Christ:

Grace to you and peace.

[2] We always give thanks to God for all of you and mention you in our prayers, constantly [3] remembering before our God and Father your work of faith and labor of love and steadfastness of hope in our Lord Jesus Christ. [4] For we know, brothers and sisters beloved by God, that he has chosen you, [5] because our message of the gospel came to you not in word only, but also in power and in the Holy Spirit and with full conviction; just as you know what kind of persons we proved to be among you for your sake. [6] And you became imitators of us and of the Lord, for in spite of persecution you received the word with joy inspired by the Holy Spirit, [7] so that you became an example to all the believers in Macedonia and in Achaia. [8] For the word of the Lord has sounded forth from you not only in Macedonia and Achaia, but in every place your faith in God has become known, so that we have no need to speak about it. [9] For the people of those regions report about us what kind of welcome we had among you, and how you turned to God from idols, to serve a living and true God, [10] and to wait for his Son from heaven, whom he raised from the dead—Jesus, who rescues us from the wrath that is coming.

Matthew 22:15-22

[15] Then the Pharisees went and plotted to entrap him in what he said. [16] So they sent their disciples to him, along with the Herodians, saying, "Teacher, we know that you are sincere, and teach the way of God in accordance with truth, and show deference to no one; for you do not regard people with partiality. [17] Tell us, then, what you think. Is it lawful to pay taxes to the emperor, or not?" [18] But Jesus, aware of their malice, said, "Why are you putting me to the test, you hypocrites? [19] Show me the coin used for the tax." And they brought him a denarius. [20] Then he said to them, "Whose head is this, and whose title?" [21] They answered, "The emperor's." Then he said to them, "Give therefore to the emperor the things that are the emperor's, and to God the things that are God's." [22] When they heard this, they were amazed; and they left him and went away.

Primary Hymns and Songs for the Day

"O Worship the King" (Pss) (O)
> B16, C17, F336, N26, P476, UM73 (PD)
>> H-3   Hbl-85; Chr-154; Desc-71; Org-82
>> S-1   #223-226. Various treatments
>
> E388, EL842 (PD), L548, VU235
>> H-3   Hbl-90, 105; Chr-221; Desc-49; Org-51
>> S-2   #71-74. Introduction and harmonizations

"He Is Exalted" (Pss, Matt)
> R238, S2070, SF2070, SP66

"O Young and Fearless Prophet" (Matt)
> UM444 (PD)
>> S-2   #27. Descant
>
> C669

"Take My Life, and Let It Be" (Matt) (C)
> B277, C609, P391
>> H-3   Chr-34, 177; Desc-51; Org-53
>> S-2   #78-80. Various treatments
>
> B283, E707, EL583/EL685, L406, R133, N448, UM399
> (PD), VU506

Additional Hymn Suggestions

"Sing Praise to God Who Reigns Above" (O) (Exod)
> B20, C6, E408, EL871, F343, N6, P483, R52, UM126 (PD),
> VU216, W528

"Immortal, Invisible, God Only Wise" (Exod)
> B6, C66, E423, EL834, F319, L526, N1, P263, R46, UM103
> (PD), VU264, W512

"Rock of Ages, Cleft for Me" (Exod)
> B342, C214, E685, EL623, F108, L327, N596, UM361 (PD)

"How Firm a Foundation" (Exod, 1 Thess) (C)
> B338, C618, E636, EL796, F32, L507, N407, P361, UM529
> (PD), VU660, W585

"Praise, My Soul, the King of Heaven" (Pss)
> B32, C23, E410, EL864/EL865, F339, L549, P478/P479,
> R53, UM66 (PD), VU240, W530

"Rejoice, the Lord Is King" (Pss)
> B197, C699, E481, EL430, F374, L171, N303, P155,
> UM715/UM716, VU213, W493

"The Battle Hymn of the Republic" (Pss)
> B633, C705, EL890, F692, L332, N610, UM717 (PD), W686

"O God Beyond All Praising" (Pss)
> EL880, S2009, SF2009, VU256, W541

"Wounded World that Cries for Healing" (Pss)
> S2177, SF2177

"Unsettled World" (Pss)
> S2183, SF2183

"Filled with the Spirit's Power" (1 Thess)
> L160, N266, UM537, VU194

"We Are God's People" (1 Thess)
> B383, F546, S2220, SF2220

"Rejoice in God's Saints" (1 Thess)
> C476, EL418, UM708

"O, How I Love Jesus" (1 Thess, Matt)
> B217, C99, F634, N52, UM170 (PD)

"Lord of the Dance" (Matt)
> P302, UM261, VU352, W636

"All Who Love and Serve Your City" (Matt, Exod)
> C670, E570/E571, EL724, L436, P413, UM433, W621

Additional Contemporary Suggestions

"I Love You, Lord" (Exod)
> B212, R36, S2068, SF2068, SP72

"In the Secret" ("I Want to Know You") (Exod)
> M38; V-3 p. 36 Vocal Solo

"Show Me Your Ways" (Exod)
> M107

"Rock of Ages" (Exod, Pss)
> M93

"El-Shaddai" (Exod, Pss)
> UM123, S-2 #54

"Awesome God" (Exod, Pss)
> R245, S2040, SF2040, SP11

"Come, All You People" ("Uyai Mose") (Pss)
> EL819, S2274, SF2274

"We Will Glorify" (Pss)
> B213, S2087, SF2087, SP68

"Lord, Be Glorified" (Pss, Matt)
> B457, EL744, S2150, SF2150, R172, SP196

"More Precious than Silver" (Matt)
> S2065, SF2065, SP99

"Make Me a Servant" (Matt)
> S2176, SF2176, SP193

"Step By Step" (Matt, Exod)
> M51

"Take This Life" (Matt, Stewardship)
> M98

Vocal Solos

"God, Our Ever Faithful Shepherd" (Exod, Pss)
V-4   p. 15
"Praise to the Lord, the Almighty" (Pss)
V-6   p. 18

Anthems

"God Is Our Refuge" (Exod)
Allen Pote; Hope A 583
SATB with keyboard (opt. trumpets)

"Take My Life, and Let It Be" (Matt)
Ruth Watson Hendson; Alfred Music VTS4064-D
SATB with keyboard

Other Suggestions

Visuals:
> **O**   Rock, cleft rock, hand
> **P**   Earthquake, cloud, footstool
> **E**   Symbols of the Holy Spirit, Trinity
> **G**   Array of coins around an empty offering plate, cross

Call to Worship: EL819, S2274, SF2274. "Come, All You People"
> ("Uyai Mose") (Pss)

Prayer: C31, C52, or UM152 (Exod)

Response: C380, UM588. "All Things Come of Thee" (Matt)

Alternate Lessons: Isa 45:1-7; Ps 96:1-9, (10-13) (*See page 3*)

Deuteronomy 34:1-12

[1] Then Moses went up from the plains of Moab to Mount Nebo, to the top of Pisgah, which is opposite Jericho, and the LORD showed him the whole land: Gilead as far as Dan, [2] all Naphtali, the land of Ephraim and Manasseh, all the land of Judah as far as the Western Sea, [3] the Negeb, and the Plain—that is, the valley of Jericho, the city of palm trees—as far as Zoar. [4] The LORD said to him, "This is the land of which I swore to Abraham, to Isaac, and to Jacob, saying, 'I will give it to your descendants'; I have let you see it with your eyes, but you shall not cross over there." [5] Then Moses, the servant of the LORD, died there in the land of Moab, at the LORD's command. [6] He was buried in a valley in the land of Moab, opposite Beth-peor, but no one knows his burial place to this day. [7] Moses was one hundred twenty years old when he died; his sight was unimpaired and his vigor had not abated. [8] The Israelites wept for Moses in the plains of Moab thirty days; then the period of mourning for Moses was ended.

[9] Joshua son of Nun was full of the spirit of wisdom, because Moses had laid his hands on him; and the Israelites obeyed him, doing as the LORD had commanded Moses.

[10] Never since has there arisen a prophet in Israel like Moses, whom the LORD knew face to face. [11] He was unequaled for all the signs and wonders that the LORD sent him to perform in the land of Egypt, against Pharaoh and all his servants and his entire land, [12] and for all the mighty deeds and all the terrifying displays of power that Moses performed in the sight of all Israel.

Psalm 90:1-6, 13-17

[1] Lord, you have been our dwelling place in all generations. [2] Before the mountains were brought forth, or ever you had formed the earth and the world, from everlasting to everlasting you are God. [3] You turn us back to dust, and say, "Turn back, you mortals." [4] For a thousand years in your sight are like yesterday when it is past, or like a watch in the night. [5] You sweep them away; they are like a dream, like grass that is renewed in the morning; [6] in the morning it flourishes and is renewed; in the evening it fades and withers.

[13] Turn, O LORD! How long? Have compassion on your servants! [14] Satisfy us in the morning with your steadfast love, so that we may rejoice and be glad all our days. [15] Make us glad as many days as you have afflicted us, and as many years as we have seen evil. [16] Let your work be manifest to your servants, and your glorious power to their children. [17] Let the favor of the Lord our God be upon us, and prosper for us the work of our hands—O prosper the work of our hands!

1 Thessalonians 2:1-8

[1] You yourselves know, brothers and sisters, that our coming to you was not in vain, [2] but though we had already suffered and been shamefully mistreated at Philippi, as you know, we had courage in our God to declare to you the gospel of God in spite of great opposition. [3] For our appeal does not spring from deceit or impure motives or trickery, [4] but just as we have been approved by God to be entrusted with the message of the gospel, even so we speak, not to please mortals, but to please God who tests our hearts. [5] As you know and as God is our witness, we never came with words of flattery or with a pretext for greed; [6] nor did we seek praise from mortals, whether from you or from others, [7] though we might have made demands as apostles of Christ. But we were gentle among you, like a nurse tenderly caring for her own children. [8] So deeply do we care for you that we are determined to share with you not only the gospel of God but also our own selves, because you have become very dear to us.

Matthew 22:34-46

[34] When the Pharisees heard that he had silenced the Sadducees, they gathered together, [35] and one of them, a lawyer, asked him a question to test him. [36] "Teacher, which commandment in the law is the greatest?" [37] He said to him, " 'You shall love the Lord your God with all your heart, and with all your soul, and with all your mind.' [38] This is the greatest and first commandment. [39] And a second is like it: 'You shall love your neighbor as yourself.' [40] On these two commandments hang all the law and the prophets."

[41] Now while the Pharisees were gathered together, Jesus asked them this question: [42] "What do you think of the Messiah? Whose son is he?" They said to him, "The son of David." [43] He said to them, "How is it then that David by the Spirit calls him Lord, saying, [44] 'The Lord said to my Lord, "Sit at my right hand, until I put your enemies under your feet" ' ? [45] If David thus calls him Lord, how can he be his son?" [46] No one was able to give him an answer, nor from that day did anyone dare to ask him any more questions.

Primary Hymns and Songs for the Day

"O God, Our Help in Ages Past" (Pss) (O)
 B74, C67, E680, EL632, F370, L320, N25, P210, UM117
 (PD), VU806, W579
  H-3 Hbl-87; Chr-60, 143; Desc-93; Org-132
  S-1 #293-296. Various treatments
"Love the Lord Your God" (Matt)
 S2168, SF2168
"Lord, I Want to Be a Christian" (Matt) (C)
 B489, C589, F421, N454, P372 (PD), R145, UM402
  H-3 Chr-130

Additional Hymn Suggestions

"I'll Praise My Maker While I've Breath" (Deut)
 B35, C20, E429 (PD), P253, UM60, VU867
"God Hath Spoken by the Prophets" (Deut)
 L238, UM108, W516
"Go Down, Moses" (Deut)
 C663, E648, N572, P334, UM448, W508
  See especially stanzas 8-11
"Beams of Heaven as I Go" (Deut)
 N447, UM524
"Swing Low, Sweet Chariot" (Deut)
 C643, UM703
"Praise, My Soul, the King of Heaven" (Pss, 1 Thess)
 B32, C23, E410, EL864/EL865, F339, L549, P478/P479,
 R53, UM66 (PD), VU240, W530
"The Care the Eagle Gives Her Young" (1 Thess)
 C76, N468, UM118, VU269
"Lord, Speak to Me" (1 Thess)
 B568, EL676, F625, L403, N531, P426, UM463 (PD), VU589
"Blest Be the Tie That Binds" (1 Thess)
 B387, C433, EL656, F560, L370, N393, P438, UM557 (PD),
 VU602
"O Master, Let Me Walk with Thee" (1 Thess, Matt)
 B279, C602, E659/E660, EL818, F442, L492, N503, P357,
 UM430 (PD), VU560
"Pass It On" (1 Thess, Matt)
 C477, F641, UM572, VU289
"The Gift of Love" (Matt)
 B423, C526, EL644, P335, R155, UM408, VU372
"More Love to Thee, O Christ" (Matt)
 B473, C527, F476, N456, P359, UM453 (PD)
"Spirit of God, Descend Upon My Heart" (Matt)
 B245, C265, EL800, F147, L486, N290, P326, UM500 (PD),
 VU378
"Where Charity and Love Prevail" (Matt)
 E581, EL359, L126, N396, UM549
"Healer of Our Every Ill" (Matt)
 C506, EL612, S2213, SF2213, VU619
"In Remembrance of Me" (Matt, Communion)
 B365, C403, S2254

Additional Contemporary Suggestions

"Jesu, Jesu" (Matt)
 B501, C600, E602, EL708, N498, P367, R289, UM432,
 VU593, W431, S-1 #63 Vocal part

"I Sing Praises to Your Name" (Matt)
 R79, S2037, SF2037, SP27
"Jesus, Name above All Names" (Matt)
 R26, S2071, SF2071, SP76
"To Know You More" (Matt)
 S2161, SF2161
"More Like You" (Matt)
 S2167, SF2167
"The Family Prayer Song" (Matt)
 M54, S2188, SF2188
"More Love, More Power" (Matt)
 M40
"Refresh My Heart" (Matt)
 M49
"Let It Be Said of Us" (Matt)
 M53
"Just Let Me Say" (Matt)
 M83
"Take This Life" (Matt)
 M98
"With All of My Heart" (Matt)
 M86, SP187

Vocal Solos

"Over Yonder" (Deut)
V-7 p. 38
"The Call" (Pss, Matt)
V-4 p. 31
"The Gift of Love" (Matt)
V-8 p. 120

Anthems

"On Jordan's Stormy Banks" (Deut)
arr. Ken Berg; Santa Barbara Music 811
SATB with piano

"Promised Land" (Deut)
Natalie Sleeth; Heritage Music Press
Three-part mixed with keyboard (#HV405)
Two-part with keyboard (#S5775)

Other Suggestions

Visuals:
 O Portrait or bust of Moses, tears
 P Tall grass, morning/evening, rejoicing, hands at
  work/praise
 E Nurturing, caring for children
 G Images of loving God, neighbor, self, worship, service
  to others, nurture, Matt 22:37, 38
Prayer: C571 or C443 (Matt) or UM268 (Deut)
Response: C523, EL642, R226, S2179, SF2179, W604. "Live in
 Charity" ("Ubi Caritas") (Matt)
Benediction: S2171, SF2171, VU684. "Make Me a Channel of
 Your Peace" (Matt)
Alternate Lessons: Lev. 19:1-2, 15-18; Ps 1 (*See page 3*)

Joshua 3:7-17

[7] The LORD said to Joshua, "This day I will begin to exalt you in the sight of all Israel, so that they may know that I will be with you as I was with Moses. [8] You are the one who shall command the priests who bear the ark of the covenant, 'When you come to the edge of the waters of the Jordan, you shall stand still in the Jordan.' "
[9] Joshua then said to the Israelites, "Draw near and hear the words of the LORD your God." [10] Joshua said, "By this you shall know that among you is the living God who without fail will drive out from before you the Canaanites, Hittites, Hivites, Perizzites, Girgashites, Amorites, and Jebusites: [11] the ark of the covenant of the Lord of all the earth is going to pass before you into the Jordan. [12] So now select twelve men from the tribes of Israel, one from each tribe. [13] When the soles of the feet of the priests who bear the ark of the LORD, the Lord of all the earth, rest in the waters of the Jordan, the waters of the Jordan flowing from above shall be cut off; they shall stand in a single heap."

[14] When the people set out from their tents to cross over the Jordan, the priests bearing the ark of the covenant were in front of the people. [15] Now the Jordan overflows all its banks throughout the time of harvest. So when those who bore the ark had come to the Jordan, and the feet of the priests bearing the ark were dipped in the edge of the water, [16] the waters flowing from above stood still, rising up in a single heap far off at Adam, the city that is beside Zarethan, while those flowing toward the sea of the Arabah, the Dead Sea, were wholly cut off. Then the people crossed over opposite Jericho. [17] While all Israel were crossing over on dry ground, the priests who bore the ark of the covenant of the LORD stood on dry ground in the middle of the Jordan, until the entire nation finished crossing over the Jordan.

Psalm 107:1-7, 33-37

[1] O give thanks to the LORD, for he is good; for his steadfast love endures forever. [2] Let the redeemed of the LORD say so, those he redeemed from trouble [3] and gathered in from the lands, from the east and from the west, from the north and from the south. [4] Some wandered in desert wastes, finding no way to an inhabited town; [5] hungry and thirsty, their soul fainted within them. [6] Then they cried to the LORD in their trouble, and he delivered them from their distress; [7] he led them by a straight way, until they reached an inhabited town.

[33] He turns rivers into a desert, springs of water into thirsty ground, [34] a fruitful land into a salty waste, because of the wickedness of its inhabitants. [35] He turns a desert into pools of water, a parched land into springs of water. [36] And there he lets the hungry live, and they establish a town to live in; [37] they sow fields, and plant vineyards, and get a fruitful yield.

1 Thessalonians 2:9-13

[9] You remember our labor and toil, brothers and sisters; we worked night and day, so that we might not burden any of you while we proclaimed to you the gospel of God. [10] You are witnesses, and God also, how pure, upright, and blameless our conduct was toward you believers. [11] As you know, we dealt with each one of you like a father with his children, [12] urging and encouraging you and pleading that you lead a life worthy of God, who calls you into his own kingdom and glory.

[13] We also constantly give thanks to God for this, that when you received the word of God that you heard from us, you accepted it not as a human word but as what it really is, God's word, which is also at work in you believers.

Matthew 23:1-12

[1] Then Jesus said to the crowds and to his disciples, [2] "The scribes and the Pharisees sit on Moses' seat; [3] therefore, do whatever they teach you and follow it; but do not do as they do, for they do not practice what they teach. [4] They tie up heavy burdens, hard to bear, and lay them on the shoulders of others; but they themselves are unwilling to lift a finger to move them. [5] They do all their deeds to be seen by others; for they make their phylacteries broad and their fringes long. [6] They love to have the place of honor at banquets and the best seats in the synagogues, [7] and to be greeted with respect in the marketplaces, and to have people call them rabbi. [8] But you are not to be called rabbi, for you have one teacher, and you are all students. [9] And call no one your father on earth, for you have one Father—the one in heaven. [10] Nor are you to be called instructors, you have one instructor, the Messiah. [11] The greatest among you will be your servant. [12] All who exalt themselves will be humbled, and all who humble themselves will be exalted."

Primary Hymns and Songs for the Day

"Guide Me, O Thou Great Jehovah" (Josh) (O)
    B56, C622, E690, EL618, F608, L343, N18/N19, P281,
    UM127 (PD), VU651 (Fr.)
        H-3 Hbl-25, 51, 58; Chr-89; Desc-26; Org-23
        S-1 #76-77. Descant and harmonization

"Every Time I Feel the Spirit" (Josh)
    C592, N282, P315, UM404

"Lord, Whose Love Through Humble Service" (Matt)
    C461, EL712, L423, UM581
        H-3 Chr-51, 67
    E610, R286, W630

"On Jordan's Stormy Banks I Stand" (Deut) (C)
    B521, EL437, N598, UM724 (PD)
        H-3 Chr-155; Org-117
        S-1 #271. Orff instrument arrangement
            #272. Transposition in D major

Additional Hymn Suggestions

"A Mighty Fortress Is Our God" (Josh, Pss, Reformation) (O)
    B8, C65, E687/E688, EL503/504/505, F118, L228/L229,
    N439/N440, P259/P260, UM110 (PD),
    VU261/VU262/VU263, W575/W576

"He Leadeth Me: O Blessed Thought" (Josh) (O)
    B52, C545, F606, L501, UM128 (PD), VU657

"Go Down, Moses" (Josh)
    C663, E648, N572, P334, UM448, W508

"Precious Lord, Take My Hand" (Josh)
    B456, C628, EL773, F611, N472, P404, UM474, VU670

"Faith, While Trees Are Still in Blossom" (Josh)
    C535, UM508, VU643

"On Jordan's Stormy Banks I Stand" (Josh) (C)
    B521, EL437, N598, UM724 (PD)

"Lift Every Voice and Sing" (Josh, Pss)
    B627, C631, E599, EL841, L562, N593, P563, UM519, W641

"You Satisfy the Hungry Heart" (Pss, Communion)
    C429, EL484, P521, UM629, R217, VU478, W736

"O Food to Pilgrims Given" (Pss, Communion)
    E308/E309, L222, UM631

"O God Beyond All Praising" (Pss)
    EL880, S2009, SF2009, VU256, W541

"Come to the Table" (Pss)
    EL481, S2264, SF2264

"Because He Lives" (Josh, Pss, 1 Thess)
    B407, C562, F292, UM364

"Thy Word Is a Lamp" (1 Thess)
    C326, R94, SP183, UM601

"Go Forth for God" (1 Thess) (C)
    E347, R291, UM670, VU418

"Ask Ye What Great Thing I Know" (1 Thess, Matt)
    B538, N49, UM163 (PD), VU338

"All Who Love and Serve Your City" (1 Thess, Matt)
    C670, E570/E571, EL724, L436, P413, UM433, W621

"I'm Gonna Live So God Can Use Me" (1 Thess, Matt)
    C614, P369, S2153, VU575

"Jesu, Jesu" (Matt)
    B501, C600, E602, EL708, N498, P367, R289, UM432,
    VU593, W431, S-1 #63 Vocal part

"Lord, Speak to Me" (Matt)
    B568, EL676, F625, L403, N531, P426, UM463 (PD), VU589

"Draw Us in the Spirit's Tether" (Matt, Communion)
    C392, EL470, N337, P504, UM632, VU479, W731

"Love the Lord Your God" (Matt)
    S2168, SF2168

"As We Gather at Your Table" (Matt, Communion)
    EL522, N332, S2268, SF2268, VU457

Additional Contemporary Suggestions

"Holy Ground" (Josh)
    B224, C112, S2272, SF2272, SP86

"Awesome In This Place" (Josh)
    M36

"In the Lord I'll Be Ever Thankful" (Pss, 1 Thess)
    S2195, SF2195

"Forever" (Pss)
    M68

"Shout to the North" (Pss)
    M99

"Sanctuary" (1 Thess)
    M52, R185, S2164, SF2164

"We Bring the Sacrifice of Praise" (1 Thess, Matt)
    R3, S2031, SF2031, SP1

"The Servant Song" (Matt)
    C490, EL659, N539, R148, S2222, SF2222, SP193, VU595

"Make Me a Servant" (Matt)
    S2176, SF2176, SP193

"Humble Thyself in the Sight of the Lord" (Matt)
    S2131, SF2131, R188, SP223

Vocal Solos

"Stan' Still Jordan" (Josh)
V-7   p. 62

"Take My Life" (Matt)
V-8   p. 262

Anthems

"Guide Me, O Thou Great Jehovah" (Josh)
Arr. John Ferguson; Hope C 5421
SATB with organ

"On Jordan's Stormy Banks I Stand" (Josh)
arr. Dale Grotenhuis; Curtis C8307
SATB with keyboard

Other Suggestions

Visuals:
    O   Flowing water
    P   Water, bubbling water, sand, grapes, wheat
    E   Man encouraging child, open Bible
    G   Christ as teacher, servanthood (bowl/pitcher/towel),
         boxes symbolizing burdens, phylacteries, chair
Benediction: C434, EL536, F523, N81, P540, UM672/UM673,
    VU422/VU423, stanza 2. "God Be with You till We Meet
    Again" (Josh)
Alternate Lessons: Mic 3:5-12 and Ps 43 (*See page 3*)

Revelation 7:9-17

⁹After this I looked, and there was a great multitude that no one could count, from every nation, from all tribes and peoples and languages, standing before the throne and before the Lamb, robed in white, with palm branches in their hands. ¹⁰ They cried out in a loud voice, saying "Salvation belongs to our God who is seated on the throne, and to the Lamb!" ¹¹ And all the angels stood around the throne and around the elders and the four living creatures, and they fell on their faces before the throne and worshiped God, ¹² singing, "Amen! Blessing and glory and wisdom and thanksgiving and honor and power and might be to our God forever and ever! Amen."

¹³ Then one of the elders addressed me, saying, "Who are these, robed in white, and where have they come from?" ¹⁴ I said to him, "Sir, you are the one that knows." Then he said to me, "These are they who have come out of the great ordeal; they have washed their robes and made them white in the blood of the Lamb. ¹⁵ For this reason they are before the throne of God, and worship him day and night within his temple, and the one who is seated on the throne will shelter them. ¹⁶ They will hunger no more, and thirst no more; the sun will not strike them, nor any scorching heat; ¹⁷ for the Lamb at the center of the throne will be their shepherd, and he will guide them to springs of the water of life, and God will wipe away every tear from their eyes."

Psalm 34:1-10, 22

¹ I will bless the Lord at all times; his praise shall continually be in my mouth. ² My soul makes its boast in the Lord; let the humble hear and be glad. ³ O magnify the Lord with me, and let us exalt his name together. ⁴ I sought the Lord, and he answered me, and delivered me from all my fears. ⁵ Look to him, and be radiant; so your faces shall never be ashamed. ⁶ This poor soul cried, and was heard by the Lord, and was saved from every trouble. ⁷ The angel of the Lord encamps around those who fear him, and delivers them. ⁸ O taste and see that the Lord is good; happy are those who take refuge in him. ⁹ O fear the Lord, you his holy ones, for those who fear him have no want. ¹⁰ The young lions suffer want and hunger, but those who seek the Lord lack no good thing.

²² The Lord redeems the life of his servants; none of those who take refuge in him will be condemned.

1 John 3:1-3

¹ See what love the Father has given us, that we should be called children of God; and that is what we are. The reason the world does not know us is that it did not know him. ²Beloved, we are God's children now; what we will be has not yet been revealed. What we do know is this; when he is revealed, we will be like him, for we will see him as he is. ³ And all who have this hope in him purify themselves, just as he is pure.

Matthew 5:1-12

¹ When Jesus saw the crowds, he went up the mountain; and after he sat down, his disciples came to him. ² Then he began to speak, and taught them, saying:

³ "Blessed are the poor in spirit, for theirs is the kingdom of heaven.

⁴ "Blessed are those who mourn, for they will be comforted.

⁵ "Blessed are the meek, for they will inherit the earth.

⁶ "Blessed are those who hunger and thirst for righteousness, for they will be filled.

⁷ "Blessed are the merciful, for they will receive mercy.

⁸ "Blessed are the pure in heart, for they will see God.

⁹ "Blessed are the peacemakers, for they will be called children of God.

¹⁰ "Blessed are those who are persecuted for righteousness' sake, for theirs is the kingdom of heaven.

¹¹ "Blessed are you when people revile you and persecute you and utter all kinds of evil against you falsely on my account. ¹²Rejoice and be glad, for your reward is great in heaven, for in the same way they persecuted the prophets who were before you."

Primary Hymns and Songs for the Day

"For All the Saints" (All Saints) (O)
   B355, C637, E287, EL422, F614, L174, N299, P526, UM711
   (PD), VU705, W705
      H-3   Hbl-58; Chr-65; Org-152
      S-1   #314-318. Various treatments
"Blest Are They" (Matt)
   R127, EL728, S2155, SF2155, VU896
"O How He Loves You and Me!" (1 John)
   B146, F622, R27, S2108, SF2108, SP113
"Rejoice in God's Saints" (Rev, All Saints) (C)
   C476, UM708
      H-3   Hbl-90, 105; Chr-221; Desc-49; Org-51
      S-2   #71-74. Introduction and harmonizations
   EL418

Additional Hymn Suggestions

"Maker, in Whom We Live" (Rev) (O)
   UM88 (PD), VU321
"Ye Servants of God" (Rev) (O) or (C)
   B589, C110, E535, EL825 (PD), F360, N305, P477, UM181
   (PD), VU342
"Ye Watchers and Ye Holy Ones" (Rev)
   E618, EL424, L175, P451, UM90, W707
"This Is the Feast of Victory" (Rev, Communion)
   E417/E418, EL165/EL166/EL167, P594, R199, UM638,
   VU904, W458
"See the Morning Sun Ascending" (Rev)
   UM674, VU406
"Come, We That Love the Lord" (Rev)
   B525, E392, N379, UM732, VU715, W552
"Marching to Zion" (Rev)
   B524, C707, EL625, F550, N382, UM733 (PD), VU714
"All Who Hunger" (Rev, Pss, Matt, Communion)
   C419, EL461, S2126, SF2126, VU460
"Come to the Table" (Rev, Pss, Communion)
   EL481, S2264, SF2264
"Taste and See" (Pss, Communion)
   EL493, S2267, SF2267
"For the Bread Which You Have Broken" (Communion)
   C411, E340/E341, EL494, L200, P508/P509, UM614/UM615,
   VU470
"Since Jesus Came into My Heart" (Matt)
   B441, F639, S2140, SF2140
"Bring Forth the Kingdom" (Matt)
   R153, S2190, SF2190
"Gather Us In" (Matt) (O)
   C284, EL532, S2236, SF2236, W665
"Christ for the World We Sing" (Matt, All Saints)
   E537, F686, R299, UM568 (PD)
"I Sing a Song of the Saints of God" (Matt, All Saints)
   E293, N712, P364, UM712 (PD)
"In Unity We Lift Our Song" (All Saints)
   S2221, SF2221
"For All the Saints" (All Saints)
   S2283, SF2283

Additional Contemporary Suggestions

"Blessing, Honour and Glory" (Rev)
   R81, M21

"To Him Who Sits on the Throne" (Rev)
   R265, SP60
"My Tribute" ("To God Be the Glory") (Rev)
   B153, C39, F365, N14, R68, UM99; V-8 p. 5 Vocal Solo
"Shepherd Me, O God" (Rev, All Saints)
   EL780, S2058, SF2058
"Joy Comes with the Dawn" (Rev)
   S2210, SF2210, VU166
"Holy Ground" (Rev)
   B224, C112, S2272, SF2272, SP86
"How Majestic Is Your Name" (Pss)
   C63, R98, S2023, SF2023, SP14
"Behold, What Manner of Love" (1 John)
   SP48
"Celebrate Love" (1 John)
   S2073, SF2073
"He Came Down" (1 John)
   EL253, S2085, SF2085
"Holy, Holy" (1 John, Matt)
   B254, F149, P140, R206, S2039, SP141
"Open Our Eyes, Lord" (Matt)
   B499, R91, S2086, SF2086, SP199
"Give Thanks" (Matt)
   C528, R266, S2036, SF2036, SP170
"Open the Eyes of My Heart" (Matt)
   M57; V-3 p. 162 Vocal Solo
"Trading My Sorrows" (Matt, All Saints)
   M75

Vocal Solos

"Ye Servants of God" (Rev)
V-1   p. 41
"In Bright Mansions Above" (All Saints)
V-4   p. 39
"How Long Train Been Gone" (All Saints)
V-7   p. 17

Anthems

"When Shall I See?" (All Saints)
Bradley Ellingboe; Kjos 6326
Two-part mixed with piano

"For All the Saints" (All Saints)
Arr. Robert Powell; Hinshaw Music HMC1878
SATB with organ and handbells

Other Suggestions

NOTE: These scriptures and ideas may be used on Nov. 6.
Visuals:
   O   White robe, palm branches
   P   "Taste & See," spices, abundance, rejoicing, refuge
   E   Images of "saints" of the congregation
   G   Images of people living the Beatitudes, mountain
Introit: S2132, SP219. "You Who Are Thirsty" (Pss, Matt)
Canticle: C185. The Beatitudes (Matt)
Prayer: C252 or UM392 (Matt)
Litany: C157 or C488 or UM713 (All Saints)
Response: C299, S2277, SF2277. "Lord, Have Mercy" (Rev)

Joshua 24:1-3a, 14-25

[1] Then Joshua gathered all the tribes of Israel to Shechem, and summoned the elders, the heads, the judges, and the officers of Israel; and they presented themselves before God. [2]And Joshua said to all the people, "Thus says the LORD, the God of Israel: Long ago your ancestors—Terah and his sons Abraham and Nahor—lived beyond the Euphrates and served other gods. [3]Then I took your father Abraham from beyond the River and led him through all the land of Canaan and made his offspring many. . . .

[14] "Now therefore revere the LORD, and serve him in sincerity and in faithfulness; put away the gods that your ancestors served beyond the River and in Egypt, and serve the LORD. [15]Now if you are unwilling to serve the LORD, choose this day whom you will serve, whether the gods your ancestors served in the region beyond the River or the gods of the Amorites in whose land you are living; but as for me and my household, we will serve the LORD."

[16] Then the people answered, "Far be it from us that we should forsake the LORD to serve other gods; [17]for it is the LORD our God who brought us and our ancestors up from the land of Egypt, out of the house of slavery, and who did those great signs in our sight. He protected us along all the way that we went, and among all the peoples through whom we passed; [18]and the LORD drove out before us all the peoples, the Amorites who lived in the land. Therefore we also will serve the LORD, for he is our God."

[19] But Joshua said to the people, "You cannot serve the LORD, for he is a holy God. He is a jealous God; he will not forgive your transgressions or your sins. [20] If you forsake the LORD and serve foreign gods, then he will turn and do you harm, and consume you, after having done you good." [21]And the people said to Joshua, "No, we will serve the LORD!" [22] Then Joshua said to the people, "You are witnesses against yourselves that you have chosen the LORD, to serve him." And they said, "We are witnesses." [23] He said, "Then put away the foreign gods that are among you, and incline your hearts to the LORD, the God of Israel." [24] The people said to Joshua, "The LORD our God we will serve, and him we will obey." [25] So Joshua made a covenant with the people that day, and made statutes and ordinances for them at Shechem.

Psalm 78:1-7

[1] Give ear, O my people, to my teaching; incline your ears to the words of my mouth. [2] I will open my mouth in a parable; I will utter dark sayings from of old, [3] things that we have heard and known, that our ancestors have told us. [4] We will not hide them from their children; we will tell to the coming generation the glorious deeds of the LORD, and his might, and the wonders that he has done. [5] He established a decree in Jacob, and appointed a law in Israel, which he commanded our ancestors to teach to their children; [6] that the next generation might know them, the children yet unborn, and rise up and tell them to their children, [7] so that they should set their hope in God, and not forget the works of God, but keep his commandments.

1 Thessalonians 4:13-18

[13] But we do not want you to be uninformed, brothers and sisters, about those who have died, so that you may not grieve as others do who have no hope. [14] For since we believe that Jesus died and rose again, even so, through Jesus, God will bring with him those who have died. [15] For this we declare to you by the word of the Lord, that we who are alive, who are left until the coming of the Lord, will by no means precede those who have died. [16] For the Lord himself, with a cry of command, with the archangel's call and with the sound of God's trumpet, will descend from heaven, and the dead in Christ will rise first. [17] Then we who are alive, who are left, will be caught up in the clouds together with them to meet the Lord in the air; and so we will be with the Lord forever. [18]Therefore encourage one another with these words.

Matthew 25:1-13

[1] "Then the kingdom of heaven will be like this. Ten bridesmaids took their lamps and went to meet the bridegroom. [2] Five of them were foolish, and five were wise. [3] When the foolish took their lamps, they took no oil with them; [4] but the wise took flasks of oil with their lamps. [5] As the bridegroom was delayed, all of them became drowsy and slept. [6] But at midnight there was a shout, 'Look! Here is the bridegroom! Come out to meet him.' [7] Then all those bridesmaids got up and trimmed their lamps. [8] The foolish said to the wise, 'Give us some of your oil, for our lamps are going out.' [9] But the wise replied, 'No! there will not be enough for you and for us; you had better go to the dealers and buy some for yourselves.' [10] And while they went to buy it, the bridegroom came, and those who were ready went with him into the wedding banquet; and the door was shut. [11] Later the other bridesmaids came also, saying, 'Lord, lord, open to us.' [12] But he replied, 'Truly I tell you, I do not know you.' [13] Keep awake therefore, for you know neither the day nor the hour."

Primary Hymns and Songs for the Day
"Stand Up and Bless the Lord" (Josh) (O)
    B30, UM662 (PD) (P491)
        H-3   Hbl-79; Chr-141; Desc-95; Org-143
        S-1   #306-308. Various treatments
        P491
"The Family Prayer Song" (Josh)
    M54, S2188, SF2188
"We Are God's People" (Josh, Matt)
    B383, F546, S2220, SF2220
"My Lord, What a Morning" (1 Thess)
    C708, EL438 (PD), P449, UM719, VU708
        H-3   Chr-139
"Wake, Awake, for Night Is Flying" (Matt) (C)
    E61, EL436, L31, P17, UM720 (PD), VU711, W371
        H-3   Chr-174, 203; Org-172

Additional Hymn Suggestions
"The God of Abraham Praise" (Josh) (O)
    B34, C24, E401, EL831, F332, L544, N24, P488, R51, UM116
    (PD), VU255, W537
"Dear Lord, Lead Me Day by Day" (Josh)
    B459, UM411, VU568
"Near to the Heart of God" (Josh)
    B295, C581, F35, P527, UM472 (PD)
"Awake, O Sleeper" (Josh, Matt)
    E547, EL452, UM551, VU566, W586
"The Battle Hymn of the Republic" (Josh, 1 Thess)
    B633, C705, EL890, F692, L332, N610, UM717 (PD), W686
"The Summons" (Josh, Matt)
    EL798, S2130, SF2130, VU567
"I'm Gonna Live So God Can Use Me" (Josh, Matt)
    C614, P369, S2153, VU575
"Christ Beside Me" (Josh, Matt)
    R164, S2166, SF2166
"Walk with Me" (Josh, Matt)
    S2242, SF2242, VU649
"Lo, He Comes with Clouds Descending" (1 Thess)
    E57, EL435, L27, P6, UM718 (PD), VU25
    B199, E58, F306
"When We All Get to Heaven" (1 Thess)
    B514, F123, UM701 (PD)
"Steal Away to Jesus" (1 Thess)
    C644, N599, UM704
"Rejoice, the Lord Is King" (1 Thess)
    B197, C699, E481, EL430, F374, L171, N303, P155,
    UM715/UM716, VU213, W493
"There Are Some Things I May Not Know" ("Yes, God Is Real")
    (1 Thess)
    N405, S2147, SF2147
"Sing with All the Saints in Glory" (1 Thess) (C)
    EL426, UM702 (PD), W467
"Let There Be Light" (Matt)
    UM440, VU679, W653
"I Love Thy Kingdom, Lord" (Matt)
    B354, C274, E524, F545, L368, N312, P441, UM540 (PD)
"I Want to Be Ready" (Matt)
    N616, UM722
"Living for Jesus" (Matt)
    B282, C610, F462, S2149, SF2149

Additional Contemporary Suggestions
"Surely the Presence of the Lord" (Josh)
    C263, R167, SP243, UM328; S-2, #200 Stanzas for soloist
"Cry of My Heart" (Josh)
    S2165, SF2165, M39
"Guide My Feet" (Josh)
    N497, P354, S2208
"One God and Father of Us All" (Josh)
    S2240, SF2240
"Holy Ground" (Josh)
    B224, C112, S2272, SF2272, SP86
"I Give You My Heart" (Josh)
    M97
"Awesome God" (Pss)
    R245, S2040, SF2040, SP11
"The Battle Belongs to the Lord" (1 Thess)
    R244, SP158
"O Freedom" (1 Thess, Matt)
    S2194, SF2194
"This Kingdom" (1 Thess, Matt)
    M17
"We Will Dance" (1 Thess, Matt)
    M140

Vocal Solos
"Here I Am" (Josh)
V-11   p. 19
"Gospel Train" (Josh, 1 Thess)
V-7   p. 74
"Prepare Thyself, Zion" (Matt)
V-9   p. 2

Anthems
"Guide My Feet" (Josh)
arr. Leck/Ellis; Hal Leonard 08745189
SATB with piano

"Keep Your Lamps!" (Matt)
arr. Andre Thomas; Hinshaw Music HMC-577
SATB with conga drums

Other Suggestions
NOTE: To celebrate All Saints Sunday today, see Nov. 1 suggestions.
Visuals:
    O   "Choose this day whom you will serve," "As for me and my
        household . . .," servanthood (bowl / pitcher / towel)
    P   Christ as teacher, open Bible
    E   Trumpet, clouds, resurrection, encouragement
    G   Ten lamps, oil, wedding garments, bouquet, clock set at
        12:00
Call to Worship: C708, EL438 (PD), P449, UM719, VU708, refrain.
    "My Lord, What a Morning" (1 Thess)
Call to Prayer: C644, N599, UM704, refrain. "Steal Away to Jesus" (1
    Thess)
Alternate Lessons: Wis 6:12-16 or Amos 5:18-24; Wis 6:17-20 or Ps 70
    (*See page 3*)
NOTE: Daylight Savings Time ends today.

Judges 4:1-7

[1] The Israelites again did what was evil in the sight of the LORD, after Ehud died. [2] So the LORD sold them into the hand of King Jabin of Canaan, who reigned in Hazor; the commander of his army was Sisera, who lived in Harosheth-ha-goiim. [3] Then the Israelites cried out to the LORD for help; for he had nine hundred chariots of iron, and had oppressed the Israelites cruelly twenty years.

[4] At that time Deborah, a prophetess, wife of Lappidoth, was judging Israel. [5] She used to sit under the palm of Deborah between Ramah and Bethel in the hill country of Ephraim; and the Israelites came up to her for judgment. [6] She sent and summoned Barak son of Abinoam from Kedesh in Naphtali, and said to him, "The LORD, the God of Israel, commands you, 'Go, take position at Mount Tabor, bringing ten thousand from the tribe of Naphtali and the tribe of Zebulun. [7] I will draw out Sisera, the general of Jabin's army, to meet you by the Wadi Kishon with his chariots and his troops; and I will give him into your hand.' "

Psalm 123

[1] To you I lift up my eyes, O you who are enthroned in the heavens! [2] As the eyes of servants look to the hand of their master, as the eyes of a maid to the hand of her mistress, so our eyes look to the LORD our God, until he has mercy upon us. [3] Have mercy upon us, O LORD, have mercy upon us, for we have had more than enough of contempt. [4] Our soul has had more than its fill of the scorn of those who are at ease, of the contempt of the proud.

1 Thessalonians 5:1-11

[1] Now concerning the times and the seasons, brothers and sisters, you do not need to have anything written to you. [2] For you yourselves know very well that the day of the Lord will come like a thief in the night. [3] When they say, "There is peace and security," then sudden destruction will come upon them, as labor pains come upon a pregnant woman, and there will be no escape! [4] But you, beloved, are not in darkness, for that day to surprise you like a thief; [5] for you are all children of light and children of the day; we are not of the night or of darkness. [6] So then let us not fall asleep as others do, but let us keep awake and be sober; [7] for those who sleep sleep at night, and those who are drunk get drunk at night. [8] But since we belong to the day, let us be sober, and put on the breastplate of faith and love, and for a helmet the hope of salvation. [9] For God has destined us not for wrath but for obtaining salvation through our Lord Jesus Christ, [10] who died for us, so that whether we are awake or asleep we may live with him. [11] Therefore encourage one another and build up each other, as indeed you are doing.

Matthew 25:14-30

[14] "For it is as if a man, going on a journey, summoned his slaves and entrusted his property to them; [15] to one he gave five talents, to another two, to another one, to each according to his ability. Then he went away. [16] The one who had received the five talents went off at once and traded with them, and made five more talents. [17] In the same way, the one who had the two talents made two more talents. [18] But the one who had received the one talent went off and dug a hole in the ground and hid his master's money. [19] After a long time the master of those slaves came and settled accounts with them. [20] Then the one who had received the five talents came forward, bringing five more talents, saying, 'Master, you handed over to me five talents; see, I have made five more talents.' [21] His master said to him, 'Well done, good and trustworthy slave; you have been trustworthy in a few things, I will put you in charge of many things; enter into the joy of your master.' [22] And the one with the two talents also came forward, saying, 'Master, you handed over to me two talents; see, I have made two more talents.' [23] His master said to him, 'Well done, good and trustworthy slave; you have been trustworthy in a few things, I will put you in charge of many things; enter into the joy of your master.' [24] Then the one who had received the one talent also came forward, saying, 'Master, I knew that you were a harsh man, reaping where you did not sow, and gathering where you did not scatter seed; [25] so I was afraid, and I went and hid your talent in the ground. Here you have what is yours.' [26] But his master replied, 'You wicked and lazy slave! You knew, did you, that I reap where I did not sow, and gather where I did not scatter? [27] Then you ought to have invested my money with the bankers, and on my return I would have received what was my own with interest. [28] So take the talent from him, and give it to the one with the ten talents. [29] For to all those who have, more will be given, and they will have an abundance; but from those who have nothing, even what they have will be taken away. [30] As for this worthless slave, throw him into the outer darkness, where there will be weeping and gnashing of teeth.' "

Primary Hymns and Songs for the Day
"I Want to Walk as a Child of the Light" (1 Thess) (O)
    E490, EL815, R152, UM206, W510
        S-2   #91. Descant
"Canta, Debora, Canta!" (Judg)
    R121, UM81
        S-1   #81. Tambourine part
"Lord, Be Glorified" (Matt)
    B457, EL744, S2150, SF2150, R172, SP196
"Take My Life, and Let It Be" (Matt)
    B277, C609, P391
        H-3   Chr-34, 177; Desc-51; Org-53
        S-2   #78-80. Various treatments
    B283, E707, EL583/EL685, L406, R133, N448, UM399
    (PD), VU506

Additional Hymn Suggestions
"God Hath Spoken by the Prophets" (Judg)
    L238, UM108, W516
"There's a Wideness in God's Mercy" (Pss)
    B25, C73, E470, EL587/EL588, F115, L290, N23, P298,
    UM121, VU271, W595
"O Morning Star, How Fair and Bright" (1 Thess)
    C105, E497, EL308, L76, N158, P69, UM247, VU98, W390
"Ah, Holy Jesus" (1 Thess)
    C210, E158, EL349, L123, N218, P93, R183, UM289 (PD),
    VU138
"Jesus, Keep Me Near the Cross" (1 Thess)
    B280, C587, EL335, N197, UM301 (PD), VU142
"Pues Si Vivimos" ("When We Are Living") (1 Thess)
    C536, EL639, N499, P400, UM356, VU581
"Awake, O Sleeper" (1 Thess)
    E547, EL452, UM551, VU566, W586
"We Are Called" (1 Thess)
    EL720, S2172, SF2172
"Lead Me, Guide Me" (1 Thess)
    C583, EL768, R176, S2214, SF2214
"Gather Us In" (1 Thess)
    C284, EL532, S2236, SF2236, W665
"Joy in the Morning" (1 Thess)
    S2284, SF2284
"Together We Serve" (1 Thess, Matt)
    S2175, SF2175
"God, Who Stretched the Spangled Heavens" (Matt) (O)
    C651, E580, EL771, L463, N556, P268, UM150, W648
"What Gift Can We Bring" (Matt)
    N370, UM87
"All Who Love and Serve Your City" (Matt)
    C670, E570/E571, EL724, L436, P413, UM433, W621
"Faith, While Trees Are Still in Blossom" (Matt)
    C535, UM508, VU643
"I'm Gonna Live So God Can Use Me" (Matt)
    C614, P369, S2153, VU575
"Lord, Whose Love Through Humble Service" (C) (Matt)
    C461, E610, EL712, R286, L423, UM581, W630

Additional Contemporary Suggestions
"Kyrie Eleison" ("Lord, Have Mercy") (Pss)
    EL151/EL152, UM483/UM484
"Freedom Is Coming" (1 Thess)
    S2192, SF2192
"O Freedom" (1 Thess)
    S2194, SF2194
"Light of the World" (1 Thess)
    S2204
"We Are Marching" ("Siyahamba") (1 Thess)
    C442, EL866, N526, R306, S2235-ab, SF2235-ab, VU646
"Shine on Us" (1 Thess)
    M19
"Hear Our Praises" (1 Thess)
    M64
"Song for the Nations" ("May We Be a Shining Light") (1 Thess)
    R303, SP144
"Here I Am to Worship" (1 Thess)
    M116
"My Life Is in You, Lord" (Matt)
    S2032, SF2032, SP204
"Let It Be Said of Us" (Matt)
    M53
"When It's All Been Said and Done" (Matt)
    M115

Vocal Solos
"I Will Lift Up Mine Eyes" (Pss)
V-11   p. 27
"Redeeming Grace" (1 Thess, Matt)
V-4   p. 47
"Fit for a King" (Matt, Stewardship)
V-10   p. 32

Anthems
"I Want to Walk as a Child of the Light" (1 Thess)
Arr. Kristina Langlois; Augsburg 9780800678197
SAB with organ

"What Gift Can We Bring" (Matt)
Jane Marshall; Hope CY 3370
SATB with keyboard

Other Suggestions
Visuals:
    O   Manacles
    P   Hand
    E   Robber's mask, light/dark, awake/asleep, lantern
    G   Three piles of coins (large, medium, small, bank bag,
           time/talent survey, nos. 1, 2, and 5 (nos. 10, 4, and 1)
Stewardship can be emphasized today, related to Matt
Response: S2275, SF2275. "Kyrie" or C299, S2277, SF2277.
    "Lord, Have Mercy" (Pss)
Baptism Response: S2249, SF2249. "God Claims You" (1 Thess)
Prayer: UM403. For True Life (1 Thess, Matt)
Prayer: UM481. Prayer of Saint Francis (Pss)
Alternate Lessons: Zeph 1:7, 12-18; Ps 90:1-12 (*See page 3.*)

Ezekiel 34:11-16, 20-24

[11] For thus says the Lord GOD: I myself will search for my sheep, and will seek them out. [12] As shepherds seek out their flocks when they are among their scattered sheep, so I will seek out my sheep. I will rescue them from all the places to which they have been scattered on a day of clouds and thick darkness. [13] I will bring them out from the peoples and gather them from the countries, and will bring them into their own land; and I will feed them on the mountains of Israel, by the watercourses, and in all the inhabited parts of the land. [14] I will feed them with good pasture, and the mountain heights of Israel shall be their pasture; there they shall lie down in good grazing land, and they shall feed on rich pasture on the mountains of Israel. [15] I myself will be the shepherd of my sheep, and I will make them lie down, says the Lord GOD. [16] I will seek the lost, and I will bring back the strayed, and I will bind up the injured, and I will strengthen the weak, but the fat and the strong I will destroy. I will feed them with justice.

[20] Therefore, thus . . . says the Lord GOD to them: I myself will judge between the fat sheep and the lean sheep. [21] Because you pushed with flank and shoulder, and butted at all the weak animals with your horns until you scattered them far and wide, [22] I will save my flock, and they shall no longer be ravaged; and I will judge between sheep and sheep.

[23] I will set up over them one shepherd, my servant David, and he shall feed them: he shall feed them and be their shepherd. [24] And I, the LORD, will be their God, and my servant David shall be prince among them; I, the LORD, have spoken.

Psalm 100

[1] Make a joyful noise to the LORD, all the earth. [2] Worship the LORD with gladness; come into his presence with singing. [3] Know that the LORD is God. It is he that made us, and we are his; we are his people, and the sheep of his pasture. [4] Enter his gates with thanksgiving, and his courts with praise. Give thanks to him, bless his name. [5] For the LORD is good; his steadfast love endures forever, and his faithfulness to all generations.

Ephesians 1:15-23

[15] I have heard of your faith in the Lord Jesus and your love toward all the saints, and for this reason [16] I do not cease to give thanks for you as I remember you in my prayers. [17] I pray that the God of our Lord Jesus Christ, the Father of glory, may give you a spirit of wisdom and revelation as you come to know him, [18] so that, with the eyes of your heart enlightened, you may know what is the hope to which he has called you, what are the riches of his glorious inheritance among the saints, [19] and what is the immeasurable greatness of his power for us who believe, according to the working of his great power.

[20] God put this power to work in Christ when he raised him from the dead and seated him at his right hand in the heavenly places, [21] far above all rule and authority and power and dominion, and above every name that is named, not only in this age but also in the age to come. [22] And he has put all things under his feet and has made him the head over all things for the church, [23] which is his body, the fullness of him who fills all in all.

Matthew 25:31-46

[31] "When the Son of Man comes in his glory, and all the angels with him, then he will sit on the throne of his glory. [32] All the nations will be gathered before him, and he will separate people one from another as a shepherd separates the sheep from the goats, [33] and he will put the sheep at his right hand and the goats at the left. [34] Then the king will say to those at his right hand, 'Come, you that are blessed by my Father, inherit the kingdom prepared for you from the foundation of the world; [35] for I was hungry and you gave me food, I was thirsty and you gave me something to drink, I was a stranger and you welcomed me, [36] I was naked and you gave me clothing, I was sick and you took care of me, I was in prison and you visited me.' [37] Then the righteous will answer him, 'Lord, when was it that we saw you hungry and gave you food, or thirsty and gave you something to drink? [38] And when was it that we saw you a stranger and welcomed you, or naked and gave you clothing? [39] And when was it that we saw you sick or in prison and visited you?' [40] And the king will answer them, 'Truly I tell you, just as you did it to one of the least of these who are members of my family, you did it to me.' [41] Then he will say to those at his left hand, 'You that are accursed, depart from me into the eternal fire prepared for the devil and his angels; [42] for I was hungry and you gave me no food, I was thirsty and you gave me nothing to drink, [43] I was a stranger and you did not welcome me, naked and you did not give me clothing, sick and in prison and you did not visit me.' [44] Then they also will answer, 'Lord, when was it that we saw you hungry or thirsty or a stranger or naked or sick or in prison, and did not take care of you?' [45] Then he will answer them, 'Truly I tell you, just as you did not do it to one of the least of these, you did not do it to me.' [46] And these will go away into eternal punishment, but the righteous into eternal life."

Primary Hymns and Songs for the Day

"All People That on Earth Do Dwell" (Pss) (O)
>B5, C18, E377 and 378, EL883, F381, L245, N7, P220,
>UM75 (PD), VU822 (Fr.), W669
>>H-3   Hbl-45; Chr-24; Desc-84, 85; Org-107
>>S-1   #257-259. Various treatments
>>S-2   #140. Descant

"When God Restored Our Common Life" (Eze, Matt)
>S2182, SF2182

"Above All" (Eph)
>M77; V-3 p. 17 Vocal Solo

"Cuando El Pobre" ("When the Poor Ones") (Matt)
>C662, EL725, P407, UM434, VU702

"Rescue the Perishing" (Matt)
>B559, F661, UM591 (PD)

"Lord, Whose Love Through Humble Service" (C) (Matt)
>C461, EL712, L423, UM581
>>H-3   Chr-51, 67
>E610, R286, W630

Additional Hymn Suggestions

"Praise, My Soul, the King of Heaven" (Eze)
>B32, C23, E410, EL864/EL865, F339, L549, P478/P479,
>R53, UM66 (PD), VU240, W530

"All My Hope Is Firmly Grounded" (Eze)
>C88, E665, EL757, N408, UM132, VU654/VU655

"Loving Spirit" (Eze)
>C244, EL397, P323, S2123, SF2123, VU387

"Why Stand So Far Away, My God?" (Eze)
>C671, S2180, SF2180

"Savior, Like a Shepherd Lead Us" (Eze, Pss)
>B61, C558, E708, EL789, F601, L481, N252, P387, UM381 (PD)

"Here Am I" (Eze, Matt)
>C654, S2178, SF2178

"Come, Thou Almighty King" (Pss, Eph, Christ the King)
>B247, C27, E365, EL408, F341, L522, N275, P139, UM61
>(PD), VU314, W487

"All Creatures of Our God and King" (Pss, Christ the King)
>B27, C22, E400, EL835, F347, L527, N17, P455, R47, UM62,
>VU217 (Fr.), W520

"O Worship the King" (Eph, Christ the King)
>B16, C17, E388, EL842 (PD), F336, L548, N26, P476, UM73
>(PD), VU235

"Holy God, We Praise Thy Name" (Eph, Christ the King)
>E366, F385, EL414 (PD), L535, N276, P460, UM79, VU894
>(Fr.), W524; See especially stanzas 1, 5-7

"Immortal, Invisible, God Only Wise" (Eph)
>B6, C66, E423, EL834, F319, L526, N1, P263, R46, UM103
>(PD), VU264, W512

"Jesus, the Very Thought of Thee" (Eph)
>B225, C102, E642, EL754, F465, L316, N507, P310, UM175 (PD)

"Hope of the World" (Eph)
>C538, E472, L493, N46, P360, UM178, VU215, W565

"For All the Saints" (Eph)
>B355, C637, E287, EL422, F614, L174, N299, P526, UM711
>(PD), VU705, W705

"There's a Spirit in the Air" (Matt)
>B393, C257, P433, N294, R282, UM192, VU582, W531

"All Who Love and Serve Your City" (Matt)
>C670, E570/E571, EL724, L436, P413, UM433, W621

"Spirit of Jesus, If I Love My Neighbor" (Matt)
>N590

"We Gather Together" (Matt, Thanksgiving) (O)
>B636, C276, E433, F387, N421, P559, UM131 (PD), W760

"All Who Hunger" (Matt, Communion)
>C419, EL461, S2126, SF2126, VU460

"As We Gather at Your Table" (Matt, Communion)
>EL522, N332, S2268, SF2268, VU457

Additional Contemporary Suggestions

"Give Thanks" (Eze, Matt)
>C528, R266, S2036, SF2036, SP170

"You Are My Hiding Place" (Eze)
>C554, S2055, SF2055

"Shepherd Me, O God"
>EL780, S2058, SF2058

"All Things Are Possible" (Eze)
>M92

"Praise, Praise, Praise the Lord" (Pss)
>EL875, S2035, SF2035

"I Will Enter His Gates" (Pss)
>S2270, SF2270, SP168

"People Need the Lord" (Matt)
>B557, S2244, SF2244

"King of Kings" (Christ the King)
>B234, R268, S2075, SF2075, SP94, VU167

Vocal Solos

"Reach Out to Your Neighbor" (Matt)
>V-8   p. 372

"Crown Him, the Risen King" (Christ the King)
>V-10   p. 55

Anthems

"Make a Joyful Noise" (Pss)
Gary Alan Smith; Abingdon Press 9780687645817
SATB, *a cappella*

"My Lord, What a Mornin' " (Matt)
Arr. Robert DeCormier; Hal Leonard HL 08745676
SSAATTBB with soli

Other Suggestions

Visuals:
>**O**   Sheep, good shepherd
>**P**   Instruments, worship, singing
>**E**   Portraits of Christ or local "saints," church history
>**G**   Christ descending, angels, food, drink, clothes, visita-
>tion, medicine bag, prison ministry, Bible, crown, rich
>fabric, Christ as king

Response: B28, E402, P468, UM93, W536. "Let All the World in
>Every Corner Sing" (Pss)

Prayer: C473. Be God's Kindness (Matt)

Prayer: UM323 (Eph) or UM721 (Christ the King)

Alternate Lessons: Eze 31:11-16, 20-24; Ps 95:1-7a (*See page 3.*)

Deuteronomy 8:7-18

⁷ For the LORD your God is bringing you into a good land, a land with flowing streams, with springs and underground waters welling up in valleys and hills, ⁸ a land of wheat and barley, of vines and fig trees and pomegranates, a land of olive trees and honey, ⁹ a land where you may eat bread without scarcity, where you will lack nothing, a land whose stones are iron and from whose hills you may mine copper. ¹⁰ You shall eat your fill and bless the LORD your God for the good land that he has given you.

¹¹ Take care that you do not forget the LORD your God, by failing to keep his commandments, his ordinances, and his statutes, which I am commanding you today. ¹² When you have eaten your fill and have built fine houses and live in them, ¹³ and when your herds and flocks have multiplied, and your silver and gold is multiplied, and all that you have is multiplied, ¹⁴ then do not exalt yourself, forgetting the LORD your God, who brought you out of the land of Egypt, out of the house of slavery, ¹⁵ who led you through the great and terrible wilderness, an arid wasteland with poisonous snakes and scorpions. He made water flow for you from flint rock, ¹⁶ and fed you in the wilderness with manna that your ancestors did not know, to humble you and to test you, and in the end to do you good. ¹⁷ Do not say to yourself, "My power and the might of my own hand have gotten me this wealth." ¹⁸ But remember the LORD your God, for it is he who gives you power to get wealth, so that he may confirm his covenant that he swore to your ancestors, as he is doing today.

Psalm 65

¹ Praise is due to you, O God, in Zion; and to you shall vows be performed, ² O you who answer prayer! To you all flesh shall come. ³ When deeds of iniquity overwhelm us, you forgive our transgressions. ⁴ Happy are those whom you choose and bring near to live in your courts. We shall be satisfied with the goodness of your house, your holy temple. ⁵ By awesome deeds you answer us with deliverance, O God of our salvation; you are the hope of all the ends of the earth and of the farthest seas. ⁶ By your strength you established the mountains; you are girded with might. ⁷ You silence the roaring of the seas, the roaring of their waves, the tumult of the peoples. ⁸ Those who live at earth's farthest bounds are awed by your signs; you make the gateways of the morning and the evening shout for joy. ⁹ You visit the earth and water it, you greatly enrich it; the river of God is full of water; you provide the people with grain, for so you have prepared it. ¹⁰ You water its furrows abundantly, settling its ridges, softening it with showers, and blessing its growth. ¹¹ You crown the year with your bounty; your wagon tracks overflow with richness. ¹² The pastures of the wilderness overflow, the hills gird themselves with joy, ¹³ the meadows clothe themselves with flocks, the valleys deck themselves with grain, they shout and sing together for joy.

2 Corinthians 9:6-15

⁶ The point is this: the one who sows sparingly will also reap sparingly, and the one who sows bountifully will also reap bountifully. ⁷ Each of you must give as you have made up your mind, not reluctantly or under compulsion, for God loves a cheerful giver. ⁸ And God is able to provide you with every blessing in abundance, so that by always having enough of everything, you may share abundantly in every good work. ⁹ As it is written, "He scatters abroad, he gives to the poor; his righteousness endures forever." ¹⁰ He who supplies seed to the sower and bread for food will supply and multiply your seed for sowing and increase the harvest of your righteousness. ¹¹ You will be enriched in every way for your great generosity, which will produce thanksgiving to God through us; ¹² for the rendering of this ministry not only supplies the needs of the saints but also overflows with many thanksgivings to God. ¹³ Through the testing of this ministry you glorify God by your obedience to the confession of the gospel of Christ and by the generosity of your sharing with them and with all others, ¹⁴ while they long for you and pray for you because of the surpassing grace of God that he has given you. ¹⁵ Thanks be to God for his indescribable gift!

Luke 17:11-19

¹¹ On the way to Jerusalem Jesus was going through the region between Samaria and Galilee. ¹² As he entered a village, ten lepers approached him. Keeping their distance, ¹³ they called out, saying, "Jesus, Master, have mercy on us!" ¹⁴ When he saw them, he said to them, "Go and show yourselves to the priests." And as they went, they were made clean. ¹⁵ Then one of them, when he saw that he was healed, turned back, praising God with a loud voice. ¹⁶ He prostrated himself at Jesus' feet and thanked him. And he was a Samaritan. ¹⁷ Then Jesus asked, "Were not ten made clean? But the other nine, where are they? ¹⁸ Was none of them found to return and give praise to God except this foreigner?" ¹⁹ Then he said to him, "Get up and go on your way; your faith has made you well."

Primary Hymns and Songs for the Day

"Come, Ye Thankful People, Come" (2 Cor) (O)
  B637, C718, E290, EL693, F392, L407, N422, P551, UM694
  (PD), VU516, W759
    H-3   Hbl-54; Chr-58; Desc-94; Org-137
    S-1   #302-303. Harmonizations with descant
"For the Beauty of the Earth" (Pss)
  B44, C56, EL879, F1, L561, P473, N28, UM92 (PD)
    H-3   Chr-33, 65; Desc-30; Org-29
    S-1   #93-96. Various treatments
  E416, VU226, W557
"Sois la Semilla" ("You Are the Seed") (2 Cor)
  C478, N528, UM583
"Give Thanks" (2 Cor)
  C528, R266, S2036, SF2036, SP170
"I'll Praise My Maker While I've Breath" (Luke) (C)
  B35, C20, E429 (PD), P253, UM60, VU867
    H-3   Chr-109; Org-105
    S-2   #141. Harmonization

Additional Hymn Suggestions

"Praise to the Lord, the Almighty" (Deut, Thanksgiving) (O)
  B14, C25, E390, EL858 (PD) and 859, F337, L543, N22, P482,
  R57, UM139, VU220 (Fr.) and VU221, W547
"Now Thank We All Our God" (Deut, Thanksgiving)
  B638, C715, E396 or 397, EL839 or 840, F525, L533 or L534,
  N419, P555, UM102 (PD), VU236 (Fr.), W560
"What Gift Can We Bring" (Deut)
  N370, UM87
"For the Fruits of This Creation" (Deut)
  B643, C714, E424, EL679, L563, N425, P553, UM97, VU227,
  W562
"Praise Our God Above" ("Harvest Song") (Deut, Pss, Thanksgiving)
  N424, P480, S2061
"The Trees of the Field" (Pss) (C)
  R302, S2279, SF2279, SP128, VU884
"Una Espiga" ("Sheaves of Summer") (Pss, Communion)
  C396, N338, UM637
"Praise, My Soul, the King of Heaven" (Luke, Thanksgiving)
  B32, C23, E410, EL864/EL865, F339, L549, P478/P479, R53,
  UM66 (PD), VU240, W530
"When Jesus the Healer Passed Through Galilee" (Luke)
  UM263, VU358
"Jesus' Hands Were Kind Hands" (Luke)
  B477, UM273, VU570
"Awake, O Sleeper" (Luke)
  E547, EL452, UM551, VU566, W586
"An Outcast Among Outcasts" (Luke)
  N201, S2104, SF2104
"Father, We Thank You" (Thanksgiving, Communion)
  E302/E303, EL478, UM563/UM565, W558
"I Come with Joy" (Thanksgiving, Communion)
  B371, C420, E304, EL482, P607, R195, UM617, W726
"Let Us Offer to the Father" ("Te Ofrecemos Padre Nuestro")
  (Thanksgiving, Communion)
  S2262, SF2262
"Time Now to Gather" (Thanksgiving, Communion)
  S2265, SF2265
"My Gratitude Now Accept, O God" ("Gracias, Señor")
  (Thanksgiving)
  S2044, SF2044

"For All the Saints" (Thanksgiving)
  S2283, SF2283

Additional Contemporary Suggestions

"Come! Come! Everybody Worship" (2 Cor)
  S2271, SF2271
"Lord, Be Glorified" (2 Cor)
  B457, EL744, S2150, SF2150, R172, SP196
"Grace Alone" (2 Cor)
  M100, S2162, SF2162
"Be Glorified" (2 Cor)
  M13
"He Is Able" (2 Cor)
  M37
"In the Lord I'll Be Ever Thankful" (2 Cor, Luke)
  S2195, SF2195
"White as Snow" (Luke)
  M35
"Something Beautiful" (Luke)
  F656, UM394
"Jesus Be Praised" (Luke)
  S2079, SF2079
"Thank You, Jesus" ("Tino tenda, Jesu") (Luke)
  S2081, SF2081
"Thank You, Lord" (Luke, Thanksgiving)
  C531, UM84

Vocal Solos

"O For a Thousand Tongues to Sing" (Luke)
  V-1   p. 32
"When I Praise" (Luke, Thanksgiving)
  V-3   p. 170
"Now Thank We All Our God" (Thanksgiving)
  V-6   p. 8

Anthems

"O For a Thousand Tongues to Sing" (Luke)
Carlton R. Young: Abingdon Press 9780687646111
SATB with piano (opt. bass and claves)

"We Plow the Fields" (Thanksgiving)
Arr. Donald McCullough; Hinshaw HMC2182
SATB with piano and flute

Other Suggestions

Visuals:
  O   Flowing water, wheat, barley, figs, etc.
  P   Cornucopia with fruit, vegetables, etc., water, sheep, sea,
         mountains, grain
  E   Seed, bread, people in ministry, 2 Cor 9:15
  G   Nos. 1 and 9, healing, praise, Luke 17:19b
Litany: C716. "A Thanksgiving" (Deut, Thanksgiving)
Thanksgiving Prayers: F391, N859, UM74.
Response: S2275, SF2275. "Kyrie" (Luke)
Response: S2081, SF2081. "Thank You, Jesus" (Luke)
Communion Hymn: N783. "As the Grains of Wheat"

ALSO AVAILABLE FROM ABINGDON PRESS

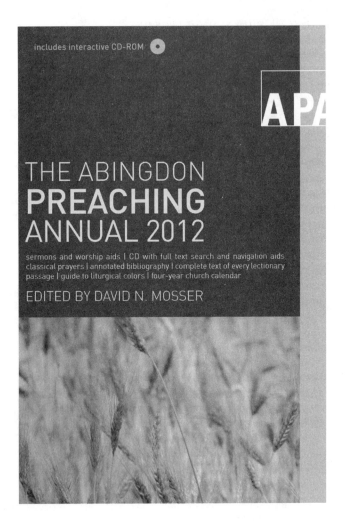

Pastors and other preachers have long turned to *The Abingdon Preaching Annual* for help with one of the central tasks of their ministry: sermon preparation.

Sermon Helps:

· Lectionary-based sermons for each Sunday and special liturgical event of the year

· Lectionary commentary on passages not used in the weekly sermon

· Topical sermon series on diverse themes

Worship Planning Aids:

· Four-year liturgical event calendar

· Guide to liturgical colors

· 2012 lectionary readings in one, easy-to-read table

· Related worship aids following each lectionary sermon and each series sermon

Searchable CD-ROM Included!

· PDF format provides ease of navigation and use

· Full text of the print edition with a hyperlinked table of contents

· Pre-sermon, offertory, and pastoral prayers

· Classical and contemporary prayers and affirmations

· Classic sermon

· Annotated bibliography hyperlinked to the sermon titles

· Full text of every lectionary passage used, hyperlinked to the weekly readings

The Abingdon Preaching Annual, always a trusted resource, is now the most comprehensive and useful aid for sermon preparation you will find.

ISBN: 9781426710186

Available from Cokesbury.com,

1-800-672-1789 or your local Cokesbury store

Abingdon Press

ALSO AVAILABLE FROM ABINGDON PRESS

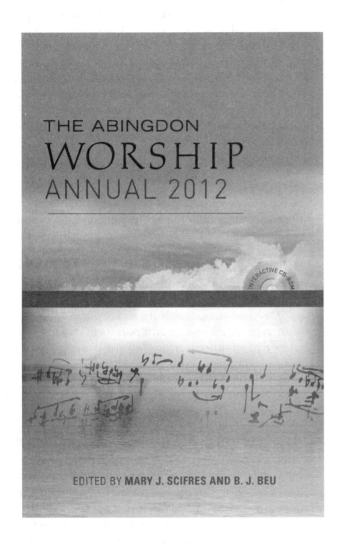

A trusted planning resource for traditional and contemporary worship . . . now includes interactive CD!

Using a Theme Idea based on the lectionary readings, each week's offering of prayers and litanies follows a basic pattern of Christian worship:

- Invitation and Gathering
- Proclamation and Response
- Thanksgiving and Communion
- Sending Forth

Plus:
- Praise Sentences
- Contemporary Gathering Words

Includes CD-ROM in searchable PDF format:
- Full print text with hyperlinked table of contents
- Song suggestions for each week
- Annotated resource list linked to worship planning websites
- Prayers and liturgies for baptism

ISBN: 9781426710193
Available from Cokesbury.com,
1-800-672-1789 or your local Cokesbury store

Abingdon Press

Isaiah 64:1-9

[1]O that you would tear open the heavens and come down, so that the mountains would quake at your presence—[2]as when fire kindles brushwood and the fire causes water to boil—to make your name known to your adversaries, so that the nations might tremble at your presence! [3]When you did awesome deeds that we did not expect, you came down, the mountains quaked at your presence. [4]From ages past no one has heard, no ear has perceived, no eye has seen any God besides you, who works for those who wait for him. [5]You meet those who gladly do right, those who remember you in your ways. But you were angry, and we sinned; because you hid yourself we transgressed. [6]We have all become like one who is unclean, and all our righteous deeds are like a filthy cloth. We all fade like a leaf, and our iniquities, like the wind, take us away. [7]There is no one who calls on your name, or attempts to take hold of you; for you have hidden your face from us, and have delivered us into the hand of our iniquity. [8]Yet, O LORD, you are our Father; we are the clay, and you are our potter; we are all the work of your hand. [9]Do not be exceedingly angry, O LORD, and do not remember iniquity forever. Now consider, we are all your people.

Psalm 80:1-7, 17-19

[1]Give ear, O Shepherd of Israel, you who lead Joseph like a flock! You who are enthroned upon the cherubim, shine forth [2]before Ephraim and Benjamin and Manasseh. Stir up your might, and come to save us! [3]Restore us, O God; let your face shine, that we may be saved. [4]O LORD God of hosts, how long will you be angry with your people's prayers? [5]You have fed them with the bread of tears, and given them tears to drink in full measure. [6]You make us the scorn of our neighbors; our enemies laugh among themselves. [7]Restore us, O God of hosts; let your face shine, that we may be saved. . . .

[17]But let your hand be upon the one at your right hand, the one whom you made strong for yourself. [18]Then we will never turn back from you; give us life, and we will call on your name. [19]Restore us, O LORD God of hosts; let your face shine, that we may be saved.

1 Corinthians 1:3-9

[3]Grace to you and peace from God our Father and the Lord Jesus Christ.

[4]I give thanks to my God always for you because of the grace of God that has been given you in Christ Jesus, [5]for in every way you have been enriched in him, in speech and knowledge of every kind—[6]just as the testimony of Christ has been strengthened among you—[7]so that you are not lacking in any spiritual gift as you wait for the revealing of our Lord Jesus Christ. [8]He will also strengthen you to the end, so that you may be blameless on the day of our Lord Jesus Christ. [9]God is faithful; by him you were called into the fellowship of his Son, Jesus Christ our Lord.

Mark 13:24-37

[24] "But in those days, after that suffering, the sun will be darkened, and the moon will not give its light, [25]and the stars will be falling from heaven, and the powers in the heavens will be shaken. [26]Then they will see 'the Son of Man coming in clouds' with great power and glory. [27]Then he will send out the angels, and gather his elect from the four winds, from the ends of the earth to the ends of heaven.

[28] "From the fig tree learn its lesson: as soon as its branch becomes tender and puts forth its leaves, you know that summer is near. [29]So also, when you see these things taking place, you know that he is near, at the very gates. [30]Truly I tell you, this generation will not pass away until all these things have taken place. [31]Heaven and earth will pass away, but my words will not pass away.

[32] "But about that day or hour no one knows, neither the angels in heaven, nor the Son, but only the Father. [33]Beware, keep alert; for you do not know when the time will come. [34]It is like a man going on a journey, when he leaves home and puts his slaves in charge, each with his work, and commands the doorkeeper to be on the watch. [35]Therefore, keep awake—for you do not know when the master of the house will come, in the evening, or at midnight, or at cockcrow, or at dawn, [36]or else he may find you asleep when he comes suddenly. [37]And what I say to you I say to all: Keep awake."

Primary Hymns and Songs for the Day

"Come, Thou Long-Expected Jesus" (Mark, Pss) (O)
  B77, C125, F168, P2, UM196 (PD)
    H-3   Hbl-46; Chr-26, 134; Desc-53; Org-56
    S-1   #168-171. Various treatments
  E66, N122, P1 (PD), VU2, W364
    H-3   Hbl-53, 81; Chr-76; Desc-99; Org-158
    S-1   #324. Descant
  EL254, L30
"Have Thine Own Way, Lord" (Isa)
  B294, C588, F400, UM382 (PD)
    S-2   #2. Instrumental descant
"Change My Heart, O God" (Isa)
  EL801, R143, SP195, S2152, SF2152
"My Lord, What a Morning" (Mark)
  C708, EL438 (PD), P449, UM719, VU708
    H-3   Chr-139
"Soon and Very Soon" (Mark) (C)
  B192, EL439, R276, UM706
    S-2   #187. Piano arrangement

Additional Hymn Suggestions

"How Like a Gentle Spirit" (Isa)
  C69, N443, UM115
"All My Hope Is Firmly Grounded" (Isa)
  C88, E665, EL757, N408, UM132, VU654/VU655
"Great Is Thy Faithfulness" (Pss, 1 Cor)
  B54, C86, EL733, F98, N423, P276, R249, UM140, VU288
"Send Your Word" (Pss, 1 Cor)
  N317, UM195
"O Morning Star, How Fair and Bright" (Pss, Mark, Advent)
  C105, E497, EL308, L76, N158, P69, UM247, VU98, W390
"I Know Whom I Have Believed" (1 Cor, Mark)
  B337, F631, UM714 (PD)
"People, Look East" (Mark)
  C142, EL248, P12, UM202, VU9, W359
"Lo, He Comes with Clouds Descending" (Mark)
  B199, E57/E58, EL435, F306, L27, P6, UM718 (PD), VU25
"Awake, O Sleeper" (Mark)
  E547, UM551, VU566, W586
"Wake, Awake, for Night Is Flying" (Mark)
  E61, EL436, L31, P17, UM720 (PD), VU711, W371
"O Day of God, Draw Nigh" (Mark, Advent)
  B623, C700, E601, N611, P452, UM730 (PD), VU688, and VU689 (Fr.)
"Joy Comes with the Dawn" (Mark)
  S2210, SF2210, VU166
"Let All Mortal Flesh Keep Silence" (Mark, Communion)
  B80, C124, E324, EL490, F166, L198, N345, P5, R229, UM626 (PD), VU473 (Fr.), W523
"Thou Didst Leave Thy Throne" (Advent)
  B121, F170, S2100, SF2100

Additional Contemporary Suggestions

"Open Our Eyes, Lord" (Isa)
  B499, R91, S2086, SF2086, SP199
"Water, River, Spirit, Grace" (Isa, Baptism)
  C366, S2253, SF2253

"The Power of Your Love" (Isa)
  M26
"Open the Eyes of My Heart" (Isa)
  M57; V-3 p. 162 Vocal Solo
"The Potter's Hand" (Isa)
  M85
"Jesus, Lover of My Soul" (Isa)
  M112
"Did You Feel the Mountains Tremble?" (Isa, Mark)
  M69; V-3 p. 140 Vocal Solo
"Shine, Jesus, Shine" (Pss, Advent)
  B579, EL671, R247, S2173, SF2173, SP142
"Let the Peace of God Reign" (1 Cor)
  M87
"There's Something About That Name" (Mark)
  B177, C115, F227, R26, SP89, UM171
"Freedom Is Coming" (Mark)
  S2192, SF2192
"O Freedom" (Mark)
  S2194, SF2194
"Ancient of Days" (Mark)
  M1
"No Greater Love" (Mark)
  M25

Vocal Solos

"But Who May Abide" (Isa, Mark)
V-2
"Then Shall the Righteous Shine Forth" (Isa, Mark)
V-8   p. 274
"Patiently Have I Waited" (Advent)
V-4   p. 24

Anthems

"Adonai" (Isa)
Mark A. Miller; Abingdon Press 9780687644308
SATB with piano (opt. solo)

"And There Will Be Signs" (Mark)
Jan Bender: Concordia 98-2082
Unison with Organ

Other Suggestions

Visuals:
  O   Fire, volcanic imagery, dirty cloth, leaf, potter, potter's wheel, lump of clay, water
  P   Angels, water (tears), dried leaves, rough cloth (burlap), shepherd
  E   Portrait of Christ, pile of gifts, 1 Cor 1:9
  G   Eclipse of sun/moon, stars, angels, fig tree, alarm clock, crowing rooster
Response: EL262, VU22. "Wait for the Lord" (Isa.)
Prayers: C19 or F189 (Advent)
Canticle: UM205. "Canticle of Light and Darkness" (Pss) See S-1, p. 383.

Isaiah 40:1-11

[1] Comfort, O comfort my people, says your God. [2] Speak tenderly to Jerusalem, and cry to her that she has served her term, that her penalty is paid, that she has received from the LORD's hand double for all her sins. [3] A voice cries out: "In the wilderness prepare the way of the LORD, make straight in the desert a highway for our God. [4] Every valley shall be lifted up, and every mountain and hill be made low; the uneven ground shall become level, and the rough places a plain. [5] Then the glory of the LORD shall be revealed, and all people shall see it together, for the mouth of the LORD has spoken." [6] A voice says, "Cry out!" And I said, "What shall I cry?" All people are grass, their constancy is like the flower of the field. [7] The grass withers, the flower fades, when the breath of the LORD blows upon it; surely the people are grass. [8] The grass withers, the flower fades; but the word of our God will stand forever. [9] Get you up to a high mountain, O Zion, herald of good tidings; lift up your voice with strength, O Jerusalem, herald of good tidings, lift it up, do not fear; say to the cities of Judah, "Here is your God!" [10] See, the Lord GOD comes with might, and his arm rules for him; his reward is with him, and his recompense before him. [11] He will feed his flock like a shepherd; he will gather the lambs in his arms, and carry them in his bosom, and gently lead the mother sheep.

Psalm 85:1-2, 8-13

[1] LORD, you were favorable to your land; you restored the fortunes of Jacob. [2] You forgave the iniquity of your people; you pardoned all their sin. . . .

[8] Let me hear what God the LORD will speak, for he will speak peace to his people, to his faithful, to those who turn to him in their hearts. [9] Surely his salvation is at hand for those who fear him, that his glory may dwell in our land. [10] Steadfast love and faithfulness will meet; righteousness and peace will kiss each other. [11] Faithfulness will spring up from the ground, and righteousness will look down from the sky. [12] The LORD will give what is good, and our land will yield its increase. [13] Righteousness will go before him, and will make a path for his steps.

2 Peter 3:8-15a

[8] But do not ignore this one fact, beloved, that with the Lord one day is like a thousand years, and a thousand years are like one day. [9] The Lord is not slow about his promise, as some think of slowness, but is patient with you, not wanting any to perish, but all to come to repentance. [10] But the day of the Lord will come like a thief, and then the heavens will pass away with a loud noise, and the elements will be dissolved with fire, and the earth and everything that is done on it will be disclosed.

[11] Since all these things are to be dissolved in this way, what sort of persons ought you to be in leading lives of holiness and godliness, [12] waiting for and hastening the coming of the day of God, because of which the heavens will be set ablaze and dissolved, and the elements will melt with fire? [13] But, in accordance with his promise, we wait for new heavens and a new earth, where righteousness is at home.

[14] Therefore, beloved, while you are waiting for these things, strive to be found by him at peace, without spot or blemish; [15] and regard the patience of our Lord as salvation.

Mark 1:1-8

[1] The beginning of the good news of Jesus Christ, the Son of God.

[2] As it is written in the prophet Isaiah, "See, I am sending my messenger ahead of you, who will prepare your way; [3] the voice of one crying out in the wilderness: 'Prepare the way of the Lord, make his paths straight,' " [4] John the baptizer appeared in the wilderness, proclaiming a baptism of repentance for the forgiveness of sins. [5] And people from the whole Judean countryside and all the people of Jerusalem were going out to him, and were baptized by him in the river Jordan, confessing their sins. [6] Now John was clothed with camel's hair, with a leather belt around his waist, and he ate locusts and wild honey. [7] He proclaimed, "The one who is more powerful than I is coming after me; I am not worthy to stoop down and untie the thong of his sandals. [8] I have baptized you with water; but he will baptize you with the Holy Spirit."

Primary Hymns and Songs for the Day

"O Come, O Come, Emmanuel" (Pss, Mark) (O)
    B76, C119, E56, EL257, F169, L34 (PD), N116, P9, UM211,
    VU1(Fr.), W357
        H-3   Hbl-14, 79; Chr-141; Org-168
        S-1   #342. Handbell accompaniment
"Prepare the Way of the Lord" (Isa, Mark)
    C121, R92, UM207, VU10, W369
"There's Something About That Name" (2 Pet, Mark)
    B177, C115, F227, R26, SP89, UM171
"Wild and Lone the Prophet's Voice" (Mark)
    P409, S2089, SF2089
"Blessed Be the God of Israel" (Isa, Mark) (C)
    C135, E444, EL250/EL552, P602, UM209, VU901

Additional Hymn Suggestions

"Toda la Tierra" ("All Earth Is Waiting") (Isa)
    C139, EL266, N121, UM210, VU5
"God Hath Spoken by the Prophets" (Isa, Mark) (O)
    L238, UM108, W516
"Hail to the Lord's Anointed" (Isa, Mark)
    C140, E616, EL311 (PD), L87, N104, P205, UM203 (PD), VU30
"People, Look East" (Isa, Advent)
    C142, EL248, P12, UM202, VU9, W359
"Blessed Quietness" (Isa, Advent)
    F145, C267, N284, S2142, SF2142
"Lift Up Your Heads, Ye Mighty Gates" (Pss, 2 Pet)
    B128, C129, E436, F239, N117, P8, R59, UM213 (PD), W363
"Fling Wide the Door" (Pss, 2 Pet)
    EL259, L32
"O God, Our Help in Ages Past" (2 Pet)
    B74, C67, E680, EL632, F370, L320, N25, P210, UM117
    (PD), VU806, W579
"Love Divine, All Loves Excelling" (2 Pet)
    B208, C517, E657, EL631 (PD), L315, P376, N43, R196,
    UM384, VU333, W588
"O Day of God, Draw Nigh" (2 Pet, Advent)
    B623, C700, E601, N611, P452, UM730 (PD), VU688, and
    VU689 (Fr.)
"This Is a Day of New Beginnings" (2 Pet, Communion)
    B370, C518, N417, UM383, W661
"Angels from the Realms of Glory" (Mark)
    B94, C149, E93, EL275, F190, L50, P22, UM220 (PD),
    VU36, W377
"Lead Me, Lord" (Mark)
    C593, N774, R175, UM473 (PD), VU662
"Now the Silence" (Communion, Advent)
    C415, E333, EL460, L205, R221, UM619, VU475, W668
"Let All Mortal Flesh Keep Silence" (Communion, Advent)
    B80, C124, E324, EL490, F166, L198, N345, P5, R229,
    UM626 (PD), VU473 (Fr.), W523
"In the Singing" (Communion, Advent)
    EL466, S2255, SF2255

Additional Contemporary Suggestions

"Lord God, Almighty" (Isa)
    R40, S2006, SF2006

"God Is Here Today" ("Dios Esta' Aqui') (Isa)
    S2049, SF2049
"O Lord, Your Tenderness" (Isa)
    S2143, SF2143
"Let It Rise" (Isa)
    M4
"Rise Up and Praise Him" (Isa)
    M62
"How Great Are You, Lord" (Isa, Pss)
    M103
"Alleluia" (Isa, Mark)
    R136, SP108, UM186; S-2 #3-4
"God Will Make a Way" (Isa, Mark)
    SP40
"Freedom Is Coming" (2 Peter)
    S2192, SF2192
"While We Are Waiting, Come" (2 Peter, Advent)
    SP130
"Jesus, Name Above All Names" (Mark)
    R26, S2071, SF2071, SP76
"Emmanuel, Emmanuel" (Advent)
    B82, C134, R28, SP75, UM204

Vocal Solos

"Comfort Ye"
"Every Valley"
"O Thou That Tellest Good Tidings to Zion" (Isa)
    V-2
"He Shall Feed His Flock Like a Shepherd" (Isa)
    V-2
    V-8   p. 334
"Lift Up Your Heads" (2 Pet, Pss)
    V-10   p. 38
"My Lord, What a Mornin'" (2 Pet)
    V-7   p. 68

Anthems

"Comfort, Comfort Now My People" (Isa)
Richard Proulx; Morningstar Music AE110
SAB with Percussion

"Lift Up Your Heads" (Pss, 2 Pet)
Mark Burrows; Abingdon Press 0687343755
SATB with piano

Other Suggestions

Visuals:
    O   God's outstretched hand, Bible, straight highway,
         wilderness, places of solitude, city streets, prairies,
         mountaintop, shepherd carrying a lamb, sheep
    P   Kiss, images of peace, reconciliation
    E   Fire, upheaval/peace, calm
    G   Wilderness, water, rough fabric, leather, honeycomb,
         sandals, fire/dove (Holy Spirit)
Introit: C121, R92, UM207, VU10, W369. "Prepare the Way" (Mark)
Canticle: C123. "The Coming of God" (Pss, Mark, Advent)
Litany: C120, UM211. Advent Antiphons (Pss, Mark)

Isaiah 61:1-4, 8-11

[1] The spirit of the Lord GOD is upon me, because the LORD has anointed me; he has sent me to bring good news to the oppressed, to bind up the brokenhearted, to proclaim liberty to the captives, and release to the prisoners; [2] to proclaim the year of the LORD's favor, and the day of vengeance of our God; to comfort all who mourn; [3] to provide for those who mourn in Zion—to give them a garland instead of ashes, the oil of gladness instead of mourning, the mantle of praise instead of a faint spirit. They will be called oaks of righteousness, the planting of the LORD, to display his glory. [4] They shall build up the ancient ruins, they shall raise up the former devastations; they shall repair the ruined cities, the devastations of many generations. . . .

[8] For I the LORD love justice, I hate robbery and wrongdoing; I will faithfully give them their recompense, and I will make an everlasting covenant with them. [9] Their descendants shall be known among the nations, and their offspring among the peoples; all who see them shall acknowledge that they are a people whom the LORD has blessed. [10] I will greatly rejoice in the LORD, my whole being shall exult in my God; for he has clothed me with the garments of salvation, he has covered me with the robe of righteousness, as a bridegroom decks himself with a garland, and as a bride adorns herself with her jewels. [11] For as the earth brings forth its shoots, and as a garden causes what is sown in it to spring up, so the Lord GOD will cause righteousness and praise to spring up before all the nations.

Psalm 126

[1] When the LORD restored the fortunes of Zion, we were like those who dream. [2] Then our mouth was filled with laughter, and our tongue with shouts of joy; then it was said among the nations, "The LORD has done great things for them." [3] The LORD has done great things for us, and we rejoiced. [4] Restore our fortunes, O LORD, like the watercourses in the Negeb. [5] May those who sow in tears reap with shouts of joy. [6] Those who go out weeping, bearing the seed for sowing, shall come home with shouts of joy, carrying their sheaves.

1 Thessalonians 5:16-24

[16] Rejoice always, [17] pray without ceasing, [18] give thanks in all circumstances; for this is the will of God in Christ Jesus for you. [19] Do not quench the Spirit. [20] Do not despise the words of prophets, [21] but test everything; hold fast to what is good; [22] abstain from every form of evil.

[23] May the God of peace himself sanctify you entirely; and may your spirit and soul and body be kept sound and blameless at the coming of our Lord Jesus Christ. [24] The one who calls you is faithful, and he will do this.

John 1:6-8, 19-28

[6] There was a man sent from God, whose name was John. [7] He came as a witness to testify to the light, so that all might believe through him. [8] He himself was not the light, but he came to testify to the light. . . .

[19] This is the testimony given by John when the Jews sent priests and Levites from Jerusalem to ask him, "Who are you?" [20] He confessed and did not deny it, but confessed, "I am not the Messiah." [21] And they asked him, "What then? Are you Elijah?" He said, "I am not." "Are you the prophet?" He answered, "No." [22] Then they said to him, "Who are you? Let us have an answer for those who sent us. What do you say about yourself?" [23] He said, "I am the voice of one crying out in the wilderness, 'Make straight the way of the Lord,' " as the prophet Isaiah said.

[24] Now they had been sent from the Pharisees. [25] They asked him, "Why then are you baptizing if you are neither the Messiah, nor Elijah, nor the prophet?" [26] John answered them, "I baptize with water. Among you stands one whom you do not know, [27] the one who is coming after me; I am not worthy to untie the thong of his sandal." [28] This took place in Bethany across the Jordan where John was baptizing.

Primary Hymns and Songs for the Day

"O For a Thousand Tongues to Sing" (Isa) (O)
B216, C5, E493, EL886, F349, L559, N42, P466, R32, UM57
(PD), VU326

    H-3   Hbl-79; Chr-142; Desc-17; Org-12
    S-1   #33-38. Various Treatments

"Hail to the Lord's Anointed" (Isa)
N104, UM203 (PD)

    H-3   Hbl-16, 22, 68; Chr-101; Desc-37
    S-1   #114. Descant
           #115. Harmonization
    C140, E616, EL311 (PD), L87, P205, VU30

"Hark! The Herald Angels Sing" (John) (C)
B88, C150, E87, EL270, F184, L60, N144, P31, UM240 (PD),
VU48, W387

    H-3   Hbl-26, 67; Chr-91; Desc-75; Org-89
    S-1   #234-6. Harmonizations and descant

Additional Hymn Suggestions

"Holy, Holy, Holy! Lord God Almighty" (Isa)
B2, C4, E362, F323, EL413, L165, N277, P138, R204, UM64 and
UM65, VU315, W485

"Come, Thou Long-Expected Jesus" (Isa)
B77, C125, E66, EL254, F168, L30, N122, P1/P2, UM196 (PD),
VU2, W364

"Tell Out, My Soul" (Isa)
B81, E437/E438, R130, UM200, W534

"O Zion, Haste" (Isa)
B583, C482, E539, EL668, F658, L397, UM573 (PD)

"Holy" ("Santo") (Isa)
EL762, S2019, SF2019

"The Spirit Sends Us Forth to Serve" (Isa) (C)
EL551, S2241, SF2241

"Spirit, Spirit of Gentleness" (Isa, Pss, John)
C249, EL396, N286, P319, S2120, VU375 (Fr.)

"We Are Called" (Isa, John)
EL720, S2172, SF2172

"Gather Us In" (Isa, John) (O)
C284, EL532, S2236, SF2236, W665

"Rejoice, Ye Pure in Heart" (Pss, 1 Thess)
B39, C15, E556/E557, EL873/EL874, F394, N55/N71, P145/
P146, UM160/UM161

"Go Forth for God" (1 Thess) (C)
E347, R291, UM670, VU418

"Christ, Whose Glory Fills the Skies" (John)
E7, EL553, F293, L265, P462, UM173 (PD), VU336

"Word of God, Come Down on Earth" (John)
E633, EL510, UM182, W513

"Christ Is the World's Light" (John)
UM188, W543

"Send Your Word" (John)
N317, UM195

"I Want to Walk as a Child of the Light" (John)
E490, EL815, R152, UM206, W510

"Savior of the Nations, Come" (John)
E54, EL263, P14 (PD), UM214, W372

"Lead Me, Guide Me" (John)
C583, EL768, R176, S2214, SF2214

"Wild and Lone the Prophet's Voice" (John, Advent)
P409, S2089, SF2089

Additional Contemporary Suggestions

"Holy Spirit, Come to Us" (Isa, Advent)
EL406, S2118, SF2118, W473

"Holy, Holy" (Isa)
B254, F149, P140, R206, S2039, SP141

"Joy Comes with the Dawn" (Isa)
S2210, SF2210, VU166

"Shout to the Lord" (Pss)
EL821, S2074, SF2074, M16; V-3 p. 56 Vocal Solo

"Come, Rejoice in God" (1 Thess)
S2017, SF2017

"Sanctuary" (1 Thess)
M52, R185, S2164, SF2164

"Song of Hope" ("Canto de Esperanza") (1 Thess)
P432, S2186, VU424

"Lord, Listen to Your Children Praying" (1 Thess)
C305, S2193, SF2193, VU400

"Jesus, We Are Here" (1 Thess)
EL529, S2273, SF2273

"Rejoice" (1 Thess)
SP150

"Prepare the Way of the Lord" (John)
C121, R92, UM207, VU10, W369

"Arise, Shine" (John)
S2005, SF2005

"Jesus, Name Above All Names" (John)
R26, S2071, SF2071, SP76

"Arise, Shine, for Your Light Is Come" (John)
R123, SP176

Vocal Solos

"Come Thou Long Expected Jesus" (Isa)
V-1   p. 5

"Rejoice Greatly, O Daughter of Zion" (Pss)
V-2

Anthems

"Thou Shalt Know Him" (Isa, John)
Mark Sirett; Augsburg 11-10645
SATB *a cappella*

"Go and Tell John" (John)
Lloyd Pfautsch, Hope CY 3334
SATB *a cappella*

Other Suggestions

Visuals:

    O   Garland, oil, mantel, oak tree, rich garments/jewelry
    P   Praise, tears of joy, sheaves of wheat
    E   Praying hands, 1 Thess 5:16-17
    G   Water/baptism, light, John 1:23 (Christ candle)

Introit: C142, EL248, P12, UM202, VU9, W359, stanza 3. "People,
    Look East" (Advent)

Prayer: C591 or UM489. "For God's Gifts" (John)

Response: C593, N774, R175, UM473 (PD), VU662. "Lead Me,
    Lord" (John)

2 Samuel 7:1-11, 16

[1] Now when the king was settled in his house, and the LORD had given him rest from all his enemies around him, [2] the king said to the prophet Nathan, "See now, I am living in a house of cedar, but the ark of God stays in a tent." [3] Nathan said to the king, "Go, do all that you have in mind; for the LORD is with you."

[4] But that same night the word of the LORD came to Nathan: [5] Go and tell my servant David: Thus says the LORD: Are you the one to build me a house to live in? [6] I have not lived in a house since the day I brought up the people of Israel from Egypt to this day, but I have been moving about in a tent and a tabernacle. [7] Wherever I have moved about among all the people of Israel, did I ever speak a word with any of the tribal leaders of Israel, whom I commanded to shepherd my people Israel, saying, "Why have you not built me a house of cedar?" [8] Now therefore thus you shall say to my servant David: Thus says the LORD of hosts: I took you from the pasture, from following the sheep to be prince over my people Israel; [9] and I have been with you wherever you went, and have cut off all your enemies from before you; and I will make for you a great name, like the name of the great ones of the earth. [10] And I will appoint a place for my people Israel and will plant them, so that they may live in their own place, and be disturbed no more; and evildoers shall afflict them no more, as formerly, [11] from the time that I appointed judges over my people Israel; and I will give you rest from all your enemies. Moreover the LORD declares to you that the LORD will make you a house. . . .

[16] Your house and your kingdom shall be made sure forever before me; your throne shall be established forever.

Luke 1:46b-55

[46b] My soul magnifies the Lord, [47] and my spirit rejoices in God my Savior, [48] for he has looked with favor on the lowliness of his servant. Surely, from now on all generations will call me blessed; [49] for the Mighty One has done great things for me, and holy is his name. [50] His mercy is for those who fear him from generation to generation. [51] He has shown strength with his arm; he has scattered the proud in the thoughts of their hearts. [52] He has brought down the powerful from their thrones, and lifted up the lowly; [53] he has filled the hungry with good things, and sent the rich away empty. [54] He has helped his servant Israel, in remembrance of his mercy, [55] according to the promise he made to our ancestors, to Abraham and to his descendants forever."

Romans 16:25-27

[25] Now to God who is able to strengthen you according to my gospel and the proclamation of Jesus Christ, according to the revelation of the mystery that was kept secret for long ages [26] but is now disclosed, and through the prophetic writings is made known to all the Gentiles, according to the command of the eternal God, to bring about the obedience of faith— [27] to the only wise God, through Jesus Christ, to whom be the glory forever! Amen.

Luke 1:26-38

[26] In the sixth month the angel Gabriel was sent by God to a town in Galilee called Nazareth, [27] to a virgin engaged to a man whose name was Joseph, of the house of David. The virgin's name was Mary. [28] And he came to her and said, "Greetings, favored one! The Lord is with you." [29] But she was much perplexed by his words and pondered what sort of greeting this might be. [30] The angel said to her, "Do not be afraid, Mary, for you have found favor with God. [31] And now, you will conceive in your womb and bear a son, and you will name him Jesus. [32] He will be great, and will be called the Son of the Most High, and the Lord God will give to him the throne of his ancestor David. [33] He will reign over the house of Jacob forever, and of his kingdom there will be no end." [34] Mary said to the angel, "How can this be, since I am a virgin?" [35] The angel said to her, "The Holy Spirit will come upon you, and the power of the Most High will overshadow you; therefore the child to be born will be holy; he will be called Son of God. [36] And now, your relative Elizabeth in her old age has also conceived a son; and this is the sixth month for her who was said to be barren. [37] For nothing will be impossible with God." [38] Then Mary said, "Here am I, the servant of the Lord; let it be with me according to your word." Then the angel departed from her.

Primary Hymns and Songs for the Day

"Hail to the Lord's Anointed" (2 Sam) (O)
C140, E616, EL311 (PD), L87, N104, P205, UM203 (PD), VU30
H-3   Hbl-16, 22, 68; Chr-101; Desc-37
S-1   #114. Descant
       #115. Harmonization
"My Soul Gives Glory to My God" (Luke)
C130, N119, P600, UM198, VU899
H-3   Chr-139, 145; Desc-77
S-1   #241-242. Orff arr. and descant
EL251
"To a Maid Engaged to Joseph" (Luke)
P19, UM215, VU14
H-3   Chr-201
S-2   #12-13. Descants
"Give Thanks" (Luke)
C528, R266, S2036, SF2036, SP170
"It Came Upon the Midnight Clear" (2 Sam, Luke) (C)
B93, C153, E89/E90, EL282, F197, L54, N131, P38, UM218 (PD), VU44, W400
H-3   Hbl-72; Chr-113; Desc-22; Org-19
S-2   #39. Descant

Additional Hymn Suggestions

"Blessed Be the God of Israel" (2 Sam)
C135, E444, EL250/EL552, P602, UM209, VU901
"O Come, O Come, Emmanuel" (2 Sam)
B76, C119, E56, EL257, F169, L34 (PD), N116, P9, UM211, VU1 (Fr.), W357
"That Boy-Child of Mary" (2 Sam, Luke)
B110, EL293, P55, UM241
"To God Be the Glory" (Rom)
B153, C39, F365, N14, R68, UM99; V-8 p. 5 Vocal Solo
"Tell Out, My Soul" (Luke)
B81, E437/E438, R130, UM200, W534
"People, Look East" (Luke)
C142, EL248, P12, UM202, VU9, W359
"Savior of the Nations, Come" (Luke)
E54, EL263, P14 (PD), UM214, W372
"Lo, How a Rose E'er Blooming" (Luke)
B78, C160, E81, EL272, F174, L58, N127, P48 (PD), UM216, VU8, W374
"In the Bleak Midwinter" (Luke)
E112, EL294, N128, P36, UM221 (PD), VU55
"He Is Born" ("Il Est Né") (Luke)
B112, UM228, VU50 (Fr.)
"O Come, All Ye Faithful" (Luke)
B89, C148, E83, EL283, F193, L45, N135, P41, UM234 (PD), VU60 (Fr.), W392
"Once in Royal David's City" (Luke)
C165, E102, EL269, N45, P49, UM250 (PD), VU62, W402
"Sing of Mary, Pure and Lowly" (Luke)
C184, E277, UM272, W404
"The First One Ever" (Luke)
E673, UM276
"The Snow Lay on the Ground" (Luke)
E110, S2093, SF2093, P57

"Joseph Dearest, Joseph Mine" (Luke)
N105, S2099, SF2099
"Spirit, Spirit of Gentleness" (Luke)
C249, EL396, N286, P319, S2120, VU375 (Fr.)
"She Comes Sailing on the Wind" (Luke)
S2122, SF2122, VU380
"I'm So Glad Jesus Lifted Me" (Luke)
C529, EL860 (PD), N474, S2151, SF2151
"Blest Are They" (Luke)
R127, EL728, S2155, SF2155, VU896

Additional Contemporary Suggestions

"He Is Able" (Rom)
M37
"Praise to the Lord" (Luke)
EL844, S2029, SF2029, VU835
"Glory to God" ("Gloria a Dios") (Luke)
EL164, S2033, SF2033
"This Kingdom" (Luke)
M17
"Holy Spirit, Rain Down" (Luke)
M88
"Shout to the North" (Luke)
M99
"You Are My All in All" (Luke)
SP220
"Good to Me" (Luke)
M164

Vocal Solos

"Glory Hallelujah to de New-Born King" (Luke)
V-7   p. 80
"Nativity Lullaby"
V-9   p. 10

Anthems

"Lo, How a Rose E'er Blooming" (Luke)
Donald Bailey; Gentry Publications JG2251
SATB *divisi, a cappella*

"Mary Had a Baby" (Luke)
Arr. Sam Batt Owens; MorningStar 50-1060
SATB *a cappella*

Other Suggestions

Visuals:
O   Cedar, crown, tent, ark of the covenant (chest)
G   Luke 1:46b, food, hungry being fed
E   Open Bible, Christ, servant, obedience
G   Luke 1:28ff., angel, Mary, annunciation, servant imagery, Luke 1:38
As an alternative to reading the Magnificat, have the choir lead the congregation in singing C130, N119, P600, UM198, VU899, "My Soul Gives Glory to My God."
Additional Magnificat Settings: C131, E269, EL314, F176, L180, N732, R131, UM199, VU898, W553 (Luke)
Response: W713. "Ave Maria" (Luke)

Isaiah 9:2-7

[2] The people who walked in darkness have seen a great light; those who lived in a land of deep darkness—on them light has shined. [3] You have multiplied the nation, you have increased its joy; they rejoice before you as with joy at the harvest, as people exult when dividing plunder. [4] For the yoke of their burden, and the bar across their shoulders, the rod of their oppressor, you have broken as on the day of Midian. [5] For all the boots of the tramping warriors and all the garments rolled in blood shall be burned as fuel for the fire. [6] For a child has been born for us, a son given to us; authority rests upon his shoulders; and he is named Wonderful Counselor, Mighty God, Everlasting Father, Prince of Peace. [7] His authority shall grow continually, and there shall be endless peace for the throne of David and his kingdom. He will establish and uphold it with justice and with righteousness from this time onward and forevermore. The zeal of the LORD of hosts will do this.

Psalm 96

[1] O sing to the LORD a new song; sing to the LORD, all the earth. [2] Sing to the LORD, bless his name; tell of his salvation from day to day. [3] Declare his glory among the nations, his marvelous works among all the peoples. [4] For great is the LORD, and greatly to be praised; he is to be revered above all gods. [5] For all the gods of the peoples are idols, but the LORD made the heavens. [6] Honor and majesty are before him; strength and beauty are in his sanctuary. [7] Ascribe to the LORD, O families of the peoples, ascribe to the LORD glory and strength. [8] Ascribe to the LORD the glory due his name; bring an offering, and come into his courts. [9] Worship the LORD in holy splendor; tremble before him, all the earth. [10] Say among the nations, "The LORD is king! The world is firmly established; it shall never be moved. He will judge the peoples with equity." [11] Let the heavens be glad, and let the earth rejoice; let the sea roar, and all that fills it; [12] let the field exult, and everything in it. Then shall all the trees of the forest sing for joy [13] before the LORD; for he is coming, for he is coming to judge the earth. He will judge the world with righteousness, and the peoples with his truth.

Titus 2:11-14

[11] For the grace of God has appeared, bringing salvation to all, [12] training us to renounce impiety and worldly passions, and in the present age to live lives that are self-controlled, upright, and godly, [13] while we wait for the blessed hope and the manifestation of the glory of our great God and Savior, Jesus Christ. [14] He it is who gave himself for us that he might redeem us from all iniquity and purify for himself a people of his own who are zealous for good deeds.

Luke 2:1-20

[1] In those days a decree went out from Emperor Augustus that all the world should be registered. [2] This was the first registration and was taken while Quirinius was governor of Syria. [3] All went to their own towns to be registered. [4] Joseph also went from the town of Nazareth in Galilee to Judea, to the city of David called Bethlehem, because he was descended from the house and family of David. [5] He went to be registered with Mary, to whom he was engaged and who was expecting a child. [6] While they were there, the time came for her to deliver her child. [7] And she gave birth to her firstborn son and wrapped him in bands of cloth, and laid him in a manger, because there was no place for them in the inn.

[8] In that region there were shepherds living in the fields, keeping watch over their flock by night. [9] Then an angel of the Lord stood before them, and the glory of the Lord shone around them, and they were terrified. [10] But the angel said to them, "Do not be afraid; for see—I am bringing you good news of great joy for all the people: [11] to you is born this day in the city of David a Savior, who is the Messiah, the Lord. [12] This will be a sign for you: you will find a child wrapped in bands of cloth and lying in a manger." [13] And suddenly there was with the angel a multitude of the heavenly host, praising God and saying, [14] "Glory to God in the highest heaven, and on earth peace among those whom he favors!"

[15] When the angels had left them and gone into heaven, the shepherds said to one another, "Let us go now to Bethlehem and see this thing that has taken place, which the Lord has made known to us." [16] So they went with haste and found Mary and Joseph, and the child lying in the manger. [17] When they saw this, they made known what had been told them about this child; [18] and all who heard it were amazed at what the shepherds told them. [19] But Mary treasured all these words and pondered them in her heart. [20] The shepherds returned, glorifying and praising God for all they had heard and seen, as it had been told them.

Primary Hymns and Songs for the Day

"O Come, All Ye Faithful" (Isa, Luke) (O)
B89, C148, E83, EL283, F193, L45, N135, P41, UM234
(PD), VU60 (Fr.), W392
> See especially stanzas 1, 3, and 4
> H-3   Hbl-78; Desc-12; Org-2
> S-1   #7-13. Various treatments

"O Little Town of Bethlehem" (Luke)
B86, C144, E78/E79, EL279, F178, L41, N133, P43/P44,
UM230, VU64, W386
> H-3   Hbl-81; Chr-145; Desc-95; Org-141
> S-1   #304. Harmonization

"We Have Heard on High" (Luke) (festive close)
B100, C155, E96, EL289, F192, L71, P23, N125, UM238,
VU38 (Fr.), W376
> H-3   Hbl-47; Chr-31; Desc-43; Org-45

"Silent Night, Holy Night" (Luke) (quiet close)
B91, C145, E111, EL281, F195, L65, N134, P60, UM239
(PD), VU67 (Fr.), W379

Additional Hymn Suggestions

"Away in a Manger" (Luke)
B103, C147, E101, EL277, F185/F187, L67, N124, P24/P25,
UM217, VU69, W378

"What Child Is This" (Luke)
B118, C162, E115, EL296, F180, L40, N148, P53, UM219
(PD), VU74, W411

"Good Christian Friends, Rejoice" (Luke)
B96, C164, E107 (PD), EL288, F177, L55, N129, P28,
UM224, VU35, W391

"The Friendly Beasts" (Luke)
UM227, VU56

"Infant Holy, Infant Lowly" (Luke)
B106, C163, EL276, F194, L44, P37, UM229, VU58, W393

"While Shepherds Watched Their Flocks" (Luke)
C154, E94/E95, F175, P58, UM236, VU75, W382

"Love Came Down at Christmas" (Luke)
B109, E84, N165, UM242

"The First Noel" (Luke)
B85, C151, E109, EL300, F179, L56, N139, P56, UM245
(PD), VU90 (Fr.) and VU91, W408

"On This Day Earth Shall Ring" (Luke)
E92, P46, UM248

"Go, Tell It on the Mountain" (Luke)
B95, C167, E99, EL290, F205, L70, N154, P29, UM251,
VU43, W397

"Like a Child" (Luke)
C133, S2092, SF2092, VU366

"The Snow Lay on the Ground" (Luke)
E110, S2093, P57

"Rise Up, Shepherd, and Follow" (Luke)
P50, S2096, SF2096, VU70

"One Holy Night in Bethlehem" (Luke)
S2097, SF2097

Additional Contemporary Suggestions

"His Name Is Wonderful" (Isa)
B203, F230, R30, SP90, UM174

"King of Kings" (Isa)
B234, R268, S2075, SF2075, SP94, VU167

"Come Now, O Prince of Peace" ("O-So-So") (Isa)
EL247, S2232, SF2232

"Light of the World" (Isa)
S2204

"How Majestic Is Your Name" (Isa)
C63, R98, S2023, SF2023, SP14

"Jesus, Name Above All Names" (Isa)
R26, S2071, SF2071, SP76

"I Sing Praises to Your Name" (Pss)
R79, S2037, SF2037, SP27

"Shout to the Lord" (Pss)
EL821, S2074, SF2074, M16; V-3 p. 56 Vocal Solo

"Lord, I Lift Your Name on High" (Luke)
EL857, M2, R4, S2088, SF2088

"Amen, Amen" (Luke)
N161, P299, S2072

Vocal Solos

"For unto Us a Child Is Born" (Isa)
V-2

"This Night in David's City" (Luke)
V-9   p. 8

"Mary Had a Baby" (Luke)
V-7   p. 46

"O Holy Night" (Luke)
V-8   p. 93

"Sing Noel!" (Christmas)
V-11   p. 13

Anthems

"A Child Is Born in Bethlehem" (Luke)
Philip Stopford; Hal Leonard 08745637
SATB with organ

"Midnight Clear" (Luke)
David Giardiniere; Hinshaw HMC2117
SATB with piano

Other Suggestions

Visuals:
> **O**   Joy, praise, Isa 9:6b
> **P**   Musical notes, sea, field, trees, branches upraised, Ps 96:12b
> **E**   Titus 2:11, Christ child, manger
> **G**   Christ child, manger, Mary, Joseph, shepherds/angels, peace, joy, Luke 2:14, 19

Introit: C166, E114, EL284, L72, N151, P61, UM244, VU71, W380, stanzas 1 and 4 "'Twas in the Moon of Wintertime" (Luke, Christmas)

Introit: EL164, S2033, SF2033, UM72. "Gloria" (Luke)

Response: S2090, SF2090 "Light the Advent Candle" (Advent)

Opening Prayer: UM231 (Luke, Christmas)

Response: UM256, stanza 1. "We Would See Jesus" (Luke)

Canticle: N757, UM82 "Canticle of God's Glory" (Luke)

Readings: B99 or F196 (Isa) and C152, F186, or F188 (Luke)

Response: B110, EL293, P55, UM241, stanzas 2 and 5. "That Boy-Child of Mary" (Luke)

Isaiah 52:7-10

[7]How beautiful upon the mountains are the feet of the messenger who announces peace, who brings good news, who announces salvation, who says to Zion, "Your God reigns." [8]Listen! Your sentinels lift up their voices, together they sing for joy; for in plain sight they see the return of the LORD to Zion. [9]Break forth together into singing, you ruins of Jerusalem; for the LORD has comforted his people, he has redeemed Jerusalem. [10]The LORD has bared his holy arm before the eyes of all the nations; and all the ends of the earth shall see the salvation of our God.

Psalm 98

[1]O sing to the LORD a new song, for he has done marvelous things. His right hand and his holy arm have gotten him victory. [2]The LORD has made known his victory; he has revealed his vindication in the sight of the nations. [3]He has remembered his steadfast love and faithfulness to the house of Israel. All the ends of the earth have seen the victory of our God. [4]Make a joyful noise to the LORD, all the earth; break forth into joyous song and sing praises.

[5]Sing praises to the LORD with the lyre, with the lyre and the sound of melody. [6]With trumpets and the sound of the horn make a joyful noise before the King, the LORD. [7]Let the sea roar, and all that fills it; the world and those who live in it. [8]Let the floods clap their hands; let the hills sing together for joy [9]at the presence of the LORD, for he is coming to judge the earth. He will judge the world with righteousness, and the peoples with equity.

Hebrews 1:1-4, (5-12)

[1]Long ago God spoke to our ancestors in many and various ways by the prophets, [2]but in these last days he has spoken to us by a Son, whom he appointed heir of all things, through whom he also created the worlds. [3]He is the reflection of God's glory and the exact imprint of God's very being, and he sustains all things by his powerful word. When he had made purification for sins, he sat down at the right hand of the Majesty on high, [4]having become as much superior to angels as the name he has inherited is more excellent than theirs. [5]For to which of the angels did God ever say, "You are my Son; today I have begotten you"? Or again, "I will be his Father, and he will be my Son"? [6]And again, when he brings the firstborn into the world, he says, "Let all God's angels worship him." [7]Of the angels he says, "He makes his angels winds, and his servants flames of fire." [8]But of the Son he says, "Your throne, O God, is forever and ever, and the righteous scepter is the scepter of your kingdom. [9]You have loved righteousness and hated wickedness; therefore God, your God, has anointed you with the oil of gladness beyond your companions." [10]And, "In the beginning, Lord, you founded the earth, and the heavens are the work of your hands; [11]they will perish, but you remain; they will all wear out like clothing; [12]like a cloak you will roll them up, and like clothing they will be changed. But you are the same, and your years will never end."

John 1:1-14

[1]In the beginning was the Word, and the Word was with God, and the Word was God. [2]He was in the beginning with God. [3]All things came into being through him, and without him not one thing came into being. What has come into being [4]in him was life, and the life was the light of all people.

[5]The light shines in the darkness, and the darkness did not overcome it. [6]There was a man sent from God, whose name was John. [7]He came as a witness to testify to the light, so that all might believe through him. [8]He himself was not the light, but he came to testify to the light. [9]The true light, which enlightens everyone, was coming into the world. [10]He was in the world, and the world came into being through him; yet the world did not know him. [11]He came to what was his own, and his own people did not accept him. [12]But to all who received him, who believed in his name, he gave power to become children of God, [13]who were born, not of blood or of the will of the flesh or of the will of man, but of God. [14]And the Word became flesh and lived among us, and we have seen his glory, the glory as of a father's only son, full of grace and truth.

Primary Hymns and Songs for the Day

"Joy to the World" (Pss) (O)
> B87, C143, E100, EL267, F171, L39, N132, P40, UM246 (PD), VU59, W399
>> H-3   Hbl-8, 29, 73; Chr-119; Desc-15; Org-6
>> S-1   #19-20. Trumpet descants

"Good Christian Friends, Rejoice" (Isa)
> B96, C164, E107 (PD), EL288, F177, L55, N129, P28, UM224, VU35, W391
>> H-3   Hbl-19, 30, 65; Chr-83; Desc-55; Org-62
>> S-1   #180. Rhythm instrument accompaniment

"Sing a New Song to the Lord" (Pss)
> S2045, SF2045, W550

"Love Came Down at Christmas" (John)
> B109, E84, N165, UM242
>> V-8   p. 90 Vocal Solo

"Jesus, Name Above All Names" (John)
> R26, S2071, SF2071, SP76

"I Want to Walk as a Child of the Light" (John) (C)
> E490, EL815, R152, UM206, W510
>> S-2   #91. Descant

"Hark! The Herald Angels Sing" (John) (C)
> B88, C150, E87, EL270, F184, L60, N144, P31, UM240 (PD), VU48, W387
>> H-3   Hbl-26, 67; Chr-91; Desc-75; Org-89
>> S-1   #234-6. Harmonizations and descant

Additional Hymn Suggestions

"Wake, Awake, for Night Is Flying" (Isa)
> E61, EL436, L31, P17, UM720 (PD), VU711, W371

"Infant Holy, Infant Lowly" (Heb)
> B106, C163, EL276, F194, L44, P37, UM229, VU58, W393

"When Christmas Morn Is Dawning" (Heb)
> L59, UM232

"Angels We Have Heard on High" (Heb)
> B100, C155, E96, EL289, F192, L71, P23, N125, UM238, VU38 (Fr.), W376

"O Come, All Ye Faithful" (Isa, Luke) (O)
> B89, C148, E83, EL283, F193, L45, N135, P41, UM234 (PD), VU60 (Fr.), W392
>> See especially stanzas 1, 2, and 6

"En el Frio Invernal" ("Cold December Flies Away") (John)
> EL299, L53, UM233

"I Sing the Almighty Power of God" (John) (O)
> B42, E398, UM152 (PD)
> C64, N12, P288 (PD), R54
> VU231 (PD), W502 (PD)

"Savior of the Nations, Come" (John)
> E54, EL263, P14 (PD), UM214, W372

"O Come, All Ye Faithful" (John)
> B89, C148, E83, EL283, F193, L45, N135, P41, UM234 (PD), VU60 (Fr.), W392

"Hark! The Herald Angels Sing" (John)
> B88, C150, E87, EL270, F184, L60, N144, P31, UM240 (PD), VU48, W387

"Womb of Life" (John)
> C14, N274, S2046, SF2046

"Word of God, Come Down on Earth" (John)
> E633, EL510, UM182, W513

"Thou Didst Leave Thy Throne" (John)
> B121, F170, S2100, SF2100

"O Holy Spirit, Root of Life" (John)
> C251, EL399, N57, S2121, SF2121, VU379

"Deck Thyself, My Soul, with Gladness" (Communion)
> E339, EL488/EL489, L224, P506, UM612 (PD), VU463

"On This Day Earth Shall Ring" (John, Communion) (C)
> E92, P46, UM248

"In the Bleak Midwinter" (Christmas)
> E112, EL294, N128, P36, UM221 (PD), VU55

"'Twas in the Moon of Wintertime" (Christmas)
> C166, E114, EL284, L72, N151, P61, UM244, VU71, W380

Additional Contemporary Suggestions

"Our God Reigns" (Isa)
> SP64

"The Lord Reigns" (Isa)
> SP58, M14

"Someone Asked the Question" (Isa)
> N523, S2144

"Sing unto the Lord a New Song" (Pss)
> SP23

"I Will Celebrate" (Pss)
> M46, R77, SP147

"Clap Your Hands" (Pss)
> S2028, SF2028

"Shout to the Lord" (Pss)
> EL821, S2074, SF2074, M16; V-3 p. 56 Vocal Solo

"Shine, Jesus, Shine" (John)
> B579, EL671, R247, S2173, SF2173, SP142

"Light of the World" (John)
> S2204, SF2204

"Shine on Us" (John)
> M19

Vocal Solos

"Hark! The Herald Angels Sing" (John)
V-1   p. 13
"Of the Father's Love Begotten" (John, Communion)
V-5   p. 17

Anthems

"Blessed Be That Maid Marie" (Christmas)
John Leavitt; Concordia 98-3784
SATB with opt. keyboard, C instrument, perc.

"Sing We Now of Christmas" (Christmas)
arr. Cary Ratcliff; G. Schirmer 50486203
SATB with keyboard

Other Suggestions

Visuals:
> O   Mountains, feet, sheet music, singing, ruins, nations
> P   Singing, hand, creation, instruments, Ps 98:11, 14
> E   Angels, scepter/crown/royal cloak, oil, flames
> G   Light/darkness, Christ candle, John 1:1, 5, 14

Prayer: UM231. "Christmas" (Heb)

NOTE: If you read Luke's Christmas story today, see Christmas Eve suggestions.

Ecclesiastes 3:1-13

[1] For everything there is a season, and a time for every matter under heaven: [2] a time to be born, and a time to die; a time to plant, and a time to pluck up what is planted; [3] a time to kill, and a time to heal; a time to break down, and a time to build up; [4] a time to weep, and a time to laugh; a time to mourn, and a time to dance; [5] a time to throw away stones, and a time to gather stones together; a time to embrace, and a time to refrain from embracing; [6] a time to seek, and a time to lose; a time to keep, and a time to throw away; [7] a time to tear, and a time to sew; a time to keep silence, and a time to speak; [8] a time to love, and a time to hate; a time for war, and a time for peace.

[9] What gain have the workers from their toil? [10] I have seen the business that God has given to everyone to be busy with. [11] He has made everything suitable for its time; moreover he has put a sense of past and future into their minds, yet they cannot find out what God has done from the beginning to the end. [12] I know that there is nothing better for them than to be happy and enjoy themselves as long as they live; [13] moreover, it is God's gift that all should eat and drink and take pleasure in all their toil.

Psalm 8

[1] O LORD, our Sovereign, how majestic is your name in all the earth! You have set your glory above the heavens. [2] Out of the mouths of babes and infants you have founded a bulwark because of your foes, to silence the enemy and the avenger. [3] When I look at your heavens, the work of your fingers, the moon and the stars that you have established; [4] what are human beings that you are mindful of them, mortals that you care for them? [5] Yet you have made them a little lower than God, and crowned them with glory and honor. [6] You have given them dominion over the works of your hands; you have put all things under their feet, [7] all sheep and oxen, and also the beasts of the field, [8] the birds of the air, and the fish of the sea, whatever passes along the paths of the seas. [9] O LORD, our Sovereign, how majestic is your name in all the earth!

Revelation 21:1-6a

[1] Then I saw a new heaven and a new earth; for the first heaven and the first earth had passed away, and the sea was no more. [2] And I saw the holy city, the new Jerusalem, coming down out of heaven from God, prepared as a bride adorned for her husband. [3] And I heard a loud voice from the throne saying, "See, the home of God is among mortals. He will dwell with them as their God; they will be his peoples, and God himself will be with them; [4] he will wipe every tear from their eyes. Death will be no more; mourning and crying and pain will be no more, for the first things have passed away."

[5] And the one who was seated on the throne said, "See, I am making all things new." Also he said, "Write this, for these words are trustworthy and true." [6] Then he said to me, "It is done! I am the Alpha and the Omega, the beginning and the end."

Matthew 25:31-46

[31] "When the Son of Man comes in his glory, and all the angels with him, then he will sit on the throne of his glory. [32] All the nations will be gathered before him, and he will separate people one from another as a shepherd separates the sheep from the goats, [33] and he will put the sheep at his right hand and the goats at the left. [34] Then the king will say to those at his right hand, 'Come, you that are blessed by my Father, inherit the kingdom prepared for you from the foundation of the world; [35] for I was hungry and you gave me food, I was thirsty and you gave me something to drink, I was a stranger and you welcomed me, [36] I was naked and you gave me clothing, I was sick and you took care of me, I was in prison and you visited me.' [37] Then the righteous will answer him, 'Lord, when was it that we saw you hungry and gave you food, or thirsty and gave you something to drink? [38] And when was it that we saw you a stranger and welcomed you, or naked and gave you clothing? [39] And when was it that we saw you sick or in prison and visited you?' [40] And the king will answer them, 'Truly I tell you, just as you did it to one of the least of these who are members of my family, you did it to me.' [41] Then he will say to those at his left hand, 'You that are accursed, depart from me into the eternal fire prepared for the devil and his angels; [42] for I was hungry and you gave me no food, I was thirsty and you gave me nothing to drink, [43] I was a stranger and you did not welcome me, naked and you did not give me clothing, sick and in prison and you did not visit me.' [44] Then they also will answer, 'Lord, when was it that we saw you hungry or thirsty or a stranger or naked or sick or in prison, and did not take care of you?' [45] Then he will answer them, 'Truly I tell you, just as you did not do it to one of the least of these, you did not do it to me.' [46] And these will go away into eternal punishment, but the righteous into eternal life."

Primary Hymns and Songs for the Day

"Hymn of Promise" (Eccl) (O)
　　C638, N433, UM707, VU703
　　　　H-3　　Chr-112; Org-117
　　　　S-1　　#270. Descant
"How Majestic Is Your Name" (Pss) (O)
　　C63, R98, S2023, SF2023, SP14
"This Is a Day of New Beginnings" (Rev, Communion)
　　B370, C518, N417, UM383, W661
　　　　H-3　　Chr-196
"There's a Spirit in the Air" (Matt)
　　B393, C257, P433, R282, VU582, W531
　　　　H-3　　Chr-194
　　N292, UM192
　　　　S-2　　#144. Orff instrument arrangement
"We've a Story to Tell to the Nations" (Rev, Matt) (C)
　　B586, C484, F659, UM569 (PD)
　　　　H-3　　Chr-210; Org-91

Additional Hymn Suggestions

"O God, Our Help in Ages Past" (Eccl) (C)
　　B74, C67, E680, EL632, F370, L320, N25, P210, UM117 (PD),
　　VU806, W579
"Beams of Heaven as I Go" (Eccl, Rev)
　　N447, UM524
"How Great Thou Art" (Pss)
　　B10, C33, EL856, F2, L532, N35, P467, R250, UM77, VU238
　　(Fr.)
"Love Divine, All Loves Excelling" (Rev)
　　B208, C517, E657, EL631 (PD), L315, P376, N43, R196,
　　UM384, VU333, W588
"Come, Ye Disconsolate" (Rev)
　　B67, C502, EL607, SF2132, UM510 (PD)
"We Shall Overcome" (Rev)
　　C630, N570, UM533
"I Want to Be Ready" (Rev)
　　N616, UM722
"O Holy City, Seen of John" (Rev)
　　E582/E583, N613, P453, UM726, VU709
"O What Their Joy and Their Glory Must Be" (Rev)
　　E623, L337, N385, UM727 (PD)
"Blessed Quietness" (Rev)
　　F145, C267, N284, S2142, SF2142
"Joy Comes with the Dawn" (Rev)
　　S2210, SF2210, VU166
"Joy in the Morning" (Rev)
　　S2284, SF2284
"For the Healing of the Nations" (Rev)
　　C668, N576, UM428, VU678, W643
"Cuando El Pobre" ("When the Poor Ones") (Matt)
　　C662, EL725, P407, UM434, VU702
"Rescue the Perishing" (Matt)
　　B559, F661, UM591 (PD)
"Star-Child" (Matt, New Year)
　　S2095, SF2095
"All Who Hunger" (Rev, Matt, Communion)
　　C419, EL461, S2126, SF2126, VU460
"Together We Serve" (Matt, Covenant Renewal)
　　S2175, SF2175

"Here Am I" (Matt)
　　C654, S2178, SF2178
"In Remembrance of Me" (Matt, Communion)
　　B365, C403, S2254
"As We Gather at Your Table" (Matt, Communion)
　　EL522, N332, S2268, SF2268, VU457

Additional Contemporary Suggestions

"In His Time" (Eccl)
　　B53, S2203, SF2203, SP39
"I Could Sing of Your Love Forever" (Eccl)
　　M63; V-3 p. 22 Vocal Solo
"Soon and Very Soon" (Rev)
　　B192, EL439, R276, UM706
"We Will Glorify" (Pss, Rev)
　　B213, S2087, SF2087, SP68
"Spirit Song" (Rev)
　　C352, R248, SP134, UM347
"There's Something About That Name" (Rev)
　　B177, C115, F227, R26, SP89, UM171
"Blessing, Honor and Glory" (Rev)
　　EL433, M21, R81
"Jehovah Reigns" (Rev)
　　M55
"I See the Lord" (Rev, Matt)
　　M31
"To Him Who Sits on the Throne" (Rev, Matt)
　　R265, SP60
"You Who Are Thirsty" (Rev, Matt)
　　S2132, SP219
"People Need the Lord" (Matt)
　　B557, S2244, SF2244

Vocal Solos

"I Will Sing of Thy Great Mercies" (Eccl)
V-4　　　p. 43
"Reach Out to Your Neighbor" (Matt)
V-8　　　p. 372

Anthems

"Now Is the Time" (Eccl)
John Horman; Abingdon Press 0687503604
Unison (opt. two-part) with keyboard and instruments

"Lead Me, Lord" (Pss)
Samuel Sebastian Wesley; Novello 29-0305
SATB with organ

Other Suggestions

NOTE: These scriptures may also be used on Sunday morning, Jan. 1.
Visuals:
　　O　　Clock, many images from text
　　P　　Infants, all ages, outer space, nature
　　E　　Butterfly, chrysalis, bride, portrait of Christ
　　G　　Shepherd, sheep, goats, ministries to others
Canticle: C702 or UM734 (Rev)
Prayer: UM607 or F508 (New Year)
Prayer: C68. Ancient Jewish Prayer (Eccl)
Benediction: B370, C518, N417, UM383, W66, stanza 4. "This Is a
　　Day of New Beginnings" (Rev)

Isaiah 61:10–62:3

[10]I will greatly rejoice in the Lord, my whole being shall exult in my God; for he has clothed me with the garments of salvation, he has covered me with the robe of righteousness, as a bridegroom decks himself with a garland, and as a bride adorns herself with her jewels. [11]For as the earth brings forth its shoots, and as a garden causes what is sown in it to spring up, so the Lord God will cause righteousness and praise to spring up before all the nations.

[1]For Zion's sake I will not keep silent, and for Jerusalem's sake I will not rest, until her vindication shines out like the dawn, and her salvation like a burning torch. [2]The nations shall see your vindication, and all the kings your glory; and you shall be called by a new name that the mouth of the Lord will give. [3]You shall be a crown of beauty in the hand of the Lord, and a royal diadem in the hand of your God.

Psalm 148

[1]Praise the Lord! Praise the Lord from the heavens; praise him in the heights! [2]Praise him, all his angels; praise him, all his host! [3]Praise him, sun and moon; praise him, all you shining stars! [4]Praise him, you highest heavens, and you waters above the heavens! [5]Let them praise the name of the Lord, for he commanded and they were created. [6]He established them forever and ever; he fixed their bounds, which cannot be passed. [7]Praise the Lord from the earth, you sea monsters and all deeps, [8]fire and hail, snow and frost, stormy wind fulfilling his command! [9]Mountains and all hills, fruit trees and all cedars! [10]Wild animals and all cattle, creeping things and flying birds! [11]Kings of the earth and all peoples, princes and all rulers of the earth! [12]Young men and women alike, old and young together! [13]Let them praise the name of the Lord, for his name alone is exalted; his glory is above earth and heaven. [14]He has raised up a horn for his people, praise for all his faithful, for the people of Israel who are close to him. Praise the Lord!

Galatians 4:4-7

[4]But when the fullness of time had come, God sent his Son, born of a woman, born under the law, [5]in order to redeem those who were under the law, so that we might receive adoption as children. [6]And because you are children, God has sent the Spirit of his Son into our hearts, crying, "Abba! Father!" [7]So you are no longer a slave but a child, and if a child then also an heir, through God.

Luke 2:22-40

[22]When the time came for their purification according to the law of Moses, they brought him up to Jerusalem to present him to the Lord [23](as it is written in the law of the Lord, "Every firstborn male shall be designated as holy to the Lord"), [24]and they offered a sacrifice according to what is stated in the law of the Lord, "a pair of turtledoves or two young pigeons."

[25]Now there was a man in Jerusalem whose name was Simeon; this man was righteous and devout, looking forward to the consolation of Israel, and the Holy Spirit rested on him. [26]It had been revealed to him by the Holy Spirit that he would not see death before he had seen the Lord's Messiah. [27]Guided by the Spirit, Simeon came into the temple; and when the parents brought in the child Jesus, to do for him what was customary under the law, [28]Simeon took him in his arms and praised God, saying, [29]"Master, now you are dismissing your servant in peace, according to your word; [30]for my eyes have seen your salvation, [31]which you have prepared in the presence of all peoples, [32]a light for revelation to the Gentiles and for glory to your people Israel."

[33]And the child's father and mother were amazed at what was being said about him. [34]Then Simeon blessed them and said to his mother Mary, "This child is destined for the falling and the rising of many in Israel, and to be a sign that will be opposed [35]so that the inner thoughts of many will be revealed—and a sword will pierce your own soul too."

[36]There was also a prophet, Anna the daughter of Phanuel, of the tribe of Asher. She was of a great age, having lived with her husband seven years after her marriage, [37]then as a widow to the age of eighty-four. She never left the temple but worshiped there with fasting and prayer night and day. [38]At that moment she came, and began to praise God and to speak about the child to all who were looking for the redemption of Jerusalem.

[39]When they had finished everything required by the law of the Lord, they returned to Galilee, to their own town of Nazareth. [40]The child grew and became strong, filled with wisdom; and the favor of God was upon him.

Primary Hymns and Songs for the Day

"All Creatures of Our God and King" (Pss) (O)
  B27, C22, E400, EL835, F347, L527, N17, P455, R47, UM62, VU217 (Fr.), W520
      H-3   Hbl-44; Chr-21; Desc-66; Org-73
      S-1   #198-204. Various treatments

"He Is Born" ("Il Est Né") (Luke, Christmas)
  B112, UM228, VU50 (Fr.)
      H-3   Chr-92
      S-1   #177. Orff instrument arrangement

"There's a Song in the Air" (Luke, Christmas) (C)
  C159, UM249 (PD)
      H-3   Chr-194
      S-2   #40. Descant

Additional Hymn Suggestions

"Deck Thyself, My Soul, with Gladness" (Isa)
  E339, EL488/EL489, L224, P506, UM612 (PD), VU463

"Lo, How a Rose E'er Blooming" (Isa)
  B78, C160, E81, EL272, F174, L58, N127, P48 (PD), UM216, VU8, W374

"Hark! The Herald Angels Sing" (Isa, Gal) (O)
  B88, C150, E87, EL270, F184, L60, N144, P31, UM240 (PD), VU48, W387

"How Great Thou Art" (Pss)
  B10, C33, EL856, F2, L532, N35, P467, R250, UM77, VU238 (Fr.)

"God Created Heaven and Earth" (Pss)
  EL738, N33, P290, UM151, VU251

"Let All Things Now Living" (Pss)
  B640, C717, EL881, F389, L557, P554, R48, S2008, VU242, W559

"Baptized in Water" (Gal, Baptism)
  B362, E294, EL456, P492, S2248, W720

"Wash, O God, Our Sons and Daughters" (Gal)
  C365, EL445, UM605, VU442

"Once in Royal David's City" (Gal, Luke)
  C165, E102, EL269, N45, P49, UM250 (PD), VU62, W402

"Sing of Mary, Pure and Lowly" (Luke)
  C184, E277, UM272, W404

"Our Parent, by Whose Name" (Luke)
  E587, EL640, L357, UM447, VU555, W570

"Let Us Now Depart in Thy Peace" (Luke) (C)
  C444, UM668

"Lord, Dismiss Us with Thy Blessing" (Luke) (C)
  C439, E344, EL545, F520, L259, N77, P538, UM671 (PD), VU425

"Lord of All Hopefulness" (Luke)
  E482, EL765, L469, R174, S2197, SF2197, W568

"Like a Child" (Luke, Christmas)
  C133, S2092, SF2092, VU366

"Joseph Dearest, Joseph Mine" (Luke, Christmas)
  N105, S2099, SF2099

"That Boy-Child of Mary" (Luke, Christmas)
  B110, EL293, P55, UM241

"Away in a Manger" (Luke, Christmas)
  B103, C147, E101, EL277, F185/F187, L67, N124, P24/P25, UM217, VU69, W378

"What Child Is This" (Luke, Christmas)
  B118, C162, E115, EL296, F180, L40, N148, P53, UM219 (PD), VU74, W411

"Sing We Now of Christmas" (Luke, Christmas)
  B111, UM237

Additional Contemporary Suggestions

"Honor and Praise" (Pss)
  S2018, SF2018

"Let Everything That Has Breath" (Pss)
  M59

"God of Wonders" (Pss)
  M80; V-3 p. 184 Vocal Solo

"Praise You" (Pss, Luke)
  M84, S2003, SF2003

"Holy, Holy" (Gal, Communion)
  B254, F149, P140, R206, S2039, SP141

"Jesus, Name Above All Names" (Luke)
  R26, S2071, SF2071, SP76

"Shine, Jesus, Shine" (Luke)
  B579, EL671, R247, S2173, SF2173, SP142

"Go Now in Peace" (Luke) (C)
  B660, C437, R293, UM665, VU964; S-1 #146 Orff arr.

"The Virgin Mary Had a Baby Boy" (Christmas)
  S2098, VU73

Vocal Solos

"Sing a Song of Joy" (Pss)
  V-4   p. 2

"Gentle Jesus, Meek and Mild" (Luke, Christmas)
  V-1   p. 11

Anthems

"Sing We Now of Christmas" (Luke, Christmas)
Prentice/Barnett; Gentry Publication JG2283
SATB and harp or piano (JB0546 *a cappella*)

"Gather 'Round God's Temple Gladly" (Christmas)
Deborah Govenor; Brookfield Press 08745574
SATB with keyboard

Other Suggestions

NOTE: You may also celebrate Epiphany of the Lord today, using Jan. 6 scriptures and ideas, or New Year's Day today, using scriptures and ideas from Dec. 31 Watch Night.
Visuals:
      O   Wedding garments, crown, garland, spring garden
      P   Celestial imagery, nature imagery, all ages of people praising
      E   Clock, open manacles, children's toys
      G   Baby, elderly man/woman, Christ candle
Introit: C166, E114, EL284, L72, N151, P61, UM244, VU71, W380, stanzas 2 and 4. "'Twas in the Moon of Wintertime" (Christmas)
Settings of Song of Simeon: C156, N734, N805-N808, P604/P605, UM225, VU902/VU903, W676/W691 (Luke)
Prayer: UM231 (Gal) or C1 (Pss)
See Christmas Eve and Day for additional Christmas carols.

Isaiah 60:1-6

[1]Arise, shine; for your light has come, and the glory of the LORD has risen upon you. [2]For darkness shall cover the earth, and thick darkness the peoples; but the LORD will arise upon you, and his glory will appear over you. [3]Nations shall come to your light, and kings to the brightness of your dawn. [4]Lift up your eyes and look around; they all gather together, they come to you; your sons shall come from far away, and your daughters shall be carried on their nurses' arms. [5]Then you shall see and be radiant; your heart shall thrill and rejoice, because the abundance of the sea shall be brought to you, the wealth of the nations shall come to you. [6]A multitude of camels shall cover you, the young camels of Midian and Ephah; all those from Sheba shall come. They shall bring gold and frankincense, and shall proclaim the praise of the LORD.

Psalm 72:1-7, 10-14

[1]Give the king your justice, O God, and your righteousness to a king's son. [2]May he judge your people with righteousness, and your poor with justice. [3]May the mountains yield prosperity for the people, and the hills, in righteousness. [4]May he defend the cause of the poor of the people, give deliverance to the needy, and crush the oppressor. [5]May he live while the sun endures, and as long as the moon, throughout all generations. [6]May he be like rain that falls on the mown grass, like showers that water the earth. [7]In his days may righteousness flourish and peace abound, until the moon is no more. . . .

[10]May the kings of Tarshish and of the isles render him tribute, may the kings of Sheba and Seba bring gifts. [11]May all kings fall down before him, all nations give him service. [12]For he delivers the needy when they call, the poor and those who have no helper. [13]He has pity on the weak and the needy, and saves the lives of the needy. [14]From oppression and violence he redeems their life; and precious is their blood in his sight.

Ephesians 3:1-12

[1]This is the reason that I Paul am a prisoner for Christ Jesus for the sake of you Gentiles— [2]for surely you have already heard of the commission of God's grace that was given me for you, [3]and how the mystery was made known to me by revelation, as I wrote above in a few words, [4]a reading of which will enable you to perceive my understanding of the mystery of Christ. [5]In former generations this mystery was not made known to humankind, as it has now been revealed to his holy apostles and prophets by the Spirit: [6]that is, the Gentiles have become fellow heirs, members of the same body, and sharers in the promise in Christ Jesus through the gospel.

[7]Of this gospel I have become a servant according to the gift of God's grace that was given me by the working of his power. [8]Although I am the very least of all the saints, this grace was given to me to bring to the Gentiles the news of the boundless riches of Christ, [9]and to make everyone see what is the plan of the mystery hidden for ages in God who created all things; [10]so that through the church the wisdom of God in its rich variety might now be made known to the rulers and authorities in the heavenly places. [11]This was in accordance with the eternal purpose that he has carried out in Christ Jesus our Lord, [12]in whom we have access to God in boldness and confidence through faith in him.

Matthew 2:1-12

[1]In the time of King Herod, after Jesus was born in Bethlehem of Judea, wise men from the East came to Jerusalem, [2]asking, "Where is the child who has been born king of the Jews? For we observed his star at its rising, and have come to pay him homage." [3]When King Herod heard this, he was frightened, and all Jerusalem with him; [4]and calling together all the chief priests and scribes of the people, he inquired of them where the Messiah was to be born. [5]They told him, "In Bethlehem of Judea; for so it has been written by the prophet: [6]'And you, Bethlehem, in the land of Judah, are by no means least among the rulers of Judah; for from you shall come a ruler who is to shepherd my people Israel.'"

[7]Then Herod secretly called for the wise men and learned from them the exact time when the star had appeared. [8]Then he sent them to Bethlehem, saying, "Go and search diligently for the child; and when you have found him, bring me word so that I may also go and pay him homage." [9]When they had heard the king, they set out; and there, ahead of them, went the star that they had seen at its rising, until it stopped over the place where the child was. [10]When they saw that the star had stopped, they were overwhelmed with joy. [11]On entering the house, they saw the child with Mary his mother; and they knelt down and paid him homage. Then, opening their treasure chests, they offered him gifts of gold, frankincense, and myrrh. [12]And having been warned in a dream not to return to Herod, they left for their own country by another road.

Primary Hymns and Songs for the Day
"Angels from the Realms of Glory" (Matt) (O)
    B94, C149, E93, EL275, F190, L50, P22, UM220 (PD),
    VU36, W377
        H-3   Chr-30, 48, 62; Desc-89; Org-121
        S-1   #280. Descant and harmonization
"What Child Is This" (Matt)
    B118, C162, E115, EL296, F180, L40, N148, P53, UM219
    (PD), VU74, W411
        H-3   Hbl-102; Chr-210; Desc-46; Org-47
        S-1   #150. Guitar chords
"We Three Kings" (Matt)
    B113, C172, E128, F206, P66, UM254 (PD), W406
        H-3   Chr-208; Org-65
"The First Noel" (Matt) (C)
    B85, C151, E109, EL300, F179, L56, N139, P56, UM245
    (PD), VU90 (Fr.) and VU91, W408
        H-3   Hbl-95; Chr-182; Desc-100; Org-161
        S-1   #328-330. Various treatments

Additional Hymn Suggestions
"Rise, Shine, You People" (Isa)
    EL665, L393, UM187
"Break Forth, O Beauteous Heavenly Light" (Isa)
    B114 (PD), E91, F207, N140, P26, UM223, VU83
"This Little Light of Mine" (Isa) (C)
    N524/N525, UM585
"Gather Us In" (Isa) (O)
    C284, EL532, S2236, SF2236, W665
"We Are Called" (Isa, Pss)
    EL720, S2172, SF2172
"O Morning Star, How Fair and Bright" (Isa, Matt)
    C105, E497, EL308, L76, N158, P69, UM247, VU98, W390
"Hail to the Lord's Anointed" (Pss)
    C140, E616, EL311 (PD), L87, N104, P205, UM203 (PD),
    VU30
"Here Am I" (Pss)
    C654, S2178, SF2178
"Immortal, Invisible, God Only Wise" (Eph)
    B6, C66, E423, EL834, F319, L526, N1, P263, R46, UM103
    (PD), VU264, W512
"Make Me a Captive, Lord" (Eph)
    B278, P378, UM421
"Lo, How a Rose E'er Blooming" (Matt)
    B78, C160, E81, EL272, F174, L58, N127, P48 (PD),
    UM216, VU8, W374
"Sing We Now of Christmas" (Matt)
    B111, UM237
"De Tierra Lejana Venimos" ("From a Distant Home") (Matt)
    P64, UM243, VU89
"On This Day Earth Shall Ring" (Matt)
    E92, P46, UM248
"We Would See Jesus" (Matt)
    UM256 (PD)
"Carol of the Epiphany" (Matt)
    S2094, SF2094
"Star-Child" (Matt)
    S2095, SF2095

"Rise Up, Shepherd, and Follow" (Matt)
    P50, S2096, SF2096, VU70
"The Virgin Mary Had a Baby Boy" (Matt)
    S2098, VU73
"Go, Tell It on the Mountain" (Eph, Matt) (C)
    B95, C167, E99, EL290, F205, L70, N154, P29, UM251,
    VU43, W397
"This Is a Day of New Beginnings" (New Year, Communion)
    B370, C518, N417, UM383, W661

Additional Contemporary Suggestions
"Arise, Shine" (Isa)
    S2005, SF2005
"Arise Shine" (Isa)
    R123, SP176
"Let It Rise" (Isa)
    M4
"Shine on Us" (Isa, Epiphany)
    M19
"Grace Alone" (Eph)
    M100, S2162, SF2162
"Honor and Praise" (Matt, Epiphany)
    S2018, SF2018
"All Hail King Jesus" (Matt, Epiphany)
    S2069, SF2069, SP63
"We Worship and Adore You" (Matt)
    SP103
"Come and Behold Him" (Matt)
    M18

Vocal Solos
"A Scottish Christmas Song" (Matt)
V-4   p. 4
"Fit for a King" (Matt, Stewardship)
V-10   p. 32

Anthems
"We Three Kings of Orient Are" (Matt)
Michael Burkhardt; MorningStar file_10-127-3E
Downloadable file at www.morningstarmusic.com

"O Lux Beatissima" (Epiphany)
Howard Helvey; Hinshaw HMC1971
SATB *a cappella*

Other Suggestions
NOTE: These lessons and ideas may be used on Jan. 1 or 8.
Visuals:
    O   Light, gold, frankincense, crown
    P   Deliverance, poor and needy being helped, sun, moon,
         rain, kings, gifts
    E   Manacles, towel, bowl/pitcher (servant)
    G   Kings, gold, frankincense, myrrh (gifts), star
Introit: C166, E114, EL284, L72, N151, P61, UM244, VU71,
    W380, stanzas 3 and 4. "'Twas in the Moon of Wintertime"
    (Matt)
Introit: S2005, SF2005. "Arise, Shine" (Isa)
For additional ideas, see *The Abingdon Worship Annual 2012.*

Genesis 1:1-5

[1] In the beginning when God created the heavens and the earth, [2] the earth was a formless void and darkness covered the face of the deep, while a wind from God swept over the face of the waters. [3] Then God said, "Let there be light"; and there was light. [4] And God saw that the light was good; and God separated the light from the darkness. [5] God called the light Day, and the darkness he called Night. And there was evening and there was morning, the first day.

Psalm 29

[1] Ascribe to the LORD, O heavenly beings, ascribe to the LORD glory and strength. [2] Ascribe to the LORD the glory of his name; worship the LORD in holy splendor. [3] The voice of the LORD is over the waters; the God of glory thunders, the LORD, over mighty waters. [4] The voice of the LORD is powerful; the voice of the LORD is full of majesty. [5] The voice of the LORD breaks the cedars; the LORD breaks the cedars of Lebanon. [6] He makes Lebanon skip like a calf, and Sirion like a young wild ox. [7] The voice of the LORD flashes forth flames of fire. [8] The voice of the LORD shakes the wilderness; the LORD shakes the wilderness of Kadesh. [9] The voice of the LORD causes the oaks to whirl, and strips the forest bare; and in his temple all say, "Glory!" [10] The LORD sits enthroned over the flood; the LORD sits enthroned as king forever. [11] May the LORD give strength to his people! May the LORD bless his people with peace!

Acts 19:1-7

[1] While Apollos was in Corinth, Paul passed through the interior regions and came to Ephesus, where he found some disciples. [2] He said to them, "Did you receive the Holy Spirit when you became believers?" They replied, "No, we have not even heard that there is a Holy Spirit." [3] Then he said, "Into what then were you baptized?" They answered, "Into John's baptism." [4] Paul said, "John baptized with the baptism of repentance, telling the people to believe in the one who was to come after him, that is, in Jesus." [5] On hearing this, they were baptized in the name of the Lord Jesus. [6] When Paul had laid his hands on them, the Holy Spirit came upon them, and they spoke in tongues and prophesied— [7] altogether there were about twelve of them.

Mark 1:4-11

[4] John the baptizer appeared in the wilderness, proclaiming a baptism of repentance for the forgiveness of sins. [5] And people from the whole Judean countryside and all the people of Jerusalem were going out to him, and were baptized by him in the river Jordan, confessing their sins. [6] Now John was clothed with camel's hair, with a leather belt around his waist, and he ate locusts and wild honey. [7] He proclaimed, "The one who is more powerful than I is coming after me; I am not worthy to stoop down and untie the thong of his sandals. [8] I have baptized you with water; but he will baptize you with the Holy Spirit."

[9] In those days Jesus came from Nazareth of Galilee and was baptized by John in the Jordan. [10] And just as he was coming up out of the water, he saw the heavens torn apart and the Spirit descending like a dove on him. [11] And a voice came from heaven, "You are my Son, the Beloved; with you I am well pleased."

Primary Hymns and Songs for the Day
"I Sing the Almighty Power of God" (Gen, Pss) (O)
    B42, E398, UM152 (PD)
        H-3   Hbl-44; Chr-21; Desc-40; Org-40
        S-1   #131-132. Introduction and descant
    C64, N12, P288 (PD), R54
        H-3   Hbl-16, 22, 68; Chr-101; Desc-37
        S-1   #115. Harmonization
    VU231 (PD), W502 (PD)
"When Jesus Came to Jordan" (Mark)
    UM252
        H-3   Chr-211
    EL305, P72, W697
"Spirit Song" (Mark)
    C352, R248, SP134, UM347
"I've Just Come from the Fountain" (Acts, Mark, Baptism) (C)
    S2250, SF2250

Additional Hymn Suggestions
"God of the Sparrow, God of the Whale" (Gen)
    C70, EL740, N32, P272, UM122, VU229
"Morning Has Broken" (Gen)
    B48, C53, E8, EL556, F5, P469, UM145, VU409, W674
"God Created Heaven and Earth" (Gen)
    EL738, N33, P290, UM151, VU251
"Wind Who Makes All Winds That Blow" (Gen)
    C236, N271, P131, UM538, VU196
"God, That Madest Earth and Heaven" (Gen)
    EL564, F4, L281, UM688 (PD)
"Womb of Life" (Gen)
    C14, N274, S2046, SF2046
"Mothering God, You Gave Me Birth" (Gen, Baptism)
    C83, EL735, N467, S2050, SF2050, VU320
"God the Sculptor of the Mountains" (Gen)
    EL736, S2060, SF2060
"Spirit, Spirit of Gentleness" (Gen, Mark)
    C249, EL396, N286, P319, S2120, VU375 (Fr.)
"Loving Spirit" (Gen, Mark, Baptism)
    C244, EL397, P323, S2123, SF2123, VU387
"Praise and Thanksgiving Be to God" (Pss, Acts, Mark)
    EL458, L191, UM604, VU441
"Holy Spirit, Come, Confirm Us" (Acts)
    N264, UM331
"Wash, O God, Our Sons and Daughters" (Acts)
    C365, EL445, UM605, VU442
"This Is the Spirit's Entry Now" (Acts, Mark)
    EL448, L195, UM608, VU451, W722
"Come, Holy Ghost, Our Souls Inspire" (Acts, Mark)
    E503/E504, L472/L473, N268, P125, UM651 (PD), VU201
"Wonder of Wonders" (Acts, Mark, Baptism)
    C378, N328, P499, S2247
"Baptized in Water" (Acts, Mark, Baptism)
    B362, E294, EL456, P492, S2248, W720
"Blessed Be the God of Israel" (Mark)
    C135, E444, EL250/EL552, P602, UM209, VU901
"O Love, How Deep" (Mark)
    E448/E449, EL322, L88, N209, P83, UM267 (PD), VU348
"You Have Put on Christ" (Mark, Baptism)
    EL211, UM609, VU452, W112

"Shall We Gather at the River" (Mark, Baptism)
    B518, C701, EL423, N597, UM723 (PD), VU710
"Wild and Lone the Prophet's Voice" (Mark)
    P409, S2089, SF2089
"At the Font We Start Our Journey" (Mark, Baptism)
    N308, S2114, SF2114

Additional Contemporary Suggestions
"Thou Art Worthy" (Gen, Mark)
    C114, R34, S2041, SF2041, SP5
"Holy Spirit, Come to Us" (Gen, Baptism)
    EL406, S2118, SF2118, W473
"Ah, Lord God" (Gen)
    R254, SP2
"God of Wonders" (Gen, Pss)
    M80; V-3 p. 184 Vocal Solo
"Please Enter My Heart, Hosanna" (Acts)
    S2154, SF2154
"We Are One in Christ Jesus" (Acts)
    C493, EL643, S2229, SF2229
"Jesus, We Are Here" ("Yesu Tawa Pano") (Acts)
    EL529, S2273, SF2273
"Jesus, Name above All Names" (Mark)
    R26, S2071, SF2071, SP76
"Water, River, Spirit, Grace" (Mark)
    C366, S2253, SF2253
"Great and Mighty Is He" (Mark)
    SP4, M11

Vocal Solos
"Spirit of Faith Come Down" (Mark)
V-1   p. 43
"This Is De Healin' Water" (Baptism)
V-7   p. 52

Anthems
"Christ, When for Us You Were Baptized" (Mark)
Michael Helman: Augsburg 9780800674052
SAB with keyboard

"Down in the River to Pray" (Mark, Baptism)
David L. Mennicke; MorningStar 50-5902
SATB *divisi a cappella*

Other Suggestions
NOTE: Include the celebration of baptisms or baptism renewal today!
Visuals:
    O   Light/darkness, water, wind, evening/morning
    P   Ps 29:2b, 11a, b; water, cedar, skipping calf, wind (bent trees)
    E   Dove, symbols of the Holy Spirit, water, baptism
    G   Sandals, water, dove, Mark 1:8, 11b
Introit: B48, C53, E8, EL556, F5, P469, UM145, VU409, W674, stanza 1. "Morning Has Broken" (Gen)
Prayer: UM146 or UM253 (Baptism, Mark)
Prayer: C698. Prayer of a Native American (Gen)
Reading: B41. "God's Work" (Gen)
Response: B243, C261, F159, N293, P398, SP136, UM334. "Sweet, Sweet Spirit" (Acts, Mark)

1 Samuel 3:1-10 (11-20)

[1] Now the boy Samuel was ministering to the LORD under Eli. The word of the LORD was rare in those days; visions were not widespread.

[2] At that time Eli, whose eyesight had begun to grow dim so that he could not see, was lying down in his room; [3] the lamp of God had not yet gone out, and Samuel was lying down in the temple of the LORD, where the ark of God was. [4] Then the LORD called, "Samuel! Samuel!" and he said, "Here I am!" [5] and ran to Eli, and said, "Here I am, for you called me." But he said, "I did not call; lie down again." So he went and lay down. [6] The LORD called again, "Samuel!" Samuel got up and went to Eli, and said, "Here I am, for you called me." But he said, "I did not call, my son; lie down again." [7] Now Samuel did not yet know the LORD, and the word of the LORD had not yet been revealed to him. [8] The LORD called Samuel again, a third time. And he got up and went to Eli, and said, "Here I am, for you called me." Then Eli perceived that the LORD was calling the boy. [9] Therefore Eli said to Samuel, "Go, lie down; and if he calls you, you shall say, 'Speak, LORD, for your servant is listening.' " So Samuel went and lay down in his place.

[10] Now the LORD came and stood there, calling as before, "Samuel! Samuel!" And Samuel said, "Speak, for your servant is listening." [11] Then the LORD said to Samuel, "See, I am about to do something in Israel that will make both ears of anyone who hears of it tingle. [12] On that day I will fulfill against Eli all that I have spoken concerning his house, from beginning to end. [13] For I have told him that I am about to punish his house forever, for the iniquity that he knew, because his sons were blaspheming God, and he did not restrain them. [14] Therefore I swear to the house of Eli that the iniquity of Eli's house shall not be expiated by sacrifice or offering forever."

[15] Samuel lay there until morning; then he opened the doors of the house of the LORD. Samuel was afraid to tell the vision to Eli. [16] But Eli called Samuel and said, "Samuel, my son." He said, "Here I am." [17] Eli said, "What was it that he told you? Do not hide it from me. May God do so to you and more also, if you hide anything from me of all that he told you." [18] So Samuel told him everything and hid nothing from him. Then he said, "It is the LORD; let him do what seems good to him."

[19] As Samuel grew up, the LORD was with him and let none of his words fall to the ground. [20] And all Israel from Dan to Beer-sheba knew that Samuel was a trustworthy prophet of the LORD.

Psalm 139:1-6, 13-18

[1] O LORD, you have searched me and known me. [2] You know when I sit down and when I rise up; you discern my thoughts from far away. [3] You search out my path and my lying down, and are acquainted with all my ways. [4] Even before a word is on my tongue, O LORD, you know it completely. [5] You hem me in, behind and before, and lay your hand upon me. [6] Such knowledge is too wonderful for me; it is so high that I cannot attain it. . . . .

[13] For it was you who formed my inward parts; you knit me together in my mother's womb. [14] I praise you, for I am fearfully and wonderfully made. Wonderful are your works; that I know very well. [15] My frame was not hidden from you, when I was being made in secret, intricately woven in the depths of the earth. [16] Your eyes beheld my unformed substance. In your book were written all the days that were formed for me, when none of them as yet existed. [17] How weighty to me are your thoughts, O God! How vast is the sum of them! [18] I try to count them—they are more than the sand; I come to the end—I am still with you.

1 Corinthians 6:12-20

[12] "All things are lawful for me," but not all things are beneficial. "All things are lawful for me," but I will not be dominated by anything. [13] "Food is meant for the stomach and the stomach for food," and God will destroy both one and the other. The body is meant not for fornication but for the Lord, and the Lord for the body. [14] And God raised the Lord and will also raise us by his power. [15] Do you not know that your bodies are members of Christ? Should I therefore take the members of Christ and make them members of a prostitute? Never! [16] Do you not know that whoever is united to a prostitute becomes one body with her? For it is said, "The two shall be one flesh." [17] But anyone united to the Lord becomes one spirit with him. [18] Shun fornication! Every sin that a person commits is outside the body; but the fornicator sins against the body itself. [19] Or do you not know that your body is a temple of the Holy Spirit within you, which you have from God, and that you are not your own? [20] For you were bought with a price; therefore glorify God in your body.

John 1:43-51

[43] The next day Jesus decided to go to Galilee. He found Philip and said to him, "Follow me." [44] Now Philip was from Bethsaida, the city of Andrew and Peter. [45] Philip found Nathanael and said to him, "We have found him about whom Moses in the law and also the prophets wrote, Jesus son of Joseph from Nazareth." [46] Nathanael said to him, "Can anything good come out of Nazareth?" Philip said to him, "Come and see." [47] When Jesus saw Nathanael coming toward him, he said of him, "Here is truly an Israelite in whom there is no deceit!" [48] Nathanael asked him, "Where did you get to know me?" Jesus answered, "I saw you under the fig tree before Philip called you." [49] Nathanael replied, "Rabbi, you are the Son of God! You are the King of Israel!" [50] Jesus answered, "Do you believe because I told you that I saw you under the fig tree? You will see greater things than these." [51] And he said to him, "Very truly, I tell you, you will see heaven opened and the angels of God ascending and descending upon the Son of Man."

Primary Hymns and Songs for the Day
"Open My Eyes, That I May See" (1 Sam) (O)
    B502, C586, F486, P324, UM454, VU371
        H-3   Chr-157; Org-108
"I Am Thine, O Lord" (1 Sam, John)
    B290, C601, F455, N455, UM419 (PD)
"The Lone, Wild Bird" (Pss)
    P320, S2052, SF2052, VU384
"Come and See" ("Kyrie") (John)
    S2127, SF2127
"Lord, Speak to Me" (1 Sam, John) (C)
    B568, EL676, F625, L403, N531, P426, UM463 (PD), VU589
        H-3   Hbl-75; Chr-131; Desc-22; Org-18
        S-1   #52. Descant

Additional Hymn Suggestions
"Come, Thou Fount of Every Blessing" (1 Sam)
    B15, C16, E686, EL807, F318, L499, N459, P356, UM400
    (PD), VU559
"Faith, While Trees Are Still in Blossom" (1 Sam)
    C535, UM508, VU643
"Here I Am, Lord" (1 Sam)
    C452, EL574, P525, R149, UM593, VU509
"Be Thou My Vision" (1 Sam, 1 Cor, John)
    B60, C595, E488, EL793, F468, N451, P339, R151, UM451,
    VU642
"Lord God, Your Love Has Called Us Here" (1 Cor)
    EL358, P353, UM579
"Praise to the Lord, the Almighty" (Pss)
    B14, C25, E390, EL858 (PD) and 859, F337, L543, N22,
    P482, R57, UM139, VU220 (Fr.) and VU221, W547
"Dear Lord, Lead Me Day by Day" (Pss)
    B459, UM411, VU568
"Precious Lord, Take My Hand" (Pss, MLKing Jr. Day)
    B456, C628, EL773, F611, N472, P404, UM474, VU670
"I Was There to Hear Your Borning Cry" (Pss)
    C75, EL732, N351, S2051, SF2051, VU644
"Loving Spirit" (Pss)
    C244, EL397, P323, S2123, SF2123, VU387
"Guide My Feet" (Pss, MLK Jr. Day)
    N497, P354, S2208
"Lead Me, Guide Me" (Pss)
    C583, EL768, R176, S2214, SF2214
"To God Be the Glory" (1 Cor)
    B153, C39, F365, N14, R68, UM99; V-8 p. 5 Vocal Solo
"Have Thine Own Way, Lord" (1 Cor)
    B294, C588, F400, UM382 (PD)
"Come, Let Us with Our Lord Arise" (1 Cor)
    E49, R18, S2084, SF2084
"He Leadeth Me: O Blessed Thought" (John)
    B52, C545, F606, L501, UM128 (PD), VU657
"O The Lamb" (John)
    N192, UM300
"Two Fishermen" (John)
    S2101, SF2101, W633
"We Need a Faith" (MLK Jr. Day)
    S2181, SF2181

"Lord, You Give the Great Commission" (1 Sam, John) (C)
    C459, E528, EL579, P429, R305, UM584, VU512, W470

Additional Contemporary Suggestions
"Let My Words Be Few" (1 Sam)
    M105
"Oh, I Know the Lord's Laid His Hands on Me"
    (1 Sam, Pss, MLK Jr. Day)
    S2139, SF2139
"He Knows My Name" (1 Sam, Pss)
    M109
"Lead Me, Lord" (1 Sam, John)
    M108
"In the Secret" ("I Want to Know You") (Pss)
    M38; V-3 p. 36 Vocal Solo
"Sanctuary" (1 Cor)
    M52, R185, S2164, SF2164
"Lord, Be Glorified" (1 Cor)
    B457, EL744, S2150, SF2150, R172, SP196
"Be Glorified" (1 Cor)
    M13
"Cry of My Heart" (John)
    S2165, SF2165, M39
"You Are Mine" (John)
    EL581, S2218, SF2218
"Come Just as You Are" (John)
    M47
"Step by Step" (John)
    M51

Vocal Solos
"Be Thou My Vision" (1 Sam, 1 Cor, John)
V-6   p. 13
"Here I Am" (1 Sam, John)
V-11   p. 19
"Sing a Song of Joy" (Pss)
V-4   p. 2

Anthems
"Here I Am, Lord" (1 Sam)
Arr. Ovid Young; Augsburg 9780800656058
SATB with keyboard

"Search Me, Lord" (Pss)
Timothy Broege; Hal Leonard 48019113
SATB with piano (opt. cello)

Other Suggestions
Visuals:
    O   Listening, service to others, 3:4b, 5b, 9b
    P   Hand, newborn child, hourglass
    E   Unity, various body shapes and sizes, circle of hands,
         1 Cor 6:19
    G   John 1:43c, "Come and see" invitation, fig tree, mission
Prayer: C19. "Prayer of an African Girl" (1 Sam, Epiphany)
Litanies: C451 (1 Cor), C157 or C664 (MLK Jr. Day)
Response: N161, P299, S2072. "Amen, Amen" (John, MLK Jr.
    Day)

Jonah 3:1-5, 10

[1] The word of the LORD came to Jonah a second time, saying, [2] "Get up, go to Nineveh, that great city, and proclaim to it the message that I tell you." [3] So Jonah set out and went to Nineveh, according to the word of the LORD. Now Nineveh was an exceedingly large city, a three days' walk across. [4] Jonah began to go into the city, going a day's walk. And he cried out, "Forty days more, and Nineveh shall be overthrown!" [5] And the people of Nineveh believed God; they proclaimed a fast, and everyone, great and small, put on sackcloth. . . .

[10] When God saw what they did, how they turned from their evil ways, God changed his mind about the calamity that he had said he would bring upon them; and he did not do it.

Psalm 62:5-12

[5] For God alone my soul waits in silence, for my hope is from him. [6] He alone is my rock and my salvation, my fortress; I shall not be shaken. [7] On God rests my deliverance and my honor; my mighty rock, my refuge is in God. [8] Trust in him at all times, O people; pour out your heart before him; God is a refuge for us. [9] Those of low estate are but a breath, those of high estate are a delusion; in the balances they go up; they are together lighter than a breath. [10] Put no confidence in extortion, and set no vain hopes on robbery; if riches increase, do not set your heart on them. [11] Once God has spoken; twice have I heard this: that power belongs to God, [12] and steadfast love belongs to you, O Lord. For you repay to all according to their work.

1 Corinthians 7:29-31

[29] I mean, brothers and sisters, the appointed time has grown short; from now on, let even those who have wives be as though they had none, [30] and those who mourn as though they were not mourning, and those who rejoice as though they were not rejoicing, and those who buy as though they had no possessions, [31] and those who deal with the world as though they had no dealings with it. For the present form of this world is passing away.

Mark 1:14-20

[14] Now after John was arrested, Jesus came to Galilee, proclaiming the good news of God, [15] and saying, "The time is fulfilled, and the kingdom of God has come near; repent, and believe in the good news."

[16] As Jesus passed along the Sea of Galilee, he saw Simon and his brother Andrew casting a net into the sea—for they were fishermen. [17] And Jesus said to them, "Follow me and I will make you fish for people." [18] And immediately they left their nets and followed him. [19] As he went a little farther, he saw James son of Zebedee and his brother John, who were in their boat mending the nets. [20] Immediately he called them; and they left their father Zebedee in the boat with the hired men, and followed him.

Primary Hymns and Songs for the Day
"Lord of the Dance" (Mark) (O)
    P302, UM261, VU352, W636
        H-3   Chr-106; Org-81
"Tu Has Venido a la Orilla" ("Lord, You Have Come to
   the Lakeshore") (Mark)
    C342, EL817, N173, P377, UM344, VU563
        H-3   Chr-133; Org-114
"Dear Lord and Father of Mankind" (Jonah, Mark)
   (Alternate Text "Parent of Us All")
    B267, C594, E652/E653, F422, L506, N502, P345, UM358
    (PD), VU608
        H-3   Hbl-56; Chr-61; Org-124
        S-2   #151. Introduction
               #152. Violin descant
"Two Fishermen" (Mark)
    S2101, SF2101, W633
"I Have Decided to Follow Jesus" (Mark)
    B305, C344, S2129, SF2129
"Jesus Calls Us" (Mark) (C)
    B293, C337, EL696, F399, L494, N172, UM398 (PD), VU562
        H-3   Chr-115
        S-2   #65. Harmonization

Additional Hymn Suggestions
"For the Healing of the Nations" (Jonah) (O)
    C668, N576, UM428, VU678, W643
"Rock of Ages, Cleft for Me" (Jonah, Pss)
    B342, C214, E685, EL623, F108, L327, N596, UM361
"It's Me, It's Me, O Lord" (Jonah, 1 Cor)
    C579, N519, UM352
"Blessed Be the God of Israel" (Jonah, Mark) (O)
    C135, E444, EL250/EL552, P602, UM209, VU901
"Depth of Mercy" (Jonah, Mark)
    B306, UM355
"Lord God, Your Love Has Called Us Here" (Jonah, Mark)
    EL358, P353, UM579
"O God Beyond All Praising" (Jonah)
    EL880, S2009, SF2009, VU256, W541
"Taste and See" (Pss, Communion)
    EL493, S2267, SF2267
"Hope of the World" (Pss)
    C538, E472, L493, N46, P360, UM178, VU215, W565
"Dear Lord, Lead Me Day by Day" (1 Cor)
    B459, UM411, VU568
"God of Grace and God of Glory" (1 Cor, Mark) (O)
    B395, C464, E594/E595, EL705, F528, L415, N436, P420,
    R301, UM577, VU686
"Forth in Thy Name, O Lord" (1 Cor, Mark) (C)
    L505, UM438, VU416
"We Would See Jesus" (Mark)
    UM256 (PD)
"Softly and Tenderly Jesus Is Calling" (Mark)
    B312, C340, EL608 (PD), F432, N449, R147, UM348
"O Jesus, I Have Promised" (Mark)
    B276, C612, E655, EL810, F402, L503, N493, P388, UM396 (PD)
"Come and See" ("Kyrie") (Mark)
    S2127, SF2127

"The Summons" (Mark)
    EL798, S2130, SF2130, VU567
"Would I Have Answered When You Called" (Mark)
    S2137, SF2137

Additional Contemporary Suggestions
"I Will Call Upon the Lord" (Jonah, Pss)
    R15, S2002, SF2002, SP224
"Rock of Ages" (Pss)
    M93
"Give Thanks" (Pss)
    C528, R266, S2036, SF2036, SP170
"Praise the Name of Jesus" (Pss, Mark)
    R7, S2066, SF2066, SP87
"Amen, Amen" (Mark)
    N161, P299, S2072
"You Are Mine" (Mark)
    EL581, S2218, SF2218
"Cry of My Heart" (Mark)
    S2165, SF2165, M39
"You're Worthy of My Praise" (Mark)
    M41
"Step by Step" (Mark)
    M51
"Lead Me, Lord" (Mark)
    M108
"Every Move I Make" (Mark)
    M122

Vocal Solos
"My Father's Heart" (Jonah, Mark)
V-3   p. 134
"Keep A-Inchin' Along" (Jonah, Mark)
V-7   p. 32
"Here I Am" (Jonah, Mark)
V-11   p. 19

Anthems
"O for a Closer Walk with God" (Jonah, Mark)
Mark Burrows; Abingdon Press 068732520X
SATB with piano

"Come Follow Me Forever" (Mark)
Haydn/ arr. Liebergen; GIA G-5387
Two-part mixed/equal voices with keyboard

Other Suggestions
Visuals:
    O   Sackcloth, empty plate, no. 40
    P   Large rock, refuge, symbols of power, Ps 62:11
    E   Ticking alarm clock
    G   Sackcloth, fish/net, fishing, nets left behind, discipling,
        multiple images of people
Call to Confession: UM366. "For Guidance"
Response: UM587. "Bless Thou the Gifts" (Jonah, Mark)
Response: N161, P299, S2072. "Amen, Amen" (Mark)
See *The Abingdon Worship Annual 2012* for additional worship
resources.

Deuteronomy 18:15-20

[15] The LORD your God will raise up for you a prophet like me from among your own people; you shall heed such a prophet. [16] This is what you requested of the LORD your God at Horeb on the day of the assembly when you said: "If I hear the voice of the LORD my God any more, or ever again see this great fire, I will die." [17] Then the LORD replied to me: "They are right in what they have said. [18] I will raise up for them a prophet like you from among their own people; I will put my words in the mouth of the prophet, who shall speak to them everything that I command. [19] Anyone who does not heed the words that the prophet shall speak in my name, I myself will hold accountable. [20] But any prophet who speaks in the name of other gods, or who presumes to speak in my name a word that I have not commanded the prophet to speak—that prophet shall die."

Psalm 111

[1] Praise the LORD! I will give thanks to the LORD with my whole heart, in the company of the upright, in the congregation. [2] Great are the works of the LORD, studied by all who delight in them. [3] Full of honor and majesty is his work, and his righteousness endures forever. [4] He has gained renown by his wonderful deeds; the LORD is gracious and merciful. [5] He provides food for those who fear him; he is ever mindful of his covenant. [6] He has shown his people the power of his works, in giving them the heritage of the nations. [7] The works of his hands are faithful and just; all his precepts are trustworthy. [8] They are established forever and ever, to be performed with faithfulness and uprightness. [9] He sent redemption to his people; he has commanded his covenant forever. Holy and awesome is his name. [10] The fear of the LORD is the beginning of wisdom; all those who practice it have a good understanding. His praise endures forever.

1 Corinthians 8:1-13

[1] Now concerning food sacrificed to idols: we know that "all of us possess knowledge." Knowledge puffs up, but love builds up. [2] Anyone who claims to know something does not yet have the necessary knowledge; [3] but anyone who loves God is known by him.

[4] Hence, as to the eating of food offered to idols, we know that "no idol in the world really exists," and that "there is no God but one." [5] Indeed, even though there may be so-called gods in heaven or on earth—as in fact there are many gods and many lords— [6] yet for us there is one God, the Father, from whom are all things and for whom we exist, and one Lord, Jesus Christ, through whom are all things and through whom we exist.

[7] It is not everyone, however, who has this knowledge. Since some have become so accustomed to idols until now, they still think of the food they eat as food offered to an idol; and their conscience, being weak, is defiled.

[8] "Food will not bring us close to God." We are no worse off if we do not eat, and no better off if we do. [9] But take care that this liberty of yours does not somehow become a stumbling block to the weak. [10] For if others see you, who possess knowledge, eating in the temple of an idol, might they not, since their conscience is weak, be encouraged to the point of eating food sacrificed to idols? [11] So by your knowledge those weak believers for whom Christ died are destroyed. [12] But when you thus sin against members of your family, and wound their conscience when it is weak, you sin against Christ. [13] Therefore, if food is a cause of their falling, I will never eat meat, so that I may not cause one of them to fall.

Mark 1:21-28

[21] They went to Capernaum; and when the sabbath came, he entered the synagogue and taught. [22] They were astounded at his teaching, for he taught them as one having authority, and not as the scribes. [23] Just then there was in their synagogue a man with an unclean spirit, [24] and he cried out, "What have you to do with us, Jesus of Nazareth? Have you come to destroy us? I know who you are, the Holy One of God." [25] But Jesus rebuked him, saying, "Be silent, and come out of him!" [26] And the unclean spirit, convulsing him and crying with a loud voice, came out of him. [27] They were all amazed, and they kept on asking one another, "What is this? A new teaching—with authority! He commands even the unclean spirits, and they obey him." [28] At once his fame began to spread throughout the surrounding region of Galilee.

Primary Hymns and Songs for the Day

"God Hath Spoken By the Prophets" (Deut) (O)
  UM108
      H-3   Chr-53; Org-33
      S-1   #109-10. Descant and harmonization
  L238, W516
"Jesus, United by Thy Grace" (1 Cor)
  UM561 (PD), VU591
      H-3   Hbl-66, 73; Chr-90; Desc-92; Org-131
      S-1   #291-292. Descant and harmonization
"Silence, Frenzied, Unclean Spirit" (Mark)
  C186, N176, UM264, VU620, W751
      Alternate Tunes: EBENEZER or BEACH SPRING
      H-3   Chr-171
"Blest Be the Tie That Binds" (1 Cor) (C)
  B387, C433, EL656, F560, L370, N393, P438, UM557 (PD),
  VU602
      H-3   Hbl-49; Chr-14; Desc-27; Org-25

Additional Hymn Suggestions

"Guide Me, O Thou Great Jehovah" (Deut)
  B56, C622, E690, EL618, F608, L343, N18/N19, P281,
  UM127 (PD), VU651 (Fr.)
"Lord, Speak to Me" (Deut)
  B568, EL676, F625, L403, N531, P426, UM463 (PD), VU589
"We Sing to You, O God" (Deut)
  EL791, N9, S2001, SF2001
"We Sing of Your Glory" (Deut)
  EL849, S2011, SF2011
"Praise the Lord Who Reigns Above" (Pss)
  B33, R253, UM96 (PD)
"All Creatures of Our God and King" (1 Cor) (O)
  B27, C22, E400, EL835, F347, L527, N17, P455, R47, UM62,
  VU217 (Fr.), W520
"We Believe in One True God" (1 Cor)
  P137, UM85 (PD)
"Christ Is the World's Light" (1 Cor)
  UM188, W543
"Forgive Our Sins as We Forgive" (1 Cor)
  E674, EL605, L307, P347, R184, UM390, W754
"Be Thou My Vision" (1 Cor)
  B60, C595, E488, EL793, F468, N451, P339, R151, UM451,
  VU642
"God Made from One Blood" (1 Cor)
  C500, N427, S2170, SF2170, VU554
"Together We Serve" (1 Cor)
  S2175, SF2175
"Baptized in Water" (1 Cor, Baptism)
  B362, E294, EL456, P492, S2248, W720
"Draw Us in the Spirit's Tether" (1 Cor, Communion)
  C392, EL470, N337, P504, UM632, VU479, W731
"O Christ, the Healer" (1 Cor, Mark)
  C503, EL610, L360, N175, P380, R191, UM265, W747
"Christ, Whose Glory Fills the Skies" (Mark)
  E7, EL553, F293, L265, P462, UM173 (PD), VU336
"Rise, Shine, You People" (Mark)
  EL665, L393, UM187

"Heal Me, Hands of Jesus" (Mark)
  C504, UM262, VU621
"When Jesus the Healer Passed Through Galilee" (Mark)
  UM263, VU358
"O Love, How Deep" (Mark)
  E448/E449, EL322, L88, N209, P83, UM267 (PD), VU348
"An Outcast Among Outcasts" (Mark)
  N201, S2104, SF2104
"Wounded World That Cries for Healing" (Mark)
  S2177, SF2177

Additional Contemporary Suggestions

"Awesome God" (Deut, Pss, Mark)
  R245, S2040, SF2040, SP11
"Majesty" (Deut, Mark)
  B215, R63, SP73, UM176
"Thank You, Lord" (Pss)
  C531, UM84
"Great Is the Lord" (Pss)
  B12, R22, S2022, SF2022, SP30
"How Majestic Is Your Name" (Pss)
  C63, R98, S2023, SF2023, SP14
"What a Mighty God We Serve" (Pss, Mark)
  R159, S2021, SF2021, SP3
"Through It All" (Pss, Mark)
  C555, F43, UM507
"Jesus, Your Name" (Mark)
  M3
"There Is None Like You" (Mark)
  M104

Vocal Solos

"Where Shall My Wondering Soul Begin?" (Mark)
V-1   p. 59
"Jesus Is Lord of All" (Mark)
V-8   p. 254

Anthems

"Song of Moses" (Deut)
John Ness Beck; G. Schirmer 11992
SATB with keyboard

"Heal Me, Hands of Christ" (Mark)
Elaine Aune; Augsburg 9780800676193
SATB with keyboard

Other Suggestions

Visuals:
  O   Bust or painting of Moses, fire, prophets, pulpit, open
         Bible
  P   Praise, food, hands, justice, Ps 111:9c, 10a, c
  E   Building, no. 1 (God, Lord), 1 Cor 8:1b, food, stum-
         bling blocks, books, healing, Christ, love
  G   Christ sitting and teaching, healing, others teaching,
         healing, Mark 1:24b, open Bible
Prayer: C394 or UM564. "For Unity" (1 Cor)
Prayer: C505 or C508 (Mark)
Response: C531, UM84. "Thank You, Lord" (Pss)

Isaiah 40:21-31

[21] Have you not known? Have you not heard? Has it not been told you from the beginning? Have you not understood from the foundations of the earth? [22] It is he who sits above the circle of the earth, and its inhabitants are like grasshoppers; who stretches out the heavens like a curtain, and spreads them like a tent to live in; [23] who brings princes to naught, and makes the rulers of the earth as nothing. [24] Scarcely are they planted, scarcely sown, scarcely has their stem taken root in the earth, when he blows upon them, and they wither, and the tempest carries them off like stubble. [25] To whom then will you compare me, or who is my equal? says the Holy One. [26] Lift up your eyes on high and see: Who created these? He who brings out their host and numbers them, calling them all by name; because he is great in strength, mighty in power, not one is missing. [27] Why do you say, O Jacob, and speak, O Israel, "My way is hidden from the LORD, and my right is disregarded by my God"? [28] Have you not known? Have you not heard? The LORD is the everlasting God, the Creator of the ends of the earth. He does not faint or grow weary; his understanding is unsearchable. [29] He gives power to the faint, and strengthens the powerless. [30] Even youths will faint and be weary, and the young will fall exhausted; [31] but those who wait for the LORD shall renew their strength, they shall mount up with wings like eagles, they shall run and not be weary, they shall walk and not faint.

Psalm 147:1-11, 20c

[1] Praise the LORD! How good it is to sing praises to our God; for he is gracious, and a song of praise is fitting. [2] The LORD builds up Jerusalem; he gathers the outcasts of Israel. [3] He heals the brokenhearted, and binds up their wounds. [4] He determines the number of the stars; he gives to all of them their names. [5] Great is our LORD, and abundant in power; his understanding is beyond measure. [6] The LORD lifts up the downtrodden; he casts the wicked to the ground. [7] Sing to the LORD with thanksgiving; make melody to our God on the lyre. [8] He covers the heavens with clouds, prepares rain for the earth, makes grass grow on the hills. [9] He gives to the animals their food, and to the young ravens when they cry. [10] His delight is not in the strength of the horse, nor his pleasure in the speed of a runner; [11] but the LORD takes pleasure in those who fear him, in those who hope in his steadfast love. . . .

[20c] Praise the LORD!

1 Corinthians 9:16-23

[16] If I proclaim the gospel, this gives me no ground for boasting, for an obligation is laid on me, and woe to me if I do not proclaim the gospel! [17] For if I do this of my own will, I have a reward; but if not of my own will, I am entrusted with a commission. [18] What then is my reward? Just this: that in my proclamation I may make the gospel free of charge, so as not to make full use of my rights in the gospel.

[19] For though I am free with respect to all, I have made myself a slave to all, so that I might win more of them. [20] To the Jews I became as a Jew, in order to win Jews. To those under the law I became as one under the law (though I myself am not under the law) so that I might win those under the law. [21] To those outside the law I became as one outside the law (though I am not free from God's law but am under Christ's law) so that I might win those outside the law. [22] To the weak I became weak, so that I might win the weak. I have become all things to all people, that I might by all means save some. [23] I do it all for the sake of the gospel, so that I may share in its blessings.

Mark 1:29-39

[29] As soon as they left the synagogue, they entered the house of Simon and Andrew, with James and John. [30] Now Simon's mother-in-law was in bed with a fever, and they told him about her at once. [31] He came and took her by the hand and lifted her up. Then the fever left her, and she began to serve them.

[32] That evening, at sundown, they brought to him all who were sick or possessed with demons. [33] And the whole city was gathered around the door. [34] And he cured many who were sick with various diseases, and cast out many demons; and he would not permit the demons to speak, because they knew him.

[35] In the morning, while it was still very dark, he got up and went out to a deserted place, and there he prayed. [36] And Simon and his companions hunted for him. [37] When they found him, they said to him, "Everyone is searching for you." [38] He answered, "Let us go on to the neighboring towns, so that I may proclaim the message there also; for that is what I came out to do." [39] And he went throughout Galilee, proclaiming the message in their synagogues and casting out demons.

Primary Hymns and Songs for the Day

"Praise to the Lord, the Almighty" (Isa, Pss) (O)
B14, C25, E390, EL858 (PD) and 859, F337, L543, N22, P482, R57, UM139, VU220 (Fr.) and VU221, W547
H-3   Hbl-89; Chr-163; Desc-69; Org-79
S-1   #218-222. Various treatments

"When Jesus the Healer Passed Through Galilee" (Mark)
UM263, VU358
S-2   #76. Flute/recorder descant

"Precious Lord, Take My Hand" (Mark, Black History)
B456, C628, EL773, F611, N472, P404, UM474, VU670
H-3   Chr-164; Org-116

"Make Me a Captive, Lord" (1 Cor) (C)
B278, P378
H-3   Hbl-61; Chr-71; Desc-93; Org-133
UM421 (PD)
H-3   Hbl-55; Chr-60; Desc-30; Org-27
S-1   #86-88. Various treatments

Additional Hymn Suggestions

"We Sing to You, O God" (Isa)
EL791, N9, S2001, SF2001

"You Alone Are Holy" ("Solo Tu Eres Santo") (Isa)
S2077, SF2077

"O Holy Spirit, Root of Life" (Isa)
C251, EL399, N57, S2121, SF2121, VU379

"In the Midst of New Dimensions" (Isa)
N391, S2238, SF2238

"Sing Praise to God Who Reigns Above" (Isa, Pss)
B20, C6, E408, EL871, F343, N6, P483, R52, UM126 (PD), VU216, W528

"All My Hope Is Firmly Grounded" (Isa, Pss)
C88, E665, EL757, N408, UM132, VU654/VU655

"O For a Thousand Tongues to Sing" (Pss) (O)
B216, C5, E493, EL886, F349, L559, N42, P466, R32, UM57 (PD), VU326

"Rejoice, Ye Pure in Heart" (Pss)
B39, C15, E556/E557, EL873/EL874, F394, N55/ N71, P145/P146, UM160/UM161

"Lord of the Dance" (1 Cor, Mark)
P302, UM261, VU352, W636

"Heal Me, Hands of Jesus" (Mark)
C504, UM262, VU621

"O Christ, the Healer" (Mark)
C503, EL610, L360, N175, P380, R191, UM265, W747

"O Love, How Deep" (Mark)
E448/E449, EL322, L88, N209, P83, UM267 (PD), VU348

"He Touched Me" (Mark)
C564, F628, UM367

"There Is a Balm in Gilead" (Mark, Black History)
B269, C501, E676, EL614 (PD), F48, N553, P394, UM375, VU612, W608

"Take Time to Be Holy" (Mark)
B446, C572, F457, UM395 (PD), VU672

"I'm So Glad Jesus Lifted Me" (Mark, Black History)
C529, EL860 (PD), N474, S2151, SF2151

Additional Contemporary Suggestions

"On Eagle's Wings" (Isa)
B71, C77, EL787, N775, R112, UM143, VU807/VU808, S-2 #143. Stanzas for soloist

"The Power of Your Love" (Isa)
M26

"Great and Mighty Is He" (Isa, Pss)
SP4, M11

"Great Are You, Lord" (Isa, Pss)
R69, SP102

"How Great Are You, Lord" (Isa, Pss)
M103

"People Need the Lord" (Isa, Mark)
B557, S2244, SF2244

"Great Is the Lord" (Pss)
B12, R22, S2022, SF2022, SP30

"Someone Asked the Question" (Pss, Black History)
N523, S2144, SF2144

"Oh Lord, You're Beautiful" (Mark)
S2064, SF2064

"Amen, Amen" (Mark, Black History)
N161, P299, S2072

"Oh, I Know the Lord's Laid His Hands on Me" (Mark, Black History)
S2139, SF2139

"My Redeemer Lives" (Mark)
M73

Vocal Solos

"Wings Like Eagles" (Isa)
V-11   p. 9

"Sing a Song of Joy" (Pss)
V-4   p. 2

Anthems

"With Wings as Eagles" (Isa)
Donald McCullough; Hinshaw HMC-1961
SATB with piano and flute

"We Come to You for Healing, Lord" (Mark)
Ruth Elaine Schram; Augsburg 9780800620202
SAB with keyboard; opt. flute

Other Suggestions

Visuals:
O   Helping the powerless, exhausted youth, Isa 40:31
P   Praising, singing, healing, stars, stringed instruments (lyre), rain clouds, grass, birds, love
E   Proclamation, ordination certificate, manacles (slave)
G   Helping older woman up, healing, sundown/early dawn

Call to Prayer: C503, EL610, L360, N175, P380, R191, UM265, W747, stanza 1. "O Christ, the Healer" (Mark)

Prayer: C332. "God of Wondrous Darkness" (Isa, Mark)

Scripture Response: B294, C588, F400, UM382 (PD), stanza 3. "Have Thine Own Way, Lord" (Pss, Mark)

Response: C30, EL846, N760, S2067, SF2067, VU431. "Amen, We Praise Your Name, O God" ("Amen Siakudumisa") (Pss, Black History)

February is Black History Month, which can be reflected in your choice of music and liturgy.

2 Kings 5:1-14

[1]Naaman, commander of the army of the king of Aram, was a great man and in high favor with his master, because by him the LORD had given victory to Aram. The man, though a great warrior, suffered from leprosy. [2]Now the Arameans on one of their raids had taken a young girl captive from the land of Israel, and she served Naaman's wife. [3]She said to her mistress, "If only my lord were with the prophet who is in Samaria! He would cure him of his leprosy." [4]So Naaman went in and told his lord just what the girl from the land of Israel said. [5]And the king of Aram said, "Go then, and I will send along a letter to the king of Israel."

He went, taking with him ten talents of silver, six thousand shekels of gold, and ten sets of garments. [6]He brought the letter to the king of Israel, which read, "When this letter reaches you, know that I have sent to you my servant Naaman, that you may cure him of his leprosy." [7]When the king of Israel read the letter, he tore his clothes and said, "Am I God, to give death or life, that this man sends word to me to cure a man of his leprosy? Just look and see how he is trying to pick a quarrel with me."

[8]But when Elisha the man of God heard that the king of Israel had torn his clothes, he sent a message to the king, "Why have you torn your clothes? Let him come to me, that he may learn that there is a prophet in Israel." [9]So Naaman came with his horses and chariots, and halted at the entrance of Elisha's house. [10]Elisha sent a messenger to him, saying, "Go, wash in the Jordan seven times, and your flesh shall be restored and you shall be clean." [11]But Naaman became angry and went away, saying, "I thought that for me he would surely come out, and stand and call on the name of the LORD his God, and would wave his hand over the spot, and cure the leprosy! [12]Are not Abana and Pharpar, the rivers of Damascus, better than all the waters of Israel? Could I not wash in them, and be clean?" He turned and went away in a rage. [13]But his servants approached and said to him, "Father, if the prophet commanded you to do something difficult, would you not have done it? How much more, when all he said to you was, 'Wash, and be clean'?" [14]So he went down and immersed himself seven times in the Jordan, according to the word of the man of God; his flesh was restored like the flesh of a young boy, and he was clean.

Psalm 30

[1] I will extol you, O LORD, for you have drawn me up, and did not let my foes rejoice over me. [2]O LORD my God, I cried to you for help, and you have healed me. [3]O LORD, you brought up my soul from Sheol, restored me to life from among those gone down to the Pit. [4]Sing praises to the LORD, O you his faithful ones, and give thanks to his holy name. [5]For his anger is but for a moment; his favor is for a lifetime. Weeping may linger for the night, but joy comes with the morning. [6]As for me, I said in my prosperity, "I shall never be moved." [7]By your favor, O LORD, you had established me as a strong mountain; you hid your face; I was dismayed. [8]To you, O LORD, I cried, and to the LORD I made supplication: [9] "What profit is there in my death, if I go down to the Pit? Will the dust praise you? Will it tell of your faithfulness? [10]Hear, O LORD, and be gracious to me! O LORD, be my helper!" [11]You have turned my mourning into dancing; you have taken off my sackcloth and clothed me with joy, [12]so that my soul may praise you and not be silent. O LORD my God, I will give thanks to you forever.

1 Corinthians 9:24-27

[24]Do you not know that in a race the runners all compete, but only one receives the prize? Run in such a way that you may win it. [25]Athletes exercise self-control in all things; they do it to receive a perishable wreath, but we an imperishable one. [26]So I do not run aimlessly, nor do I box as though beating the air; [27]but I punish my body and enslave it, so that after proclaiming to others I myself should not be disqualified.

Mark 1:40-45

[40]A leper came to him begging him, and kneeling he said to him, "If you choose, you can make me clean." [41]Moved with pity, Jesus stretched out his hand and touched him, and said to him, "I do choose. Be made clean!" [42]Immediately the leprosy left him, and he was made clean. [43] After sternly warning him he sent him away at once, [44]saying to him, "See that you say nothing to anyone; but go, show yourself to the priest, and offer for your cleansing what Moses commanded, as a testimony to them." [45]But he went out and began to proclaim it freely, and to spread the word, so that Jesus could no longer go into a town openly, but stayed out in the country; and people came to him from every quarter.

Primary Hymns and Songs for the Day
"Marching to Zion" (Pss, Black History) (O)
　B524, C707, EL625, F550, N382, UM733 (PD), VU714
　　H-3　Chr-298
"Just as I Am" (Mark)
　B303/B307, C339, E693, EL592, F417, L296, N207, P370, R140,
　UM357 (PD), VU508
　　H-3　Chr-120; Org-186
"He Touched Me" (Mark)
　C564, F628, UM367
"Oh Lord, You're Beautiful" (Mark)
　S2064, SF2064
"Guide My Feet" (1 Cor, Black History) (C)
　N497, P354, S2208

Additional Hymn Suggestions
"Lord God, Your Love Has Called Us Here" (2 Kgs)
　EL358, P353, UM579
"If Thou But Suffer God to Guide Thee" (2 Kgs)
　B57, C565, E635, EL769, L453, N410, P282, UM142 (PD),
　VU285/VU286
"Praise to the Lord, the Almighty" (2 Kgs, Pss)
　B14, C25, E390, EL858 (PD) and 859, F337, L543, N22, P482,
　R57, UM139, VU220 (Fr.) and VU221, W547
"Praise, My Soul, the King of Heaven" (2 Kgs, Pss, Mark)
　B32, C23, E410, EL864/EL865, F339, L549, P478/P479, R53,
　UM66 (PD), VU240, W530
"This Is a Day of New Beginnings" (2 Kgs, Mark)
　B370, C518, N417, UM383, W661
"Wash, O God, Our Sons and Daughters" (2 Kgs, Mark)
　C365, EL445, UM605, VU442
"Water, River, Spirit, Grace" (2 Kgs, Baptism)
　C366, S2253, SF2253
"Come, We That Love the Lord" (Pss)
　B525, E392, N379, UM732, VU715, W552
"I'll Fly Away" (Pss)
　N595, S2282, SF2282
"Joy in the Morning" (Pss)
　S2284, SF2284
"Faith Is Patience in the Night" (Pss, 1 Cor)
　S2211, SF2211
"I Want to Walk as a Child of the Light" (1 Cor)
　E490, EL815, R152, UM206, W510
"When We All Get to Heaven" (1 Cor)
　B514, F123, UM701 (PD)
"When Jesus the Healer Passed Through Galilee" (Mark)
　UM263, VU358
"O Christ, the Healer" (Mark)
　C503, EL610, L360, N175, P380, R191, UM265, W747
"Nothing but the Blood" (Mark)
　B135, F266, UM362 (PD)
"O Happy Day, That Fixed My Choice" (Mark)
　B349, F647, UM391 (PD)
"My Hope Is Built" (Mark) (C)
　B406, C537, EL596, F92, L293/L294, N368, P379, UM368 (PD)

Additional Contemporary Suggestions
"Wade in the Water" (2 Kgs)
　C371, EL459 (PD), S2107, SF2107

"Give Thanks" (Pss)
　C528, R266, S2036, SF2036, SP170
"I Exalt You" (Pss)
　R44, SP18
"I Could Sing of Your Love Forever" (Pss)
　M63; V-3 p. 22 Vocal Solo
"Someone Asked the Question" (Pss, Black History)
　N523, S2144
"O Freedom" (Pss, Black History)
　S2194, SF2194
"Soon and Very Soon" (Pss, Black History)
　B192, EL439, R276, UM706
"He Who Began a Good Work in You" (1 Cor)
　S2163, SF2163, SP180, R134
"I Will Never Be (the Same Again)" (1 Cor)
　M34
"In the Secret" ("I Want to Know You") (1 Cor)
　M38; V-3 p. 36 Vocal Solo
"Turn Your Eyes upon Jesus" (1 Cor, Mark)
　B320, F621, SP218, UM349
"Through It All" (Mark)
　C555, F43, UM507
"People Need the Lord" (Mark)
　B557, S2244, SF2244
"White as Snow" (Mark)
　M35

Vocal Solos
"Ev'ry Time I Feel De Spirit" (1 Kgs)
V-7　　p. 78
"Praise to the Lord, the Almighty" (1 Kgs, Pss)
V-6　　p. 18
"Clean Before My Lord" (1 Kgs, Mark)
V-8　　p. 233

Anthems
"I Will Sing unto the Lord" (Pss)
Kenney Potter; Choristers Guild CGA1178
SATB with keyboard; opt. trumpet

"Jesus' Hands Were Kind Hands" (Mark)
Sue Ellen Page; Choristers Guild CGA 485
Unison with Keyboard

Other Suggestions
Visuals:
　O　Leper, young girl, riches/gold, letter, torn clothes, no. 7
　P　Praying hands, healing, singing, Ps 30:5b (weeping/joy)
　E　Runners/race, trophy, athletes training, laurel wreath,
　　　boxer
　G　Leper, kneeling, outstretched hand, offering, Mark 1:44
Introit: S2271, SF2271. "Come! Come! Everybody Worship" (Pss)
Offering Response: S2195, SF2195. "In the Lord I'll Be Ever Thankful" (Pss)
Response: M87. "Let the Peace of God Reign" (1 Cor)

2 Kings 2:1-12

[1] Now when the Lord was about to take Elijah up to heaven by a whirlwind, Elijah and Elisha were on their way from Gilgal. [2] Elijah said to Elisha, "Stay here; for the Lord has sent me as far as Bethel." But Elisha said, "As the Lord lives, and as you yourself live, I will not leave you." So they went down to Bethel. [3] The company of prophets who were in Bethel came out to Elisha, and said to him, "Do you know that today the Lord will take your master away from you?" And he said, "Yes, I know; keep silent."

[4] Elijah said to him, "Elisha, stay here; for the Lord has sent me to Jericho." But he said, "As the Lord lives, and as you yourself live, I will not leave you." So they came to Jericho. [5] The company of prophets who were at Jericho drew near to Elisha, and said to him, "Do you know that today the Lord will take your master away from you?" And he answered, "Yes, I know; be silent."

[6] Then Elijah said to him, "Stay here; for the Lord has sent me to the Jordan." But he said, "As the Lord lives, and as you yourself live, I will not leave you." So the two of them went on. [7] Fifty men of the company of prophets also went, and stood at some distance from them, as they both were standing by the Jordan. [8] Then Elijah took his mantle and rolled it up, and struck the water; the water was parted to the one side and to the other, until the two of them crossed on dry ground.

[9] When they had crossed, Elijah said to Elisha, "Tell me what I may do for you, before I am taken from you." Elisha said, "Please let me inherit a double share of your spirit." [10] He responded, "You have asked a hard thing; yet, if you see me as I am being taken from you, it will be granted you; if not, it will not." [11] As they continued walking and talking, a chariot of fire and horses of fire separated the two of them, and Elijah ascended in a whirlwind into heaven. [12] Elisha kept watching and crying out, "Father, father! The chariots of Israel and its horsemen!" But when he could no longer see him, he grasped his own clothes and tore them in two pieces.

Psalm 50:1-6

[1] The mighty one, God the Lord, speaks and summons the earth from the rising of the sun to its setting. [2] Out of Zion, the perfection of beauty, God shines forth. [3] Our God comes and does not keep silence, before him is a devouring fire, and a mighty tempest all around him. [4] He calls to the heavens above and to the earth, that he may judge his people: [5] "Gather to me my faithful ones, who made a covenant with me by sacrifice!" [6] The heavens declare his righteousness, for God himself is judge.

2 Corinthians 4:3-6

[3] And even if our gospel is veiled, it is veiled to those who are perishing. [4] In their case the god of this world has blinded the minds of the unbelievers, to keep them from seeing the light of the gospel of the glory of Christ, who is the image of God. [5] For we do not proclaim ourselves; we proclaim Jesus Christ as Lord and ourselves as your slaves for Jesus' sake. [6] For it is the God who said, "Let light shine out of darkness," who has shone in our hearts to give the light of the knowledge of the glory of God in the face of Jesus Christ.

Mark 9:2-9

[2] Six days later, Jesus took with him Peter and James and John, and led them up a high mountain apart, by themselves. And he was transfigured before them, [3] and his clothes became dazzling white, such as no one on earth could bleach them. [4] And there appeared to them Elijah with Moses, who were talking with Jesus. [5] Then Peter said to Jesus, "Rabbi, it is good for us to be here; let us make three dwellings, one for you, one for Moses, and one for Elijah." [6] He did not know what to say, for they were terrified. [7] Then a cloud overshadowed them, and from the cloud there came a voice, "This is my Son, the Beloved; listen to him!" [8] Suddenly when they looked around, they saw no one with them any more, but only Jesus.

[9] As they were coming down the mountain, he ordered them to tell no one about what they had seen, until after the Son of Man had risen from the dead.

Primary Hymns and Songs for the Day
"Christ, Whose Glory Fills the Skies" (Mark) (O)
    E7, EL553, F293, L265, P462, UM173 (PD), VU336
        H-3   Hbl-51; Chr-206; Desc-89; Org-120
        S-1   #278-279. Harmonizations
"Shine, Jesus, Shine" (2 Cor, Mark)
    B579, EL671, R247, S2173, SF2173, SP142
        H-3   Chr-171
"O Wondrous Sight! O Vision Fair" (Mark)
    E137, UM258 (PD)
        H-3   Hbl-84, 93; Chr-60, 84; Desc-102; Org-175
        S-2   #191. Harmonization
    EL316 (PD), L80, N184, P75
        H-3   Org-145
        S-1   #82-84. Various treatments
    E136 (PD)
"We Have Come at Christ's Own Bidding" (Mark)
    N182, S2103, SF2103, VU104
        H-3   Hbl-46; Chr-26, 134; Desc-53; Org-56
        S-1   #168-171. Various treatments
"Swing Low, Sweet Chariot" (2 Kgs, Black History) (C)
    C643, UM703
        H-3   Chr-177

Additional Hymn Suggestions
"Hail to the Lord's Anointed" (2 Kgs, Mark) (O)
    C140, E616, EL311 (PD), L87, N104, P205, UM203 (PD), VU30
"Steal Away to Jesus" (2 Kgs, Mark, Black History)
    C644, N599, UM704
"I Want to Walk as a Child of the Light" (2 Cor)
    E490, EL815, R152, UM206, W510
"Be Thou My Vision" (2 Cor)
    B60, C595, E488, EL793, F468, N451, P339, R151, UM451, VU642
"Open My Eyes, That I May See" (2 Cor)
    B502, C586, F486, P324, UM454, VU371
"This Little Light of Mine" (2 Cor)
    N524/N525, UM585
"Christ Beside Me" (2 Cor)
    R164, S2166, SF2166
"You Are Mine" (2 Cor)
    EL581, S2218, SF2218
"Christ Is the World's Light" (2 Cor, Mark) (C)
    UM188, W543
"Jesus Shall Reign" (Mark)
    B587, C95, E544, EL434, F238, L530, N157, P423, R296, UM157 (PD), VU330, W492
"Christ, Upon the Mountain Peak" (Mark)
    E129/E130, EL317, P74, UM260, VU102, W701
"I Stand Amazed in the Presence" (Mark)
    B547, F223, UM371 (PD)
"This Is the Feast of Victory" (Mark, Communion)
    E417/E418, EL165/EL166/EL167, P594, R199, UM638, VU904, W458
"Mine Eyes Have Seen the Glory" (Mark, Transfiguration)
    B633, C705, EL890, F692, L332, N610, UM717 (PD), W686
"You Alone Are Holy" (Mark)
    S2077, SF2077

"Come, Let Us with Our Lord Arise" (Mark)
    E49, R18, S2084, SF2084
"Swiftly Pass the Clouds of Glory" (Mark)
    P73, S2102
"As We Gather at Your Table" (Mark, Communion)
    EL522, N332, S2268, SF2268, VU457

Additional Contemporary Suggestions
"Praise to the Lord" (Pss)
    EL844, S2029, SF2029, VU835
"God Is Here Today" (Pss, Transfiguration)
    S2049, SF2049
"Shine on Us" (2 Cor)
    M19
"Turn Your Eyes upon Jesus" (Mark)
    B320, F621, SP218, UM349
"Jesus, We Are Here" ("Yesu Tawa Pano") (Mark)
    EL529, S2273, SF2273
"Holy Ground" (Mark)
    B224, C112, S2272, SF2272, SP86
"He Is Exalted" (Mark, Transfiguration)
    R238, S2070, SF2070, SP66
"When I Look into Your Holiness" (Mark, Transfiguration)
    R41, SP71
"We Declare Your Majesty" (Mark, Transfiguration)
    M43
"Great and Mighty Is He" (Transfiguration)
    SP4, M11
"Awesome in this Place" (Transfiguration)
    M36
"All Hail King Jesus" (Transfiguration)
    S2069, SF2069, SP63
"Honor and Praise" (Transfiguration)
    S2018, SF2018

Vocal Solos
"I Saw the Lord, and All Beside Was Darkness" (Mark)
V-8   p. 268
"Show Me Your Glory" (Mark, Transfiguration)
V-3   p. 178

Anthems
"This Little Light of Mine" (2 Cor)
arr. David L. Bone; Hinshaw HMC1966
SATB *divisi a cappella*

"The Lord Is My Light" (Mark)
Michael Bedford; Choristers Guild CGA878
Unison/two part with keyboard; opt. flute

Other Suggestions
Visuals:
    O   Light, whirlwind, fire, mantel/stole, generations
    P   Sunrise/set, fire, scales of justice, Ps 50:6a
    E   Manacles, light/darkness, Christ
    G   White robe, cloud, transfigured Christ, Elijah, Moses
Introit: S2005, SF2005. "Arise, Shine" (2 Kgs, Mark)
Call to Prayer: S2202, SF2202. "Come Away" (Mark)
Prayer: C591, UM489, or UM259 (1 Cor, Mark)

Joel 2:1-2, 12-17

[1]Blow the trumpet in Zion; sound the alarm on my holy mountain! Let all the inhabitants of the land tremble, for the day of the LORD is coming, it is near— [2] a day of darkness and gloom, a day of clouds and thick darkness! Like blackness spread upon the mountains a great and powerful army comes; their like has never been from of old, nor will be again after them in ages to come. . . .

[12] Yet even now, says the LORD, return to me with all your heart, with fasting, with weeping, and with mourning; [13]rend your hearts and not your clothing. Return to the LORD, your God, for he is gracious and merciful, slow to anger, and abounding in steadfast love, and relents from punishing. [14]Who knows whether he will not turn and relent, and leave a blessing behind him, a grain offering and a drink offering for the LORD, your God? [15]Blow the trumpet in Zion; sanctify a fast; call a solemn assembly; [16]gather the people. Sanctify the congregation; assemble the aged; gather the children, even infants at the breast. Let the bridegroom leave his room, and the bride her canopy. [17]Between the vestibule and the altar let the priests, the ministers of the LORD, weep. Let them say, "Spare your people, O LORD, and do not make your heritage a mockery, a byword among the nations. Why should it be said among the peoples, 'Where is their God?' "

Psalm 51:1-17

[1] Have mercy on me, O God, according to your steadfast love; according to your abundant mercy blot out my transgressions. [2]Wash me thoroughly from my iniquity, and cleanse me from my sin. [3]For I know my transgressions, and my sin is ever before me. [4]Against you, you alone, have I sinned, and done what is evil in your sight, so that you are justified in your sentence and blameless when you pass judgment. [5] Indeed, I was born guilty, a sinner when my mother conceived me. [6]You desire truth in the inward being; therefore teach me wisdom in my secret heart. [7]Purge me with hyssop, and I shall be clean; wash me, and I shall be whiter than snow. [8]Let me hear joy and gladness; let the bones that you have crushed rejoice. [9]Hide your face from my sins, and blot out all my iniquities. [10]Create in me a clean heart, O God, and put a new and right spirit within me. [11]Do not cast me away from your presence, and do not take your holy spirit from me. [12]Restore to me the joy of your salvation, and sustain in me a willing spirit. [13]Then I will teach transgressors your ways, and sinners will return to you. [14]Deliver me from bloodshed, O God, O God of my salvation, and my tongue will sing aloud of your deliverance. [15]O Lord, open my lips, and my mouth will declare your praise. [16]For you have no delight in sacrifice; if I were to give a burnt offering, you would not be pleased. [17]The sacrifice acceptable to God is a broken spirit; a broken and contrite heart, O God, you will not despise.

2 Corinthians 5:20b–6:10

[20b]We entreat you on behalf of Christ, be reconciled to God. [21]For our sake he made him to be sin who knew no sin, so that in him we might become the righteousness of God.

[1] As we work together with him, we urge you also not to accept the grace of God in vain. [2]For he says, "At an acceptable time I have listened to you, and on a day of salvation I have helped you." See, now is the acceptable time; see, now is the day of salvation! [3]We are putting no obstacle in anyone's way, so that no fault may be found with our ministry, [4]but as servants of God we have commended ourselves in every way: through great endurance, in afflictions, hardships, calamities, [5]beatings, imprisonments, riots, labors, sleepless nights, hunger; [6]by purity, knowledge, patience, kindness, holiness of spirit, genuine love, [7]truthful speech, and the power of God; with the weapons of righteousness for the right hand and for the left; [8]in honor and dishonor, in ill repute and good repute. We are treated as impostors, and yet are true; [9]as unknown, and yet are well known; as dying, and see—we are alive; as punished, and yet not killed; [10] as sorrowful, yet always rejoicing; as poor, yet making many rich; as having nothing, and yet possessing everything.

Matthew 6:1-6, 16-21

[1] "Beware of practicing your piety before others in order to be seen by them; for then you have no reward from your Father in heaven.

[2] "So whenever you give alms, do not sound a trumpet before you, as the hypocrites do in the synagogues and in the streets, so that they may be praised by others. Truly I tell you, they have received their reward. [3]But when you give alms, do not let your left hand know what your right hand is doing, [4]so that your alms may be done in secret; and our Father who sees in secret will reward you. . . .

[5] "And whenever you pray, do not be like the hypocrites; for they love to stand and pray in the synagogues and at the street corners, so that they may be seen by others. Truly I tell you, they have received their reward. [6]But whenever you pray, go into your room and shut the door and pray to your Father who is in secret; and your Father who sees in secret will reward you.

[16] "And whenever you fast, do not look dismal, like the hypocrites, for they disfigure their faces so as to show others that they are fasting. Truly I tell you, they have received their reward. [17]But when you fast, put oil on your head and wash your face, [18] so that your fasting may be seen not by others but by your Father who is in secret; and your Father who sees in secret will reward you.

[19] "Do not store up for yourselves treasures on earth, where moth and rust consume and where thieves break in and steal; [20]but store up for yourselves treasures in heaven, where neither moth nor rust consumes and where thieves do not break in and steal. [21]For where your treasure is, there your heart will be also."

Primary Hymns and Songs for the Day

"Lord, Who Throughout These Forty Days" (Matt) (O)
C180, E142, N211, P81, W417 (PD)
  H-3 Chr-132; Desc-94; Org-137
 UM269
  H-3 Chr-106; Desc-65; Org-72
  S-2 #105. Flute/violin descant
     #106. Harmonization
 EL319, L99
"More Love to Thee, O Christ" (Matt)
B473, C527, F476, N456, P359, UM453 (PD)
  H-3 Org-94
"Come and Find the Quiet Center" (Matt)
C575, S2128, SF2128, VU374
"Sunday's Palms Are Wednesday's Ashes" (Ash Wed.)
S2138, SF2138, VU107
  H-3 Hbl-14, 64; Chr-132, 203
  S-2 #22. Descant
(NOTE: The last two suggestions use the same tune.)
"Lord, I Want to Be a Christian" (Joel, Matt) (C)
B489, C589, F421, N454, P372 (PD), R145, UM402
  H-3 Chr-130

Additional Hymn Suggestions

"There's a Wideness in God's Mercy" (Joel)
B25, C73, E470, EL587/EL588, F115, L290, N23, P298, UM121, VU271, W595
"Sing My Tongue, the Glorious Battle" (Joel)
E165/E166, L118, N220, UM296 (PD), W437
"Alas! And Did My Savior Bleed" (2 Cor)
B139/B145, C204, EL337, F274, L98, N199/N200, P78, UM294/UM359
"Lead On, O King Eternal" (2 Cor)
B621, C632, E555, EL805, F595, L495, N573, P447/P448, R298, UM580
"Lead On, O Cloud of Presence" (2 Cor, Lent)
C633, S2234, SF2234, VU421
"In the Singing" (2 Cor, Communion)
EL466, S2255, SF2255
"Love Divine, All Loves Excelling" (2 Cor, Matt) (O)
B208, C517, E657, EL631 (PD), L315, P376, N43, R196, UM384, VU333, W588
"It's Me, It's Me, O Lord" (Matt, Black History)
C579, N519, UM352
"Just as I Am, Without One Plea" (Matt)
B303/B307, C339, E693, EL592, F417, L296, N207, P370, R140, UM357 (PD), VU508
"Take Time to Be Holy" (Matt)
B446, C572, F457, UM395 (PD), VU672
"Near to the Heart of God" (Matt)
B295, C581, F35, P527, UM472 (PD)
"Prayer Is the Soul's Sincere Desire" (Matt)
F446 (PD), N508, UM492
"Sweet Hour of Prayer" (Matt)
B445, C570, F439, N505, UM496 (PD)
"Come Away with Me" (Matt)
S2202, SF2202
"The Fragrance of Christ" (Matt)
S2205, SF2205

"What Wondrous Love Is This" (2 Cor) (C)
B143 (PD), C200, E439, EL666, F283, L385, N223, P85, R277, UM292, VU147 (Fr.), W600

Additional Contemporary Suggestions

"Open Our Eyes, Lord" (Pss)
B499, R91, S2086, SF2086, SP199
"Give Me a Clean Heart" (Pss)
C515, N188, S2133, SF2133
"Change My Heart, O God" (Pss)
EL801, R143, SP195, S2152, SF2152
"Please Enter My Heart, Hosanna" (Pss)
S2154, SF2154
"Come and Fill Our Hearts" (Pss)
EL538, S2157, SF2157, W561
"Lord, Have Mercy" (Pss)
C299, S2277, SF2277
"Refiner's Fire" (Pss)
M50
"The Power of Your Love" (Pss)
M26
"White as Snow" (Pss)
M35
"Purify My Heart" (Pss)
R187, M90
"You Are My Hiding Place" (Pss, Matt)
C554, S2055, SF2055
"Lord, Listen to Your Children Praying" (Matt)
C305, S2193, SF2193, VU400
"I Want to Know You" ("In the Secret") (Matt)
M38; V-3 p. 36 Vocal Solo

Vocal Solos

"If with All Your Hearts" (Joel)
V-8 p. 277
"A Contrite Heart" (Pss)
V-4 p. 10

Anthems

"O My God, Bestow Thy Tender Mercy" (Pss)
Pergolesi/Hopson; Carl Fisher CM7974
Two-part mixed with keyboard

"The Lord's Prayer" (Matt)
Mark A. Miller; Abingdon Press 0687491444
SATB with piano

Other Suggestions

Visuals:
 O Black cloth, grain, wine, trumpet, empty plate
 P Water, snow, rejoicing, Ps 51:10, 15, 17, heart
 E Clock, calendar with today's date, rejoicing, black/gold
 G Praying hands, oil/water, closed door, empty plate, rust
Prayer: C574, N846 or UM353 (Pss)
Response: S2275, SF2275 or N784 (Pss)
Prayer: C456, C567, or N769 (Matt)
Response: C299, S2277, SF2277. "Lord, Have Mercy" (Pss)

Genesis 9:8-17

[8] Then God said to Noah and to his sons with him, [9] "As for me, I am establishing my covenant with you and your descendants after you, [10] and with every living creature that is with you, the birds, the domestic animals, and every animal of the earth with you, as many as came out of the ark. [11] I establish my covenant with you, that never again shall all flesh be cut off by the waters of a flood, and never again shall there be a flood to destroy the earth." [12] God said, "This is the sign of the covenant that I make between me and you and every living creature that is with you, for all future generations: [13] I have set my bow in the clouds, and it shall be a sign of the covenant between me and the earth. [14] When I bring clouds over the earth and the bow is seen in the clouds, [15] I will remember my covenant that is between me and you and every living creature of all flesh; and the waters shall never again become a flood to destroy all flesh. [16] When the bow is in the clouds, I will see it and remember the everlasting covenant between God and every living creature of all flesh that is on the earth." [17] God said to Noah, "This is the sign of the covenant that I have established between me and all flesh that is on the earth."

Psalm 25:1-10

[1] To you, O LORD, I lift up my soul. [2] O my God, in you I trust; do not let me be put to shame; do not let my enemies exult over me. [3] Do not let those who wait for you be put to shame; let them be ashamed who are wantonly treacherous. [4] Make me to know your ways, O LORD; teach me your paths. [5] Lead me in your truth, and teach me, for you are the God of my salvation; for you I wait all day long. [6] Be mindful of your mercy, O LORD, and of your steadfast love, for they have been from of old. [7] Do not remember the sins of my youth or my transgressions; according to your steadfast love remember me, for your goodness' sake, O LORD! [8] Good and upright is the LORD; therefore he instructs sinners in the way. [9] He leads the humble in what is right, and teaches the humble his way. [10] All the paths of the LORD are steadfast love and faithfulness, for those who keep his covenant and his decrees.

1 Peter 3:18-22

[18] For Christ also suffered for sins once for all, the righteous for the unrighteous, in order to bring you to God. He was put to death in the flesh, but made alive in the spirit, [19] in which also he went and made a proclamation to the spirits in prison, [20] who in former times did not obey, when God waited patiently in the days of Noah, during the building of the ark, in which a few, that is, eight persons, were saved through water. [21] And baptism, which this prefigured, now saves you—not as a removal of dirt from the body, but as an appeal to God for a good conscience, through the resurrection of Jesus Christ, [22] who has gone into heaven and is at the right hand of God, with angels, authorities, and powers made subject to him.

Mark 1:9-15

[9] In those days Jesus came from Nazareth of Galilee and was baptized by John in the Jordan. [10] And just as he was coming up out of the water, he saw the heavens torn apart and the Spirit descending like a dove on him. [11] And a voice came from heaven, "You are my Son, the Beloved; with you I am well pleased."

[12] And the Spirit immediately drove him out into the wilderness. [13] He was in the wilderness forty days, tempted by Satan; and he was with the wild beasts; and the angels waited on him.

[14] Now after John was arrested, Jesus came to Galilee, proclaiming the good news of God, [15] and saying, "The time is fulfilled, and the kingdom of God has come near; repent, and believe in the good news."

Primary Hymns and Songs for the Day
"Lord, Who Throughout These Forty Days" (Mark) (O)
    C180, E142, N211, P81, W417 (PD)
        H-3   Chr-132; Desc-94; Org-137
    UM269
        H-3   Chr-106; Desc-65; Org-72
        S-2   #105. Flute/violin descant
                #106. Harmonization
    EL319, L99
"In the Midst of New Dimensions" (Gen)
    N391, S2238, SF2238
"Cry of My Heart" (Pss)
    S2165, SF2165, M39
"When Jesus Came to Jordan" (Mark)
    UM252
        H-3   Chr-211
    EL305, P72, W697
"Spirit Song" (1 Pet, Mark)
    C352, R248, SP134, UM347
"Thy Holy Wings, O Savior" (Gen, 1 Pet) (C)
    EL613, UM502
        S-1   #47-#49. Various treatments

Additional Hymn Suggestions
"God of the Sparrow" (Gen)
    C70, EL740, N32, P272, UM122, VU229
"O Love That Wilt Not Let Me Go" (Gen)
    B292, C540, F404, L324, N485, P384, UM480 (PD), VU658
"Faith, While Trees Are Still in Blossom" (Gen)
    C535, UM508, VU643
"God Made from One Blood" (Gen)
    C500, N427, S2170, SF2170, VU554
"As a Fire Is Meant for Burning" (Gen)
    S2237, SF2237, VU578
"Lead Me, Guide Me" (Pss)
    C583, EL768, R176, S2214, SF2214
"Ah, Holy Jesus" (1 Pet)
    C210, E158, EL349, L123, N218, P93, R183, UM289 (PD), VU138
"Hail, Thou Once Despised Jesus" (1 Pet)
    E495, UM325 (PD)
"Come, Thou Almighty King" (1 Pet, Mark)
    B247, C27, E365, EL408, F341, L522, N275, P139, UM61 (PD), VU314, W487
"Wonder of Wonders" (1 Pet, Mark, Baptism)
    C378, N328, P499, S2247
"Baptized in Water" (1 Pet, Mark, Baptism)
    B362, E294, EL456, P492, S2248, W720
"O Love, How Deep" (Mark)
    E448/E449, EL322, L88, N209, P83, UM267 (PD), VU348
"We'll Understand It Better By and By" (Mark)
    N444, UM525 (PD)
"Wild and Lone the Prophet's Voice" (Mark)
    P409, S2089, SF2089
"Jesus, Tempted in the Desert" (Mark)
    S2105, SF2105, VU115
"Jesus Walked This Lonesome Valley" (Mark)
    C211, F217, P80, S2112, W427
"She Comes Sailing on the Wind" (Mark)
    S2122, SF2122, VU380

Additional Contemporary Suggestions
"To Know You More" (Pss)
    S2161, SF2161
"More Like You" (Pss)
    S2167, SF2167
"Lord, Have Mercy" (Pss)
    C299, S2277, SF2277
"I Want to Know You" ("In the Secret") (Pss)
    M38; V-3 p. 36 Vocal Solo
"Knowing You" (Pss, Mark)
    M30
"I Could Sing of Your Love Forever" (Pss)
    M63; V-3 p. 22 Vocal Solo
"Show Me Your Ways" (Pss)
    M107
"Lead Me, Lord" (Pss)
    M108
"I've Just Come from the Fountain" (1 Pet, Mark)
    S2250, SF2250
"Holy Ground" (Mark, Lent)
    B224, C112, S2272, SF2272, SP86
"Jesus, Name Above All Names" (Mark)
    R26, S2071, SF2071, SP76

Vocal Solos
"Ah, Holy Jesus" (1 Pet)
V-6   p. 24
"I Walked Today Where Jesus Walked" (Mark, Lent)
V-8   p. 14

Anthems
"A Lenten Prayer" (Gen, 1 Peter)
David Ashley White; Paraclete Press PPM09208
Two-part with keyboard (opt. flute)

"Jesus Walked This Lonesome Valley" (Mark)
arr. Ken Berg; Choristers Guild CGA 979
SATB *a cappella*

Other Suggestions
Visuals:
    O   Water, Noah's ark, animals, rainbow
    P   Praying hands, Ps 25:1, 9a
    E   Baptism, cross, resurrection, open Bible, prison
    G   Rocks, sand, bones, Holy Spirit, no. 40, wild animals, angels
Introit: B143 (PD), C200, E439, EL666, F283, L385, N223, P85, R277, UM292, VU147 (Fr.), W600, stanza 1. "What Wondrous Love Is This" (Lent)
Scripture Response: B406, C537, EL596, F92, L293/L294, N368, P379, UM368 (PD), stanza 3. "My Hope Is Built" (Gen)
Response: S2275, SF2275. "Kyrie" (Pss)
Prayer: UM253 (Mark), UM493 or UM705 (Pss, Lent)
Prayer: C178 or F218 (Mark, Lent)

Genesis 17:1-7, 15-16

[1] When Abram was ninety-nine years old, the LORD appeared to Abram, and said to him, "I am God Almighty; walk before me, and be blameless. [2] And I will make my covenant between me and you, and will make you exceedingly numerous." [3] Then Abram fell on his face; and God said to him, [4] "As for me, this is my covenant with you: You shall be the ancestor of a multitude of nations. [5] No longer shall your name be Abram, but your name shall be Abraham; for I have made you the ancestor of a multitude of nations. [6] I will make you exceedingly fruitful; and I will make nations of you, and kings shall come from you. [7] I will establish my covenant between me and you, and your offspring after you throughout their generations, for an everlasting covenant, to be God to you and to your offspring after you." . . .

[15] God said to Abraham, "As for Sarai your wife, you shall not call her Sarai, but Sarah shall be her name. [16] I will bless her, and moreover I will give you a son by her. I will bless her, and she shall give rise to nations; kings of peoples shall come from her."

Psalm 22:23-31

[23] You who fear the LORD, praise him! All you offspring of Jacob, glorify him; stand in awe of him, all you offspring of Israel! [24] For he did not despise or abhor the affliction of the afflicted; he did not hide his face from me, but heard when I cried to him. [25] From you comes my praise in the great congregation; my vows I will pay before those who fear him. [26] The poor shall eat and be satisfied; those who seek him shall praise the LORD. May your hearts live forever! [27] All the ends of the earth shall remember and turn to the LORD; and all the families of the nations shall worship before him. [28] For dominion belongs to the LORD, and he rules over the nations. [29] To him, indeed, shall all who sleep in the earth bow down; before him shall bow all who go down to the dust, and I shall live for him. [30] Posterity will serve him; future generations will be told about the Lord, [31] and proclaim his deliverance to a people yet unborn, saying that he has done it.

Romans 4:13-25

[13] For the promise that he would inherit the world did not come to Abraham or to his descendants through the law but through the righteousness of faith. [14] If it is the adherents of the law who are to be the heirs, faith is null and the promise is void. [15] For the law brings wrath; but where there is no law, neither is there violation.

[16] For this reason it depends on faith, in order that the promise may rest on grace and be guaranteed to all his descendants, not only to the adherents of the law but also to those who share the faith of Abraham (for he is the father of all of us, [17] as it is written, "I have made you the father of many nations")—in the presence of the God in whom he believed, who gives life to the dead and calls into existence the things that do not exist. [18] Hoping against hope, he believed that he would become "the father of many nations," according to what was said, "So numerous shall your descendants be." [19] He did not weaken in faith when he considered his own body, which was already as good as dead (for he was about a hundred years old), or when he considered the barrenness of Sarah's womb. [20] No distrust made him waver concerning the promise of God, but he grew strong in his faith as he gave glory to God, [21] being fully convinced that God was able to do what he had promised. [22] Therefore his faith "was reckoned to him as righteousness." [23] Now the words, "it was reckoned to him," were written not for his sake alone, [24] but for ours also. It will be reckoned to us who believe in him who raised Jesus our Lord from the dead, [25] who was handed over to death for our trespasses and was raised for our justification.

Mark 8:31-38

[31] Then he began to teach them that the Son of Man must undergo great suffering, and be rejected by the elders, the chief priests, and the scribes, and be killed, and after three days rise again. [32] He said all this quite openly. And Peter took him aside and began to rebuke him. [33] But turning and looking at his disciples, he rebuked Peter and said, "Get behind me, Satan! For you are setting your mind not on divine things but on human things."

[34] He called the crowd with his disciples, and said to them, "If any want to become my followers, let them deny themselves and take up their cross and follow me. [35] For those who want to save their life will lose it, and those who lose their life for my sake, and for the sake of the gospel, will save it. [36] For what will it profit them to gain the whole world and forfeit their life? [37] Indeed, what can they give in return for their life? [38] Those who are ashamed of me and of my words in this adulterous and sinful generation, of them the Son of Man will also be ashamed when he comes in the glory of his Father with the holy angels."

Primary Hymns and Songs for the Day

"The God of Abraham Praise" (Gen, Pss, Mark) (O)
   B34, C24, E401, EL831, F332, L544, N24, P488, R51, UM116
   (PD), VU255, W537
      H-3   Hbl-62, 95; Chr-59; Org-77
      S-1   #211. Harmonization
"Take Up Thy Cross" (Mark)
   B494, E675, EL667, L398, N204, P393, UM415, VU561, W634
"Must Jesus Bear the Cross Alone" (Mark)
   B475, F504, SF2112, UM424 (PD)
"I Have Decided to Follow Jesus" (Mark)
   B305, C344, S2129, SF2129
"Where He Leads Me" (Mark) (C)
   B288, C346, F607, UM338 (PD)

Additional Hymn Suggestions

"God, Whose Love Is Reigning O'er Us" (Gen) (O)
   UM100, VU399
"Deep in the Shadows of the Past" (Gen)
   N320, P330, S2246
"Be Thou My Vision" (Gen, Rom)
   B60, C595, E488, EL793, F468, N451, P339, R151, UM451,
   VU642
"Faith, While Trees Are Still in Blossom" (Gen, Rom)
   C535, UM508, VU643
"The Church of Christ, in Every Age" (Gen, Rom, Mark)
   B402, C475, EL729, L433, N306, P421, UM589, VU601, W626
"You Satisfy the Hungry Heart" (Pss, Communion)
   C429, EL484, P521, UM629, R217, VU478, W736
"Standing on the Promises" (Rom)
   B335, C552, F69, UM374 (PD)
"Through It All" (Rom)
   C555, F43, UM507
"Faith of Our Fathers" (Rom)
   B352, C635, EL812 and 813, F526, L500, N381, UM710 (PD),
   VU580, W571
"There Are Some Things I May Not Know" (Rom)
   N405, S2147, SF2147
"We Walk by Faith" (Rom)
   N256, P399, S2196, SF2196, W572
"In the Singing" (Rom, Communion)
   EL466, S2255, SF2255
"Lord of the Dance" (Mark)
   P302, UM261, VU352, W636
"Beneath the Cross of Jesus" (Mark)
   B291, C197, E498, EL338, F253, L107, N190, P92, UM297
   (PD), VU135
"Weary of All Trumpeting" (Mark)
   E572, UM442, W635
"My Song Is Love Unknown" (Mark, Lent)
   E458, EL343, L94, N222, P76, S2083, SF2083, VU143, W439
"Swiftly Pass the Clouds of Glory" (Mark)
   P73, S2102
"Living for Jesus" (Mark)
   B282, C610, F462, S2149, SF2149
"Forth in Thy Name, O Lord" (Mark) (C)
   L505, UM438, VU416

Additional Contemporary Suggestions

"El-Shaddai" (Gen)
   UM123, S-2 #54
"Give Thanks" (Pss)
   C528, R266, S2036, SF2036, SP170
"My Tribute" ("To God Be the Glory") (Rom)
   B153, C39, F365, N14, R68, UM99; V-8 p. 5 Vocal Solo
"O How He Loves You and Me!" (Rom)
   B146, F622, R27, S2108, SF2108, SP113
"Sing Alleluia to the Lord" (Rom)
   B214, C32, S2258, SF2258, R202, SP93
"Here Is Bread, Here Is Wine" (Rom, Communion)
   EL483, S2266, SF2266
"There Is a Redeemer" (Rom, Lent)
   R232, SP111
"Knowing You" ("All I Once Held Dear") (Mark, Lent)
   M30
"The Wonderful Cross" (Mark, Lent)
   M76
"I Stand Amazed" (Mark, Lent)
   M79
"Take This Life" (Mark, Lent)
   M98
"I Come to the Cross" (Mark, Lent)
   M106

Vocal Solos

"Redeeming Grace" (Rom)
V-4   p. 47
"Lead Me to Calvary" (Mark)
V-8   p. 226

Anthems

"Be Thou My Vision" (Gen, Rom)
Arr. Dan Forrest; Brookfield Press 08745013
SATB with piano

"Take Up Your Cross" (Mark)
Jonathan Shippey; Hinshaw HMC2073
Two-part mixed with piano or opt. hammered dulcimer

Other Suggestions

Visuals:
   O   Elderly man/woman, people of all nations, covenant
   P   Praising, hungry being fed, people of all nations,
       deliverance
   E   Elderly person holding a child, all nations, resurrection
   G   Wooden cross, crucifix, resurrection, sandals (follow)
Introit: B143 (PD), C200, E439, EL666, F283, L385, N223, P85,
   R277, UM292, VU147 (Fr.), W600, stanza 1. "What Wondrous
   Love Is This."
Response: C299, S2277, SF2277. "Lord, Have Mercy" (Mark, Lent)
Prayer: UM268 or UM403 (Mark)

Exodus 20:1-17

[1] Then God spoke all these words:

[2] I am the LORD your God, who brought you out of the land of Egypt, out of the house of slavery; [3] you shall have no other gods before me.

[4] You shall not make for yourself an idol, whether in the form of anything that is in heaven above, or that is on the earth beneath, or that is in the water under the earth. [5] You shall not bow down to them or worship them; for I the LORD your God am a jealous God, punishing children for the iniquity of parents, to the third and the fourth generation of those who reject me, [6] but showing steadfast love to the thousandth generation of those who love me and keep my commandments.

[7] You shall not make wrongful use of the name of the LORD your God, for the LORD will not acquit anyone who misuses his name.

[8] Remember the sabbath day, and keep it holy. [9] Six days you shall labor and do all your work. [10] But the seventh day is a sabbath to the LORD your God; you shall not do any work—you, your son or your daughter, your male or female slave, your livestock, or the alien resident in your towns. [11] For in six days the LORD made heaven and earth, the sea, and all that is in them, but rested the seventh day; therefore the LORD blessed the sabbath day and consecrated it.

[12] Honor your father and your mother, so that your days may be long in the land that the LORD your God is giving you.

[13] You shall not murder.

[14] You shall not commit adultery.

[15] You shall not steal.

[16] You shall not bear false witness against your neighbor.

[17] You shall not covet your neighbor's house; you shall not covet your neighbor's wife, or male or female slave, or ox, or donkey, or anything that belongs to your neighbor.

Psalm 19

[1] The heavens are telling the glory of God; and the firmament proclaims his handiwork. [2] Day to day pours forth speech, and night to night declares knowledge. [3] There is no speech, nor are there words; their voice is not heard; [4] yet their voice goes out through all the earth, and their words to the end of the world. In the heavens he has set a tent for the sun, [5] which comes out like a bridegroom from his wedding canopy, and like a strong man runs its course with joy. [6] Its rising is from the end of the heavens, and its circuit to the end of them; and nothing is hid from its heat. [7] The law of the LORD is perfect, reviving the soul; the decrees of the LORD are sure, making wise the simple; [8] the precepts of the LORD are right, rejoicing the heart; the commandment of the LORD is clear, enlightening the eyes; [9] the fear of the LORD is pure, enduring forever; the ordinances of the LORD are true and righteous altogether. [10] More to be desired are they than gold, even much fine gold; sweeter also than honey, and drippings of the honeycomb. [11] Moreover by them is your servant warned; in keeping them there is great reward. [12] But who can detect their errors? Clear me from hidden faults. [13] Keep back your servant also from the insolent; do not let them have dominion over me. Then I shall be blameless, and innocent of great transgression. [14] Let the words of my mouth and the meditation of my heart be acceptable to you, O LORD, my rock and my redeemer.

1 Corinthians 1:18-25

[18] For the message about the cross is foolishness to those who are perishing, but to us who are being saved it is the power of God. [19] For it is written, "I will destroy the wisdom of the wise, and the discernment of the discerning I will thwart." [20] Where is the one who is wise? Where is the scribe? Where is the debater of this age? Has not God made foolish the wisdom of the world? [21] For since, in the wisdom of God, the world did not know God through wisdom, God decided, through the foolishness of our proclamation, to save those who believe. [22] For Jews demand signs and Greeks desire wisdom, [23] but we proclaim Christ crucified, a stumbling block to Jews and foolishness to Gentiles, [24] but to those who are the called, both Jews and Greeks, Christ the power of God and the wisdom of God. [25] For God's foolishness is wiser than human wisdom, and God's weakness is stronger than human strength.

John 2:13-22

[13] The Passover of the Jews was near, and Jesus went up to Jerusalem. [14] In the temple he found people selling cattle, sheep, and doves, and the money changers seated at their tables. [15] Making a whip of cords, he drove all of them out of the temple, both the sheep and the cattle. He also poured out the coins of the money changers and overturned their tables. [16] He told those who were selling the doves, "Take these things out of here! Stop making my Father's house a marketplace!" [17] His disciples remembered that it was written, "Zeal for your house will consume me." [18] The Jews then said to him, "What sign can you show us for doing this?" [19] Jesus answered them, "Destroy this temple, and in three days I will raise it up." [20] The Jews then said, "This temple has been under construction for forty-six years, and will you raise it up in three days?" [21] But he was speaking of the temple of his body. [22] After he was raised from the dead, his disciples remembered that he had said this; and they believed the scripture and the word that Jesus had spoken.

Primary Hymns and Songs for the Day

"How Great Thou Art" (Pss) (O)
  B10, C33, EL856, F2, L532, N35, P467, R250, UM77, VU238
  (Fr.)
    H-3   Chr-103; Org-105
    S-1   #163. Harmonization
"In the Cross of Christ I Glory" (1 Cor)
  B554, C207, E441, EL324, F251, L104, N193, P84, UM295 (PD)
    H-3   Hbl-72; Chr-113; Desc-89; Org-119
    S-1   #276-277. Harmonization with descant
  E442, N194
"Jesus Walked This Lonesome Valley" (John)
  C211, F217, P80, S2112, W427
"The Old Rugged Cross" (1 Cor) (C)
  B141, C548, F256, N195, UM504 (PD)
    H-3   Chr-190; Org-163

Additional Hymn Suggestions

"O Come, O Come, Emmanuel" (Exod)
  See especially stanzas 2 and 3.
  B76, C119, E56, EL257, F169, L34 (PD), N116, P9, UM211,
  VU1 (Fr.), W357
"O For a Heart to Praise My God" (Exod)
  F357, UM417 (PD), W591
"You Alone Are Holy" (Exod)
  S2077, SF2077
"Spirit, Spirit of Gentleness" (Exod)
  C249, EL396, N286, P319, S2120, VU375 (Fr.)
"Take Time to Be Holy" (Exod, John)
  B446, C572, F457, UM395 (PD), VU672
"Praise the Source of Faith and Learning" (Pss, 1 Cor)
  N411, S2004, SF2004
"Let Us with a Joyful Mind" (Pss)
  E389, L521, P244, N16, S2012, SF2012, VU234
"All My Hope Is Firmly Grounded" (1 Cor)
  C88, E665, EL757, N408, UM132, VU654/VU655
"Rejoice, Ye Pure in Heart" (1 Cor)
  B39, C15, E556/E557, EL873/EL874, F394, N55/N71, P145/
  P146, UM160/UM161
"Sing, My Tongue, the Glorious Battle" (1 Cor)
  E165/E166, L118, N220, UM296 (PD), W437
"God of Grace and God of Glory" (1 Cor) (C)
  B395, C464, E594/E595, EL705, F528, L415, N436, P420, R301,
  UM577, VU686
"O Christ, the Healer" (1 Cor, John)
  C503, EL610, L360, N175, P380, R191, UM265, W747
"Beneath the Cross of Jesus" (1 Cor, John)
  B291, C197, E498, EL338, F253, L107, N190, P92, UM297
  (PD), VU135
"Lord of the Dance" (John)
  P302, UM261, VU352, W636
"O Love, How Deep" (John)
  E448/E449, EL322, L88, N209, P83, UM267 (PD), VU348
"Lord, Who Throughout These Forty Days" (John)
  C180, E142, EL319, L99, N211, P81, UM269, W417 (PD)
"Ah, Holy Jesus" (John)
  C210, E158, EL349, L123, N218, P93, R183, UM289 (PD),
  VU138
"Where Cross the Crowded Ways of Life" (John)
  C665, E609, EL719, F665, L429, N543, P408, UM427 (PD), VU681

"All Who Love and Serve Your City" (John)
  C670, E570/E571, EL724, L436, P413, UM433, W621
"Wild and Lone the Prophet's Voice" (John)
  P409, S2089, SF2089

Additional Contemporary Suggestions

"Every Time I Feel the Spirit" (Exod)
  C592, N282, P315, UM404
"Honor and Praise" (Exod)
  S2018, SF2018
"I Will Call Upon the Lord" (Pss)
  R15, S2002, SF2002, SP224
"All Heaven Declares" (Pss)
  R163, M58
"God of Wonders" (Pss)
  M80; V-3 p. 184 Vocal Solo
"Shout to the North" (1 Cor)
  M99
"The Wonderful Cross" (1 Cor)
  M76
"Here Is Bread, Here Is Wine" (1 Cor, Communion)
  EL483, S2266, SF2266
"You Are My All in All" (1 Cor, John)
  SP220
"More Precious Than Silver" (John)
  S2065, SF2065, SP99
"Sanctuary" (John)
  M52, R185, S2164, SF2164
"The Heart of Worship" (John)
  M71

Vocal Solos

"The Heavens Declare His Glory" (Pss)
V-8   p. 248
"Ah, Holy Jesus" (John)
V-6   p. 24

Anthems

"Keep My Commandments" (Exod)
Kenney Potter; Hinshaw HMC1882
SATB *a cappella*

"Expectans expectavi" (John)
Charles Wood: Free download at www.CPDL.org
SATB with organ

Other Suggestions

Visuals:
    O   Tablet/Ten Commandments, open manacles
    P   Celestial images, tent, wedding canopy, bridegroom,
             runner
    E   Wooden cross, clown or jester, (stumbling) block
    G   Animals, whip, overturned table, spilled coins, cross
Reading: C203 (1 Cor) or F420 (Exod)
Prayer: UM268 (Exod) or UM429 (1 Cor, John)

Numbers 21:4-9

[4] From Mount Hor they set out by the way to the Red Sea, to go around the land of Edom; but the people became impatient on the way. [5] The people spoke against God and against Moses, "Why have you brought us up out of Egypt to die in the wilderness? For there is no food and no water, and we detest this miserable food." [6] Then the LORD sent poisonous serpents among the people, and they bit the people, so that many Israelites died. [7] The people came to Moses and said, "We have sinned by speaking against the LORD and against you; pray to the LORD to take away the serpents from us." So Moses prayed for the people. [8] And the LORD said to Moses, "Make a poisonous serpent, and set it on a pole; and everyone who is bitten shall look at it and live." [9] So Moses made a serpent of bronze, and put it upon a pole; and whenever a serpent bit someone, that person would look at the serpent of bronze and live.

Psalm 107:1-3, 17-22

[1] O give thanks to the LORD, for he is good; for his steadfast love endures forever. [2] Let the redeemed of the LORD say so, those he redeemed from trouble [3] and gathered in from the lands, from the east and from the west, from the north and from the south. . . .

[17] Some were sick through their sinful ways, and because of their iniquities endured affliction; [18] they loathed any kind of food, and they drew near to the gates of death. [19] Then they cried to the LORD in their trouble, and he saved them from their distress; [20] he sent out his word and healed them, and delivered them from destruction. [21] Let them thank the LORD for his steadfast love, for his wonderful works to humankind. [22] And let them offer thanksgiving sacrifices, and tell of his deeds with songs of joy.

Ephesians 2:1-10

[1] You were dead through the trespasses and sins [2] in which you once lived, following the course of this world, following the ruler of the power of the air, the spirit that is now at work among those who are disobedient. [3] All of us once lived among them in the passions of our flesh, following the desires of flesh and senses, and we were by nature children of wrath, like everyone else. [4] But God, who is rich in mercy, out of the great love with which he loved us [5] even when we were dead through our trespasses, made us alive together with Christ—by grace you have been saved— [6] and raised us up with him and seated us with him in the heavenly places in Christ Jesus, [7] so that in the ages to come he might show the immeasurable riches of his grace in kindness toward us in Christ Jesus. [8] For by grace you have been saved through faith, and this is not your own doing; it is the gift of God— [9] not the result of works, so that no one may boast. [10] For we are what he has made us, created in Christ Jesus for good works, which God prepared beforehand to be our way of life.

John 3:14-21

[14] "And just as Moses lifted up the serpent in the wilderness, so must the Son of Man be lifted up, [15] that whoever believes in him may have eternal life.

[16] "For God so loved the world that he gave his only Son, so that everyone who believes in him may not perish but may have eternal life.

[17] "Indeed, God did not send the Son into the world to condemn the world, but in order that the world might be saved through him. [18] Those who believe in him are not condemned; but those who do not believe are condemned already, because they have not believed in the name of the only Son of God. [19] And this is the judgment, that the light has come into the world, and people loved darkness rather than light because their deeds were evil. [20] For all who do evil hate the light and do not come to the light, so that their deeds may not be exposed. [21] But those who do what is true come to the light, so that it may be clearly seen that their deeds have been done in God."

Primary Hymns and Songs for the Day

"We Bring the Sacrifice of Praise" (Pss) (O)
 R3, S2031, SF2031, SP1
"Amazing Grace" (Eph, Communion)
 B330, C546, E671, EL779, F107, L448, N547/N548, P280,
 R189, UM378 (PD), VU266 (Fr.), W583
  H-3 Hbl-14, 46; Chr-27; Desc-14; Org-4
  S-2 #5-7. Various treatments
"Grace Alone" (Eph)
 M100, S2162, SF2162
"I Want to Walk as a Child of the Light" (John)
 E490, EL815, R152, UM206, W510
"What Wondrous Love Is This" (John) (C)
 B143 (PD), C200, E439, EL666, F283, L385, N223, P85, R277,
 UM292, VU147 (Fr.), W600
  H-3 Hbl-102; Chr-212; Org-185
  S-1 #347. Harmonization

Additional Hymn Suggestions

"If Thou But Suffer God to Guide Thee" (Num)
 B57, C565, E635, EL769, L453, N410, P282, UM142 (PD),
 VU285/VU286
"God Hath Spoken by the Prophets" (Num, John)
 L238, UM108, W516
"There's a Wideness in God's Mercy" (Eph)
 B25, C73, E470, EL587/EL588, F115, L290, N23, P298, UM121,
 VU271, W595
"Just as I Am, Without One Plea" (Eph)
 B303/B307, C339, E693, EL592, F417, L296, N207, P370, R140,
 UM357 (PD), VU508
"Rock of Ages, Cleft for Me" (Eph)
 B342, C214, E685, EL623, F108, L327, N596, UM361
"And Can It Be That I Should Gain" (Eph)
 B147, F260, R193, UM363 (PD)
"Savior, Like a Shepherd Lead Us" (Eph)
 B61, C558, E708, EL789, F601, L481, N252, P387, UM381 (PD)
"We Walk by Faith" (Eph)
 N256, P399, S2196, SF2196, W572
"To God Be the Glory" (John)
 B153, C39, F365, N14, R68, UM99; V-8 p. 5 Vocal Solo
"Of the Father's Love Begotten" (John)
 B251, C104, E82, EL295, F172 (PD), L42, N118, P309, R252,
 UM184, VU61, W398
"When Morning Gilds the Skies" (John)
 B221, C100, E427, EL853 (PD), F322, L546, N86, P487,
 UM185, VU339 (Fr.), W675
"O Love, How Deep" (John)
 E448/E449, EL322, L88, N209, P83, UM267 (PD), VU348
"Because He Lives" (John)
 B407, C562, F292, UM364
"Come, Let Us with Our Lord Arise" (John)
 E49, R18, S2084, SF2084
"He Came Down" (John)
 EL253, S2085, SF2085
"O Holy Spirit, Root of Life" (John)
 C251, EL399, N57, S2121, SF2121, VU379
"Living for Jesus" (John)
 B282, C610, F462, S2149, SF2149
"Victim Divine" (John, Lent)
 L202, S2259, SF2259

Additional Contemporary Suggestions

"How Great Are You, Lord" (Num, Eph)
 M103
"Give Thanks" (Num, Pss)
 C528, R266, S2036, SF2036, SP170
"Forever" (Pss)
 M68
"Majesty" (Eph)
 B215, R63, SP73, UM176
"Hallelujah" ("Your Love Is Amazing") (Eph, John)
 M118
"Celebrate Love" (Eph, John)
 S2073, SF2073
"Sing Alleluia to the Lord" (Eph, John)
 B214, C32, S2258, SF2258, R202, SP93
"O How He Loves You and Me!" (John)
 B146, F622, R27, S2108, SF2108, SP113
"There Is a Redeemer" (John)
 R232, SP111
"I Believe in Jesus" (John)
 M7
"No Greater Love" (John)
 M25
"Above All" (John)
 M77; V-3 p. 17 Vocal Solo
"You Are My King" ("Amazing Love") (John)
 M82
"That's Why We Praise Him" (John)
 M94
"I Come to the Cross" (John, Lent)
 M106

Vocal Solos

"And Can It Be That I Should Gain" (Eph)
V-1 p. 29
"Redeeming Grace" (Eph)
V-4 p. 47

Anthems

"What Wondrous Love Is This" (John)
arr. Drew Collins; Kjos 6319
Two-part mixed with keyboard

"When Morning Gilds the Skies" (John)
Arr. David Schwoebel; Choristers Guild CGA1174
Unison with organ; opt. flute

Other Suggestions

Visuals:
 O Serpent on a pole, wilderness, empty bowl/cup
 P Ps 107:2, map/globe, praying hands, thanks, singing
 E Death (black), resurrection, gift
 G Light/darkness, wooden cross, crucifix, John 3:16, life
  preserver (salvation)
Song of Assurance: S2141, SF2141. "There's a Song" (Eph)
Reading: C205. "Behold the Love, the Grace of God" (John)

Jeremiah 31:31-34

[31] The days are surely coming, says the LORD, when I will make a new covenant with the house of Israel and the house of Judah. [32] It will not be like the covenant that I made with their ancestors when I took them by the hand to bring them out of the land of Egypt—a covenant that they broke, though I was their husband, says the LORD. [33] But this is the covenant that I will make with the house of Israel after those days, says the LORD: I will put my law within them, and I will write it on their hearts; and I will be their God, and they shall be my people. [34] No longer shall they teach one another, or say to each other, "Know the LORD," for they shall all know me, from the least of them to the greatest, says the LORD; for I will forgive their iniquity, and remember their sin no more.

Psalm 51:1-12

[1] Have mercy on me, O God, according to your steadfast love; according to your abundant mercy blot out my transgressions. [2] Wash me thoroughly from my iniquity, and cleanse me from my sin. [3] For I know my transgressions, and my sin is ever before me. [4] Against you, you alone, have I sinned, and done what is evil in your sight, so that you are justified in your sentence and blameless when you pass judgment. [5] Indeed, I was born guilty, a sinner when my mother conceived me. [6] You desire truth in the inward being; therefore teach me wisdom in my secret heart. [7] Purge me with hyssop, and I shall be clean; wash me, and I shall be whiter than snow. [8] Let me hear joy and gladness; let the bones that you have crushed rejoice. [9] Hide your face from my sins, and blot out all my iniquities. [10] Create in me a clean heart, O God, and put a new and right spirit within me. [11] Do not cast me away from your presence, and do not take your holy spirit from me. [12] Restore to me the joy of your salvation, and sustain in me a willing spirit.

Hebrews 5:5-10

[5] So also Christ did not glorify himself in becoming a high priest, but was appointed by the one who said to him, "You are my Son, today I have begotten you"; [6] as he says also in another place, "You are a priest forever, according to the order of Melchizedek."

[7] In the days of his flesh, Jesus offered up prayers and supplications, with loud cries and tears, to the one who was able to save him from death, and he was heard because of his reverent submission. [8] Although he was a Son, he learned obedience through what he suffered; [9] and having been made perfect, he became the source of eternal salvation for all who obey him, [10] having been designated by God a high priest according to the order of Melchizedek.

John 12:20-33

[20] Now among those who went up to worship at the festival were some Greeks. [21] They came to Philip, who was from Bethsaida in Galilee, and said to him, "Sir, we wish to see Jesus." [22] Philip went and told Andrew; then Andrew and Philip went and told Jesus. [23] Jesus answered them, "The hour has come for the Son of Man to be glorified. [24] Very truly, I tell you, unless a grain of wheat falls into the earth and dies, it remains just a single grain; but if it dies, it bears much fruit. [25] Those who love their life lose it, and those who hate their life in this world will keep it for eternal life. [26] Whoever serves me must follow me, and where I am, there will my servant be also. Whoever serves me, the Father will honor.

[27] "Now my soul is troubled. And what should I say—'Father, save me from this hour'? No, it is for this reason that I have come to this hour. [28] Father, glorify your name." Then a voice came from heaven, "I have glorified it, and I will glorify it again." [29] The crowd standing there heard it and said that it was thunder. Others said, "An angel has spoken to him." [30] Jesus answered, "This voice has come for your sake, not for mine. [31] Now is the judgment of this world; now the ruler of this world will be driven out. [32] And I, when I am lifted up from the earth, will draw all people to myself." [33] He said this to indicate the kind of death he was to die.

Primary Hymns and Songs for the Day

"Jesus Shall Reign" (Heb, John) (O)
　　B587, C95, E544, EL434, F238, L530, N157, P423, R296,
　　UM157 (PD), VU330, W492
　　　　H-3　　Hbl-29, 57; Chr-117; Desc-31; Org-31
　　　　S-1　　#100-103. Various treatments.
"This Is a Day of New Beginnings" (Jer, John)
　　B370, C518, N417, UM383, W661
"Give Me a Clean Heart" (Jer, Pss)
　　C515, N188, S2133, SF2133
"Change My Heart, O God" (Jer, Pss)
　　EL801, R143, SP195, S2152, SF2152
"My Song Is Love Unknown" (Heb)
　　E458, EL343, L94, N222, P76, S2083, SF2083, VU143, W439
"I Have Decided to Follow Jesus" (John) (C)
　　B305, C344, S2129, SF2129

Additional Hymn Suggestions

"Breathe on Me, Breath of God" (Jer)
　　B241, C254, E508, F161, L488, N292, P316, UM420 (PD),
　　VU382 (Fr.), W725
"O Love That Wilt Not Let Me Go" (Jer)
　　B292, C540, F404, L324, N485, P384, UM480 (PD), VU658
"Here I Am, Lord" (Jer)
　　C452, EL574, P525, R149, UM593, VU509
"Since Jesus Came Into My Heart" (Jer, Pss)
　　B441, F639, S2140, SF2140
"God the Sculptor of the Mountains" (Jer Communion)
　　EL736, S2060, SF2060
"Wonder of Wonders" (Jer, Baptism)
　　C378, N328, P499, S2247
"Ah, Holy Jesus" (Heb)
　　C210, E158, EL349, L123, N218, P93, R183, UM289 (PD),
　　VU138
"O the Lamb" (Heb)
　　N192, UM300
"Living for Jesus" (Heb)
　　B282, C610, F462, S2149, SF2149
"Victim Divine" (Heb, Communion, Lent)
　　L202, S2259, SF2259
"Lift High the Cross" (John)
　　B594, C108, E473, EL660, L377, N198, P371, R297, UM159,
　　VU151, W704
"Hallelujah! What a Savior" (John)
　　B175, F246, UM165 (PD)
"Go to Dark Gethsemane" (John)
　　C196, E171, EL347, F281, L109, N219, P97, UM290 (PD),
　　VU133
"Beneath the Cross of Jesus" (John)
　　B291, C197, E498, EL338, F253, L107, N190, P92, UM297
　　(PD), VU135
"Where He Leads Me" (John)
　　B288, C346, F607, UM338 (PD)
"O Jesus, I Have Promised" (John)
　　B276, C612, E655, EL810, F402, L503, N493, P388, UM396
　　(PD)

"Jesus Calls Us" (John)
　　B293, C337, EL696, F399, L494, N172, UM398 (PD), VU562
"Must Jesus Bear the Cross Alone" (John)
　　B475, F504, SF2112, UM424 (PD)
"Take Up Thy Cross" (John) (C)
　　B494, E675, EL667, L398, N204, P393, UM415, VU561,
　　W634

Additional Contemporary Suggestions

"The Potter's Hand" (Jer)
　　M85
"I Give You My Heart" (Jer, Pss)
　　M97
"Refresh My Heart" (Jer, Pss)
　　M49
"Before the Throne of God Above" (Jer, Heb)
　　M65
"Come and Fill Our Hearts" (Jer, John)
　　EL538, S2157, SF2157, W561
"Purify My Heart" (Pss)
　　R187, M90
"Take My Life" (Pss, John)
　　M91
"That's Why We Praise Him" (Heb)
　　M94
"Glorify Thy Name" (John)
　　B249, R37, S2016, SF2016, SP19
"The Servant Song" (John)
　　C490, EL659, N539, R148, S2222, SF2222, SP193, VU595
"We Want to See Jesus Lifted High" (John)
　　M67

Vocal Solos

"A Contrite Heart" (Pss)
V-4　　p. 10
"Clean Before My Lord" (Pss)
V-8　　p. 233

Anthems

"Create in Me" (Pss)
Michael Burkhardt; MorningStar 50-3060
Multiple voicings with piano; opt. handbells

"Beneath the Cross of Jesus" (John)
arr. Bradley Ellingboe; Kjos 9043
SATB and Clarinet (or C-instrument) with piano

Other Suggestions

Visuals:
　　O　　Heart, Exodus, open Bible, love at work
　　P　　Water, bones, Ps 51:7b, 10; rejoicing
　　E　　Miter/chasuble, praying hands, crucifix, cross
　　G　　Clock or hourglass, Crucifixion, bowl/pitcher/towel
　　　　　　(service)
Response: C299, S2277, SF2277. "Lord, Have Mercy" (Jer, Pss)
Scripture Response: B180, C542, E699, F222, N546, P303,
　　UM479, VU669, stanza 4. "Jesus, Lover of My Soul" (Jer)
Litany: C209. "The Wondrous Cross" (John)

Mark 11:1-11 (Palms)

[1] When they were approaching Jerusalem, at Bethphage and Bethany, near the Mount of Olives, he sent two of his disciples [2] and said to them, "Go into the village ahead of you, and immediately as you enter it, you will find tied there a colt that has never been ridden; untie it and bring it. [3] If anyone says to you, 'Why are you doing this?' just say this, 'The Lord needs it and will send it back here immediately.'" [4] They went away and found a colt tied near a door, outside in the street. As they were untying it, [5] some of the bystanders said to them, "What are you doing, untying the colt?" [6] They told them what Jesus had said; and they allowed them to take it. [7] Then they brought the colt to Jesus and threw their cloaks on it; and he sat on it. [8] Many people spread their cloaks on the road, and others spread leafy branches that they had cut in the fields. [9] Then those who went ahead and those who followed were shouting, "Hosanna! Blessed is the one who comes in the name of the Lord! [10] Blessed is the coming kingdom of our ancestor David! Hosanna in the highest heaven!"

[11] Then he entered Jerusalem and went into the temple; and when he had looked around at everything, as it was already late, he went out to Bethany with the twelve.

Psalm 118:1-2, 19-29 (Palms)

[1] O give thanks to the LORD, for he is good; his steadfast love endures forever! [2] Let Israel say, "His steadfast love endures forever." . . .

[19] Open to me the gates of righteousness, that I may enter through them and give thanks to the LORD. [20] This is the gate of the LORD; the righteous shall enter through it. [21] I thank you that you have answered me and have become my salvation. [22] The stone that the builders rejected has become the chief cornerstone. [23] This is the LORD's doing; it is marvelous in our eyes. [24] This is the day that the LORD has made; let us rejoice and be glad in it. [25] Save us, we beseech you, O LORD! O LORD, we beseech you, give us success! [26] Blessed is the one who comes in the name of the LORD. We bless you from the house of the LORD. [27] The LORD is God, and he has given us light. Bind the festal procession with branches, up to the horns of the altar. [28] You are my God, and I will give thanks to you; you are my God, I will extol you. [29] O give thanks to the LORD, for he is good, for his steadfast love endures forever.

Isaiah 50:4-9a

[4] The Lord GOD has given me the tongue of a teacher, that I may know how to sustain the weary with a word. Morning by morning he wakens—wakens my ear to listen as those who are taught. [5] The Lord GOD has opened my ear, and I was not rebellious, I did not turn backward. [6] I gave my back to those who struck me, and my cheeks to those who pulled out the beard; I did not hide my face from insult and spitting. [7] The Lord GOD helps me; therefore I have not been disgraced; therefore I have set my face like flint, and I know that I shall not be put to shame; [8] he who vindicates me is near. Who will contend with me? Let us stand up together. Who are my adversaries? Let them confront me. [9a] It is the Lord GOD who helps me.

Psalm 31:9-16

[9] Be gracious to me, O LORD, for I am in distress; my eye wastes away from grief, my soul and body also. [10] For my life is spent with sorrow, and my years with sighing; my strength fails because of my misery, and my bones waste away. [11] I am the scorn of all my adversaries, a horror to my neighbors, an object of dread to my acquaintances; those who see me in the street flee from me. [12] I have passed out of mind like one who is dead; I have become like a broken vessel. [13] For I hear the whispering of many—terror all around!—as they scheme together against me, as they plot to take my life. [14] But I trust in you, O LORD; I say, "You are my God." [15] My times are in your hand; deliver me from the hand of my enemies and persecutors. [16] Let your face shine upon your servant; save me in your steadfast love.

Philippians 2:5-11

[5] Let the same mind be in you that was in Christ Jesus, [6] who, though he was in the form of God, did not regard equality with God as something to be exploited, [7] but emptied himself, taking the form of a slave, being born in human likeness. And being found in human form, [8] he humbled himself and became obedient to the point of death—even death on a cross. [9] Therefore God also highly exalted him and gave him the name that is above every name, [10] so that at the name of Jesus every knee should bend, in heaven and on earth and under the earth, [11] and every tongue should confess that Jesus Christ is Lord, to the glory of God the Father.

Mark 14:1–15:47
or Mark 15:1-39 (40-47)

[1] It was two days before the Passover and the festival of Unleavened Bread. The chief priests and the scribes were looking for a way to arrest Jesus by stealth and kill him; [2] for they said, "Not during the festival, or there may be a riot among the people."

[3] While he was at Bethany in the house of Simon the leper, as he sat at the table, a woman came with an alabaster jar of very costly ointment of nard, and she broke open the jar and poured the ointment on his head. [4] But some were there who said to one another in anger, "Why was the ointment wasted in this way? [5] For this ointment could have been sold for more than three hundred denarii, and the money given to the poor." And they scolded her. [6] But Jesus said, "Let her alone; why do you trouble her? She has performed a good service for me. [7] For you always have the poor with you, and you can show kindness to them whenever you wish; but you will not always have me. [8] She has done what she could; she has anointed my body beforehand for its burial.

[9] Truly I tell you, wherever the good news is proclaimed in the whole world, what she has done will be told in remembrance of her."

[10] Then Judas Iscariot, who was one of the twelve, went to the chief priests in order to betray him to them. [11] When they heard it, they were greatly pleased, and promised to give him money. So he began to look for an opportunity to betray him.

[12] On the first day of Unleavened Bread, when the Passover lamb is sacrificed, his disciples said to him, "Where do you want us to go and make the preparations for you to eat the Passover?" [13] So he sent two of his disciples, saying to them, "Go into the city, and a man carrying a jar of water will meet you; follow him, [14] and wherever he enters, say to the owner of the house, 'The Teacher asks, Where is my guest room where I may eat the Passover with my disciples?' [15] He will show you a large room upstairs, furnished and ready. Make preparations for us there."

[16] So the disciples set out and went to the city, and found everything as he had told them; and they prepared the Passover meal.

[17] When it was evening, he came with the twelve. [18] And when they had taken their places and were eating, Jesus said, "Truly I tell you, one of you will betray me, one who is eating with me." [19] They began to be distressed and to say to him one after another, "Surely, not I?" [20] He said to them, "It is one of the twelve, one who is dipping bread into the bowl with me. [21] For the Son of Man goes as it is written of him, but woe to that one by whom the Son of Man is betrayed! It would have been better for that one not to have been born."

[22] While they were eating, he took a loaf of bread, and after blessing it he broke it, gave it to them, and said, "Take; this is my body." [23] Then he took a cup, and after giving thanks he gave it to them, and all of them drank from it. [24] He said to them, "This is my blood of the covenant, which is poured out for many. [25] Truly I tell you, I will never again drink of the fruit of the vine until that day when I drink it new in the kingdom of God."

[26] When they had sung the hymn, they went out to the Mount of Olives. [27] And Jesus said to them, "You will all become deserters; for it is written, 'I will strike the shepherd, and the sheep will be scattered.' [28] But after I am raised up, I will go before you to Galilee." [29] Peter said to him, "Even though all become deserters, I will not." [30] Jesus said to him, "Truly I tell you, this day, this very night, before the cock crows twice, you will deny me three times." [31] But he said vehemently, "Even though I must die with you, I will not deny you." And all of them said the same.

[32] They went to a place called Gethsemane; and he said to his disciples, "Sit here while I pray." [33] He took with him Peter and James and John, and began to be distressed and agitated. [34] And he said to them, "I am deeply grieved, even to death; remain here, and keep awake." [35] And going a little farther, he threw himself on the ground and prayed that, if it were possible, the hour might pass from him.

[36] He said, "Abba, Father, for you all things are possible; remove this cup from me; yet, not what I want, but what you want." [37] He came and found them sleeping; and he said to Peter, "Simon, are you asleep? Could you not keep awake one hour? [38] Keep awake and pray that you may not come into the time of trial; the spirit indeed is willing, but the flesh is weak." [39] And again he went away and prayed, saying the same words. [40] And once more he came and found them sleeping, for their eyes were very heavy; and they did not know what to say to him. [41] He came a third time and said to them, "Are you still sleeping and taking your rest? Enough! The hour has come; the Son of Man is betrayed into the hands of sinners. [42] Get up, let us be going. See, my betrayer is at hand."

[43] Immediately, while he was still speaking, Judas, one of the twelve, arrived; and with him there was a crowd with swords and clubs, from the chief priests, the scribes, and the elders. [44] Now the betrayer had given them a sign, saying, "The one I will kiss is the man; arrest him and lead him away under guard." [45] So when he came, he went up to him at once and said, "Rabbi!" and kissed him. [46] Then they laid hands on him and arrested him. [47] But one of those who stood near drew his sword and struck the slave of the high priest, cutting off his ear. [48] Then Jesus said to them, "Have you come out with swords and clubs to arrest me as though I were a bandit? [49] Day after day I was with you in the temple teaching, and you did not arrest me. But let the scriptures be fulfilled." [50] All of them deserted him and fled.

[51] A certain young man was following him, wearing nothing but a linen cloth. They caught hold of him, [52] but he left the linen cloth and ran off naked.

[53] They took Jesus to the high priest; and all the chief priests, the elders, and the scribes were assembled. [54] Peter had followed him at a distance, right into the courtyard of the high priest; and he was sitting with the guards, warming himself at the fire. [55] Now the chief priests and the whole council were looking for testimony against Jesus to put him to death; but they found none. [56] For many gave false testimony against him, and their testimony did not agree. [57] Some stood up and gave false testimony against him, saying, [58] "We heard him say, 'I will destroy this temple that is made with hands, and in three days I will build another, not made with hands.' " [59] But even on this point their testimony did not agree. [60] Then the high priest stood up before them and asked Jesus, "Have you no answer? What is it that they testify against you?" [61] But he was silent and did not answer. Again the high priest asked him, "Are you the Messiah, the Son of the Blessed One?" [62] Jesus said, "I am; and 'you will see the Son of Man seated at the right hand of the Power,' and 'coming with the clouds of heaven.' " [63] Then the high priest tore his clothes and said, "Why do we still need witnesses? [64] You have heard his blasphemy! What is your decision?" All of them condemned him as

deserving death. [65]Some began to spit on him, to blind-fold him, and to strike him, saying to him, "Prophesy!" The guards also took him over and beat him.

[66]While Peter was below in the courtyard, one of the servant-girls of the high priest came by. [67]When she saw Peter warming himself, she stared at him and said, "You also were with Jesus, the man from Nazareth." [68]But he denied it, saying, "I do not know or understand what you are talking about." And he went out into the forecourt. Then the cock crowed. [69]And the servant-girl, on seeing him, began again to say to the bystanders, "This man is one of them." [70]But again he denied it. Then after a little while the bystanders again said to Peter, "Certainly you are one of them; for you are a Galilean." [71]But he began to curse, and he swore an oath, "I do not know this man you are talking about." [72]At that moment the cock crowed for the second time. Then Peter remembered that Jesus had said to him, "Before the cock crows twice, you will deny me three times." And he broke down and wept.

[1]As soon as it was morning, the chief priests held a con-sultation with the elders and scribes and the whole coun-cil. They bound Jesus, led him away, and handed him over to Pilate. [2]Pilate asked him, "Are you the King of the Jews?" He answered him, "You say so." [3]Then the chief priests accused him of many things. [4]Pilate asked him again, "Have you no answer? See how many charges they bring against you." [5]But Jesus made no further reply, so that Pilate was amazed.

[6]Now at the festival he used to release a prisoner for them, anyone for whom they asked. [7]Now a man called Barabbas was in prison with the rebels who had com-mitted murder during the insurrection. [8]So the crowd came and began to ask Pilate to do for them according to his custom. [9]Then he answered them, "Do you want me to release for you the King of the Jews?" [10]For he realized that it was out of jealousy that the chief priests had handed him over. [11]But the chief priests stirred up the crowd to have him release Barabbas for them instead. [12]Pilate spoke to them again, "Then what do you wish me to do with the man you call the King of the Jews?" [13]They shouted back, "Crucify him!" [14]Pilate asked them, "Why, what evil has he done?" But they shouted all the more, "Crucify him!" [15]So Pilate, wishing to satisfy the crowd, released Barabbas for them; and after flogging Jesus, he handed him over to be crucified.

[16]Then the soldiers led him into the courtyard of the palace (that is, the governor's headquarters); and they called together the whole cohort. [17]And they clothed him in a purple cloak; and after twisting some thorns into a crown, they put it on him. [18]And they began saluting him, "Hail, King of the Jews!" [19]They struck his head with a reed, spat upon him, and knelt down in homage to him. [20]After mock-ing him, they stripped him of the purple cloak and put his own clothes on him. Then they led him out to crucify him.

[21]They compelled a passer-by, who was coming in from the country, to carry his cross; it was Simon of Cyrene, the father of Alexander and Rufus. [22]Then they brought Jesus to the place called Golgotha (which means the place of a skull). [23]And they offered him wine mixed with myrrh; but he did not take it. [24]And they crucified him, and divided his clothes among them, casting lots to decide what each should take.

[25]It was nine o'clock in the morning when they cruci-fied him. [26]The inscription of the charge against him read, "The King of the Jews." [27]And with him they cruci-fied two bandits, one on his right and one on his left. [29]Those who passed by derided him, shaking their heads and saying, "Aha! You who would destroy the temple and build it in three days, [30]save yourself, and come down from the cross!" [31]In the same way the chief priests, along with the scribes, were also mocking him among them-selves and saying, "He saved others; he cannot save him-self. [32]Let the Messiah, the King of Israel, come down from the cross now, so that we may see and believe." Those who were crucified with him also taunted him.

[33]When it was noon, darkness came over the whole land until three in the afternoon. [34]At three o'clock Jesus cried out with a loud voice, "Eloi, Eloi, lema sabachthani?" which means, "My God, my God, why have you forsaken me?" [35]When some of the bystanders heard it, they said, "Listen, he is calling for Elijah." [36]And some-one ran, filled a sponge with sour wine, put it on a stick, and gave it to him to drink, saying, "Wait, let us see whether Elijah will come to take him down." [37]Then Jesus gave a loud cry and breathed his last. [38]And the curtain of the temple was torn in two, from top to bottom. [39]Now when the centurion, who stood facing him, saw that in this way he breathed his last, he said, "Truly this man was God's Son!"

[40]There were also women looking on from a distance; among them were Mary Magdalene, and Mary the mother of James the younger and of Joses, and Salome. [41]These used to follow him and provided for him when he was in Galilee; and there were many other women who had come up with him to Jerusalem.

[42]When evening had come, and since it was the day of Preparation, that is, the day before the sabbath, [43]Joseph of Arimathea, a respected member of the council, who was also himself waiting expectantly for the kingdom of God, went boldly to Pilate and asked for the body of Jesus. [44]Then Pilate wondered if he were already dead; and sum-moning the centurion, he asked him whether he had been dead for some time. [45]When he learned from the centurion that he was dead, he granted the body to Joseph. [46]Then Joseph bought a linen cloth, and taking down the body, wrapped it in the linen cloth, and laid it in a tomb that had been hewn out of the rock. He then rolled a stone against the door of the tomb. [47]Mary Magdalene and Mary the mother of Joses saw where the body was laid.

Primary Hymns and Songs for the Day

"Hosanna, Loud Hosanna" (Palms Gospel) (O)
    B130, F248, N213, P89, UM278 (PD), VU123
        H-3   Hbl-16, 22, 68; Chr-101; Desc-37
        S-1   #115. Harmonization
"All Glory, Laud, and Honor" (Palms Gospel)
    B126, C192, E154, EL344, F249, L108, N216, P88, UM280
    (PD), VU122, W428
        H-3   Hbl-45; Chr-22; Desc-96; Org-144
        S-1   #309-310. Harmonization with descant
    E155, N217, W805
"Sing, My Tongue, the Glorious Battle" (Passion)
    E165/E166, L118, N220, UM296 (PD), W437
"When I Survey the Wondrous Cross" (Passion) (C)
    B144, C195, EL803, F258, N224, P101, R236, UM298 (PD)
        H-3   Hbl-6, 102; Chr-213; Desc-49; Org-49
        S-1   #155. Descant
    E474, L482, P100, UM299 (PD), VU149 (Fr.), W433
        H-3   Hbl-47; Chr-32, 76, 214; Desc-90; Org-127
        S-1   #288. Transposition to E-flat major

Additional Hymn Suggestions

"Tell Me the Stories of Jesus" (Palms Gospel)
    B129, C190, F212, UM277 (PD), VU357
"My Song Is Love Unknown" (Palm Sunday)
    E458, EL343, L94, N222, P76, S2083, SF2083, VU143, W439
"At the Name of Jesus" (Phil)
    B198 (PD), E435, F351, L179, P148, R133, UM168, VU335,
    W499
"Thou Didst Leave Thy Throne" (Phil)
    B121, F170, S2100, SF2100
"We Sang Our Glad Hosannas" (Palms and Passion)
    S2111, SF2111
"He Never Said a Mumbalin' Word" (Isa, Passion)
    C208, EL350, P95 (PD), UM291, VU141
"O Love, How Deep" (Passion Gospel)
    E448/E449, EL322, L88, N209, P83, UM267 (PD), VU348
"To Mock Your Reign, O Dearest Lord" (Passion)
    E170, UM285
"O Sacred Head, Now Wounded" (Passion Gospel)
    B137, C202, E168 or E169, EL351 (PD) or EL352, F284, L116
    or L117, N226, P98, R235, UM286, VU145, W434
"Were You There" (Passion Gospel)
    B156, C198, E172, EL353, F287, L92, N230, P102, UM288,
    VU144, W436
"Lord, Whose Love Through Humble Service" (Passion)
    C461, E610, EL712, R286, L423, UM581, W630
"The Bread of Life for All Is Broken" (Passion, Communion)
    E342, N333, UM633
"An Outcast Among Outcasts" (Passion Gospel)
    N201, S2104, SF2104
"Why Has God Forsaken Me?" (Passion Gospel)
    P406, S2110, VU154
"Lift High the Cross" (Passion Gospel) (C)
    B594, C108, E473, EL660, L377, N198, P371, R297, UM159,
    VU151, W704

Additional Contemporary Suggestions

"All Hail King Jesus" (Palms Gospel)
    S2069, SF2069, SP63

"King of Kings" (Palm Sunday)
    B234, R268, S2075, SF2075, SP94, VU167
"The King of Glory Comes" (Palm Sunday)
    B127, R267, S2091, SF2091, W501
"Hosanna" (Palms Gospel)
    R71, SP82
"He Is Exalted" (Phil)
    R238, S2070, SF2070, SP66
"Jesus, Name Above All Names" (Phil)
    R26, S2071, SF2071, SP76
"He Is Lord" (Phil)
    B178, C117, F234, R29, SP122, UM177
"At the Name of Jesus" (Phil)
    R133/R279, SP234
"Come, Now Is the Time to Worship" (Phil)
    M56; V-3 p. 114 Vocal Solo
"The Heavens Shall Declare" (Phil, Palm Sunday)
    M111
"Above All" (Passion Gospel)
    M77; V-3 p. 17 Vocal Solo
"Lord of the Dance" (Passion Gospel)
    P302, UM261, VU352, W636
"Stay with Me" ("Nohu pu") (Passion Gospel)
    EL348, S2198, SF2198

Vocal Solos

"Ride On, Jesus" (Palm Sunday)
V-7   p. 8
"The Holy City" (Palm/Passion Sunday)
V-8   p. 195

Anthems

"Sing Glad Hosannas"
Mark Patterson; Choristers Guild CGA1179
Unison with keyboard; opt. handbells

"O Vos Omnes" (Mark, Passion)
Pablo Casals; Broude AB 128
SATB *a cappella*

Other Suggestions

Visuals:

Palms G	Colt, palms, cloaks, Hosanna
Ps 118	Gates, cornerstone, Ps 118:24, 26a, 29
O	Jesus teaching, Christ's passion, flint
Ps 31	Praying hands, grief, broken pottery
E	Manacles, cross, crucifix, resurrection, Phil 2:9-10
Passion G	Perfume bottle, water jar, cup/bread/wine, cock crowing, sword, bowl of water, wooden cross, placard, purple cloak, sponge/vinegar, torn curtain, shroud, hourglass

Introit: B359, C286, N84, SP236, UM657, VU412. "This Is the Day"
    (Ps 118)
Canticle C96, UM167. "Song of Christ's Obedience" (Phil)
Prayer: C201 or UM281 (Passion/Palm Sunday)

Exodus 12:1-4 (5-10), 11-14

[1] The LORD said to Moses and Aaron in the land of Egypt: [2] This month shall mark for you the beginning of months; it shall be the first month of the year for you. [3] Tell the whole congregation of Israel that on the tenth of this month they are to take a lamb for each family, a lamb for each household. [4] If a household is too small for a whole lamb, it shall join its closest neighbor in obtaining one; the lamb shall be divided in proportion to the number of people who eat of it. [5] Your lamb shall be without blemish, a year-old male; you may take it from the sheep or from the goats. [6] You shall keep it until the fourteenth day of this month; then the whole assembled congregation of Israel shall slaughter it at twilight. [7] They shall take some of the blood and put it on the two doorposts and the lintel of the houses in which they eat it. [8] They shall eat the lamb that same night; they shall eat it roasted over the fire with unleavened bread and bitter herbs. [9] Do not eat any of it raw or boiled in water, but roasted over the fire, with its head, legs, and inner organs. [10] You shall let none of it remain until the morning; anything that remains until the morning you shall burn. [11] This is how you shall eat it: your loins girded, your sandals on your feet, and your staff in your hand; and you shall eat it hurriedly. It is the passover of the LORD. [12] For I will pass through the land of Egypt that night, and I will strike down every firstborn in the land of Egypt, both human beings and animals; on all the gods of Egypt I will execute judgments: I am the LORD. [13] The blood shall be a sign for you on the houses where you live: when I see the blood, I will pass over you, and no plague shall destroy you when I strike the land of Egypt.

[14] This day shall be a day of remembrance for you. You shall celebrate it as a festival to the LORD; throughout your generations you shall observe it as a perpetual ordinance.

Psalm 116:1-4, 12-19

[1] I love the LORD, because he has heard my voice and my supplications. [2] Because he inclined his ear to me, therefore I will call on him as long as I live. [3] The snares of death encompassed me; the pangs of Sheol laid hold on me; I suffered distress and anguish. [4] Then I called on the name of the LORD: "O LORD, I pray, save my life!" . . .

[12] What shall I return to the LORD for all his bounty to me? [13] I will lift up the cup of salvation and call on the name of the LORD, [14] I will pay my vows to the LORD in the presence of all his people. [15] Precious in the sight of the LORD is the death of his faithful ones. [16] O LORD, I am your servant; I am your servant, the child of your serving girl. You have loosed my bonds. [17] I will offer to you a thanksgiving sacrifice and call on the name of the LORD. [18] I will pay my vows to the LORD in the presence of all his people, [19] in the courts of the house of the LORD, in your midst, O Jerusalem. Praise the LORD!

1 Corinthians 11:23-26

[23] For I received from the Lord what I also handed on to you, that the Lord Jesus on the night when he was betrayed took a loaf of bread, [24] and when he had given thanks, he broke it and said, "This is my body that is for you. Do this in remembrance of me." [25] In the same way he took the cup also, after supper, saying, "This cup is the new covenant in my blood. Do this, as often as you drink it, in remembrance of me." [26] For as often as you eat this bread and drink the cup, you proclaim the Lord's death until he comes.

John 13:1-17, 31b-35

[1] Now before the festival of the Passover, Jesus knew that his hour had come to depart from this world and go to the Father. Having loved his own who were in the world, he loved them to the end. [2] The devil had already put it into the heart of Judas son of Simon Iscariot to betray him. And during supper [3] Jesus, knowing that the Father had given all things into his hands, and that he had come from God and was going to God, [4] got up from the table, took off his outer robe, and tied a towel around himself. [5] Then he poured water into a basin and began to wash the disciples' feet and to wipe them with the towel that was tied around him. [6] He came to Simon Peter, who said to him, "Lord, are you going to wash my feet?" [7] Jesus answered, "You do not know now what I am doing, but later you will understand." [8] Peter said to him, "You will never wash my feet." Jesus answered, "Unless I wash you, you have no share with me." [9] Simon Peter said to him, "Lord, not my feet only but also my hands and my head!" [10] Jesus said to him, "One who has bathed does not need to wash, except for the feet, but is entirely clean. And you are clean, though not all of you." [11] For he knew who was to betray him; for this reason he said, "Not all of you are clean."

[12] After he had washed their feet, had put on his robe, and had returned to the table, he said to them, "Do you know what I have done to you? [13] You call me Teacher and Lord—and you are right, for that is what I am. [14] So if I, your Lord and Teacher, have washed your feet, you also ought to wash one another's feet. [15] For I have set you an example, that you also should do as I have done to you. [16] Very truly, I tell you, servants are not greater than their master, nor are messengers greater than the one who sent them. [17] If you know these things, you are blessed if you do them. . . .

[31b] "Now the Son of Man has been glorified, and God has been glorified in him. [32] If God has been glorified in him, God will also glorify him in himself and will glorify him at once. [33] Little children, I am with you only a little longer. You will look for me; and as I said to the Jews so now I say to you, 'Where I am going, you cannot come.' [34] I give you a new commandment, that you love one another. Just as I have loved you, you also should love one another. [35] By this everyone will know that you are my disciples, if you have love for one another."

Primary Hymns and Songs for the Day

"What Wondrous Love Is This" (John) (O)
 B143 (PD), C200, E439, EL666, F283, L385, N223, P85, R277, UM292, VU147 (Fr.), W600
  H-3 Hbl-102; Chr-212; Org-185
  S-1 #347. Harmonization

"For the Bread Which You Have Broken" (1 Cor)
 C411, E340/E341, EL494, L200, P508/P509, UM614/UM615, VU470
  H-3 Chr-67
  S-2 #63-64. Descant and harmonization

"In Remembrance of Me" (1 Cor, Communion)
 B365, C403, S2254

"Broken for Me" (1 Cor, Communion)
 S2263, SF2263

"Jesu, Jesu" (John) (C)
 B501, C600, E602, EL708, N498, P367, R289, UM432, VU593, W431, S-1 #63 Vocal part
  H-3 Chr-114; Org-19
  S-1 #63. Vocal part

Additional Hymn Suggestions

"Go Down, Moses" (Exod)
 C663, E648, N572, P334, UM448, W508

"God the Sculptor of the Mountains" (Exod, Communion)
 EL736, S2060, SF2060

"Deep in the Shadows of the Past" (Exod)
 N320, P330, S2246

"Let Us Break Bread Together" (1 Cor, Communion)
 B366, C425, EL471 (PD), F564, L212, N330, P513, UM618, VU480, W727

"Mothering God, You Gave Me Birth" (1 Cor, Communion)
 C83, EL735, N467, S2050, SF2050, VU320

"Una Espiga" ("Sheaves of Summer") (1 Cor, John, Communion)
 C396, N338, UM637

"Bread of the World" (John, Communion)
 C387, E301, N346, P502, UM624, VU461

"O Love, How Deep" (John)
 E448/E449, EL322, L88, N209, P83, UM267 (PD), VU348

"O Sacred Head, Now Wounded" (John)
 B137, C202, E168 or E169, EL351 (PD) or EL352, F284, L116 or L117, N226, P98, R235, UM286, VU145, W434

"O Jesus, I Have Promised" (John)
 B276, C612, E655, EL810, F402, L503, N493, P388, UM396 (PD)

"O Master, Let Me Walk with Thee" (John)
 B279, C602, E659/E660, EL818, F442, L492, N503, P357, UM430 (PD), VU560

"Where Charity and Love Prevail" (John)
 E581, EL359, L126, N396, UM549

"Lord God, Your Love Has Called Us Here" (John)
 EL358, P353, UM579

"Lord, Whose Love Through Humble Service" (John)
 C461, E610, EL712, R286, L423, UM581, W630

"We Sang Our Glad Hosannas" (Holy Thursday)
 S2111, SF2111

"Together We Serve" (John)
 S2175, SF2175

"Healer of Our Every Ill" (John)
 C506, EL612, S2213, SF2213, VU619

"As We Gather at Your Table" (John, Communion)
 EL522, N332, S2268, SF2268, VU457

Additional Contemporary Suggestions

"El-Shaddai" (Exod)
 UM123, S-2 #54

"I Will Call Upon the Lord" (Pss)
 R15, S2002, SF2002, SP224

"I Love You, Lord" (Pss)
 B212, R36, S2068, SF2068, SP72

"Take Our Bread" (1 Cor, Communion)
 C413, UM640

"Make Me a Servant" (John)
 S2176, SF2176, SP193

"Live in Charity" ("Ubi Caritas") (John)
 C523, EL642, R226, S2179, SF2179, W604

"The Servant Song" (John)
 C490, EL659, N539, R148, S2222, SF2222, SP193, VU595

"They'll Know We Are Christians" (John)
 C494, S2223, SF2223

"Stay with Me" ("Nohu pu") (Holy Thursday)
 EL348, S2198, SF2198

"One Bread, One Body" (Communion)
 C393, EL496, UM620, VU467

Vocal Solos

"Wondrous Love" (John)
V-6 p. 47

"O the Deep, Deep Love of Jesus" (John, Communion)
V-8 p. 247

"He Breaks the Bread, He Pours the Wine" (John, Communion)
V-10 p. 43

Anthems

"Seek to Serve" (John)
Lloyd Pfautsch; Hope APM 003
Two-part mixed with keyboard

"Let Us Break Bread Together" (John, Communion)
John Helgen; MorningStar 50-8314
SATB with piano

Other Suggestions

Visuals:
 O Lamb, sandals, staff, Passover meal
 P Cup or goblet, open manacles
 E Bread/wine/pottery chalice, Passover meal
 G Passover meal, outer garment, towel/basin/water/pitcher, 12 disciples, Last Supper, stripping of the altar, darkness

Prayer: UM283. "Holy Thursday" (John, 1 Cor)
Prayer: C653, UM639. "Bread and Justice" (John)
Response: C385, P94, VU130. "An Upper Room Did Our Lord Prepare." (Use stanza 1 as Call to Worship, stanza 2 as Call to Communion, stanzas 3-4 as Benediction.)
Response: EL529, S2273, SF2273. "Jesus, We Are Here" (John)

Isaiah 52:13–53:12

[13] See, my servant shall prosper; he shall be exalted and lifted up, and shall be very high. [14] Just as there were many who were astonished at him—so marred was his appearance, beyond human semblance, and his form beyond that of mortals— [15] so he shall startle many nations; kings shall shut their mouths because of him; for that which had not been told them they shall see, and that which they had not heard they shall contemplate.

[1] Who has believed what we have heard? And to whom has the arm of the Lord been revealed? [2] For he grew up before him like a young plant, and like a root out of dry ground; he had no form or majesty that we should look at him, nothing in his appearance that we should desire him. [3] He was despised and rejected by others; a man of suffering and acquainted with infirmity; and as one from whom others hide their faces he was despised, and we held him of no account. [4] Surely he has borne our infirmities and carried our diseases; yet we accounted him stricken, struck down by God, and afflicted. [5] But he was wounded for our transgressions, crushed for our iniquities; upon him was the punishment that made us whole, and by his bruises we are healed. [6] All we like sheep have gone astray; we have all turned to our own way, and the Lord has laid on him the iniquity of us all. [7] He was oppressed, and he was afflicted, yet he did not open his mouth; like a lamb that is led to the slaughter, and like a sheep that before its shearers is silent, so he did not open his mouth. [8] By a perversion of justice he was taken away. Who could have imagined his future? For he was cut off from the land of the living, stricken for the transgression of my people. [9] They made his grave with the wicked and his tomb with the rich, although he had done no violence, and there was no deceit in his mouth. [10] Yet it was the will of the Lord to crush him with pain. When you make his life an offering for sin, he shall see his offspring, and shall prolong his days; through him the will of the Lord shall prosper. [11] Out of his anguish he shall see light; he shall find satisfaction through his knowledge. The righteous one, my servant, shall make many righteous, and he shall bear their iniquities. [12] Therefore I will allot him a portion with the great, and he shall divide the spoil with the strong; because he poured out himself to death, and was numbered with the transgressors; yet he bore the sin of many, and made intercession for the transgressors.

Psalm 22

[1] My God, my God, why have you forsaken me? Why are you so far from helping me, from the words of my groaning? [2] O my God, I cry by day, but you do not answer; and by night, but find no rest. [3] Yet you are holy, enthroned on the praises of Israel. [4] In you our ancestors trusted; they trusted, and you delivered them. [5] To you they cried, and were saved; in you they trusted, and were not put to shame. [6] But I am a worm, and not human; scorned by others, and despised by the people. [7] All who see me

mock at me; they make mouths at me, they shake their heads; [8] "Commit your cause to the Lord; let him deliver—let him rescue the one in whom he delights!" [9] Yet it was you who took me from the womb; you kept me safe on my mother's breast. [10] On you I was cast from my birth, and since my mother bore me you have been my God. [11] Do not be far from me, for trouble is near and there is no one to help. [12] Many bulls encircle me, strong bulls of Bashan surround me; [13] they open wide their mouths at me, like a ravening and roaring lion. [14] I am poured out like water, and all my bones are out of joint; my heart is like wax; it is melted within my breast; [15] my mouth is dried up like a potsherd, and my tongue sticks to my jaws; you lay me in the dust of death. [16] For dogs are all around me; a company of evildoers encircles me. My hands and feet have shriveled; [17] I can count all my bones. They stare and gloat over me; [18] they divide my clothes among themselves, and for my clothing they cast lots. [19] But you, O Lord, do not be far away! O my help, come quickly to my aid! [20] Deliver my soul from the sword, my life from the power of the dog! [21] Save me from the mouth of the lion! From the horns of the wild oxen you have rescued me. [22] I will tell of your name to my brothers and sisters; in the midst of the congregation I will praise you: [23] You who fear the Lord, praise him! All you offspring of Jacob, glorify him; stand in awe of him, all you offspring of Israel! [24] For he did not despise or abhor the affliction of the afflicted; he did not hide his face from me, but heard when I cried to him. [25] From you comes my praise in the great congregation; my vows I will pay before those who fear him. [26] The poor shall eat and be satisfied; those who seek him shall praise the Lord. May your hearts live forever! [27] All the ends of the earth shall remember and turn to the Lord; and all the families of the nations shall worship before him. [28] For dominion belongs to the Lord, and he rules over the nations. [29] To him, indeed, shall all who sleep in the earth bow down; before him shall bow all who go down to the dust, and I shall live for him. [30] Posterity will serve him; future generations will be told about the Lord, [31] and proclaim his deliverance to a people yet unborn, saying that he has done it.

Hebrews 10:16-25

[16] "This is the covenant that I will make with them after those days, says the Lord: I will put my laws in their hearts, and I will write them on their minds," [17] he also adds, "I will remember their sins and their lawless deeds no more." [18] Where there is forgiveness of these, there is no longer any offering for sin.

[19] Therefore, my friends, since we have confidence to enter the sanctuary by the blood of Jesus, [20] by the new and living way that he opened for us through the curtain (that is, through his flesh), [21] and since we have a great priest over the house of God, [22] let us approach with a true heart in full assurance of faith, with our hearts sprinkled clean from an

evil conscience and our bodies washed with pure water. [23] Let us hold fast to the confession of our hope without wavering, for he who has promised is faithful. [24] And let us consider how to provoke one another to love and good deeds, [25] not neglecting to meet together, as is the habit of some, but encouraging one another, and all the more as you see the Day approaching.

John 18:1–19:42

[1] After Jesus had spoken these words, he went out with his disciples across the Kidron valley to a place where there was a garden, which he and his disciples entered. [2] Now Judas, who betrayed him, also knew the place, because Jesus often met there with his disciples. [3] So Judas brought a detachment of soldiers together with police from the chief priests and the Pharisees, and they came there with lanterns and torches and weapons. [4] Then Jesus, knowing all that was to happen to him, came forward and asked them, "Whom are you looking for?" [5] They answered, "Jesus of Nazareth." Jesus replied, "I am he." Judas, who betrayed him, was standing with them. [6] When Jesus said to them, "I am he," they stepped back and fell to the ground. [7] Again he asked them, "Whom are you looking for?" And they said, "Jesus of Nazareth." [8] Jesus answered, "I told you that I am he. So if you are looking for me, let these men go." [9] This was to fulfill the word that he had spoken, "I did not lose a single one of those whom you gave me." [10] Then Simon Peter, who had a sword, drew it, struck the high priest's slave, and cut off his right ear. The slave's name was Malchus. [11] Jesus said to Peter, "Put your sword back into its sheath. Am I not to drink the cup that the Father has given me?"

[12] So the soldiers, their officer, and the Jewish police arrested Jesus and bound him. [13] First they took him to Annas, who was the father-in-law of Caiaphas, the high priest that year. [14] Caiaphas was the one who had advised the Jews that it was better to have one person die for the people.

[15] Simon Peter and another disciple followed Jesus. Since that disciple was known to the high priest, he went with Jesus into the courtyard of the high priest, [16] but Peter was standing outside at the gate. So the other disciple, who was known to the high priest, went out, spoke to the woman who guarded the gate, and brought Peter in. [17] The woman said to Peter, "You are not also one of this man's disciples, are you?" He said, "I am not." [18] Now the slaves and the police had made a charcoal fire because it was cold, and they were standing around it and warming themselves. Peter also was standing with them and warming himself.

[19] Then the high priest questioned Jesus about his disciples and about his teaching. [20] Jesus answered, "I have spoken openly to the world; I have always taught in synagogues and in the temple, where all the Jews come together. I have said nothing in secret. [21] Why do you ask me? Ask those who heard what I said to them; they know what I said." [22] When he had said this, one of the police standing nearby struck Jesus on the face, saying, "Is that how you answer the high priest?" [23] Jesus answered, "If I have spoken wrongly, testify to the wrong. But if I have spoken rightly, why do you strike me?" [24] Then Annas sent him bound to Caiaphas the high priest.

[25] Now Simon Peter was standing and warming himself. They asked him, "You are not also one of his disciples, are you?" He denied it and said, "I am not." [26] One of the slaves of the high priest, a relative of the man whose ear Peter had cut off, asked, "Did I not see you in the garden with him?" [27] Again Peter denied it, and at that moment the cock crowed.

[28] Then they took Jesus from Caiaphas to Pilate's headquarters. It was early in the morning. They themselves did not enter the headquarters, so as to avoid ritual defilement and to be able to eat the Passover. [29] So Pilate went out to them and said, "What accusation do you bring against this man?" [30] They answered, "If this man were not a criminal, we would not have handed him over to you." [31] Pilate said to them, "Take him yourselves and judge him according to your law." The Jews replied, "We are not permitted to put anyone to death." [32] (This was to fulfill what Jesus had said when he indicated the kind of death he was to die.)

[33] Then Pilate entered the headquarters again, summoned Jesus, and asked him, "Are you the King of the Jews?" [34] Jesus answered, "Do you ask this on your own, or did others tell you about me?" [35] Pilate replied, "I am not a Jew, am I? Your own nation and the chief priests have handed you over to me. What have you done?" [36] Jesus answered, "My kingdom is not from this world. If my kingdom were from this world, my followers would be fighting to keep me from being handed over to the Jews. But as it is, my kingdom is not from here." [37] Pilate asked him, "So you are a king?" Jesus answered, "You say that I am a king. For this I was born, and for this I came into the world, to testify to the truth. Everyone who belongs to the truth listens to my voice." [38] Pilate asked him, "What is truth?"

After he had said this, he went out to the Jews again and told them, "I find no case against him. [39] But you have a custom that I release someone for you at the Passover. Do you want me to release for you the King of the Jews?" [40] They shouted in reply, "Not this man, but Barabbas!" Now Barabbas was a bandit.

[1] Then Pilate took Jesus and had him flogged. [2] And the soldiers wove a crown of thorns and put it on his head, and they dressed him in a purple robe. [3] They kept coming up to him, saying, "Hail, King of the Jews!" and striking him on the face. [4] Pilate went out again and said to them, "Look, I am bringing him out to you to let you know that I find no case against him." [5] So Jesus came out, wearing the crown of thorns and the purple robe. Pilate said to them, "Here is the man!" [6] When the chief priests and the police saw him, they shouted, "Crucify him! Crucify him!" Pilate said to them, "Take him yourselves and crucify him; I find no case against him." [7] The Jews answered him, "We have a law, and according to that law

he ought to die because he has claimed to be the Son of God."

[8] Now when Pilate heard this, he was more afraid than ever. [9] He entered his headquarters again and asked Jesus, "Where are you from?" But Jesus gave him no answer. [10] Pilate therefore said to him, "Do you refuse to speak to me? Do you not know that I have power to release you, and power to crucify you?" [11] Jesus answered him, "You would have no power over me unless it had been given you from above; therefore the one who handed me over to you is guilty of a greater sin." [12] From then on Pilate tried to release him, but the Jews cried out, "If you release this man, you are no friend of the emperor. Everyone who claims to be a king sets himself against the emperor."

[13] When Pilate heard these words, he brought Jesus outside and sat on the judge's bench at a place called The Stone Pavement, or in Hebrew Gabbatha. [14] Now it was the day of Preparation for the Passover; and it was about noon. He said to the Jews, "Here is your King!" [15] They cried out, "Away with him! Away with him! Crucify him!" Pilate asked them, "Shall I crucify your King?" The chief priests answered, "We have no king but the emperor." [16] Then he handed him over to them to be crucified.

So they took Jesus; [17] and carrying the cross by himself, he went out to what is called The Place of the Skull, which in Hebrew is called Golgotha. [18] There they crucified him, and with him two others, one on either side, with Jesus between them. [19] Pilate also had an inscription written and put on the cross. It read, "Jesus of Nazareth, the King of the Jews." [20] Many of the Jews read this inscription, because the place where Jesus was crucified was near the city; and it was written in Hebrew, in Latin, and in Greek. [21] Then the chief priests of the Jews said to Pilate, "Do not write, 'The King of the Jews,' but, 'This man said, I am King of the Jews.'" [22] Pilate answered, "What I have written I have written." [23] When the soldiers had crucified Jesus, they took his clothes and divided them into four parts, one for each soldier. They also took his tunic; now the tunic was seamless, woven in one piece from the top. [24] So they said to one another, "Let us not tear it, but cast lots for it to see who will get it." This was to fulfill what the scripture says, "They divided my clothes among themselves, and for my clothing they cast lots." [25] And that is what the soldiers did.

Meanwhile, standing near the cross of Jesus were his mother, and his mother's sister, Mary the wife of Clopas, and Mary Magdalene. [26] When Jesus saw his mother and the disciple whom he loved standing beside her, he said to his mother, "Woman, here is your son." [27] Then he said to the disciple, "Here is your mother." And from that hour the disciple took her into his own home.

[28] After this, when Jesus knew that all was now finished, he said (in order to fulfill the scripture), "I am thirsty." [29] A jar full of sour wine was standing there. So they put a sponge full of the wine on a branch of hyssop and held it to his mouth. [30] When Jesus had received the wine, he said, "It is finished." Then he bowed his head and gave up his spirit.

[31] Since it was the day of Preparation, the Jews did not want the bodies left on the cross during the sabbath, especially because that sabbath was a day of great solemnity. So they asked Pilate to have the legs of the crucified men broken and the bodies removed. [32] Then the soldiers came and broke the legs of the first and of the other who had been crucified with him. [33] But when they came to Jesus and saw that he was already dead, they did not break his legs. [34] Instead, one of the soldiers pierced his side with a spear, and at once blood and water came out. [35] (He who saw this has testified so that you also may believe. His testimony is true, and he knows that he tells the truth.) [36] These things occurred so that the scripture might be fulfilled, "None of his bones shall be broken." [37] And again another passage of scripture says, "They will look on the one whom they have pierced."

[38] After these things, Joseph of Arimathea, who was a disciple of Jesus, though a secret one because of his fear of the Jews, asked Pilate to let him take away the body of Jesus. Pilate gave him permission; so he came and removed his body. [39] Nicodemus, who had at first come to Jesus by night, also came, bringing a mixture of myrrh and aloes, weighing about a hundred pounds. [40] They took the body of Jesus and wrapped it with the spices in linen cloths, according to the burial custom of the Jews. [41] Now there was a garden in the place where he was crucified, and in the garden there was a new tomb in which no one had ever been laid. [42] And so, because it was the Jewish day of Preparation, and the tomb was nearby, they laid Jesus there.

Primary Hymns and Songs for the Day
"Were You There (John) (O)
B156, C198, E172, EL353, F287, L92, N230, P102, UM288, VU144, W436
H-3 Hbl-101; Chr-209
S-2 #195-196. Descant and harmonization
"Hallelujah! What a Savior" (Isa)
B175, F246, UM165 (PD)
H-3 Chr-134
"O Sacred Head, Now Wounded" (John)
B137, C202, E168 or E169, EL351 (PD) or EL352, F284, L116 or L117, N226, P98, R235, UM286, VU145, W434
H-3 Hbl-82; Chr-148; Desc-86; Org-111
"When I Survey the Wondrous Cross" (John) (C)
B144, C195, EL803, F258, N224, P101, R236, UM298 (PD)
H-3 Hbl-6, 102; Chr-213; Desc-49; Org-49
S-1 #155. Descant
E474, L482, P100, UM299 (PD), VU149 (Fr.), W433
H-3 Hbl-47; Chr-32, 76, 214; Desc-90; Org-127
S-1 #288. Transposition to E-flat major

Additional Hymn Suggestions
"He Never Said a Mumbalin' Word" (Isa, John)
C208, EL350, P95 (PD), UM291, VU141
"Why Stand So Far Away, My God?" (Pss, John)
C671, S2180, SF2180
"Ah, Holy Jesus" (Heb)
C210, E158, EL349, L123, N218, P93, R183, UM289 (PD), VU138
"I Am Thine, O Lord" (Heb)
B290, C601, F455, N455, UM419 (PD)
"Near to the Heart of God" (Heb)
B295, C581, F35, P527, UM472 (PD)
"Victim Divine" (Heb, Communion)
L202, S2259, SF2259
"Alas! And Did My Savior Bleed" (John) (O)
B139/B145, C204, EL337, F274, L98, N199/N200, P78, UM294/UM359
"Woman in the Night" (John)
C188, UM274
"'Tis Finished! The Messiah Dies" (John)
B148, UM282 (PD)
"To Mock Your Reign, O Dearest Lord" (John)
E170, UM285
"Go to Dark Gethsemane" (John)
C196, E171, EL347, F281, L109, N219, P97, UM290 (PD), VU133
"The Bread of Life for All Is Broken" (John, Communion)
E342, N333, UM633
"Thou Didst Leave Thy Throne" (John)
B121, F170, S2100, SF2100
"When Jesus Wept" (John)
C199, E715, P312, S2106, SF2106, VU146
"Why Has God Forsaken Me?" (John)
P406, S2110, VU154
"We Sang Our Glad Hosannas" (John)
S2111, SF2111
"Goodness Is Stronger Than Evil" (Good Friday)
EL721, S2219, SF2219

"In the Cross of Christ I Glory" (John) (C)
B554, C207, E441/E442, EL324, F251, L104, N193/N194, P84, UM295 (PD)

Additional Contemporary Suggestions
"Our God Reigns" (Isa)
SP64
"Amazing Love" (Heb, John)
R272, M81
"You Are My King" ("Amazing Love") (Heb, John)
M82
"I Come to the Cross" (Heb, John)
M106
"O How He Loves You and Me!" (John)
B146, F622, R27, S2108, SF2108, SP113
"Lord of the Dance" (John)
P302, UM261, VU352, W636
"Jesus, Remember Me" (John)
C569, EL616, P599, R227, UM488, VU148, W423
"Above All" (John)
M77; V-3 p. 17 Vocal Solo

Vocal Solos
"Ah, Holy Jesus" (Isa, John)
V-6 p. 24
"'Tis Finished! The Messiah Dies" (John)
V-1 p. 63
"Were You There?" (John)
V-7 p. 60
"The Shepherd Became a Lamb" (John)
V-10 p. 48

Anthems
"O Sacred Head, Now Wounded" (John, Good Friday)
Michael Larkin; Augsburg 9780806697345
SATB with piano

"Agnus Dei" (John, Good Friday)
Paul Basler; Walton Music HL08501577
SATB with piano

Other Suggestions
Visuals:
Black draping the cross, black paraments, or none
  O Plant, root, suffering, crucifix, lamb, darkness/light,
  P Exodus, mother breast-feeding, water, bones, sword, dog
  E Heb 10:16b, crucifix
  G Sword, charcoal fire, cock crowing, whip, purple robe, rugged cross, tunic, crucifix, nails, Crown of thorns, ladder, sponge on branch, spear, shroud
Introit: S2199, SF2199. "Stay with Us" (John)
Response: EL336, S2113, SF2113. "Lamb of God" (John)
Litany: C201. Litany of the Passion (John)
Scripture Response: C196, E171, EL347, F281, L109, N219, P97, UM290 (PD), VU133. "Go to Dark Gethsemane." Use this to supplement the John reading. Stanza 1 before beginning 18:1. Sing stanza 2 after 19:3. Sing stanza 3 after 19:30. Sing UM288, stanza 5, at end of reading.

Acts 10:34-43

[34] Then Peter began to speak to them: "I truly understand that God shows no partiality, [35] but in every nation anyone who fears him and does what is right is acceptable to him. [36] You know the message he sent to the people of Israel, preaching peace by Jesus Christ—he is Lord of all. [37] That message spread throughout Judea, beginning in Galilee after the baptism that John announced: [38] how God anointed Jesus of Nazareth with the Holy Spirit and with power; how he went about doing good and healing all who were oppressed by the devil, for God was with him. [39] We are witnesses to all that he did both in Judea and in Jerusalem. They put him to death by hanging him on a tree; [40] but God raised him on the third day and allowed him to appear, [41] not to all the people but to us who were chosen by God as witnesses, and who ate and drank with him after he rose from the dead. [42] He commanded us to preach to the people and to testify that he is the one ordained by God as judge of the living and the dead. [43] All the prophets testify about him that everyone who believes in him receives forgiveness of sins through his name."

Psalm 118:1-2, 14-24

[1] O give thanks to the LORD, for he is good; his steadfast love endures forever! [2] Let Israel say, "His steadfast love endures forever." . . .

[14] The LORD is my strength and my might; he has become my salvation. [15] There are glad songs of victory in the tents of the righteous: "The right hand of the LORD does valiantly; [16] the right hand of the LORD is exalted; the right hand of the LORD does valiantly." [17] I shall not die, but I shall live, and recount the deeds of the LORD. [18] The LORD has punished me severely, but he did not give me over to death. [19] Open to me the gates of righteousness, that I may enter through them and give thanks to the LORD. [20] This is the gate of the LORD; the righteous shall enter through it. [21] I thank you that you have answered me and have become my salvation. [22] The stone that the builders rejected has become the chief cornerstone. [23] This is the LORD's doing; it is marvelous in our eyes. [24] This is the day that the LORD has made; let us rejoice and be glad in it.

1 Corinthians 15:1-11

[1] Now I would remind you, brothers and sisters, of the good news that I proclaimed to you, which you in turn received, in which also you stand, [2] through which also you are being saved, if you hold firmly to the message that I proclaimed to you—unless you have come to believe in vain.

[3] For I handed on to you as of first importance what I in turn had received: that Christ died for our sins in accordance with the scriptures, [4] and that he was buried, and that he was raised on the third day in accordance with the scriptures, [5] and that he appeared to Cephas, then to the twelve. [6] Then he appeared to more than five hundred brothers and sisters at one time, most of whom are still alive, though some have died. [7] Then he appeared to James, then to all the apostles. [8] Last of all, as to one untimely born, he appeared also to me. [9] For I am the least of the apostles, unfit to be called an apostle, because I persecuted the church of God. [10] But by the grace of God I am what I am, and his grace toward me has not been in vain. On the contrary, I worked harder than any of them—though it was not I, but the grace of God that is with me. [11] Whether then it was I or they, so we proclaim and so you have come to believe.

John 20:1-18 (or Mark 16:1-8)

[1] Early on the first day of the week, while it was still dark, Mary Magdalene came to the tomb and saw that the stone had been removed from the tomb. [2] So she ran and went to Simon Peter and the other disciple, the one whom Jesus loved, and said to them, "They have taken the Lord out of the tomb, and we do not know where they have laid him." [3] Then Peter and the other disciple set out and went toward the tomb. [4] The two were running together, but the other disciple outran Peter and reached the tomb first. [5] He bent down to look in and saw the linen wrappings lying there, but he did not go in. [6] Then Simon Peter came, following him, and went into the tomb. He saw the linen wrappings lying there, [7] and the cloth that had been on Jesus' head, not lying with the linen wrappings but rolled up in a place by itself. [8] Then the other disciple, who reached the tomb first, also went in, and he saw and believed; [9] for as yet they did not understand the scripture, that he must rise from the dead. [10] Then the disciples returned to their homes.

[11] But Mary stood weeping outside the tomb. As she wept, she bent over to look into the tomb; [12] and she saw two angels in white, sitting where the body of Jesus had been lying, one at the head and the other at the feet. [13] They said to her, "Woman, why are you weeping?" She said to them, "They have taken away my Lord, and I do not know where they have laid him." [14] When she had said this, she turned around and saw Jesus standing there, but she did not know that it was Jesus. [15] Jesus said to her, "Woman, why are you weeping? Whom are you looking for?" Supposing him to be the gardener, she said to him, "Sir, if you have carried him away, tell me where you have laid him, and I will take him away." [16] Jesus said to her, "Mary!" She turned and said to him in Hebrew, "Rabbouni!" (which means Teacher). [17] Jesus said to her, "Do not hold on to me, because I have not yet ascended to the Father. But go to my brothers and say to them, 'I am ascending to my Father and your Father, to my God and your God.' " [18] Mary Magdalene went and announced to the disciples, "I have seen the Lord"; and she told them that he had said these things to her.

Primary Hymns and Songs for the Day
"Christ the Lord Is Risen Today" (1 Cor, John) (O)
>B159, C216, F289, N233, UM302 (PD), VU155 and VU157
>>H-3   Hbl-8, 51; Chr-49; Desc-31; Org-32
>>S-1   #104-108. Various treatments
>P113, W463
>>H-3   Hbl-72; Chr-50; Desc-69; Org-78
>>S-1   #213. Descant
>EL373, L130, W462

"Christ Has Risen" (1 Cor, John)
>S2115, SF2115

"Crown Him with Many Crowns" (John) (C)
>B161, C234, E494, EL855, F345, L170, N301, P151, R56,
>UM327 (PD), VU211
>>H-3   Hbl-55; Chr-60; Desc-30; Org-27
>>S-1   #86-88. Various treatments

Additional Hymn Suggestions
"We Know That Christ Is Raised" (Acts, Baptism)
>E296, EL449, L189, P495, UM610, VU448, W721

"We Meet You, O Christ" (Acts)
>C183, P311, UM257, VU183

"Come, Let Us with Our Lord Arise" (Pss, John)
>E49, R18, S2084, SF2084

"The Strife Is O'er, the Battle Done" (1 Cor)
>B171, C221, E208, EL366, L135, N242, P119, UM306, VU159,
>W451

"Sing with All the Saints in Glory" (1 Cor) (C)
>EL426, UM702 (PD), W467

"Easter People, Raise Your Voices" (1 Cor, John) (O)
>B360, UM304

"The Day of Resurrection" (1 Cor, John)
>B164, C228, E210, EL361, L141, N245, P118, UM303, VU164

"He Lives" (1 Cor, John)
>B533, C226, F299, UM310

"Cristo Vive" ("Christ Is Risen") (1 Cor, John)
>B167, N235, P109, UM313

"Something Beautiful" (1 Cor)
>F656, UM394

"Christ Is Risen" (1 Cor, John, Communion)
>C222, P104, UM307

"Christ the Lord Is Risen" (John)
>S2116, SF2116

"Thine Be the Glory" (John)
>B163, C218, EL376, F291, L145, N253, P122, UM308, VU173

"In the Garden" (John)
>B187, C227, F588, N237, UM314

"Walk with Me" (John, Mark)
>S2242, SF2242, VU649

"O Sons and Daughters, Let Us Sing" (John, Mark)
>C220, E203, EL386/E387, L139, N244, P116 (PD), UM317,
>VU170, W447

"Christ Is Alive" (Mark)
>B173, E182, EL389, L363, P108, R300, UM318, VU158

"Christ Jesus Lay in Death's Strong Bands" (Mark)
>E186, EL370, L134, P110, UM319 (PD)

"Up from the Grave He Arose" (Mark)
>B160, C224, UM322 (PD)

"Because He Lives" (Mark)
>B407, C562, F292, UM364

Additional Contemporary Suggestions
"Holy and Anointed One" (Acts)
>M32

"Forever" (Pss)
>M68

"I Will Enter His Gates" (Pss)
>S2270, SF2270, SP168

"Grace Alone" (1 Cor)
>M100, S2162, SF2162

"Lord, I Lift Your Name on High" (1 Cor, John)
>EL857, M2, R4, S2088, SF2088

"Our God Reigns" (John)
>SP64

"Jesus Is Alive" (John)
>M20

"Sing Alleluia to the Lord" (John, Mark, Easter)
>B214, C32, S2258, SF2258, R202, SP93

"Alleluia" (Easter)
>B223, C106, F361, N765, R136, SP108, UM186; S-2 #3-4,
>S2078, SF2078 (Alternate Text & Tune)

"Blessing, Honor and Glory" (Easter)
>EL433, M21, R81

"That's Why We Praise Him" (Easter)
>M94

"My Redeemer Lives" (Easter)
>M73

Vocal Solos
"Crown Him, the Risen King" (Easter)
>V-10   p. 55

"The First Day of My Life" (Easter)
>V-11   p. 22

Anthems
"Alleluia! Christ the Lord Is Risen!" (John)
Taylor Davis; Choristers Guild CGA1186
SATB with piano

"Easter Alleluia!" (John)
Mark A. Miller; Abingdon Press 9780687644209
SATB with piano (opt. children's choir)

Other Suggestions
Visuals:
>**Acts**   crucifixion/Resurrection, Acts 10:39a
>**P**   Cornerstone
>**E**   Butterfly, empty tomb, open Bible, empty cross in shroud
>**G**   Basket of spices, stone, angels, shroud, risen Christ

Introit: C41, N236, S139, S2026, SF2026. "Halle, Halle, Halleluja"
>(Easter)

Introit: E175, EL394, L142, N262, UM324, VU163, W444. "Hail
>Thee, Festival Day" (Mark)

Response: B254, F149, P140, R206, S2039, SP141, stanza 5. "Holy,
>Holy" (Easter)

Acts 4:32-35

[32] Now the whole group of those who believed were of one heart and soul, and no one claimed private ownership of any possessions, but everything they owned was held in common. [33] With great power the apostles gave their testimony to the resurrection of the Lord Jesus, and great grace was upon them all. [34] There was not a needy person among them, for as many as owned lands or houses sold them and brought the proceeds of what was sold. [35] They laid it at the apostles' feet, and it was distributed to each as any had need.

Psalm 133

[1] How very good and pleasant it is when kindred live together in unity! [2] It is like the precious oil on the head, running down upon the beard, on the beard of Aaron, running down over the collar of his robes. [3] It is like the dew of Hermon, which falls on the mountains of Zion. For there the LORD ordained his blessing, life forevermore.

1 John 1:1–2:2

[1] We declare to you what was from the beginning, what we have heard, what we have seen with our eyes, what we have looked at and touched with our hands, concerning the word of life— [2] this life was revealed, and we have seen it and testify to it, and declare to you the eternal life that was with the Father and was revealed to us— [3] we declare to you what we have seen and heard so that you also may have fellowship with us; and truly our fellowship is with the Father and with his Son Jesus Christ. [4] We are writing these things so that our joy may be complete.

[5] This is the message we have heard from him and proclaim to you, that God is light and in him there is no darkness at all. [6] If we say that we have fellowship with him while we are walking in darkness, we lie and do not do what is true; [7] but if we walk in the light as he himself is in the light, we have fellowship with one another, and the blood of Jesus his Son cleanses us from all sin. [8] If we say that we have no sin, we deceive ourselves, and the truth is not in us. [9] If we confess our sins, he who is faithful and just will forgive us our sins and cleanse us from all unrighteousness. [10] If we say that we have not sinned, we make him a liar, and his word is not in us.

[1] My little children, I am writing these things to you so that you may not sin. But if anyone does sin, we have an advocate with the Father, Jesus Christ the righteous; [2] and he is the atoning sacrifice for our sins, and not for ours only but also for the sins of the whole world.

John 20:19-31

[19] When it was evening on that day, the first day of the week, and the doors of the house where the disciples had met were locked for fear of the Jews, Jesus came and stood among them and said, "Peace be with you." [20] After he said this, he showed them his hands and his side. Then the disciples rejoiced when they saw the Lord. [21] Jesus said to them again, "Peace be with you. As the Father has sent me, so I send you." [22] When he had said this, he breathed on them and said to them, "Receive the Holy Spirit. [23] If you forgive the sins of any, they are forgiven them; if you retain the sins of any, they are retained."

[24] But Thomas (who was called the Twin), one of the twelve, was not with them when Jesus came. [25] So the other disciples told him, "We have seen the Lord." But he said to them, "Unless I see the mark of the nails in his hands, and put my finger in the mark of the nails and my hand in his side, I will not believe."

[26] A week later his disciples were again in the house, and Thomas was with them. Although the doors were shut, Jesus came and stood among them and said, "Peace be with you." [27] Then he said to Thomas, "Put your finger here and see my hands. Reach out your hand and put it in my side. Do not doubt but believe." [28] Thomas answered him, "My Lord and my God!" [29] Jesus said to him, "Have you believed because you have seen me? Blessed are those who have not seen and yet have come to believe."

[30] Now Jesus did many other signs in the presence of his disciples, which are not written in this book. [31] But these are written so that you may come to believe that Jesus is the Messiah, the Son of God, and that through believing you may have life in his name.

Primary Hymns and Songs for the Day

"Christ Is Risen" (John) (O)
    C222, UM307
        H-3   Chr-113; Desc-102; Org-171
        S-1   #345. Handbell/keyboard arrangement
    P104
"O Look and Wonder" ("Miren Que Bueno!") (Pss)
    C292, EL649, S2231, SF2231, VU856
"Breathe on Me, Breath of God" (John)
    B241, C254, E508, F161, L488, N292, P316, UM420 (PD),
    VU382 (Fr.), W725
        H-3   Hbl-49; Chr-45; Desc-101; Org-166
"We Walk by Faith" (John)
    N256, P399, W572
        H-3   Chr-67
    S2196, SF2196
        H-3   Chr-21
"Without Seeing You" (John)
    S2206, SF2206
"I Want to Walk as a Child of the Light" (1 John) (C)
    E490, EL815, R152, UM206, W510
        S-2   #91. Descant

Additional Hymn Suggestions

"Forward Through the Ages" (Acts)
    N355, UM555 (PD)
"Help Us Accept Each Other" (Acts)
    C487, N388, P358, UM560, W656
"Blest Be the Tie That Binds" (Acts) (C)
    B387, C433, EL656, F560, L370, N393, P438, UM557 (PD),
    VU602
"Trust and Obey" (1 John)
    B447, C556, F454, UM467 (PD)
"Wash, O God, Our Sons and Daughters" (1 John)
    C365, EL445, UM605, VU442
"This Is the Spirit's Entry Now" (1 John, Baptism)
    EL448, L195, UM608, VU451, W722
"Draw Us in the Spirit's Tether" (1 John, Communion)
    C392, EL470, N337, P504, UM632, VU479, W731
"Living for Jesus" (1 John)
    B282, C610, F462, S2149, SF2149
"Just a Closer Walk with Thee" (1 John)
    B448, C557, EL697, F591, S2158, SF2158
"Walk with Me" (1 John, John)
    S2242, SF2242, VU649
"Of All the Spirit's Gifts to Me" (John)
    B442, C270, UM336
"Love Divine, All Loves Excelling" (John)
    B208, C517, E657, EL631 (PD), L315, P376, N43, R196,
    UM384, VU333, W588
"Holy Spirit, Truth Divine" (John)
    C241, EL398, L257, N63, P321, UM465 (PD), VU368
"Come Down, O Love Divine" (John)
    C582, E516, EL804, L508, N289, P313, UM475 (PD), VU367,
    W472
"Let It Breathe on Me" (John)
    C260, N288, UM503
"O Breath of Life" (John)
    C250, UM543, VU202

"Here, O My Lord, I See Thee" (John, Communion)
    C416, E318, F567, L211, N336, P520, UM623, VU459
"Faith Is Patience in the Night" (John)
    S2211, SF2211

Additional Contemporary Suggestions

"We Are the Church" (Acts)
    UM558
"Grace Alone" (Acts)
    S2162, SF2162
"We Are Marching" ("Siyahamba") (1 John)
    C442, EL866, N526, R306, S2235-ab, SF2235-ab, VU646
"Here I Am to Worship" (1 John)
    M116
"Holy, Holy" (1 John)
    B254, F149, P140, R206, S2039, SP141
"Celebrate Love" (1 John, Easter)
    S2073, SF2073
"You Are My King" ("Amazing Love") (1 John)
    M82
"Open Our Eyes, Lord" (John)
    B499, R91, S2086, SF2086, SP199
"The Power of Your Love" (John)
    M26
"I Believe In Jesus" (John)
    M7
"Surely the Presence of the Lord" (John)
    C263, R167, SP243, UM328; S-2, #200 Stanzas for soloist
"Dona Nobis Pacem" (John)
    C297, E712, EL753, R240, UM376 (PD)

Vocal Solos

"Just a Closer Walk with Thee" (1 John)
    V-8   p. 323
"I Know That My Redeemer Liveth" (John, Easter)
    V-2

Anthems

"We Walk by Faith" (John)
Michael Helman; Augsburg 9780800659752
SATB with piano; opt. flute and handbells

"Dona Nobis Pacem" (John)
arr. Hal Hopson; Hope c5181
Two-part with keyboard

Other Suggestions

Visuals:
    Acts Offering plates filled with money
    P   Oil, clasped hands, dew
    E   Light/darkness, water (cleansing), briefcase (advocate),
        1 John 2:1b
    G   Lock, wind (breath) (Holy Spirit), risen Christ, question
        mark, dove, peace
Reading: C238. "I Want to Be Counted in the Upper Room" (Acts)
Prayer: C653, UM639. "Bread and Justice" (Acts, Pss)
Response: C260, N288, UM503. "Let It Breathe on Me" (John)

Acts 3:12-19

[12] When Peter saw it, he addressed the people, "You Israelites, why do you wonder at this, or why do you stare at us, as though by our own power or piety we had made him walk? [13] The God of Abraham, the God of Isaac, and the God of Jacob, the God of our ancestors has glorified his servant Jesus, whom you handed over and rejected in the presence of Pilate, though he had decided to release him. [14] But you rejected the Holy and Righteous One and asked to have a murderer given to you, [15] and you killed the Author of life, whom God raised from the dead. To this we are witnesses. [16] And by faith in his name, his name itself has made this man strong, whom you see and know; and the faith that is through Jesus has given him this perfect health in the presence of all of you.

[17] "And now, friends, I know that you acted in ignorance, as did also your rulers. [18] In this way God fulfilled what he had foretold through all the prophets, that his Messiah would suffer. [19] Repent therefore, and turn to God so that your sins may be wiped out."

Psalm 4

[1] Answer me when I call, O God of my right! You gave me room when I was in distress. Be gracious to me, and hear my prayer. [2] How long, you people, shall my honor suffer shame? How long will you love vain words, and seek after lies? [3] But know that the LORD has set apart the faithful for himself; the LORD hears when I call to him. [4] When you are disturbed, do not sin; ponder it on your beds, and be silent. [5] Offer right sacrifices, and put your trust in the LORD. [6] There are many who say, "O that we might see some good! Let the light of your face shine on us, O LORD!" [7] You have put gladness in my heart more than when their grain and wine abound. [8] I will both lie down and sleep in peace; for you alone, O LORD, make me lie down in safety.

1 John 3:1-7

[1] See what love the Father has given us, that we should be called children of God; and that is what we are. The reason the world does not know us is that it did not know him. [2] Beloved, we are God's children now; what we will be has not yet been revealed. What we do know is this: when he is revealed, we will be like him, for we will see him as he is. [3] And all who have this hope in him purify themselves, just as he is pure.

[4] Everyone who commits sin is guilty of lawlessness; sin is lawlessness. [5] You know that he was revealed to take away sins, and in him there is no sin. [6] No one who abides in him sins; no one who sins has either seen him or known him. [7] Little children, let no one deceive you. Everyone who does what is right is righteous, just as he is righteous.

Luke 24:36b-48

[36b] Jesus himself stood among them and said to them, "Peace be with you." [37] They were startled and terrified, and thought that they were seeing a ghost. [38] He said to them, "Why are you frightened, and why do doubts arise in your hearts? [39] Look at my hands and my feet; see that it is I myself. Touch me and see; for a ghost does not have flesh and bones as you see that I have." [40] And when he had said this, he showed them his hands and his feet. [41] While in their joy they were disbelieving and still wondering, he said to them, "Have you anything here to eat?" [42] They gave him a piece of broiled fish, [43] and he took it and ate in their presence.

[44] Then he said to them, "These are my words that I spoke to you while I was still with you—that everything written about me in the law of Moses, the prophets, and the psalms must be fulfilled." [45] Then he opened their minds to understand the scriptures, [46] and he said to them, "Thus it is written, that the Messiah is to suffer and to rise from the dead on the third day, [47] and that repentance and forgiveness of sins is to be proclaimed in his name to all nations, beginning from Jerusalem. [48] You are witnesses of these things."

Primary Hymns and Songs for the Day
"Thine Be the Glory" (Luke) (O)
  B163, C218, EL376, F291, L145, N253, P122, UM308, VU173
    H-3   Hbl-98; Chr-195; Desc-59
    S-1   #190. Arr. for choir, handbells, tpts., organ
    S-2   #95. Various treatments
"Lead Me, Lord" (Pss)
  C593, N774, R175, UM473 (PD), VU662
"O How He Loves You and Me!" (1 John)
  B146, F622, R27, S2108, SF2108, SP113
"Christ Is Alive" (Acts, Luke) (C)
  B173, E182, EL389, L363, P108, R300, UM318, VU158
    H-3   Hbl-50; Chr-47; Desc-101; Org-167
    S-1   #334-35. Descant and harmonization

Additional Hymn Suggestions
"Come, Ye Sinners, Poor and Needy" (Acts)
  B323 (PD), R141, UM340, W756
"And Can It Be That I Should Gain" (Acts)
  B147, F260, R193, UM363 (PD)
"He Lives" (Acts, Luke)
  B533, C226, F299, UM310
"God of Grace and God of Glory" (Acts)
  B395, C464, E594/E595, EL705, F528, L415, N436, P420, R301,
  UM577, VU686
"Lead Me, Guide Me" (Pss)
  C583, EL768, R176, S2214, SF2214
"The Strife Is O'er, the Battle Done" (1 John)
  B171, C221, E208, EL366, L135, N242, P119, UM306, VU159,
  W451
"He Came Down" (1 John)
  EL253, S2085, SF2085
"There Are Some Things I May Not Know" (1 John)
  N405, S2147, SF2147
"Baptized in Water" (1 John, Baptism)
  B362, E294, EL456, P492, S2248, W720
"Jesus, the Very Thought of Thee" (1 John, Luke)
  B225, C102, E642, EL754, F465, L316, N507, P310, UM175
  (PD)
"O Love, How Deep" (1 John, Luke)
  E448/E449, EL322, L88, N209, P83, UM267 (PD), VU348
"Easter People, Raise Your Voices" (Luke) (O)
  B360, UM304
"Heleluyan" (Luke)
  EL171, P595, R137, UM78
"We Meet You, O Christ" (Luke)
  C183, P311, UM257, VU183
"Come, Ye Faithful, Raise the Strain" (Luke)
  C215, E199, EL363, L132, N230, P115, UM315 (PD), VU165,
  W456
"Christ Has Risen" (Luke)
  S2115, SF2115
"He Touched Me" (Luke)
  C564, F628, UM367
"'Tis So Sweet to Trust in Jesus" (Luke)
  B411, F91, UM462 (PD)
"Blessed Jesus, at Thy Word" (Luke)
  E440, EL520, N74, P454, R93, UM596 (PD), VU500
"Sent Out in Jesus' Name" (Luke)
  EL538, S2184, SF2184

"Here, O My Lord, I See Thee" (Luke, Communion)
  C416, E318, F567, L211, N336, P520, UM623, VU459
"Come, Share the Lord" (Luke, Communion)
  C408, S2269, SF2269, VU469

Additional Contemporary Suggestions
"We Bring the Sacrifice of Praise" (Pss)
  R3, S2031, SF2031, SP1
"Holy, Holy" (1 John)
  B254, F149, P140, R206, S2039, SP141
"Celebrate Love" (1 John)
  S2073, SF2073
"Behold, What Manner of Love" (1 John)
  SP48
"Above All" (1 John, Luke, Easter)
  M77; V-3 p. 17 Vocal Solo
"Open the Eyes of My Heart" (Luke)
  M57; V-3 p. 162 Vocal Solo
"Jesus Is Alive" (Luke, Easter)
  M20
"Lord God, Almighty" (Luke)
  R40, S2006, SF2006
"Open Our Eyes, Lord" (Luke)
  B499, R91, S2086, SF2086, SP199
"Jesus, We Are Here" (Luke)
  EL529, S2273, SF2273
"Turn Your Eyes upon Jesus" (Luke)
  B320, F621, SP218, UM349
"Shalom to You" (Luke)
  C436, UM666

Vocal Solos
"Author of Life Divine" (Acts)
V-1   p. 39
"I Walked Today Where Jesus Walked" (Luke, Easter)
V-8   p. 14

Anthems
"As Tenderly as a Father" (1 John)
John Shepherd; Hinshaw HMC-472
Two-part with keyboard

"O Sacrum Convivium" (Luke)
James Biery; Morningstar MSM60-8311
SATB *a cappella*

Other Suggestions
Visuals:
  Acts Portrait of Christ crucified, risen, names given to Jesus,
        eraser (forgiveness)
  P   Praying hands, person pondering, light, rejoicing
  E   Children, risen Christ, 1 John 3:1
  G   Risen Christ, fear, broiled fish, open Bible, Luke 24:36c,
        48, witnessing
Introit: EL529, S2273, SF2273. "Jesus, We Are Here" (Luke)
Response: EL751, S2200, SF2200. "O Lord, Hear My Prayer" (Pss)

Acts 4:5-12

[5] The next day their rulers, elders, and scribes assembled in Jerusalem, [6] with Annas the high priest, Caiaphas, John, and Alexander, and all who were of the high-priestly family. [7] When they had made the prisoners stand in their midst, they inquired, "By what power or by what name did you do this?" [8] Then Peter, filled with the Holy Spirit, said to them, "Rulers of the people and elders, [9] if we are questioned today because of a good deed done to someone who was sick and are asked how this man has been healed, [10] let it be known to all of you, and to all the people of Israel, that this man is standing before you in good health by the name of Jesus Christ of Nazareth, whom you crucified, whom God raised from the dead. [11] This Jesus is 'the stone that was rejected by you, the builders; it has become the cornerstone.' [12] There is salvation in no one else, for there is no other name under heaven given among mortals by which we must be saved."

Psalm 23

[1] The LORD is my shepherd, I shall not want. [2] He makes me lie down in green pastures; he leads me beside still waters; [3] he restores my soul. He leads me in right paths for his name's sake. [4] Even though I walk through the darkest valley, I fear no evil; for you are with me; your rod and your staff—they comfort me. [5] You prepare a table before me in the presence of my enemies; you anoint my head with oil; my cup overflows. [6] Surely goodness and mercy shall follow me all the days of my life, and I shall dwell in the house of the LORD my whole life long.

1 John 3:16-24

[16] We know love by this, that he laid down his life for us—and we ought to lay down our lives for one another. [17] How does God's love abide in anyone who has the world's goods and sees a brother or sister in need and yet refuses help?

[18] Little children, let us love, not in word or speech, but in truth and action. [19] And by this we will know that we are from the truth and will reassure our hearts before him [20] whenever our hearts condemn us; for God is greater than our hearts, and he knows everything. [21] Beloved, if our hearts do not condemn us, we have boldness before God; [22] and we receive from him whatever we ask, because we obey his commandments and do what pleases him.

[23] And this is his commandment, that we should believe in the name of his Son Jesus Christ and love one another, just as he has commanded us. [24] All who obey his commandments abide in him, and he abides in them. And by this we know that he abides in us, by the Spirit that he has given us.

John 10:11-18

[11] "I am the good shepherd. The good shepherd lays down his life for the sheep. [12] The hired hand, who is not the shepherd and does not own the sheep, sees the wolf coming and leaves the sheep and runs away—and the wolf snatches them and scatters them. [13] The hired hand runs away because a hired hand does not care for the sheep. [14] I am the good shepherd. I know my own and my own know me, [15] just as the Father knows me and I know the Father. And I lay down my life for the sheep. [16] I have other sheep that do not belong to this fold. I must bring them also, and they will listen to my voice. So there will be one flock, one shepherd. [17] For this reason the Father loves me, because I lay down my life in order to take it up again. [18] No one takes it from me, but I lay it down of my own accord. I have power to lay it down, and I have power to take it up again. I have received this command from my Father."

Primary Hymns and Songs for the Day

"The Church's One Foundation" (Acts) (O)
  B350, C272, E525, EL654, F547, L369, N386, P442, UM545
  (PD) and UM 546, VU332 (Fr.)
    H-3   Hbl-94; Chr-180; Desc-16; Org-9
    S-1   #25-26. Descant and harmonization
"The King of Love My Shepherd Is" (Pss, 1 John, John)
  E645, EL502, L456, P171, R106, UM138 (PD), VU273, W609
    H-3   Hbl-96; Chr-188, 221; Desc-93; Org-135
    S-1   #298-299. Harmonizations
"Savior, Like a Shepherd Lead Us" (Pss, John)
  B61, C558, E708, EL789, F601, L481, N252, P387, UM381 (PD)
    H-3   Chr-167; Org-15
    S-2   #29. Harmonization
"Lead Me, Guide Me" (Pss)
  C583, EL768, R176, S2214, SF2214
"Shepherd Me, O God" (Pss, John)
  EL780, S2058, SF2058
"Christ Is Made the Sure Foundation" (Acts) (C)
  C275, E518, EL645, P416, UM559 (PD), VU325, W617
    H-3   Chr-49; Desc-103; Org-180
    S-1   #346. Descant
  F557, N400, P417
    H-3   Chr-30, 48, 62; Desc-89; Org-121
    S-1   #280. Descant and harmonization
  B356 (PD), L367

Additional Hymn Suggestions

"At the Name of Jesus" (Acts)
  B198 (PD), E435, F351, L179, P148, R133, UM168, VU335, W499
"We Are God's People" (Acts)
  B383, F546, S2220, SF2220
"He Leadeth Me: O Blessed Thought" (Pss) (O)
  B52, C545, F606, L501, UM128 (PD), VU657
"The Lord's My Shepherd, I'll Not Want" (Pss)
  C79, EL778, F40/F42, L451, N479, P170, UM136, VU748
"Close to Thee" (Pss)
  B464, F405, UM407 (PD)
"Precious Lord, Take My Hand" (Pss)
  B456, C628, EL773, F611, N472, P404, UM474, VU670
"Send Me, Lord" (Pss)
  C447, EL809, N360, R308, UM497, VU572
"Jesus Walked This Lonesome Valley" (Pss)
  C211, F217, P80, S2112, W427
"Abide with Me" (Pss, 1 John, John) (C)
  B63, C636, E662, EL629, F500, L272, N99, P543, UM700
  (PD), VU436
"The Gift of Love" (1 John)
  B423, C526, EL644, P335, R155, UM408, VU372
"Cuando El Pobre" ("When the Poor Ones") (1 John)
  C662, EL725, P407, UM434, VU702
"Where Charity and Love Prevail" (1 John)
  E581, EL359, L126, N396, UM549
"My Song Is Love Unknown" (1 John)
  E458, EL343, L94, N222, P76, S2083, SF2083, VU143, W439
"They'll Know We Are Christians" (1 John)
  C494, S2223, SF2223

"How Like a Gentle Spirit" (John)
  C69, N443, UM115
"Ah, Holy Jesus" (John)
  C210, E158, EL349, L123, N218, P93, R183, UM289 (PD),
  VU138
"I Am Thine, O Lord" (John)
  B290, C601, F455, N455, UM419 (PD)

Additional Contemporary Suggestions

"Grace Alone" (Acts)
  M100, S2162, SF2162
"In Christ Alone" (Acts, Easter)
  M138
"Nothing Can Trouble" ("Nada Te Turbe") (Pss)
  S2054, SF2054, VU290
"Lamb of God" (Pss)
  EL336, S2113, SF2113
"Father, I Adore You" (1 John)
  B256, F414, S2038, SF2038, SP194
"Make Us One" (1 John)
  S2224, SF2224, SP137
"Bind Us Together" (1 John)
  R292, S2226, SF2226, SP140
"I Could Sing of Your Love Forever" (1 John)
  M63; V-3 p. 22 Vocal Solo
"His Name Is Wonderful" (1 John)
  B203, F230, R30, SP90, UM174
"People Need the Lord" (1 John, John)
  B557, S2244, SF2244

Vocal Solos

"How Firm a Foundation" (Acts)
V-6   p. 31
"God, Our Ever Faithful Shepherd" (Pss)
V-4   p. 15
"My Shepherd Will Supply My Need" (Pss)
V-10   p. 4

Anthems

"The Lord Is My Shepherd" (Pss)
Randall Thompson; E.C. Schirmer 2688
SATB with keyboard or harp

"My Shepherd Will Supply My Need" (Pss)
Mack Wilburg; Hinshaw HMC1424
SATB with flute, oboe, harp (keyboard)

Other Suggestions

Visuals:
    Acts   Stone, cornerstone
    P   Shepherd, Christ as a shepherd, sheep, water, path
    E   Cross, people sacrificing for others,
             pitcher/bowl/towel
    G   Christ the Shepherd, sheep, wolf, crucifix, John 10:11
Prayer: UM457 (Acts) or UM460 (Pss)
Response: C523, EL642, R226, S2179, SF2179, W604. "Live in
  Charity" (1 John)

Acts 8:26-40

26 Then an angel of the Lord said to Philip, "Get up and go toward the south to the road that goes down from Jerusalem to Gaza." (This is a wilderness road.) 27 So he got up and went. Now there was an Ethiopian eunuch, a court official of the Candace, queen of the Ethiopians, in charge of her entire treasury. He had come to Jerusalem to worship 28 and was returning home; seated in his chariot, he was reading the prophet Isaiah. 29 Then the Spirit said to Philip, "Go over to this chariot and join it." 30 So Philip ran up to it and heard him reading the prophet Isaiah. He asked, "Do you understand what you are reading?" 31 He replied, "How can I, unless someone guides me?" And he invited Philip to get in and sit beside him. 32 Now the passage of the scripture that he was reading was this: "Like a sheep he was led to the slaughter, and like a lamb silent before its shearer, so he does not open his mouth. 33 In his humiliation justice was denied him. Who can describe his generation? For his life is taken away from the earth." 34 The eunuch asked Philip, "About whom, may I ask you, does the prophet say this, about himself or about someone else?" 35 Then Philip began to speak, and starting with this scripture, he proclaimed to him the good news about Jesus. 36 As they were going along the road, they came to some water; and the eunuch said, "Look, here is water! What is to prevent me from being baptized?" 38 He commanded the chariot to stop, and both of them, Philip and the eunuch, went down into the water, and Philip baptized him. 39 When they came up out of the water, the Spirit of the Lord snatched Philip away; the eunuch saw him no more, and went on his way rejoicing. 40 But Philip found himself at Azotus, and as he was passing through the region, he proclaimed the good news to all the towns until he came to Caesarea.

Psalm 22:25-31

25 From you comes my praise in the great congregation; my vows I will pay before those who fear him. 26 The poor shall eat and be satisfied; those who seek him shall praise the LORD. May your hearts live forever! 27 All the ends of the earth shall remember and turn to the LORD; and all the families of the nations shall worship before him. 28 For dominion belongs to the LORD, and he rules over the nations. 29 To him, indeed, shall all who sleep in the earth bow down; before him shall bow all who go down to the dust, and I shall live for him. 30 Posterity will serve him; future generations will be told about the Lord, 31 and proclaim his deliverance to a people yet unborn, saying that he has done it.

1 John 4:7-21

7 Beloved, let us love one another, because love is from God; everyone who loves is born of God and knows God. 8 Whoever does not love does not know God, for God is love. 9 God's love was revealed among us in this way: God sent his only Son into the world so that we might live through him. 10 In this is love, not that we loved God but that he loved us and sent his Son to be the atoning sacrifice for our sins. 11 Beloved, since God loved us so much, we also ought to love one another. 12 No one has ever seen God; if we love one another, God lives in us, and his love is perfected in us.

13 By this we know that we abide in him and he in us, because he has given us of his Spirit. 14 And we have seen and do testify that the Father has sent his Son as the Savior of the world. 15 God abides in those who confess that Jesus is the Son of God, and they abide in God. 16 So we have known and believe the love that God has for us.

God is love, and those who abide in love abide in God, and God abides in them. 17 Love has been perfected among us in this: that we may have boldness on the day of judgment, because as he is, so are we in this world. 18 There is no fear in love, but perfect love casts out fear; for fear has to do with punishment, and whoever fears has not reached perfection in love. 19 We love because he first loved us. 20 Those who say, "I love God," and hate their brothers or sisters, are liars; for those who do not love a brother or sister whom they have seen, cannot love God whom they have not seen. 21 The commandment we have from him is this: those who love God must love their brothers and sisters also.

John 15:1-8

1 "I am the true vine, and my Father is the vinegrower. 2 He removes every branch in me that bears no fruit. Every branch that bears fruit he prunes to make it bear more fruit. 3 You have already been cleansed by the word that I have spoken to you. 4 Abide in me as I abide in you. Just as the branch cannot bear fruit by itself unless it abides in the vine, neither can you unless you abide in me. 5 I am the vine, you are the branches. Those who abide in me and I in them bear much fruit, because apart from me you can do nothing. 6 Whoever does not abide in me is thrown away like a branch and withers; such branches are gathered, thrown into the fire, and burned. 7 If you abide in me, and my words abide in you, ask for whatever you wish, and it will be done for you. 8 My Father is glorified by this, that you bear much fruit and become my disciples."

Primary Hymns and Songs for the Day
"We Know That Christ Is Raised" (Acts, Baptism) (O)
    E296, EL449, L189, P495, UM610, VU448, W721
       H-3   Hbl-100; Chr-214; Desc-38; Org-37
       S-1   #118-127. Various treatments
"I Need Thee Every Hour" (John)
    B450, C578, F443, N517, UM397 (PD), VU671
       H-3   Chr-107
"O Blessed Spring" (John)
    EL447, S2076, SF2076, VU632
"Go, Make of All Disciples" (Acts) (C)
    UM571, W628
       H-3   Hbl-74; Chr-123; Desc-64; Org-71
       S-1   #9-197. Various treatments

Additional Hymn Suggestions
"Hallelujah! What a Savior" (Acts)
    B175, F246, UM165 (PD)
"Ah, Holy Jesus" (Acts)
    C210, E158, EL349, L123, N218, P93, R183, UM289 (PD), VU138
"Deep in the Shadows of the Past" (Acts)
    N320, P330, S2246
"Wonder of Wonders" (Acts, Baptism)
    C378, N328, P499, S2247
"Baptized in Water" (Acts, Baptism)
    B362, E294, EL456, P492, S2248, W720
"Loving Spirit" (Acts)
    C244, EL397, P323, S2123, SF2123, VU387
"Stand Up, and Bless the Lord" (Pss, 1 John)
    B30, P491, UM662 (PD)
"For the Beauty of the Earth" (1 John)
    B44, C56, E416, EL879, F1, L561, P473, N28, UM92 (PD), VU226, W557
"To God Be the Glory" (1 John)
    B153, C39, F365, N14, R68, UM99; V-8 p. 5 Vocal Solo
"There's a Wideness in God's Mercy" (1 John)
    B25, C73, E470, EL587/EL588, F115, L290, N23, P298, UM121, VU271, W595
"My Jesus, I Love Thee" (1 John)
    B210, C349, F456, R275, UM172 (PD)
"Jesu, Thy Boundless Love to Me" (1 John)
    B123, L336, P366, UM183, VU631
"Of the Father's Love Begotten" (1 John)
    B251, C104, E82, EL295, F172 (PD), L42, N118, P309, R252, UM184, VU61, W398
"Where Charity and Love Prevail" (1 John)
    E581, EL359, L126, N396, UM549
"What Wondrous Love Is This" (1 John)
    B143 (PD), C200, E439, EL666, F283, L385, N223, P85, R277, UM292, VU147 (Fr.), W600
"Camina, Pueblo de Dios" ("Walk On, O People of God") (1 John, Easter)
    N614, P296, UM305
"O Perfect Love" (1 John)
    B512, F530, L287, P533, UM645, VU491
"Your Love, O God, Has Called Us Here" (1 John)
    EL358, P353, UM579
"How Firm a Foundation" (John)
    B338, C618, E636, EL796, F32, L507, N407, P361, UM529 (PD), VU660, W585
"Like the Murmur of the Dove's Song" (John)
    C245, E513, EL403, N270, P314, R280, UM544, VU205
"Mothering God, You Gave Me Birth" (John)
    C83, EL735, N467, S2050, SF2050, VU320
"God the Sculptor of the Mountains" (John)
    EL736, S2060, SF2060

Additional Contemporary Suggestions
"I've Just Come from the Fountain" (Acts, Baptism)
    S2250, SF2250
"Great Is the Lord" (1 John)
    B12, R22, S2022, SF2022, SP30
"Live in Charity" ("Ubi Caritas") (1 John)
    C523, EL642, R226, S2179, SF2179, W604
"They'll Know We Are Christians" (1 John)
    C494, S2223, SF2223
"Make Us One" (1 John)
    S2224, SF2224, SP137
"Bind Us Together" (1 John)
    R292, S2226, SF2226, SP140
"No Greater Love" (1 John)
    M25
"I Could Sing of Your Love Forever" (1 John)
    M63; V-3 p. 22 Vocal Solo
"You Are My King" ("Amazing Love") (1 John)
    M82
"Be Glorified" (John)
    M13
"Lord, Be Glorified" (John)
    B457, EL744, S2150, SF2150, R172, SP196

Vocal Solos
"Wondrous Love" (1 John)
V-6   p. 47
"I Am the Vine" (John)
V-8   p. 280

Anthems
"Let Us Love One Another" (1 John)
Sherman/ arr. Lau Lorenz 10/2788S
SATB with keyboard

"Thou Art the Vine" (John)
Andrew Carter; MorningStar 50-8504
SATB with keyboard, opt. handbells

Other Suggestions
Visuals:
  Acts Open scroll/Bible open to Isaiah, water (baptism)
  P Poor being fed, globe, flags of nations, earth from space
  E Cross, sacrificial love, Christ, 1 John 4:16b, 18a
  G Grapevine, grapes, pruned branches, fire, John 15:5
Canticle: C525. "Song of Love" (John)
Prayer: C98 (John) or UM401 (1 John)

Acts 10:44-48

[44] While Peter was still speaking, the Holy Spirit fell upon all who heard the word. [45] The circumcised believers who had come with Peter were astounded that the gift of the Holy Spirit had been poured out even on the Gentiles, [46] for they heard them speaking in tongues and extolling God. Then Peter said, [47] "Can anyone withhold the water for baptizing these people who have received the Holy Spirit just as we have?" [48] So he ordered them to be baptized in the name of Jesus Christ. Then they invited him to stay for several days.

Psalm 98

[1] O sing to the LORD a new song, for he has done marvelous things. His right hand and his holy arm have gotten him victory. [2] The LORD has made known his victory; he has revealed his vindication in the sight of the nations. [3] He has remembered his steadfast love and faithfulness to the house of Israel. All the ends of the earth have seen the victory of our God. [4] Make a joyful noise to the LORD, all the earth; break forth into joyous song and sing praises. [5] Sing praises to the LORD with the lyre, with the lyre and the sound of melody. [6] With trumpets and the sound of the horn make a joyful noise before the King, the LORD. [7] Let the sea roar, and all that fills it; the world and those who live in it. [8] Let the floods clap their hands; let the hills sing together for joy [9] at the presence of the LORD, for he is coming to judge the earth. He will judge the world with righteousness, and the peoples with equity.

1 John 5:1-6

[1] Everyone who believes that Jesus is the Christ has been born of God, and everyone who loves the parent loves the child. [2] By this we know that we love the children of God, when we love God and obey his commandments. [3] For the love of God is this, that we obey his commandments. And his commandments are not burdensome, [4] for whatever is born of God conquers the world. And this is the victory that conquers the world, our faith. [5] Who is it that conquers the world but the one who believes that Jesus is the Son of God?

[6] This is the one who came by water and blood, Jesus Christ, not with the water only but with the water and the blood. And the Spirit is the one that testifies, for the Spirit is the truth.

John 15:9-17

[9] "As the Father has loved me, so I have loved you; abide in my love. [10] If you keep my commandments, you will abide in my love, just as I have kept my Father's commandments and abide in his love. [11] I have said these things to you so that my joy may be in you, and that your joy may be complete.

[12] "This is my commandment, that you love one another as I have loved you. [13] No one has greater love than this, to lay down one's life for one's friends. [14] You are my friends if you do what I command you. [15] I do not call you servants any longer, because the servant does not know what the master is doing; but I have called you friends, because I have made known to you everything that I have heard from my Father. [16] You did not choose me but I chose you. And I appointed you to go and bear fruit, fruit that will last, so that the Father will give you whatever you ask him in my name. [17] I am giving you these commands so that you may love one another."

Primary Hymns and Songs for the Day

"Praise to the Lord, the Almighty" (Pss) (O)
B14, C25, E390, EL858 (PD) and 859, F337, L543, N22, P482, R57, UM139, VU220 (Fr.) and VU221, W547
  H-3   Hbl-89; Chr-163; Desc-69; Org-79
  S-1   #218-222. Various treatments

"Spirit of the Living God" (Acts)
B244, C259, F155, N283, P322, R90, SP131, UM393, VU376
  H-3   Chr-176
  S-1   #212. Vocal descant idea

"Sing a New Song to the Lord" (Pss)
S2045, SF2045, W550

"Blest Be the Tie That Binds" (1 Cor, Christian Home) (C)
B387, C433, EL656, F560, L370, N393, P438, UM557 (PD), VU602
  H-3   Hbl-49; Chr-14; Desc-27; Org-25

Additional Hymn Suggestions

"At the Font We Start Our Journey" (Acts, Baptism)
N308, S2114, SF2114

"Wonder of Wonders" (Acts, Baptism)
C378, N328, P499, S2247

"Baptized in Water" (Acts, Baptism)
B362, E294, EL456, P492, S2248, W720

"We Were Baptized in Christ Jesus" (Acts, Baptism)
EL451, S2251, SF2251

"Like the Murmur of the Dove's Song" (Acts)
C245, E513, EL403, N270, P314, R280, UM544, VU205

"In Christ There Is No East or West" (Acts, John)
B385, C687, E529, EL650 (PD), F685, L359, N394/N395, P439/P440, UM548, VU606, W659

"Help Us Accept Each Other" (Acts, John) (C)
C487, N388, P358, UM560, W656

"Come Down, O Love Divine" (Acts, John)
C582, E516, EL804, L508, N289, P313, UM475 (PD), VU367, W472

"Filled with the Spirit's Power" (Acts, John)
L160, N266, UM537, VU194

"Here, O Lord, Your Servants Gather" (Acts, John)
B179, C278, EL530, N72, P465, UM552, VU362 (Fr.)

"Praise the Lord Who Reigns Above" (Pss)
B33, R253, UM96 (PD)

"Blessed Assurance" (1 John)
B334, C543, EL638, F67, N473, P341, UM369 (PD), VU337

"For the Healing of the Nations" (1 John)
C668, N576, UM428, VU678, W643

"Weary of All Trumpeting" (1 John)
E572, UM442, W635

"Our Parent, by Whose Name" (1 John, Christian Home)
E587, EL640, L357, UM447, VU555, W570

"I Come with Joy" (John, Communion)
B371, C420, E304, EL482, P607, R195, UM617, W726

"Blessed Quietness" (John)
F145, C267, N284, S2142, SF2142

"Healer of Our Every Ill" (John)
C506, EL612, S2213, SF2213, VU619

"Let Us Be Bread" (John, Communion)
S2260, SF2260

"A Mother Lined a Basket" (Mother's Day)
S2189, SF2189

Additional Contemporary Suggestions

"I've Just Come from the Fountain" (Acts, Baptism)
S2250, SF2250

"Shout to the Lord" (Pss)
EL821, S2074, SF2074, M16; V-3 p. 56 Vocal Solo

"I Will Celebrate" (Pss)
R77, M46, SP147

"Jesus, Draw Me Close" (1 John)
S2159, SF2159, M48

"Goodness Is Stronger Than Evil" (1 John)
EL721, S2219, SF2219

"They'll Know We Are Christians" (John)
C494, S2223, SF2223

"Bind Us Together" (John)
R292, S2226, SF2226, SP140

"Make Us One" (John)
S2224, SF2224, SP137

"Live in Charity" ("Ubi Caritas") (John)
C523, EL642, R226, S2179, SF2179, W604

"No Greater Love" (John)
M25

"I Could Sing of Your Love Forever" (John)
M63; V-3 p. 22 Vocal Solo

"The Family Prayer Song" (Christian Home)
M54, S2188, SF2188

Vocal Solos

"I Will Sing of Thy Great Mercies" (John)
V-4   p. 43

"This Is My Commandment" (John)
V-8   p. 284

Anthems

"Welcome" (Acts, John)
Mark A. Miller; Abingdon Press 9780687644407
SATB with solo (opt.) with piano

"Those Who Love and Care for Me" (Mother's Day)
Vicki Hancock Wright; Choristers Guild CGA1185
Unison with piano

Other Suggestions

Visuals:
  Acts Dove/flames (Holy Spirit), water (baptism)
  P   Lyre, sheet music, trumpet, sea, floods, hills, scales of justice
  E   Water, wine, symbols of the Holy Spirit
  G   Sacrificial love, cross, friendship, fruit (love enacted), John 15:9c
Greeting: Ps 98:1. "Sing to the Lord."
Opening Prayer: UM335 (Acts)
Prayer: C364 or F542 (Christian Home)
Prayer: UM481 (1 John, John)
Canticle: UM646. "Canticle of Love" (John). See S-1, p. 387
Blessing: N873 (Mother's Day)

Acts 1:1-11

[1] In the first book, Theophilus, I wrote about all that Jesus did and taught from the beginning [2] until the day when he was taken up to heaven, after giving instructions through the Holy Spirit to the apostles whom he had chosen. [3] After his suffering he presented himself alive to them by many convincing proofs, appearing to them during forty days and speaking about the kingdom of God. [4] While staying with them, he ordered them not to leave Jerusalem, but to wait there for the promise of the Father. "This," he said, "is what you have heard from me; [5] for John baptized with water, but you will be baptized with the Holy Spirit not many days from now."

[6] So when they had come together, they asked him, "Lord, is this the time when you will restore the kingdom to Israel?" [7] He replied, "It is not for you to know the times or periods that the Father has set by his own authority. [8] But you will receive power when the Holy Spirit has come upon you; and you will be my witnesses in Jerusalem, in all Judea and Samaria, and to the ends of the earth." [9] When he had said this, as they were watching, he was lifted up, and a cloud took him out of their sight. [10] While he was going and they were gazing up toward heaven, suddenly two men in white robes stood by them. [11] They said, "Men of Galilee, why do you stand looking up toward heaven? This Jesus, who has been taken up from you into heaven, will come in the same way as you saw him go into heaven."

Psalm 47

[1] Clap your hands, all you peoples; shout to God with loud songs of joy. [2] For the LORD, the Most High, is awesome, a great king over all the earth. [3] He subdued peoples under us, and nations under our feet. [4] He chose our heritage for us, the pride of Jacob whom he loves. [5] God has gone up with a shout, the LORD with the sound of a trumpet. [6] Sing praises to God, sing praises; sing praises to our King, sing praises. [7] For God is the king of all the earth; sing praises with a psalm. [8] God is king over the nations; God sits on his holy throne. [9] The princes of the peoples gather as the people of the God of Abraham. For the shields of the earth belong to God; he is highly exalted.

Ephesians 1:15-23

[15] I have heard of your faith in the Lord Jesus and your love toward all the saints, and for this reason [16] I do not cease to give thanks for you as I remember you in my prayers. [17] I pray that the God of our Lord Jesus Christ, the Father of glory, may give you a spirit of wisdom and revelation as you come to know him, [18] so that, with the eyes of your heart enlightened, you may know what is the hope to which he has called you, what are the riches of his glorious inheritance among the saints, [19] and what is the immeasurable greatness of his power for us who believe, according to the working of his great power. [20] God put this power to work in Christ when he raised him from the dead and seated him at his right hand in the heavenly places, [21] far above all rule and authority and power and dominion, and above every name that is named, not only in this age but also in the age to come. [22] And he has put all things under his feet and has made him the head over all things for the church, [23] which is his body, the fullness of him who fills all in all.

Luke 24:44-53

[44] Then he said to them, "These are my words that I spoke to you while I was still with you—that everything written about me in the law of Moses, the prophets, and the psalms must be fulfilled." [45] Then he opened their minds to understand the scriptures, [46] and he said to them, "Thus it is written, that the Messiah is to suffer and to rise from the dead on the third day, [47] and that repentance and forgiveness of sins is to be proclaimed in his name to all nations, beginning from Jerusalem. [48] You are witnesses of these things. [49] And see, I am sending upon you what my Father promised; so stay here in the city until you have been clothed with power from on high."

[50] Then he led them out as far as Bethany, and, lifting up his hands, he blessed them. [51] While he was blessing them, he withdrew from them and was carried up into heaven. [52] And they worshiped him, and returned to Jerusalem with great joy; [53] and they were continually in the temple blessing God.

Primary Hymns and Songs for the Day

"Hail the Day That Sees Him Rise" (Acts, Luke) (O)
  E214, UM312, W471 (PD)
    H-3   Hbl-72; Chr-50; Desc-69; Org-78
    S-1   #213. Descant
  B165, N260, VU189
"Shout to the Lord" (Pss)
  EL821, S2074, SF2074, M16; V-3 p. 56 Vocal Solo
"Crown Him with Many Crowns" (Pss, Eph, Luke)
  B161, C234, E494, EL855, F345, L170, N301, P151, R56,
  UM327 (PD), VU211
    H-3   Hbl-55; Chr-60; Desc-30; Org-27
    S-1   #86-88. Various treatments
"Jesus Shall Reign" (Pss, Eph) (C)
  B587, C95, E544, EL434, F238, L530, N157, P423, R296,
  UM157 (PD), VU330, W492
    H-3   Hbl-29, 57; Chr-117; Desc-31; Org-31
    S-1   #100-103. Various treatments.

Additional Hymn Suggestions

"Swing Low, Sweet Chariot" (Acts)
  C643, UM703
"Wonder of Wonders" (Acts, Baptism)
  C378, N328, P499, S2247
"Ask Ye What Great Thing I Know" (Acts, Luke)
  B538, N49, UM163 (PD), VU338
"Christ, Whose Glory Fills the Skies" (Acts, Luke)
  E7, EL553, F293, L265, P462, UM173 (PD), VU336
"Christ the Lord Is Risen Today" (Acts, Luke)
  B159, C216, EL373, F289, L130, N233, P113, UM302 (PD),
  VU155 and VU157, W462/W463
"Easter People, Raise Your Voices" (Acts, Luke)
  B360, UM304
"Thine Be the Glory" (Acts, Luke)
  B163, C218, EL376, F291, L145, N253, P122, UM308, VU173
"He Lives" (Acts, Luke)
  B533, C226, F299, UM310
"Christ Is Alive" (Acts, Luke)
  B173, E182, EL389, L363, P108, R300, UM318, VU158
"Christ Jesus Lay in Death's Strong Bands" (Acts, Luke)
  E186, EL370, L134, P110, UM319 (PD)
"Hail Thee, Festival Day" (Acts, Luke)
  E216, EL394, L142, N262, P120, UM324, VU163
"For All the Saints" (Acts, Eph)
  B355, C637, E287, EL422, F614, L174, N299, P526, UM711
  (PD), VU705, W705
"Jesus, the Very Thought of Thee" (Eph)
  B225, C102, E642, EL754, F465, L316, N507, P310, UM175 (PD)
"Hope of the World" (Eph)
  C538, E472, L493, N46, P360, UM178, VU215, W565
"My Hope Is Built" (Eph)
  B406, C537, EL596, F92, L293/L294, N368, P379, UM368 (PD)
"There Are Some Things I May Not Know" (Eph)
  N405, S2147, SF2147
"We Are God's People" (Eph)
  B383, F546, S2220, SF2220
"Come, Share the Lord" (Eph, Communion)
  C408, S2269, SF2269, VU469
"Sent Out in Jesus' Name" (Luke)
  EL538, S2184, SF2184

"As We Gather at Your Table" (Luke, Communion)
  EL522, N332, S2268, SF2268, VU457
"I'll Fly Away" (Luke, Ascension)
  N595, S2282, SF2282

Additional Contemporary Suggestions

"Holy Spirit, Come to Us" (Acts)
  EL406, S2118, SF2118, W473
"Kumbayah" ("Come By Here") (Acts)
  C590, P338, UM494
"Holy Spirit, Rain Down" (Acts)
  M88
"Shout to the Lord" (Pss)
  EL821, S2074, SF2074, M16; V-3 p. 56 Vocal Solo
"He Is Exalted" (Pss, Ascension)
  R238, S2070, SF2070, SP66
"Above All" (Eph, Ascension)
  M77; V-3 p. 17 Vocal Solo
"Lord God, Almighty" (Luke)
  R40, S2006, SF2006
"Christ the Lord Is Risen" (Luke, Ascension)
  S2116, SF2116
"Lord, I Lift Your Name on High" (Ascension)
  EL857, M2, R4, S2088, SF2088
"Once Again" (Ascension)
  M78
"In Christ Alone" (Ascension)
  M138

Vocal Solos

"Jesus Christ Is Risen Today" (Acts, Luke)
V-1   p. 50
"Ride On, Jesus" (Ascension)
V-7   p. 8
"Rejoice Now, My Spirit" (Ascension)
V-9   p. 30

Anthems

"Gaelic Benediction" (Acts, Luke)
Jerry Ulrich; Abingdon Press 9780687114845
SAB with piano (opt. C Instrument)

"Christus Paradox" (Ascension)
Alfred Fedak; GIA G-5463
SATB with organ

Other Suggestions

Visuals:
  Acts   Water, dove, flames, shell (baptism)
  P   Clapping hands, feet, trumpet, singing, shield
  E   Witnessing, Ascension, risen Christ, saints
  G   Bible, risen Christ, map or globe, Ascension, Luke 24:48
Introit: EL529, S2273, SF2273. "Jesus, We Are Here" (Acts)
Litany: C240. Pentecost Prayer (Luke)
Alternate Lessons for the Seventh Sunday of Easter: Acts 1:15-17,
  21-26; Ps 1; 1 John 5:9-13; John 17:6-19 (*See page 3.*)

Acts 2:1-21

[1] When the day of Pentecost had come, they were all together in one place. [2] And suddenly from heaven there came a sound like the rush of a violent wind, and it filled the entire house where they were sitting. [3] Divided tongues, as of fire, appeared among them, and a tongue rested on each of them. [4] All of them were filled with the Holy Spirit and began to speak in other languages, as the Spirit gave them ability.

[5] Now there were devout Jews from every nation under heaven living in Jerusalem. [6] And at this sound the crowd gathered and was bewildered, because each one heard them speaking in the native language of each. [7] Amazed and astonished, they asked, "Are not all these who are speaking Galileans? [8] And how is it that we hear, each of us, in our own native language? [9] Parthians, Medes, Elamites, and residents of Mesopotamia, Judea and Cappadocia, Pontus and Asia, [10] Phrygia and Pamphylia, Egypt and the parts of Libya belonging to Cyrene, and visitors from Rome, both Jews and proselytes, [11] Cretans and Arabs—in our own languages we hear them speaking about God's deeds of power." [12] All were amazed and perplexed, saying to one another, "What does this mean?" [13] But others sneered and said, "They are filled with new wine."

[14] But Peter, standing with the eleven, raised his voice and addressed them, "Men of Judea and all who live in Jerusalem, let this be known to you, and listen to what I say. [15] Indeed, these are not drunk, as you suppose, for it is only nine o'clock in the morning. [16] No, this is what was spoken through the prophet Joel: [17] 'In the last days it will be, God declares, that I will pour out my Spirit upon all flesh, and your sons and your daughters shall prophesy, and your young men shall see visions, and your old men shall dream dreams. [18] Even upon my slaves, both men and women, in those days I will pour out my Spirit; and they shall prophesy. [19] And I will show portents in the heaven above and signs on the earth below, blood, and fire, and smoky mist. [20] The sun shall be turned to darkness and the moon to blood, before the coming of the Lord's great and glorious day. [21] Then everyone who calls on the name of the Lord shall be saved.' "

Psalm 104:24-34, 35*b*

[24] O LORD, how manifold are your works! In wisdom you have made them all; the earth is full of your creatures. [25] Yonder is the sea, great and wide, creeping things innumerable are there, living things both small and great. [26] There go the ships, and Leviathan that you formed to sport in it. [27] These all look to you to give them their food in due season; [28] when you give to them, they gather it up; when you open your hand, they are filled with good things. [29] When you hide your face, they are dismayed; when you take away their breath, they die and return to their dust. [30] When you send forth your spirit, they are created; and you renew the face of the ground. [31] May the glory of the LORD endure forever; may the LORD rejoice in his works— [32] who looks on the earth and it trembles, who touches the mountains and they smoke. [33] I will sing to the LORD as long as I live; I will sing praise to my God while I have being. [34] May my meditation be pleasing to him, for I rejoice in the LORD. . . .

[35b] Bless the LORD, O my soul. Praise the LORD!

Romans 8:22-27

[22] We know that the whole creation has been groaning in labor pains until now; [23] and not only the creation, but we ourselves, who have the first fruits of the Spirit, groan inwardly while we wait for adoption, the redemption of our bodies. [24] For in hope we were saved. Now hope that is seen is not hope. For who hopes for what is seen? [25] But if we hope for what we do not see, we wait for it with patience.

[26] Likewise the Spirit helps us in our weakness; for we do not know how to pray as we ought, but that very Spirit intercedes with sighs too deep for words. [27] And God, who searches the heart, knows what is the mind of the Spirit, because the Spirit intercedes for the saints according to the will of God.

John 15:26-27; 16:4b-15

[26] "When the Advocate comes, whom I will send to you from the Father, the Spirit of truth who comes from the Father, he will testify on my behalf. [27] You also are to testify because you have been with me from the beginning. . . .

[4b] "I did not say these things to you from the beginning, because I was with you. [5] But now I am going to him who sent me; yet none of you asks me, 'Where are you going?' [6] But because I have said these things to you, sorrow has filled your hearts. [7] Nevertheless I tell you the truth: it is to your advantage that I go away, for if I do not go away, the Advocate will not come to you; but if I go, I will send him to you. [8] And when he comes, he will prove the world wrong about sin and righteousness and judgment: [9] about sin, because they do not believe in me; [10] about righteousness, because I am going to the Father and you will see me no longer; [11] about judgment, because the ruler of this world has been condemned.

[12] "I still have many things to say to you, but you cannot bear them now. [13] When the Spirit of truth comes, he will guide you into all the truth; for he will not speak on his own, but will speak whatever he hears, and he will declare to you the things that are to come. [14] He will glorify me, because he will take what is mine and declare it to you. [15] All that the Father has is mine. For this reason I said that he will take what is mine and declare it to you."

Primary Hymns and Songs for the Day

"Spirit of the Living God" (Acts, John) (O)
　　B244, C259, F155, N283, P322, R90, SP131, UM393, VU376
　　　　H-3　　Chr-176
　　　　S-1　　#212. Vocal descant idea
"Spirit Song" (Acts, John)
　　C352, R248, SP134, UM347
"O Spirit of the Living God" (Acts) (C)
　　UM539
　　　　H-3　　Hbl-44; Chr-21; Desc-40; Org-40
　　　　S-1　　#131-132. Introduction and descant
　　N263

Additional Hymn Suggestions

"Gather Us In" (Acts, Communion) (O)
　　C284, EL532, S2236, SF2236, W665
"Hail Thee, Festival Day" (Acts)
　　E225, EL394, L142, N262, UM324, VU163
"Sweet, Sweet Spirit" (Acts)
　　B243, C261, F159, N293, P398, SP136, UM334
"Breathe on Me, Breath of God" (Acts)
　　B241, C254, E508, F161, L488, N292, P316, UM420 (PD),
　　VU382 (Fr.), W725
"Filled with the Spirit's Power" (Acts)
　　L160, N266, UM537, VU194
"Wind Who Makes All Winds that Blow" (Acts)
　　C236, N271, P131, UM538, VU196
"O Breath of Life" (Acts)
　　C250, UM543, VU202
"Like the Murmur of the Dove's Song" (Acts)
　　C245, E513, EL403, N270, P314, R280, UM544, VU205
"Now Praise the Hidden God of Love" (Acts)
　　P402, S2027, SF2027
"Spirit of God" (Acts)
　　S2117, SF2117
"She Comes Sailing on the Wind" (Acts)
　　S2122, SF2122, VU380
"Loving Spirit" (Acts, Pentecost)
　　C244, EL397, P323, S2123, SF2123, VU387
"As a Fire Is Meant for Burning" (Acts)
　　S2237, SF2237, VU578
"In the Midst of New Dimensions" (Acts, Pentecost)
　　N391, S2238, SF2238
"Deep in the Shadows of the Past" (Acts)
　　N320, P330, S2246
"Come, Share the Lord" (Acts, Communion)
　　C408, S2269, SF2269, VU469
"Spirit, Spirit of Gentleness" (Acts, Rom)
　　C249, EL396, N286, P319, S2120, VU375 (FR.)
"My Hope Is Built" (Acts, Rom)
　　B406, C537, EL596, F92, L293/L294, N368, P379, UM368 (PD)
"Spirit of God, Descend Upon My Heart" (Acts, Rom)
　　B245, C265, EL800, F147, L486, N290, P326, UM500 (PD),
　　VU378
"Come Down, O Love Divine" (Acts, John)
　　C582, E516, EL804, L508, N289, P313, UM475 (PD),
　　VU367, W472

"Come, Holy Ghost, Our Souls Inspire" (Acts, John)
　　E503/E504, L472/L473, N268, P125, UM651 (PD), VU201
"Every Time I Feel the Spirit" (Rom)
　　C592, N282, P315, UM404
"O Holy Spirit, Root of Life" (Rom)
　　C251, EL399, N57, S2121, SF2121, VU379
"Open My Eyes, That I May See" (John)
　　B502, C586, F486, P324, UM454, VU371

Additional Contemporary Suggestions

"Holy, Holy" (Acts)
　　B254, F149, P140, R206, S2039, SP141
"Where the Spirit of the Lord Is" (Acts)
　　C264, S2119, SF2119
"Holy Ground" (Acts)
　　B224, C112, S2272, SF2272, SP86
"Open the Eyes of My Heart" (Acts)
　　M57; V-3 p. 162 Vocal Solo
"Shout to the North" (Acts, Rom)
　　M99
"Holy Spirit, Rain Down" (Acts, John)
　　M88
"Surely the Presence of the Lord" (Acts, John)
　　C263, R167, SP243, UM328; S-2, #200 Stanzas for soloist
"Let It Rise" (Pss)
　　M4
"Cry of My Heart" (Rom)
　　S2165, SF2165, M39

Vocal Solos

"Consume Me" (Acts)
　　V-3　　p. 148
"Ev'ry Time I Feel De Spirit" (Acts, Pentecost)
　　V-7　　p. 78
"New Wind Blowin'" (Acts, Pentecost)
　　V-8　　p. 192

Anthems

"There's a Spirit of Love in This Place" (Acts)
Mark A. Miller; Abingdon Press 9780687644629
SATB with piano (opt. solo)

"If Ye Love Me" (John)
Philip Stopford; Hal Leonard 08745638
SSATBB *a cappella*

Other Suggestions

Visuals:
　　Acts　Wind, tongues of fire, praising, all races of people
　　P　　Sea/ships, whales, dove, volcano, singing, Ps 104:35b
　　E　　Praying hands, Holy Spirit (flames, dove)
　　G　　Briefcase (Advocate), Trinity (triangle, trefoil, others)
Prayer: N827, UM329, UM542, or UM574 (Acts, Pentecost)
Prayer: C52, C235, C243, C281, or N857 (Acts)
Litany: C246. "Litany of the Spirit" (Pentecost)
Benediction Response: EL551, S2241, SF2241. "The Spirit Sends
　　Us Forth to Serve" (Acts, Pentecost)

Isaiah 6:1-8

[1] In the year that King Uzziah died, I saw the Lord sitting on a throne, high and lofty; and the hem of his robe filled the temple. [2] Seraphs were in attendance above him; each had six wings: with two they covered their faces, and with two they covered their feet, and with two they flew. [3] And one called to another and said: "Holy, holy, holy is the LORD of hosts; the whole earth is full of his glory." [4] The pivots on the thresholds shook at the voices of those who called, and the house filled with smoke. [5] And I said: "Woe is me! I am lost, for I am a man of unclean lips, and I live among a people of unclean lips; yet my eyes have seen the King, the LORD of hosts!"

[6] Then one of the seraphs flew to me, holding a live coal that had been taken from the altar with a pair of tongs. [7] The seraph touched my mouth with it and said: "Now that this has touched your lips, your guilt has departed and your sin is blotted out." [8] Then I heard the voice of the Lord saying, "Whom shall I send, and who will go for us?" And I said, "Here am I; send me!"

Psalm 29

[1] Ascribe to the LORD, O heavenly beings, ascribe to the LORD glory and strength. [2] Ascribe to the LORD the glory of his name; worship the LORD in holy splendor. [3] The voice of the LORD is over the waters; the God of glory thunders, the LORD, over mighty waters. [4] The voice of the LORD is powerful; the voice of the LORD is full of majesty. [5] The voice of the LORD breaks the cedars; the LORD breaks the cedars of Lebanon. [6] He makes Lebanon skip like a calf, and Sirion like a young wild ox. [7] The voice of the LORD flashes forth flames of fire. [8] The voice of the LORD shakes the wilderness; the LORD shakes the wilderness of Kadesh. [9] The voice of the LORD causes the oaks to whirl, and strips the forest bare; and in his temple all say, "Glory!" [10] The LORD sits enthroned over the flood; the LORD sits enthroned as king forever. [11] May the LORD give strength to his people! May the LORD bless his people with peace!

Romans 8:12-17

[12] So then, brothers and sisters, we are debtors, not to the flesh, to live according to the flesh— [13] for if you live according to the flesh, you will die; but if by the Spirit you put to death the deeds of the body, you will live. [14] For all who are led by the Spirit of God are children of God. [15] For you did not receive a spirit of slavery to fall back into fear, but you have received a spirit of adoption. When we cry, "Abba! Father!" [16] it is that very Spirit bearing witness with our spirit that we are children of God, [17] and if children, then heirs, heirs of God and joint heirs with Christ—if, in fact, we suffer with him so that we may also be glorified with him.

John 3:1-17

[1] Now there was a Pharisee named Nicodemus, a leader of the Jews. [2] He came to Jesus by night and said to him, "Rabbi, we know that you are a teacher who has come from God; for no one can do these signs that you do apart from the presence of God." [3] Jesus answered him, "Very truly, I tell you, no one can see the kingdom of God without being born from above." [4] Nicodemus said to him, "How can anyone be born after having grown old? Can one enter a second time into the mother's womb and be born?" [5] Jesus answered, "Very truly, I tell you, no one can enter the kingdom of God without being born of water and Spirit. [6] What is born of the flesh is flesh, and what is born of the Spirit is spirit. [7] Do not be astonished that I said to you, 'You must be born from above.' [8] The wind blows where it chooses, and you hear the sound of it, but you do not know where it comes from or where it goes. So it is with everyone who is born of the Spirit." [9] Nicodemus said to him, "How can these things be?" [10] Jesus answered him, "Are you a teacher of Israel, and yet you do not understand these things?

[11] "Very truly, I tell you, we speak of what we know and testify to what we have seen; yet you do not receive our testimony. [12] If I have told you about earthly things and you do not believe, how can you believe if I tell you about heavenly things? [13] No one has ascended into heaven except the one who descended from heaven, the Son of Man. [14] And just as Moses lifted up the serpent in the wilderness, so must the Son of Man be lifted up, [15] that whoever believes in him may have eternal life.

[16] "For God so loved the world that he gave his only Son, so that everyone who believes in him may not perish but may have eternal life.

[17] "Indeed, God did not send the Son into the world to condemn the world, but in order that the world might be saved through him."

Primary Hymns and Songs for the Day

"Holy, Holy, Holy! Lord God Almighty" (Isa, Trinity) (O)
> B2, C4, E362, F323, EL413, L165, N277, P138, R204,
> UM64/UM65, VU315, W485
>> H-3   Hbl-68; Chr-99; Desc-80; Org-97
>> S-1   #245-248. Various treatments

"Holy, Holy, Holy Lord" ("Sanctus") (Isa, Communion)
> S2256, SF2256

"Lift High the Cross" (John)
> B594, C108, E473, EL660, L377, N198, P371, R297, UM159,
> VU151, W704

"Holy Spirit, Come, Confirm Us" (Trinity) (C)
> N264, UM331
>> H-3   Chr-67
>> S-2   #63-64. Descant and harmonization

"Stand Up and Bless the Lord" (Isa) (C)
> B30, P491, UM662 (PD)
>> H-3   Hbl-79; Chr-141; Desc-95; Org-143
>> S-1   #306-308. Various treatments

Additional Hymn Suggestions

"Ye Watchers and Ye Holy Ones" (Isa, Trinity)
> E618, EL424, L175, P451, UM90, W707

"Send Me, Lord" (Isa)
> C447, EL809, N360, R308, UM497, VU572

"Here I Am, Lord" (Isa)
> C452, EL574, P525, R149, UM593, VU509

"Let All Mortal Flesh Keep Silence" (Isa, Communion)
> B80, C124, E324, EL490, F166, L198, N345, P5, R229, UM626
> (PD), VU473 (Fr.), W523

"This Is the Feast of Victory" (Isa, Communion)
> E417/E418, EL165/EL166/EL167, P594, R199, UM638,
> VU904, W458

"Holy" ("Santo") (Isa)
> EL762, S2019, SF2019

"Every Time I Feel the Spirit" (Rom)
> C592, N282, P315, UM404

"The Lone, Wild Bird" (Rom)
> P320, S2052, SF2052, VU384

"Creating God, Your Fingers Trace" (Rom, Trinity)
> C335, E394/E395, EL684, N462, P134, UM109, VU265

"Mothering God, You Gave Me Birth" (Rom, John)
> C83, EL735, N467, S2050, SF2050, VU320

"Baptized in Water" (Rom, Baptism)
> B362, E294, EL456, P492, S2248, W720

"To God Be the Glory" (John)
> B153, C39, F365, N14, R68, UM99; V-8 p. 5 Vocal Solo

"Of the Father's Love Begotten" (John, Trinity)
> B251, C104, E82, EL295, F172 (PD), L42, N118, P309, R252,
> UM184, VU61, W398

"O Love, How Deep" (John, Trinity)
> E448/E449, EL322, L88, N209, P83, UM267 (PD), VU348

"Wash, O God, Our Sons and Daughters" (John, Baptism)
> C365, EL445, UM605, VU442

"We Know That Christ Is Raised" (John, Baptism)
> E296, EL449, L189, P495, UM610, VU448, W721

"Womb of Life" (John, Trinity)
> C14, N274, S2046, SF2046

"He Came Down" (John)
> EL253, S2085, SF2085

"We Are God's People" (John)
> B383, F546, S2220, SF2220

"Gather Us In" (John)
> C284, EL532, S2236, SF2236, W665

Additional Contemporary Suggestions

"Above All" (Isa, John)
> M77; V-3 p. 17 Vocal Solo

"Santo, Santo, Santo" ("Holy, Holy, Holy") (Isa)
> C111, EL473, N793, S2007, SF2007

"Because We Believe" (Isa)
> M6

"Holy, Holy, Holy" (Isa)
> R208, SP37, M95

"Holy, Holy" (Isa, Rom)
> B254, F149, P140, R206, S2039, SP141

"Spirit of the Living God" (Rom)
> B244, C259, F155, N283, P322, R90, SP131, UM393, VU376, S-1
> #212 Vocal descant

"You Are My King" ("Amazing Love") (Rom, John)
> M82

"They'll Know We Are Christians" (Rom, Trinity)
> C494, S2223, SF2223

"O How He Loves You and Me!" (John)
> B146, F622, R27, S2108, SF2108, SP113

"There Is a Redeemer" (John, Trinity)
> R232, SP111

"Lord God, Almighty" (Trinity)
> R40, S2006, SF2006

Vocal Solos

"Alleluia" (Isa, Trinity)
V-8   p. 358
"Abba Father" (Rom)
V-3   p. 109

Anthems

"Ev'ry Time I Feel the Spirit" (Rom)
arr. Moses Hogan; Hal Leonard 08745536
Two-part with piano

"Come, Join the Dance of Trinity" (Trinity)
Arr. Roy Hopp; Augsburg 9780800678296
SATB with piano

Other Suggestions

Visuals:
> O   Seraphs, incense, glowing coals
> P   Storm, flames, lightning, wind, skipping calf
> E   Crown (heirs), open manacles (handcuffs)
> G   wind, white garment, water, flame/dove (Holy Spirit)

Call to Worship: B89, C148, E83, EL283, F193, L45, N135, P41,
> UM234 (PD), VU60 (Fr.), W392, stanzas 2 and 3. "O Come, All
> Ye Faithful" (John, Trinity)

Affirmation of Faith: The Nicene Creed (Trinity)
Response: C45. "Diso Padre, Dios Hijo" (Trinity)
Blessing: N873 (Trinity)

1 Samuel 8:4-20 (11:14-15)

[4]Then all the elders of Israel gathered together and came to Samuel at Ramah, [5]and said to him, "You are old and your sons do not follow in your ways; appoint for us, then, a king to govern us, like other nations." [6]But the thing displeased Samuel when they said, "Give us a king to govern us." Samuel prayed to the LORD, [7]and the LORD said to Samuel, "Listen to the voice of the people in all that they say to you; for they have not rejected you, but they have rejected me from being king over them. [8]Just as they have done to me, from the day I brought them up out of Egypt to this day, forsaking me and serving other gods, so also they are doing to you. [9]Now then, listen to their voice; only—you shall solemnly warn them, and show them the ways of the king who shall reign over them." [10]So Samuel reported all the words of the LORD to the people who were asking him for a king. [11]He said, "These will be the ways of the king who will reign over you: he will take your sons and appoint them to his chariots and to be his horsemen, and to run before his chariots; [12]and he will appoint for himself commanders of thousands and commanders of fifties, and some to plow his ground and to reap his harvest, and to make his implements of war and the equipment of his chariots. [13]He will take your daughters to be perfumers and cooks and bakers. [14]He will take the best of your fields and vineyards and olive orchards and give them to his courtiers. [15]He will take one-tenth of your grain and of your vineyards and give it to his officers and his courtiers. [16]He will take your male and female slaves, and the best of your cattle and donkeys, and put them to his work. [17]He will take one-tenth of your flocks, and you shall be his slaves. [18]And in that day you will cry out because of your king, whom you have chosen for yourselves; but the LORD will not answer you in that day." [19]But the people refused to listen to the voice of Samuel; they said, "No! but we are determined to have a king over us, [20]so that we also may be like other nations, and that our king may govern us and go out before us and fight our battles."

[14]Samuel said to the people, "Come, let us go to Gilgal and there renew the kingship." [15]So all the people went to Gilgal, and there they made Saul king before the LORD in Gilgal. There they sacrificed offerings of well-being before the LORD, and there Saul and all the Israelites rejoiced greatly.

Psalm 138

[1]I give you thanks, O LORD, with my whole heart; before the gods I sing your praise; [2]I bow down toward your holy temple and give thanks to your name for your steadfast love and your faithfulness; for you have exalted your name and your word above everything. [3]On the day I called, you answered me, you increased my strength of soul. [4]All the kings of the earth shall praise you, O LORD, for they have heard the words of your mouth. [5]They shall sing of the ways of the LORD, for great is the glory of the LORD. [6]For though the LORD is high, he regards the lowly; but the haughty he perceives from far away. [7]Though I walk in the midst of trouble, you preserve me against the wrath of my enemies; you stretch out your hand, and your right hand delivers me. [8]The LORD will fulfill his purpose for me; your steadfast love, O LORD, endures forever. Do not forsake the work of your hands.

2 Corinthians 4:13–5:1

[13]But just as we have the same spirit of faith that is in accordance with scripture—"I believed, and so I spoke" —we also believe, and so we speak, [14]because we know that the one who raised the Lord Jesus will raise us also with Jesus, and will bring us with you into his presence. [15]Yes, everything is for your sake, so that grace, as it extends to more and more people, may increase thanksgiving, to the glory of God. [16]So we do not lose heart. Even though our outer nature is wasting away, our inner nature is being renewed day by day. [17]For this slight momentary affliction is preparing us for an eternal weight of glory beyond all measure, [18]because we look not at what can be seen but at what cannot be seen; for what can be seen is temporary, but what cannot be seen is eternal.

[1]For we know that if the earthly tent we live in is destroyed, we have a building from God, a house not made with hands, eternal in the heavens.

Mark 3:20-35

[20]And the crowd came together again, so that they could not even eat. [21]When his family heard it, they went out to restrain him, for people were saying, "He has gone out of his mind." [22]And the scribes who came down from Jerusalem said, "He has Beelzebul, and by the ruler of the demons he casts out demons." [23]And he called them to him, and spoke to them in parables, "How can Satan cast out Satan? [24]If a kingdom is divided against itself, that kingdom cannot stand. [25]And if a house is divided against itself, that house will not be able to stand. [26]And if Satan has risen up against himself and is divided, he cannot stand, but his end has come. [27]But no one can enter a strong man's house and plunder his property without first tying up the strong man; then indeed the house can be plundered.

[28]"Truly I tell you, people will be forgiven for their sins and whatever blasphemies they utter; [29]but whoever blasphemes against the Holy Spirit can never have forgiveness, but is guilty of an eternal sin"— [30]for they had said, "He has an unclean spirit."

[31]Then his mother and his brothers came; and standing outside, they sent to him and called him. [32]A crowd was sitting around him; and they said to him, "Your mother and your brothers and sisters are outside, asking for you." [33]And he replied, "Who are my mother and my brothers?" [34]And looking at those who sat around him, he said, "Here are my mother and my brothers! [35]Whoever does the will of God is my brother and sister and mother."

Primary Hymns and Songs for the Day
"If Thou But Suffer God to Guide Thee" (1 Sam, Pss, 1 Cor) (O)
    B57, C565, E635, EL769, L453, N410, P282, UM142 (PD),
    VU285/VU286
        H-3   Chr-108; Desc-103; Org-179
"In Christ There Is No East or West" (Acts, John)
    E529, EL650 (PD), L359, N394, P440, UM548, VU606, W659
        H-3   Chr-111; Desc-74; Org-88
        S-1   #231-233. Various treatments
    B385, C687, F685, N394, P439
        H-3   Hbl-71, 104; Chr-111-112; Desc-95; Org-143
        S-2   #162. Harmonization
"We Shall Overcome" (1 Cor)
    C630, N570, UM533
"Lead On, O Cloud of Presence" (1 Sam, Mark) (C)
    C633, S2234, SF2234, VU421
"They'll Know We Are Christians" (Mark) (C)
    C494, S2223, SF2223

Additional Hymn Suggestions
"All My Hope Is Firmly Grounded" (1 Sam)
    C88, E665, EL757, N408, UM132, VU654/VU655
"O God of Every Nation" (1 Sam)
    C680, E607, EL713, L416, P289, UM435, VU677, W650
"O God Who Shaped Creation" (1 Sam)
    UM443, VU276
"God Made from One Blood" (1 Sam)
    C500, N427, S2170, SF2170, VU554
"All Hail the Power of Jesus' Name" (1 Sam, 1 Cor) (O)
    B200/B201/B202, C91/C92, E450/E451, EL634,
    F325/F326/F327, L328/L329, N304, P142/P143, R45,
    UM154/UM155, VU334, W494
"Open My Eyes, That I May See" (1 Sam, 1 Cor)
    B502, C586, F486, P324, UM454, VU371
"'Tis the Old Ship of Zion" (1 Sam, Pss, 1 Cor)
    B577, C539, N310, UM345
"I Will Give Thanks with My Whole Heart" (Pss)
    P247
"The Fragrance of Christ" (Pss)
    S2205, SF2205
"Jesus, Lover of My Soul" (1 Cor)
    B180, C542, E699, F222, N546, P303, UM479 (PD), VU669
"Am I a Soldier of the Cross" (1 Cor)
    B481, F411, UM511
"By Gracious Powers" (1 Cor)
    E695/E696, EL626, N413, P342, UM517, W577
"I Know That My Redeemer Lives!" (1 Cor)
    EL619 (PD), F295, L352, W445
"Be Still, My Soul" (1 Cor)
    C566, F77, N488, UM534, VU652
"We Know That Christ Is Raised" (1 Cor)
    C376, E296, EL449, L189, P495, UM610, VU448, W721
"Without Seeing You" (1 Cor)
    S2206, SF2206
"We Walk by Faith and Not by Sight" (1 Cor)
    E209, EL635, N256, P399, S2196, SF2196, W572
"Here, O My Lord, I See Thee" (1 Cor, Communion)
    C416, E318, F567, L211, N336, P520, UM623, VU459
"O Jesus, My King" ("Jesus Es Mi Rey Soberano") (Mark)
    C109, P157, UM180

"Lord of the Dance" (Mark)
    P302, UM261, VU352, W636
"Rise Up, O Men of God" (Mark)
    B411, C611, E551, F398, UM576 (PD)
"Who Is My Mother, Who Is My Brother?" (Mark)
    C486, S2225, SF2225

Additional Contemporary Suggestions
"Bring Forth the Kingdom" (1 Sam, 1 Cor)
    R153, S2190, SF2190
"The Family Prayer Song" ("As for Me and My House")
    (1 Sam, Mark)
    M54, S2188, SF2188
"Glorify Thy Name" (Pss)
    B249, R37, S2016, SF2016, SP19
"We Bow Down" (Pss)
    R38, SP65
"Let It Rise" (Pss)
    M4
"Forever" (Pss)
    M68
"My Redeemer Lives" (1 Cor)
    M73
"Open the Eyes of My Heart" (1 Cor)
    M57, V-3 p. 162 Vocal Solo
"I'm So Glad Jesus Lifted Me" (Mark)
    C529, EL860 (PD), N474, S2151, SF2151

Vocal Solos
"Reason" (1 Sam, Pss)
V-3   p. 102
"And Can It Be That I Should Gain" (1 Cor, Mark)
V-1   p. 29

Anthems
"They'll Know We Are Christians" (Mark)
Arr. Lloyd Larson; Lorenz 10/3481L
SATB with Piano and opt. percussion

"Lord, for Thy Tender Mercy's Sake" (Mark)
Richard Farrant; Pavanne HL 08301649
SATB *a cappella*

Other Suggestions
Visuals:
    O   crown, purple, Samuel, symbols of political power
    P   crown, rejoicing, victory
    E   Bible, new growth coming out of decay, heavenly home
    G   crowns, kingdoms/house divided, chains, strength, family
Call to Worship: C486, S2225, SF2225, stanza 1. "Who Is My Mother,
    Who Is My Brother"
Prayer: UM429 or UM495 (1 Sam)
Prayer of Confession: C483 (1 Sam)
Alternate Lessons: Gen 3:8-15; Ps 130 (*See page 3.*)

1 Samuel 15:34–16:13

[34]Then Samuel went to Ramah; and Saul went up to his house in Gibeah of Saul. [35]Samuel did not see Saul again until the day of his death, but Samuel grieved over Saul. And the LORD was sorry that he had made Saul king over Israel.

[1]The LORD said to Samuel, "How long will you grieve over Saul? I have rejected him from being king over Israel. Fill your horn with oil and set out; I will send you to Jesse the Bethlehemite, for I have provided for myself a king among his sons." [2]Samuel said, "How can I go? If Saul hears of it, he will kill me." And the LORD said, "Take a heifer with you, and say, 'I have come to sacrifice to the LORD.' [3]Invite Jesse to the sacrifice, and I will show you what you shall do; and you shall anoint for me the one whom I name to you." [4]Samuel did what the LORD commanded, and came to Bethlehem. The elders of the city came to meet him trembling, and said, "Do you come peaceably?" [5]He said, "Peaceably; I have come to sacrifice to the LORD; sanctify yourselves and come with me to the sacrifice." And he sanctified Jesse and his sons and invited them to the sacrifice.

[6]When they came, he looked on Eliab and thought, "Surely the LORD's anointed is now before the LORD." [7]But the LORD said to Samuel, "Do not look on his appearance or on the height of his stature, because I have rejected him; for the LORD does not see as mortals see; they look on the outward appearance, but the LORD looks on the heart." [8]Then Jesse called Abinadab, and made him pass before Samuel. He said, "Neither has the LORD chosen this one." [9] Then Jesse made Shammah pass by. And he said, "Neither has the LORD chosen this one." [10]Jesse made seven of his sons pass before Samuel, and Samuel said to Jesse, "The LORD has not chosen any of these." [11]Samuel said to Jesse, "Are all your sons here?" And he said, "There remains yet the youngest, but he is keeping the sheep." And Samuel said to Jesse, "Send and bring him; for we will not sit down until he comes here." [12]He sent and brought him in. Now he was ruddy, and had beautiful eyes, and was handsome. The LORD said, "Rise and anoint him; for this is the one." [13]Then Samuel took the horn of oil, and anointed him in the presence of his brothers; and the spirit of the LORD came mightily upon David from that day forward. Samuel then set out and went to Ramah.

Psalm 20

[1]The LORD answer you in the day of trouble! The name of the God of Jacob protect you! [2]May he send you help from the sanctuary, and give you support from Zion. [3]May he remember all your offerings, and regard with favor your burnt sacrifices. [4]May he grant you your heart's desire, and fulfill all your plans. [5]May we shout for joy over your victory, and in the name of our God set up our banners. May the LORD fulfill all your petitions. [6]Now I know that the LORD will help his anointed; he will answer him from his holy heaven with mighty victories by his right hand. [7]Some take pride in chariots, and some in horses, but our pride is in the name of the LORD our God. [8]They will collapse and fall, but we shall rise and stand upright. [9]Give victory to the king, O LORD; answer us when we call.

2 Corinthians 5:6-10 (11-13), 14-17

[6]So we are always confident; even though we know that while we are at home in the body we are away from the Lord— [7]for we walk by faith, not by sight. [8]Yes, we do have confidence, and we would rather be away from the body and at home with the Lord. [9]So whether we are at home or away, we make it our aim to please him. [10]For all of us must appear before the judgment seat of Christ, so that each may receive recompense for what has been done in the body, whether good or evil.

[11]Therefore, knowing the fear of the Lord, we try to persuade others; but we ourselves are well known to God, and I hope that we are also well known to your consciences. [12]We are not commending ourselves to you again, but giving you an opportunity to boast about us, so that you may be able to answer those who boast in outward appearance and not in the heart. [13]For if we are beside ourselves, it is for God; if we are in our right mind, it is for you. [14]For the love of Christ urges us on, because we are convinced that one has died for all; therefore all have died. [15]And he died for all, so that those who live might live no longer for themselves, but for him who died and was raised for them.

[16]From now on, therefore, we regard no one from a human point of view; even though we once knew Christ from a human point of view, we know him no longer in that way. [17]So if anyone is in Christ, there is a new creation: everything old has passed away; see, everything has become new!

Mark 4:26-34

[26]He also said, "The kingdom of God is as if someone would scatter seed on the ground, [27]and would sleep and rise night and day, and the seed would sprout and grow, he does not know how. [28]The earth produces of itself, first the stalk, then the head, then the full grain in the head. [29]But when the grain is ripe, at once he goes in with his sickle, because the harvest has come."

[30]He also said, "With what can we compare the kingdom of God, or what parable will we use for it? [31]It is like a mustard seed, which, when sown upon the ground, is the smallest of all the seeds on earth; [32]yet when it is sown it grows up and becomes the greatest of all shrubs, and puts forth large branches, so that the birds of the air can make nests in its shade."

[33]With many such parables he spoke the word to them, as they were able to hear it; [34]he did not speak to them except in parables, but he explained everything in private to his disciples.

Primary Hymns and Songs for the Day

"The Church's One Foundation" (2 Cor) (O)
    B350, C272, E525, EL654, F547, L369, N386, P442, UM545
    (PD) and UM 546, VU332 (Fr.)
"This Is a Day of New Beginnings" (2 Cor)
    B370, C518, N417, UM383, W661
        H-3   Chr-196
"We Walk by Faith" (2 Cor, Mark)
    N256, P399, W572
        H-3   Chr-67
    S2196, SF2196
        H-3   Chr-21
"Pues Si Vivimos" ("When We Are Living") (2 Cor, Mark) (C)
    C536, EL639, N499, P400, UM356, VU581
        S-1   #320. Orff instrument arrangement
        H-3   Chr-218; Org-155

Additional Hymn Suggestions

"Hail to the Lord's Anointed" (1 Sam)
    C140, E616, EL311 (PD), L87, N104, P205, UM203 (PD), VU30
"Open My Eyes, that I May See" (1 Sam)
    B502, C586, F486, P324, UM454, VU371
"Send Me, Lord" (1 Sam)
    C447, EL809, N360, R308, UM497, VU572
"Here I Am, Lord" (1 Sam)
    C452, EL574, P525, R149, UM593, VU509
"Loving Spirit" (1 Sam, Father's Day)
    C244, EL397, P323, S2123, SF2123, VU387
"In the Midst of New Dimensions" (1 Sam)
    N391, S2238, SF2238
"Rejoice, Ye Pure in Heart" (Pss)
    B39, C15, E556/E557, EL873/EL874, F394, N55/ N71, P145/
    P146, UM160/UM161
"What Wondrous Love Is This" (2 Cor)
    B143 (PD), C200, E439, EL666, F283, L385, N223, P85, R277,
    UM292, VU147 (Fr.), W600
"Love Divine, All Loves Excelling" (2 Cor)
    B208, C517, E657, EL631 (PD), L315, P376, N43, R196,
    UM384, VU333, W588
"My Song Is Love Unknown" (2 Cor)
    E458, EL343, L94, N222, P76, S2083, SF2083, VU143, W439
"Just a Closer Walk with Thee" (2 Cor)
    B448, C557, EL697, F591, S2158, SF2158
"I'll Fly Away" (2 Cor)
    N595, S2282, SF2282
"For the Fruits of This Creation" (Mark)
    B643, C714, E424, EL679, L563, N425, P553, UM97, VU227,
    W562
"The Care the Eagle Gives Her Young" (Mark)
    C76, N468, UM118, VU269
"Sois la Semilla" ("You Are the Seed") (Mark)
    C478, N528, UM583
"Come, Ye Thankful People, Come" (Mark)
    B637, C718, E290, EL693, F392, L407, N422, P551, UM694
    (PD), VU516, W759
"Hymn of Promise" (Mark)
    C638, N433, UM707, VU703
"God the Sculptor of the Mountains" (Mark)
    EL736, S2060, SF2060

"Bring Forth the Kingdom" (Mark)
    R153, S2190, SF2190
"Faith Is Patience in the Night" (Mark)
    S2211, SF2211

Additional Contemporary Suggestions

"Spirit of the Living God" (1 Sam)
    B244, C259, F155, N283, P322, R90, SP131, UM393, VU376;
    S-1#212 Vocal descant idea
"Sanctuary" (1 Sam)
    M52, R185, S2164, SF2164
"Awesome in This Place" (1 Sam)
    M36
"Shout to the Lord" (Pss)
    EL821, S2074, SF2074, M16; V-3 p. 56 Vocal Solo
"Jesus, Draw Me Close" (2 Cor)
    M48, S2159, SF2159
"We Want to See Jesus Lifted High" (2 Cor)
    M67
"You Are My King" ("Amazing Love") (2 Cor)
    M82
"The Battle Belongs to the Lord" (2 Cor)
    R244, SP158
"I Will Not Forget You" (Mark)
    M211
"This Kingdom" (Mark)
    M17

Vocal Solos

"Just a Closer Walk with Thee" (2 Cor)
    V-8   p. 323
"Father, We Thank You" (Mark)
    E302/E303, EL478, UM563/UM565, W558

Anthems

"My Song Is Love Unknown" (2 Cor)
Edwin T. Childs; MorningStar 50-3044
SATB with keyboard

"The Mustard Seed" (Mark)
Anna Laura Page; Choristers Guild CGA1011
Unison with piano (opt. flute)

Other Suggestions

Visuals:
    O   Several vials of oil, anointing
    P   Vials of oil, rejoicing, victory
    E   Cross with white cloth, resurrection, reconciliation
    G   Bag of seeds, small plants, larger plant, wheat stalks
Call to Worship: S2124, SF2124, VU383. "Come, O Holy Spirit,
    Come" (1 Sam)
Call to Prayer: UM388, stanza 1. "O Come and Dwell in Me" (2 Cor)
Benediction: EL551, S2241, SF2241. "The Spirit Sends Us Forth to
    Serve" (1 Sam)
Alternate Lessons: Eze 17:22-24; Ps 92:1-4, 12-15 (*See page 3.*)

1 Samuel 17:(1a, 4-11, 19-23) 32-49

[1a] Now the Philistines gathered their armies for battle.

[4] And there came out from the camp of the Philistines a champion named Goliath, of Gath, whose height was six cubits and a span. [5] He had a helmet of bronze on his head, and he was armed with a coat of mail; the weight of the coat was five thousand shekels of bronze. [6] He had greaves of bronze on his legs and a javelin of bronze slung between his shoulders. [7] The shaft of his spear was like a weaver's beam, and his spear's head weighed six hundred shekels of iron; and his shield-bearer went before him. [8] He stood and shouted to the ranks of Israel, "Why have you come out to draw up for battle? Am I not a Philistine, and are you not servants of Saul? Choose a man for yourselves, and let him come down to me. [9] If he is able to fight with me and kill me, then we will be your servants; but if I prevail against him and kill him, then you shall be our servants and serve us." [10] And the Philistine said, "Today I defy the ranks of Israel! Give me a man, that we may fight together." [11] When Saul and all Israel heard these words of the Philistine, they were dismayed and greatly afraid. . . .

[19] Now Saul, and they, and all the men of Israel, were in the valley of Elah, fighting with the Philistines. [20] David rose early in the morning, left the sheep with a keeper, took the provisions, and went as Jesse had commanded him. He came to the encampment as the army was going forth to the battle line, shouting the war cry. [21] Israel and the Philistines drew up for battle, army against army. [22] David left the things in charge of the keeper of the baggage, ran to the ranks, and went and greeted his brothers. [23] As he talked with them, the champion, the Philistine of Gath, Goliath by name, came up out of the ranks of the Philistines, and spoke the same words as before. And David heard him. . . .

[32] David said to Saul, "Let no one's heart fail because of him; your servant will go and fight with this Philistine." [33] Saul said to David, "You are not able to go against this Philistine to fight with him; for you are just a boy, and he has been a warrior from his youth." [34] But David said to Saul, "Your servant used to keep sheep for his father; and whenever a lion or a bear came, and took a lamb from the flock, [35] I went after it and struck it down, rescuing the lamb from its mouth; and if it turned against me, I would catch it by the jaw, strike it down, and kill it. [36] Your servant has killed both lions and bears; and this uncircumcised Philistine shall be like one of them, since he has defied the armies of the living God." [37] David said, "The Lord, who saved me from the paw of the lion and from the paw of the bear, will save me from the hand of this Philistine." So Saul said to David, "Go, and may the Lord be with you!"

[38] Saul clothed David with his armor; he put a bronze helmet on his head and clothed him with a coat of mail. [39] David strapped Saul's sword over the armor, and he tried in vain to walk, for he was not used to them. Then David said to Saul, "I cannot walk with these; for I am not used to them." So David removed them. [40] Then he took his staff in his hand, and chose five smooth stones from the wadi, and put them in his shepherd's bag, in the pouch; his sling was in his hand, and he drew near to the Philistine.

[41] The Philistine came on and drew near to David, with his shield-bearer in front of him. [42] When the Philistine looked and saw David, he disdained him, for he was only a youth, ruddy and handsome in appearance. [43] The Philistine said to David, "Am I a dog, that you come to me with sticks?" And the Philistine cursed David by his gods. [44] The Philistine said to David, "Come to me, and I will give your flesh to the birds of the air and to the wild animals of the field." [45] But David said to the Philistine, "You come to me with sword and spear and javelin; but I come to you in the name of the Lord of hosts, the God of the armies of Israel, whom you have defied. [46] This very day the Lord will deliver you into my hand, and I will strike you down and cut off your head; and I will give the dead bodies of the Philistine army this very day to the birds of the air and to the wild animals of the earth, so that all the earth may know that there is a God in Israel, [47] and that all this assembly may know that the Lord does not save by sword and spear; for the battle is the Lord's and he will give you into our hand." [48] When the Philistine drew nearer to meet David, David ran quickly toward the battle line to meet the Philistine. [49] David put his hand in his bag, took out a stone, slung it, and struck the Philistine on his forehead; the stone sank into his forehead, and he fell face down on the ground.

Psalm 9:9-20

[9] The Lord is a stronghold for the oppressed, a stronghold in times of trouble. [10] And those who know your name put their trust in you, for you, O Lord, have not forsaken those who seek you. [11] Sing praises to the Lord, who dwells in Zion. Declare his deeds among the peoples. [12] For he who avenges blood is mindful of them; he does not forget the cry of the afflicted. [13] Be gracious to me, O Lord. See what I suffer from those who hate me; you are the one who lifts me up from the gates of death, [14] so that I may recount all your praises, and, in the gates of daughter Zion, rejoice in your deliverance. [15] The nations have sunk in the pit that they made; in the net that they hid has their own foot been caught. [16] The Lord has made himself known, he has executed judgment; the wicked are snared in the work of their own hands. [17] The wicked shall depart to Sheol, all the nations that forget God. [18] For the needy shall not always be forgotten, nor the hope of the poor perish forever. [19] Rise up, O Lord! Do not let mortals prevail; let the nations be judged before you. [20] Put them in fear, O Lord; let the nations know that they are only human.

---

2 Corinthians 6:1-13

[1] As we work together with him, we urge you also not to accept the grace of God in vain. [2] For he says, "At an acceptable time I have listened to you, and on a day of salvation I have helped you." See, now is the acceptable time; see, now is the day of salvation! [3] We are putting no obstacle in anyone's way, so that no fault may be found with our ministry, [4] but as servants of God we have commended ourselves in every way: through great endurance, in afflictions, hardships, calamities, [5] beatings, imprisonments, riots, labors, sleepless nights, hunger; [6] by purity, knowledge, patience, kindness, holiness of spirit, genuine love, [7] truthful speech, and the power of God; with the weapons of righteousness for the right hand and for the left; [8] in honor and dishonor, in ill repute and good repute. We are treated as impostors, and yet are true; [9] as unknown, and yet are well known; as dying, and see—we are alive; as punished, and yet not killed; [10] as sorrowful, yet always rejoicing; as poor, yet making many rich; as having nothing, and yet possessing everything.

[11] We have spoken frankly to you Corinthians; our heart is wide open to you. [12] There is no restriction in our affections, but only in yours. [13] In return—I speak as to children—open wide your hearts also.

Mark 4:35-41

[35] On that day, when evening had come, he said to them, "Let us go across to the other side." [36] And leaving the crowd behind, they took him with them in the boat, just as he was. Other boats were with him. [37] A great windstorm arose, and the waves beat into the boat, so that the boat was already being swamped. [38] But he was in the stern, asleep on the cushion; and they woke him up and said to him, "Teacher, do you not care that we are perishing?" [39] He woke up and rebuked the wind, and said to the sea, "Peace! Be still!" Then the wind ceased, and there was a dead calm. [40] He said to them, "Why are you afraid? Have you still no faith?" [41] And they were filled with great awe and said to one another, "Who then is this, that even the wind and the sea obey him?"

Primary Hymns and Songs for the Day
"Lift Every Voice and Sing" (1 Sam, 2 Cor) (O)
   B627, C631, E599, EL841, L562, N593, P563, UM519, W641
      H-3   Chr-128
"It Is Well with My Soul" (2 Cor, Mark)
   B410, C561, E785, F495, L346, N438, UM377
      H-3   Chr-113
"Eternal Father, Strong to Save" (Mark)
   B69, C85, E579/E608, EL756, F679, L467, P562 (PD), S2191,
   VU659
      H-3   Chr-63; Desc-74; Org-89
"Stand By Me" (Mark) (C)
   C629, UM512
      H-3   Chr-177

Additional Hymn Suggestions
"Lead Me, Lord" (1 Sam)
   C593, N774, R175, UM473 (PD), VU662
"A Mighty Fortress Is Our God" (1 Sam, Pss, Mark)
   B8, C65, E687/E688, EL503/EL504/EL505, F118, L228/L229,
   N439/N440, P259/P260, UM110 (PD), VU261/VU262/VU263,
   W575/W576
"By Gracious Powers" (1 Sam, Pss)
   E695/E696, EL626, N413, P342, UM517, W577
"God of Grace and God of Glory" (1 Sam, Pss, Mark)
   B395, C464, E594/E595, EL705, F528, L415, N436, P420, R301,
   UM577, VU686
"We Sing to You, O God" (Pss)
   EL791, N9, S2001, SF2001
"Come, Ye Disconsolate" (2 Cor)
   B67, C502, EL607, SF2132, UM510 (PD)
"Am I a Soldier of the Cross" (2 Cor)
   B481, F411, UM511
"Stand Up, Stand Up for Jesus" (2 Cor)
   B485/B487, C613, E561, F616, L389, UM514 (PD)
"O Day of God, Draw Nigh" (2 Cor)
   B623, C700, E601, N611, P452, UM730 (PD), VU688, and
   VU689 (Fr.)
"God of the Sparrow, God of the Whale" (Mark)
   C70, EL740, N32, P272, UM122, VU229
"My Hope Is Built" (Mark)
   B406, C537, EL596, F92, L293/L294, N368, P379, UM368 (PD)
"Lonely the Boat" (Mark)
   P373, UM476
"Jesus, Savior, Pilot Me" (Mark)
   EL755, L334, N441, UM509 (PD), VU637
"We'll Understand It Better By and By" (Mark)
   N444, UM525 (PD)
"How Firm a Foundation" (Mark)
   B338, C618, E636, EL796, F32, L507, N407, P361, UM529
   (PD), VU660, W585
"Jesus, Priceless Treasure" (Mark)
   E701, EL775, F277, L457, N480, P365, UM532 (PD), VU667
   and VU668 (Fr.)
"Be Still, My Soul" (Mark)
   C566, F77, N488, UM534, VU652
"Jesus, Lover of My Soul" (Mark)
   B180, C542, E699, F222, N546, P303, UM479 (PD), VU669
"Blessed Quietness" (Mark)
   F145, C267, N284, S2142, SF2142

"My Life Flows On" (Mark)
   C619, EL763, N476, S2212, SF2212, VU716

Additional Contemporary Suggestions
"Oh, I Know the Lord's Laid His Hands on Me" (1 Sam)
   S2139, SF2139
"Nothing Can Trouble" (1 Sam, Pss)
   S2054, SF2054, VU290
"Ah, Lord God" (1 Sam, Pss)
   R254, SP2
"What Mighty God We Serve" (1 Sam, Pss)
   SP3, S2021, SF2021, R159
"Great and Mighty Is He" (1 Sam, Pss)
   SP4, M11
"The Battle Belongs to the Lord" (1 Sam, 2 Cor)
   R244, SP158
"We Want to See Jesus Lifted High" (2 Cor)
   M67
"Through It All" (2 Cor)
   C555, F43, UM507
"Awesome God" (1 Sam, Mark)
   R245, S2040, SF2040, SP11
"Be Still and Know That I Am God" (Mark)
   S2057, SF2057, SP49, R10
"Healer of Our Every Ill" (Mark)
   C506, EL612, S2213, SF2213, VU619
"In Christ Alone" (Mark)
   M138

Vocal Solos
"What God Hath Promised" (2 Cor)
V-8   p. 297
"Jesus, Lover of My Soul" (Mark)
V-1   p. 37

Anthems
"Who Can This Be?" (Mark)
David Haas; GIA Publications G-3499
Unison, two equal or mixed voices with keyboard

"It Is Well with My Soul" (Mark)
arr. John Helgen; Kjos 9051
SATB *divisi* with piano

Other Suggestions
Visuals:
   O   Armor, sword/spear, slingshot, stones, bag
   P   Globe, scales of justice, rejoicing
   E   Clock set for worship hour, enduring hardship
   G   Boat, storm, fear, calm, sleeping, Jesus in command
Call to Prayer: C181. "The Storm Is Strong" (Mark)
Prayer: C624. "We Ask Not for Easy Lives" (Mark)
Scripture Response: C566, F77, N488, UM534, VU652, stanza 2. "Be
   Still, My Soul" (Mark)
Alternate Lessons: Job 38:1-11; Ps 107:1-3, 23-32 (*See page 3.*)

2 Samuel 1:1, 17-27

[1] After the death of Saul, when David had returned from defeating the Amalekites, David remained two days in Ziklag. . . .

[17] David intoned this lamentation over Saul and his son Jonathan. [18] (He ordered that The Song of the Bow be taught to the people of Judah; it is written in the Book of Jashar.) He said: [19] Your glory, O Israel, lies slain upon your high places! How the mighty have fallen! [20] Tell it not in Gath, proclaim it not in the streets of Ashkelon; or the daughters of the Philistines will rejoice, the daughters of the uncircumcised will exult. [21] You mountains of Gilboa, let there be no dew or rain upon you, nor bounteous fields! For there the shield of the mighty was defiled, the shield of Saul, anointed with oil no more. [22] From the blood of the slain, from the fat of the mighty, the bow of Jonathan did not turn back, nor the sword of Saul return empty. [23] Saul and Jonathan, beloved and lovely! In life and in death they were not divided; they were swifter than eagles, they were stronger than lions. [24] O daughters of Israel, weep over Saul, who clothed you with crimson, in luxury, who put ornaments of gold on your apparel. [25] How the mighty have fallen in the midst of the battle! Jonathan lies slain upon your high places. [26] I am distressed for you, my brother Jonathan; greatly beloved were you to me; your love to me was wonderful, passing the love of women. [27] How the mighty have fallen, and the weapons of war perished!

Psalm 130

[1] Out of the depths I cry to you, O LORD. [2] Lord, hear my voice! Let your ears be attentive to the voice of my supplications! [3] If you, O LORD, should mark iniquities, Lord, who could stand? [4] But there is forgiveness with you, so that you may be revered. [5] I wait for the LORD, my soul waits, and in his word I hope; [6] my soul waits for the Lord more than those who watch for the morning, more than those who watch for the morning. [7] O Israel, hope in the LORD! For with the LORD there is steadfast love, and with him is great power to redeem. [8] It is he who will redeem Israel from all its iniquities.

2 Corinthians 8:7-15

[7] Now as you excel in everything—in faith, in speech, in knowledge, in utmost eagerness, and in our love for you—so we want you to excel also in this generous undertaking.

[8] I do not say this as a command, but I am testing the genuineness of your love against the earnestness of others. [9] For you know the generous act of our Lord Jesus Christ, that though he was rich, yet for your sakes he became poor, so that by his poverty you might become rich. [10] And in this matter I am giving my advice: it is appropriate for you who began last year not only to do something but even to desire to do something— [11] now finish doing it, so that your eagerness may be matched by completing it according to your means. [12] For if the eagerness is there, the gift is acceptable according to what one has—not according to what one does not have. [13] I do not mean that there should be relief for others and pressure on you, but it is a question of a fair balance between [14] your present abundance and their need, so that their abundance may be for your need, in order that there may be a fair balance. [15] As it is written, "The one who had much did not have too much, and the one who had little did not have too little."

Mark 5:21-43

[21] When Jesus had crossed again in the boat to the other side, a great crowd gathered around him; and he was by the sea. [22] Then one of the leaders of the synagogue named Jairus came and, when he saw him, fell at his feet [23] and begged him repeatedly, "My little daughter is at the point of death. Come and lay your hands on her, so that she may be made well, and live." [24] So he went with him.

And a large crowd followed him and pressed in on him. [25] Now there was a woman who had been suffering from hemorrhages for twelve years. [26] She had endured much under many physicians, and had spent all that she had; and she was no better, but rather grew worse. [27] She had heard about Jesus, and came up behind him in the crowd and touched his cloak, [28] for she said, "If I but touch his clothes, I will be made well." [29] Immediately her hemorrhage stopped; and she felt in her body that she was healed of her disease. [30] Immediately aware that power had gone forth from him, Jesus turned about in the crowd and said, "Who touched my clothes?" [31] And his disciples said to him, "You see the crowd pressing in on you; how can you say, 'Who touched me?' " [32] He looked all around to see who had done it. [33] But the woman, knowing what had happened to her, came in fear and trembling, fell down before him, and told him the whole truth. [34] He said to her, "Daughter, your faith has made you well; go in peace, and be healed of your disease."

[35] While he was still speaking, some people came from the leader's house to say, "Your daughter is dead. Why trouble the teacher any further?" [36] But overhearing what they said, Jesus said to the leader of the synagogue, "Do not fear, only believe." [37] He allowed no one to follow him except Peter, James, and John, the brother of James. [38] When they came to the house of the leader of the synagogue, he saw a commotion, people weeping and wailing loudly. [39] When he had entered, he said to them, "Why do you make a commotion and weep? The child is not dead but sleeping." [40] And they laughed at him. Then he put them all outside, and took the child's father and mother and those who were with him, and went in where the child was. [41] He took her by the hand and said to her, "Talitha cum," which means, "Little girl, get up!" [42] And immediately the girl got up and began to walk about (she was twelve years of age). At this they were overcome with amazement. [43] He strictly ordered them that no one should know this, and told them to give her something to eat.

Primary Hymns and Songs for the Day

"O God, Our Help in Ages Past" (2 Sam) (O)
> B74, C67, E680, EL632, F370, L320, N25, P210, UM117 (PD),
> VU806, W579
>> H-3   Hbl-87; Chr-60, 143; Desc-93; Org-132
>> S-1   #293-296. Various treatments

"Where Cross the Crowded Ways of Life" (2 Cor, Mark)
> C665, E609, EL719, F665, L429, N543, P408, UM427 (PD),
> VU681
>> H-3   Chr-178, 180; Org-44
>> S-1   #141-43 Various treatments

"Cuando El Pobre" ("When the Poor Ones") (2 Cor, Mark)
> C662, EL725, P407, UM434, VU702

"Precious Lord, Take My Hand" (2 Sam, Pss, Mark)
> B456, C628, EL773, F611, N472, P404, UM474, VU670

"Be Still, My Soul" (2 Sam, Pss, Mark)
> C566, F77, N488, UM534, VU652
>> H-3   Chr-36

"I'm Gonna Live So God Can Use Me" (2 Cor) (C)
> C614, P369, S2153, VU575

Additional Hymn Suggestions

"Rejoice in God's Saints" (2 Sam) (O)
> C476, EL418, UM708

"Come, Ye Disconsolate" (2 Sam, Pss, Communion)
> B67, C502, EL607, SF2132, UM510 (PD)

"Out of the Depths I Cry to You" (2 Sam, Pss)
> EL600, L295, N483, P240, UM515

"Abide with Me" (2 Sam, Pss)
> B63, C636, E662, EL629, F500, L272, N99, P543, UM700 (PD),
> VU436

"Why Has God Forsaken Me?" (2 Sam, Pss)
> P406, S2110, VU154

"Out of the Depths" (2 Sam, Pss)
> C510, N554, S2136, SF2136, VU611

"Healer of Our Every Ill" (2 Sam, Pss)
> C506, EL612, S2213, SF2213, VU619

"Heal Me, Hands of Jesus" (Mark)
> C504, UM262, VU621

"When Jesus the Healer Passed Through Galilee" (Mark)
> UM263, VU358

"O Christ, the Healer" (Mark)
> C503, EL610, L360, N175, P380, R191, UM265, W747

"Only Trust Him" (Mark)
> B317, F629, UM337 (PD)

"Come, Ye Sinners, Poor and Needy" (Mark)
> B323 (PD), R141, UM340, W756

"Pass Me Not, O Gentle Savior" (Mark)
> B308, F416, N551, UM351 (PD), VU665

"Just as I Am, Without One Plea" (Mark)
> B303/B307, C339, E693, EL592, F417, L296, N207, P370, R140,
> UM357 (PD), VU508

"He Touched Me" (Mark)
> C564, F628, UM367

"Victory in Jesus" (Mark)
> B426, F82, UM370

"An Outcast Among Outcasts" (Mark)
> N201, S2104, SF2104

"Draw Us in the Spirit's Tether" (Mark, Communion)
> C392, EL470, N337, P504, UM632, VU479, W731

Additional Contemporary Suggestions

"Cares Chorus" (2 Sam, Pss)
> S2215, SF2215, SP221

"People Need the Lord" (Pss, Mark)
> B557, S2244, SF2244

"Give Thanks" (2 Cor)
> C528, R266, S2036, SF2036, SP170

"He Who Began a Good Work in You" (2 Cor)
> S2163, SF2163, SP180, R134

"Make Me a Servant" (2 Cor)
> S2176, SF2176, SP193

"Take This Life" (2 Cor)
> M98

"These Hands" (2 Cor)
> M101

"Oh Lord, You're Beautiful" (Mark)
> S2064, SF2064

"El-Shaddai" (Mark)
> UM123, S-2 #54

"Surely the Presence of the Lord" (Mark)
> C263, R167, SP243, UM328; S-2, #200 Stanzas for soloist

"Spirit Song" (Mark)
> C352, R248, SP134, UM347

"Turn Your Eyes upon Jesus" (Mark)
> B320, F621, SP218, UM349

"Awesome God" (Mark)
> R245, S2040, SF2040, SP11

"I'm So Glad Jesus Lifted Me" (Mark)
> C529, EL860 (PD), N474, S2151, SF2151

Vocal Solos

"Like a Child" (2 Sam, Pss)
> V-8   p. 356

"Jesus, Thou Art Watching Ever" (Pss)
> V-4   p. 6

Anthems

"When to Our World the Savior Came" (Mark)
Joseph Herl; MorningStar 50-5807
SATB with keyboard; opt. Congregation

"I Heard the Voice of Jesus Say" (Mark)
John Helgen; Choristers Guild CGA1177
SAB with keyboard

Other Suggestions

Visuals:
> **O**   Bow/sword, mourning, dead soldiers
> **P**   Darkness, prayer, patient waiting, dawn, Ps 130:5-6
> **E**   Kindness, Jesus, poverty/wealth, full offering plate
> **G**   Boat, child dead/woman reaching, child well/woman
>   rejoicing, Jesus healing

Prayer: C660, UM446. "Serving the Poor" (2 Cor)
Benediction: B660, C437, R293, UM665, VU964. "Go Now in Peace"
> (Mark)
Alternate Lessons: Wis 1:13-15; 2:23-24; Lam 3:23-33 or Ps 30 (*See
> page 3.*)

2 Samuel 5:1-5, 9-10

[1] Then all the tribes of Israel came to David at Hebron, and said, "Look, we are your bone and flesh. [2] For some time, while Saul was king over us, it was you who led out Israel and brought it in. The LORD said to you: It is you who shall be shepherd of my people Israel, you who shall be ruler over Israel." [3] So all the elders of Israel came to the king at Hebron; and King David made a covenant with them at Hebron before the LORD, and they anointed David king over Israel. [4] David was thirty years old when he began to reign, and he reigned forty years. [5] At Hebron he reigned over Judah seven years and six months; and at Jerusalem he reigned over all Israel and Judah thirty-three years. . . .

[9] David occupied the stronghold, and named it the city of David. David built the city all around from the Millo inward. [10] And David became greater and greater, for the LORD, the God of hosts, was with him.

Psalm 48

[1] Great is the LORD and greatly to be praised in the city of our God. His holy mountain, [2] beautiful in elevation, is the joy of all the earth, Mount Zion, in the far north, the city of the great King. [3] Within its citadels God has shown himself a sure defense. [4] Then the kings assembled, they came on together. [5] As soon as they saw it, they were astounded; they were in panic, they took to flight; [6] trembling took hold of them there, pains as of a woman in labor, [7] as when an east wind shatters the ships of Tarshish. [8] As we have heard, so have we seen in the city of the LORD of hosts, in the city of our God, which God establishes forever. [9] We ponder your steadfast love, O God, in the midst of your temple. [10] Your name, O God, like your praise, reaches to the ends of the earth. Your right hand is filled with victory. [11] Let Mount Zion be glad, let the towns of Judah rejoice because of your judgments. [12] Walk about Zion, go all around it, count its towers, [13] consider well its ramparts; go through its citadels, that you may tell the next generation [14] that this is God, our God forever and ever. He will be our guide forever.

2 Corinthians 12:2-10

[2] I know a person in Christ who fourteen years ago was caught up to the third heaven—whether in the body or out of the body I do not know; God knows. [3] And I know that such a person—whether in the body or out of the body I do not know; God knows— [4] was caught up into Paradise and heard things that are not to be told, that no mortal is permitted to repeat. [5] On behalf of such a one I will boast, but on my own behalf I will not boast, except of my weaknesses. [6] But if I wish to boast, I will not be a fool, for I will be speaking the truth. But I refrain from it, so that no one may think better of me than what is seen in me or heard from me, [7] even considering the exceptional character of the revelations. Therefore, to keep me from being too elated, a thorn was given me in the flesh, a messenger of Satan to torment me, to keep me from being too elated. [8] Three times I appealed to the Lord about this, that it would leave me, [9] but he said to me, "My grace is sufficient for you, for power is made perfect in weakness." So, I will boast all the more gladly of my weaknesses, so that the power of Christ may dwell in me. [10] Therefore I am content with weaknesses, insults, hardships, persecutions, and calamities for the sake of Christ; for whenever I am weak, then I am strong.

Mark 6:1-13

[1] He left that place and came to his hometown, and his disciples followed him. [2] On the sabbath he began to teach in the synagogue, and many who heard him were astounded. They said, "Where did this man get all this? What is this wisdom that has been given to him? What deeds of power are being done by his hands! [3] Is not this the carpenter, the son of Mary and brother of James and Joses and Judas and Simon, and are not his sisters here with us?" And they took offense at him. [4] Then Jesus said to them, "Prophets are not without honor, except in their hometown, and among their own kin, and in their own house." [5] And he could do no deed of power there, except that he laid his hands on a few sick people and cured them. [6] And he was amazed at their unbelief.

Then he went about among the villages teaching. [7] He called the twelve and began to send them out two by two, and gave them authority over the unclean spirits. [8] He ordered them to take nothing for their journey except a staff; no bread, no bag, no money in their belts; [9] but to wear sandals and not to put on two tunics. [10] He said to them, "Wherever you enter a house, stay there until you leave the place. [11] If any place will not welcome you and they refuse to hear you, as you leave, shake off the dust that is on your feet as a testimony against them." [12] So they went out and proclaimed that all should repent. [13] They cast out many demons, and anointed with oil many who were sick and cured them.

Primary Hymns and Songs for the Day

"Come, Thou Fount of Every Blessing" (2 Cor) (O)
   B15, C16, E686, EL807, F318, L499, N459, P356, UM400 (PD),
   VU559
        H-3   Chr-57; Desc-79; Org-96
        S-1   #244. Descant
"I Sing Praises to Your Name" (Pss)
   R79, S2037, SF2037, SP27
"Christ for the World We Sing" (Mark)
   E537, F686, R299, UM568 (PD)
        H-3   Hbl-28, 49, 53; Chr-56; Desc-57; Org-63
        S-1   #185-186. Descant and harmonization
"The Summons" (Mark)
   EL798, S2130, SF2130, VU567
"Lord, You Give the Great Commission" (Mark) (C)
   C459, E528, EL579, P429, R305, UM584, VU512, W470
        H-3   Hbl-61; Chr-132; Org-2
        S-1   #4-5. Instrumental and vocal descants

Additional Hymn Suggestions

"I Want to Walk as a Child of the Light" (2 Sam)
   E490, EL815, R152, UM206, W510
"Come, We That Love the Lord" (2 Sam, Pss)
   B525, E392, N379, UM732, VU715, W552
"Marching to Zion" (2 Sam, Pss)
   B524, C707, EL625, F550, N382, UM733 (PD), VU714
"Praise to the Lord, the Almighty" (Pss)
   B14, C25, E390, EL858 (PD) and 859, F337, L543, N22, P482,
   R57, UM139, VU220 (Fr.) and VU221, W547
"Glorious Things of Thee Are Spoken" (Pss)
   B398, C709, E522/E523, EL647, F376, L358, N307, P446,
   UM731 (PD)
"Guide My Feet" (Pss, 2 Cor, Mark)
   N497, P354, S2208, SF2208
"Come, Ye Sinners, Poor and Needy" (2 Cor)
   B323 (PD), R141, UM340, W756
"Amazing Grace" (2 Cor)
   B330, C546, E671, EL779, F107, L448, N547/N548, P280,
   R189, UM378 (PD), VU266 (Fr.), W583
"O Love That Wilt Not Let Me Go" (2 Cor)
   B292, C540, F404, L324, N485, P384, UM480 (PD), VU658
"Through It All" (2 Cor)
   C555, F43, UM507
"Lord, Whose Love Through Humble Service" (2 Cor, Mark)
   C461, E610, EL712, R286, L423, UM581, W630
"Living for Jesus" (2 Cor, Mark)
   B282, C610, F462, S2149, SF2149
"We Meet You, O Christ" (Mark)
   C183, P311, UM257, VU183
"Dear Lord and Father of Mankind" (Mark)
        (Alternate Text "Parent of Us All")
   B267, C594, E652/E653, F422, L506, N502, P345, UM358
   (PD), VU608
"Send Me, Lord" (Mark)
   C447, EL809, N360, R308, UM497, VU572
"Lord of All Hopefulness" (Mark)
   E482, EL765, L469, R174, S2197, SF2197, W568
"We All Are One in Mission" (Mark)
   EL576, P435, S2243, SF2243

"The Spirit Sends Us Forth to Serve" (Mark) (C)
   EL551, S2241, SF2241
"Sent Forth by God's Blessing" (Mark) (C)
   EL547, L221, N76, R307, UM664, VU481

Additional Contemporary Suggestions

"How Great Are You, Lord" (Pss)
   M103
"Great Is the Lord" (Pss)
   B12, R22, S2022, SF2022, SP30
"Give Thanks" (2 Cor)
   C528, R266, S2036, SF2036, SP170
"Grace Alone" (2 Cor)
   M100, S2162, SF2162
"You Are My Hiding Place" (2 Cor)
   C554, S2055, SF2055
"The Power of Your Love" (2 Cor)
   M26
"You Are My All in All" (2 Cor)
   SP220
"All Things Are Possible" (2 Cor)
   M92
"Shout to the North" (2 Cor)
   M99
"Carry the Light" (Mark)
   SP143
"Awesome God" (Mark)
   R245, S2040, SF2040, SP11
"Sent Out in Jesus' Name" (Mark) (C)
   EL538, S2184, SF2184
"Song of Hope" (Mark) (C)
   P432, S2186, VU424

Vocal Solos

"What God Hath Promised" (2 Cor)
V-8   p. 297
"Gospel Train" (Mark)
V-7   p. 74

Anthems

"Amazing Grace" (2 Cor)
Mark A. Miller; Abingdon Press 0687493870
Unison/two-part with keyboard (opt. solo)

"Dear Lord and Father of Mankind" (Mark)
Austin Lovelace; Hinshaw HMC1374
SATB with organ

Other Suggestions

Visuals:
   O   Shepherd, crown, oil
   P   People at worship, fear, globe, right hand
   E   Clay vessels, conditions, handicap sign
   G   Teams of two, staff, sandals, tunic, oil
Litany: C451 or C460. "On Mission and Ministry" (Mark)
Response to Scripture: E490, EL815, R152, UM206, W510, refrain.
   "I Want to Walk as a Child of the Light" (2 Sam)
Choral Response: B10, C33, EL856, F2, L532, N35, P467, R250,
   UM77, VU238, stanza 1. "How Great Thou Art" (Pss)
Alternate Lessons: Eze 2:1-5; Ps 123 (*See page 3.*)

2 Samuel 6:1-5, 12b-19

[1] David again gathered all the chosen men of Israel, thirty thousand. [2] David and all the people with him set out and went from Baale-judah, to bring up from there the ark of God, which is called by the name of the LORD of hosts who is enthroned on the cherubim. [3] They carried the ark of God on a new cart, and brought it out of the house of Abinadab, which was on the hill. Uzzah and Ahio, the sons of Abinadab, were driving the new cart [4] with the ark of God; and Ahio went in front of the ark. [5] David and all the house of Israel were dancing before the LORD with all their might, with songs and lyres and harps and tambourines and castanets and cymbals. . . .

[12b] So David went and brought up the ark of God from the house of Obed-edom to the city of David with rejoicing; [13] and when those who bore the ark of the LORD had gone six paces, he sacrificed an ox and a fatling. [14] David danced before the LORD with all his might; David was girded with a linen ephod. [15] So David and all the house of Israel brought up the ark of the LORD with shouting, and with the sound of the trumpet.

[16] As the ark of the LORD came into the city of David, Michal daughter of Saul looked out of the window, and saw King David leaping and dancing before the LORD; and she despised him in her heart.

[17] They brought in the ark of the LORD, and set it in its place, inside the tent that David had pitched for it; and David offered burnt offerings and offerings of well-being before the LORD. [18] When David had finished offering the burnt offerings and the offerings of well-being, he blessed the people in the name of the LORD of hosts, [19] and distributed food among all the people, the whole multitude of Israel, both men and women, to each a cake of bread, a portion of meat, and a cake of raisins. Then all the people went back to their homes.

Psalm 24

[1] The earth is the LORD's and all that is in it, the world, and those who live in it; [2] for he has founded it on the seas, and established it on the rivers. [3] Who shall ascend the hill of the LORD? And who shall stand in his holy place? [4] Those who have clean hands and pure hearts, who do not lift up their souls to what is false, and do not swear deceitfully. [5] They will receive blessing from the LORD, and vindication from the God of their salvation. [6] Such is the company of those who seek him, who seek the face of the God of Jacob. [7] Lift up your heads, O gates! and be lifted up, O ancient doors! that the King of glory may come in. [8] Who is the King of glory? The LORD, strong and mighty, the LORD, mighty in battle. [9] Lift up your heads, O gates! and be lifted up, O ancient doors! that the King of glory may come in. [10] Who is this King of glory? The LORD of hosts, he is the King of glory.

Ephesians 1:3-14

[3] Blessed be the God and Father of our Lord Jesus Christ, who has blessed us in Christ with every spiritual blessing in the heavenly places, [4] just as he chose us in Christ before the foundation of the world to be holy and blameless before him in love. [5] He destined us for adoption as his children through Jesus Christ, according to the good pleasure of his will, [6] to the praise of his glorious grace that he freely bestowed on us in the Beloved. [7] In him we have redemption through his blood, the forgiveness of our trespasses, according to the riches of his grace [8] that he lavished on us. With all wisdom and insight [9] he has made known to us the mystery of his will, according to his good pleasure that he set forth in Christ, [10] as a plan for the fullness of time, to gather up all things in him, things in heaven and things on earth. [11] In Christ we have also obtained an inheritance, having been destined according to the purpose of him who accomplishes all things according to his counsel and will, [12] so that we, who were the first to set our hope on Christ, might live for the praise of his glory. [13] In him you also, when you had heard the word of truth, the gospel of your salvation, and had believed in him, were marked with the seal of the promised Holy Spirit; [14] this is the pledge of our inheritance toward redemption as God's own people, to the praise of his glory.

Mark 6:14-29

[14] King Herod heard of it, for Jesus' name had become known. Some were saying, "John the baptizer has been raised from the dead; and for this reason these powers are at work in him." [15] But others said, "It is Elijah." And others said, "It is a prophet, like one of the prophets of old." [16] But when Herod heard of it, he said, "John, whom I beheaded, has been raised."

[17] For Herod himself had sent men who arrested John, bound him, and put him in prison on account of Herodias, his brother Philip's wife, because Herod had married her. [18] For John had been telling Herod, "It is not lawful for you to have your brother's wife." [19] And Herodias had a grudge against him, and wanted to kill him. But she could not, [20] for Herod feared John, knowing that he was a righteous and holy man, and he protected him. When he heard him, he was greatly perplexed; and yet he liked to listen to him. [21] But an opportunity came when Herod on his birthday gave a banquet for his courtiers and officers and for the leaders of Galilee. [22] When his daughter Herodias came in and danced, she pleased Herod and his guests; and the king said to the girl, "Ask me for whatever you wish, and I will give it." [23] And he solemnly swore to her, "Whatever you ask me, I will give you, even half of my kingdom." [24] She went out and said to her mother, "What should I ask for?" She replied, "The head of John the baptizer." [25] Immediately she rushed back to the king and requested, "I want you to give me at once the head of John the Baptist on a platter." [26] The king was deeply grieved; yet out of regard for his oaths and for the guests, he did not want to refuse her. [27] Immediately the king sent a soldier of the guard with orders to bring John's head. He went and beheaded him in the prison, [28] brought his head on a platter, and gave it to the girl. Then the girl gave it to her mother. [29] When his disciples heard about it, they came and took his body, and laid it in a tomb.

Primary Hymns and Songs for the Day

"Lift Up Your Heads, Ye Mighty Gates" (Pss) (O)
    B128, C129, E436, F239, N117, P8, R59, UM213 (PD), W363
        H-3   Hbl-50; Chr-129; Desc-101; Org-167
        S-1   #334-35. Descant and harmonization
"The King of Glory Comes" (Pss)
    B127, R267, S2091, SF2091, W501
"My Tribute" ("To God Be the Glory") (Eph)
    B153, C39, F365, N14, R68, UM99; V-8 p. 5 Vocal Solo
        S-2   #130. Stanza for soloist
"It Is Well with My Soul" (Eph) (C)
    B410, C561, EL785, F495, L346, N438, UM377
        H-3   Chr-113

Additional Hymn Suggestions

"When in Our Music God Is Glorified" (2 Sam)
    B435, C7, E420, EL850/EL851, L555, N561, P264, R62, UM68,
    VU533, W549
"What Gift Can We Bring" (2 Sam, Pss)
    N370, UM87
"Let All the World in Every Corner Sing" (2 Sam, Pss)
    B28, E402, P468, UM93, W536
"Cantemos al Señor" ("Let's Sing unto the Lord") (2 Sam, Pss)
    B38, C60, EL555, N39, R11, UM149
"My Gratitude Now Accept, O God" (Pss)
    S2044, SF2044
"There's a Wideness in God's Mercy" (Eph)
    B25, C73, E470, EL587/EL588, F115, L290, N23, P298, UM121,
    VU271, W595
"Children of the Heavenly Father" (Eph)
    B55, EL781, F89, L474, N487, UM141
"Word of God, Come Down on Earth" (Eph)
    E633, EL510, UM182, W513
"Morning Glory, Starlit Sky" (Eph)
    E585, UM194, W587
"Nothing but the Blood" (Eph)
    B135, F266, UM362 (PD)
"Blessed Assurance" (Eph)
    B334, C543, EL638, F67, N473, P341, UM369 (PD), VU337
"Amazing Grace" (Eph)
    B330, C546, E671, EL779, F107, L448, N547/N548, P280,
    R189, UM378 (PD), VU266 (Fr.), W583
"God Hath Spoken by the Prophets" (Mark)
    L238, UM108, W516
"We'll Understand It Better By and By" (Mark)
    N444, UM525 (PD)
"How Firm a Foundation" (Mark)
    B338, C618, E636, EL796, F32, L507, N407, P361, UM529
    (PD), VU660, W585
"Be Still, My Soul" (Mark)
    C566, F77, N488, UM534, VU652
"For All the Saints" (Mark)
    B355, C637, E287, EL422, F614, L174, N299, P526, UM711
    (PD), VU705, W705
"Wild and Lone the Prophet's Voice" (Mark)
    P409, S2089, SF2089
"Blest Are They" (Mark)
    R127, EL728, S2155, SF2155, VU896

Additional Contemporary Suggestions

"Clap Your Hands" (2 Sam)
    S2028, SF2028
"I Could Sing of Your Love Forever" (2 Sam)
    M63; V-3 p. 22 Vocal Solo
"We Will Dance" (2 Sam)
    M140
"Awesome in This Place" (2 Sam, Pss)
    M36
"Holy Ground" (2 Sam, Pss)
    B224, C112, S2272, SF2272, SP86
"Holy, Holy" (Eph)
    B254, F149, P140, R206, S2039, SP141
"Grace Alone" (Eph)
    M100, S2162, SF2162
"We Fall Down" (Eph)
    M66
"You Are My King" ("Amazing Love") (Eph)
    M82
"Hallelujah" ("Your Love Is Amazing") (Eph)
    M118
"Through It All" (Mark)
    C555, F43, UM507
"We Shall Overcome" (Mark)
    C630, N570, UM533

Vocal Solos

"I Will Sing of Thy Great Mercies" (2 Sam, Eph)
    V-4   p. 43
"Lift Up Your Heads" (Pss)
    V-10   p. 38
"Amazing Grace" (Eph)
    V-5   p. 8
    V-8   p. 56

Anthems

"Let All the World in Every Corner Sing" (2 Sam, Pss)
David T. Childs; Kjos 6321
Two-part with organ

"Blest Are They" (Mark)
David Haas; GIA Publications G-2958
SAB with keyboard, opt. C Instruments

Other Suggestions

NOTE: This would be a good day to celebrate music ministry!
Visuals:
    O   Ark of covenant, man dancing (video "David")
    P   Earth/sea/river, bowl/water/towel, hand, heart, gates
    E   Adoption papers, last will and testament, rejoicing
    G   Feasting, dancing, dinner platter
Prayer: UM69, C9 (2 Sam, Eph) or 713 (Mark)
Scripture Response: P302, UM261, VU352, W636, refrain. "Lord of
    the Dance" (2 Sam)
Scripture Response: E293, N712, P364, UM712 (PD), stanza 1. "I
    Sing a Song of the Saints of God" (Mark)
Benediction: M87. "Let the Peace of God Reign" (Eph)
Alternate Lessons: Amos 7:7-15; Ps 85:8-13 (*See page 3.*)

2 Samuel 7:1-14a

[1] Now when the king was settled in his house, and the LORD had given him rest from all his enemies around him, [2] the king said to the prophet Nathan, "See now, I am living in a house of cedar, but the ark of God stays in a tent." [3] Nathan said to the king, "Go, do all that you have in mind; for the LORD is with you."

[4] But that same night the word of the LORD came to Nathan: [5] Go and tell my servant David: Thus says the LORD: Are you the one to build me a house to live in? [6] I have not lived in a house since the day I brought up the people of Israel from Egypt to this day, but I have been moving about in a tent and a tabernacle. [7] Wherever I have moved about among all the people of Israel, did I ever speak a word with any of the tribal leaders of Israel, whom I commanded to shepherd my people Israel, saying, "Why have you not built me a house of cedar?" [8] Now therefore thus you shall say to my servant David: Thus says the LORD of hosts: I took you from the pasture, from following the sheep to be prince over my people Israel; [9] and I have been with you wherever you went, and have cut off all your enemies from before you; and I will make for you a great name, like the name of the great ones of the earth. [10] And I will appoint a place for my people Israel and will plant them, so that they may live in their own place, and be disturbed no more; and evildoers shall afflict them no more, as formerly, [11] from the time that I appointed judges over my people Israel; and I will give you rest from all your enemies. Moreover the LORD declares to you that the LORD will make you a house. [12] When your days are fulfilled and you lie down with your ancestors, I will raise up your offspring after you, who shall come forth from your body, and I will establish his kingdom. [13] He shall build a house for my name, and I will establish the throne of his kingdom forever. [14] I will be a father to him, and he shall be a son to me.

Psalm 89:20-37

[20] "I have found my servant David; with my holy oil I have anointed him; [21] my hand shall always remain with him; my arm also shall strengthen him. [22] The enemy shall not outwit him, the wicked shall not humble him. [23] I will crush his foes before him and strike down those who hate him. [24] My faithfulness and steadfast love shall be with him; and in my name his horn shall be exalted. [25] I will set his hand on the sea and his right hand on the rivers. [26] He shall cry to me, 'You are my Father, my God, and the Rock of my salvation!' [27] I will make him the firstborn, the highest of the kings of the earth. [28] Forever I will keep my steadfast love for him, and my covenant with him will stand firm. [29] I will establish his line forever, and his throne as long as the heavens endure. [30] If his children forsake my law and do not walk according to my ordinances, [31] if they violate my statutes and do not keep my commandments, [32] then I will punish their transgression with the rod and their iniquity with scourges; [33] but I will not remove from him my steadfast love, or be false to my faithfulness. [34] I will not violate my covenant, or alter the word that went forth from my lips. [35] Once and for all I have sworn by my holiness; I will not lie to David. [36] His line shall continue forever, and his throne endure before me like the sun. [37] It shall be established forever like the moon, an enduring witness in the skies."

Ephesians 2:11-22

[11] So then, remember that at one time you Gentiles by birth, called "the uncircumcision" by those who are called "the circumcision"—a physical circumcision made in the flesh by human hands— [12] remember that you were at that time without Christ, being aliens from the commonwealth of Israel, and strangers to the covenants of promise, having no hope and without God in the world. [13] But now in Christ Jesus you who once were far off have been brought near by the blood of Christ. [14] For he is our peace; in his flesh he has made both groups into one and has broken down the dividing wall, that is, the hostility between us. [15] He has abolished the law with its commandments and ordinances, that he might create in himself one new humanity in place of the two, thus making peace, [16] and might reconcile both groups to God in one body through the cross, thus putting to death that hostility through it. [17] So he came and proclaimed peace to you who were far off and peace to those who were near; [18] for through him both of us have access in one Spirit to the Father. [19] So then you are no longer strangers and aliens, but you are citizens with the saints and also members of the household of God, [20] built upon the foundation of the apostles and prophets, with Christ Jesus himself as the cornerstone. [21] In him the whole structure is joined together and grows into a holy temple in the Lord; [22] in whom you also are built together spiritually into a dwelling place for God.

Mark 6:30-34, 53-56

[30] The apostles gathered around Jesus, and told him all that they had done and taught. [31] He said to them, "Come away to a deserted place all by yourselves and rest a while." For many were coming and going, and they had no leisure even to eat. [32] And they went away in the boat to a deserted place by themselves. [33] Now many saw them going and recognized them, and they hurried there on foot from all the towns and arrived ahead of them. [34] As he went ashore, he saw a great crowd; and he had compassion for them, because they were like sheep without a shepherd; and he began to teach them many things. . . .

[53] When they had crossed over, they came to land at Gennesaret and moored the boat. [54] When they got out of the boat, people at once recognized him, [55] and rushed about that whole region and began to bring the sick on mats to wherever they heard he was. [56] And wherever he went, into villages or cities or farms, they laid the sick in the marketplaces, and begged him that they might touch even the fringe of his cloak; and all who touched it were healed.

Primary Hymns and Songs for the Day

"The God of Abraham Praise" (2 Sam) (O)
    B34, C24, E401, EL831, F332, L544, N24, P488, R51,
    UM116 (PD), VU255, W537
        H-3   Hbl-62, 95; Chr-59; Org-77
        S-1   #211. Harmonization

"I Love Thy Kingdom, Lord" (2 Sam, Eph)
    B354, C274, E524, F545, L368, N312, P441, UM540 (PD)
        H-3   Hbl-16; Chr-106, 167; Desc-97; Org-147
        S-1   #311. Descant and harmonization

"The Church's One Foundation" (Eph) (C)
    B350, C272, E525, EL654, F547, L369, N386, P442, UM545
    (PD) and UM 546, VU332 (Fr.)
        H-3   Hbl-94; Chr-180; Desc-16; Org-9
        S-1   #25-26. Descant and harmonization

Additional Hymn Suggestions

"Lead On, O King Eternal" (2 Sam)
    B621, C632, E555, EL805 F595, L495, N573, P447/P448,
    R298, UM580

"How Like a Gentle Spirit" (2 Sam, Eph)
    C69, N443, UM115

"Lord, Speak to Me" (2 Sam, Pss)
    B568, EL676, F625, L403, N531, P426, UM463 (PD), VU589

"How Firm a Foundation" (Pss, Eph)
    B338, C618, E636, EL796, F32, L507, N407, P361, UM529
    (PD), VU660, W585

"Christ Is Made the Sure Foundation" (Eph) (O) or (C)
    B356 (PD), C275, E518, EL645, F557, L367, N400,
    P416/P417, UM559 (PD), VU325, W617

"Christ Is the World's Light" (Eph)
    UM188, W543

"It Is Well with My Soul" (Eph)
    B410, C561, EL785, F495, L346, N438, UM377

"Here, O Lord, Your Servants Gather" (Eph)
    B179, C278, EL530, N72, P465, UM552, VU362 (Fr.)

"Come and Find the Quiet Center" (Eph)
    C575, S2128, SF2128, VU374

"When Cain Killed Abel" (Eph)
    S2135, SF2135

"Just a Closer Walk with Thee" (Eph)
    B448, C557, EL697, F591, S2158, SF2158

"Together We Serve" (Eph)
    S2175, SF2175

"For One Great Peace" (Eph)
    S2185, SF2185

"You Are Mine" (Eph)
    EL581, S2218, SF2218

"We Are God's People" (Eph)
    B383, F546, S2220, SF2220

"Sacred the Body" (Eph)
    S2228, SF2228

"Hope of the World" (Eph, Mark)
    C538, E472, L493, N46, P360, UM178, VU215, W565

"Rise, Shine, You People" (Mark)
    EL665, L393, UM187

"Lord of the Dance" (Mark)
    P302, UM261, VU352, W636

"When Jesus the Healer Passed Through Galilee" (Mark)
    UM263, VU358

"Near to the Heart of God" (Mark)
    B295, C581, F35, P527, UM472 (PD)

"Dear Lord and Father of Mankind" (Mark) (O) or (C)
    (Alternate Text "Parent of Us All")
    B267, C594, E652/E653, F422, L506, N502, P345, UM358
    (PD), VU608

Additional Contemporary Suggestions

"Oh, I Know the Lord's Laid His Hands on Me" (2 Sam)
    S2139, SF2139

"I Will Call Upon the Lord" (Pss)
    R15, S2002, SF2002, SP224

"On Eagle's Wings" (Pss)
    B71, C77, EL787, N775, R112, UM143, VU807/VU808, S-2
    #143. Stanzas for soloist

"Jesus, Draw Me Close" (Eph)
    M48, S2159, SF2159

"Bind Us Together" (Eph)
    R292, S2226, SF2226, SP140

"Sanctuary" (Eph)
    M52, R185, S2164, SF2164

"Cornerstone" (Eph)
    SP177

"Firm Foundation" (Eph)
    M9

"People Need the Lord" (Mark)
    B557, S2244, SF2244

"There Is None Like You" (Mark)
    M104

Vocal Solos

"How Firm a Foundation" (Eph)
V-6   p. 31

"Just a Closer Walk with Thee" (Eph)
V-8   p. 323

Anthems

"The Church's One Foundation" (Eph)
arr. Craig Courtney; Beckenhorst BP1353
SATB with keyboard

"Loving Shepherd of Thy Sheep" (Mark)
John Rutter; Hinshaw HMC1192
SATB *a cappella*

Other Suggestions

Visuals:
    O   Cedar, churches under construction
    P   Rock, star of David, oil, genealogical chart, father/son
    E   Walls crumbling, family, Christian unity, cornerstone
    G   Resting, boat, sheep, healing, cloak with fringe
Call to Worship: S2057, SF2057, SP49, R10. "Be Still and Know
    That I Am God" (Eph)
Alternate Lessons: Jer 23:1-6; Ps 23 (*See page 3.*)

2 Samuel 11:1-15

[1] In the spring of the year, the time when kings go out to battle, David sent Joab with his officers and all Israel with him; they ravaged the Ammonites, and besieged Rabbah. But David remained at Jerusalem.

[2] It happened, late one afternoon, when David rose from his couch and was walking about on the roof of the king's house, that he saw from the roof a woman bathing; the woman was very beautiful. [3] David sent someone to inquire about the woman. It was reported, "This is Bathsheba daughter of Eliam, the wife of Uriah the Hittite." [4] So David sent messengers to get her, and she came to him, and he lay with her. (Now she was purifying herself after her period.) Then she returned to her house. [5] The woman conceived; and she sent and told David, "I am pregnant."

[6] So David sent word to Joab, "Send me Uriah the Hittite." And Joab sent Uriah to David. [7] When Uriah came to him, David asked how Joab and the people fared, and how the war was going. [8] Then David said to Uriah, "Go down to your house, and wash your feet." Uriah went out of the king's house, and there followed him a present from the king. [9] But Uriah slept at the entrance of the king's house with all the servants of his lord, and did not go down to his house. [10] When they told David, "Uriah did not go down to his house," David said to Uriah, "You have just come from a journey. Why did you not go down to your house?" [11] Uriah said to David, "The ark and Israel and Judah remain in booths; and my lord Joab and the servants of my lord are camping in the open field; shall I then go to my house, to eat and to drink, and to lie with my wife? As you live, and as your soul lives, I will not do such a thing." [12] Then David said to Uriah, "Remain here today also, and tomorrow I will send you back." So Uriah remained in Jerusalem that day. On the next day, [13] David invited him to eat and drink in his presence and made him drunk; and in the evening he went out to lie on his couch with the servants of his lord, but he did not go down to his house.

[14] In the morning David wrote a letter to Joab, and sent it by the hand of Uriah. [15] In the letter he wrote, "Set Uriah in the forefront of the hardest fighting, and then draw back from him, so that he may be struck down and die."

Psalm 14

[1] Fools say in their hearts, "There is no God." They are corrupt, they do abominable deeds; there is no one who does good. [2] The LORD looks down from heaven on humankind to see if there are any who are wise, who seek after God. [3] They have all gone astray, they are all alike perverse; there is no one who does good, no, not one. [4] Have they no knowledge, all the evildoers who eat up my people as they eat bread, and do not call upon the LORD? [5] There they shall be in great terror, for God is with the company of the righteous. [6] You would confound the plans of the poor, but the LORD is their refuge. [7] O that deliverance for Israel would come from Zion! When the LORD restores the fortunes of his people, Jacob will rejoice; Israel will be glad.

Ephesians 3:14-21

[14] For this reason I bow my knees before the Father, [15] from whom every family in heaven and on earth takes its name. [16] I pray that, according to the riches of his glory, he may grant that you may be strengthened in your inner being with power through his Spirit, [17] and that Christ may dwell in your hearts through faith, as you are being rooted and grounded in love. [18] I pray that you may have the power to comprehend, with all the saints, what is the breadth and length and height and depth, [19] and to know the love of Christ that surpasses knowledge, so that you may be filled with all the fullness of God.

[20] Now to him who by the power at work within us is able to accomplish abundantly far more than all we can ask or imagine, [21] to him be glory in the church and in Christ Jesus to all generations, forever and ever. Amen.

John 6:1-21

[1] After this Jesus went to the other side of the Sea of Galilee, also called the Sea of Tiberias. [2] A large crowd kept following him, because they saw the signs that he was doing for the sick. [3] Jesus went up the mountain and sat down there with his disciples. [4] Now the Passover, the festival of the Jews, was near. [5] When he looked up and saw a large crowd coming toward him, Jesus said to Philip, "Where are we to buy bread for these people to eat?" [6] He said this to test him, for he himself knew what he was going to do. [7] Philip answered him, "Six months' wages would not buy enough bread for each of them to get a little." [8] One of his disciples, Andrew, Simon Peter's brother, said to him, [9] "There is a boy here who has five barley loaves and two fish. But what are they among so many people?" [10] Jesus said, "Make the people sit down." Now there was a great deal of grass in the place; so they sat down, about five thousand in all. [11] Then Jesus took the loaves, and when he had given thanks, he distributed them to those who were seated; so also the fish, as much as they wanted. [12] When they were satisfied, he told his disciples, "Gather up the fragments left over, so that nothing may be lost." [13] So they gathered them up, and from the fragments of the five barley loaves, left by those who had eaten, they filled twelve baskets. [14] When the people saw the sign that he had done, they began to say, "This is indeed the prophet who is to come into the world."

[15] When Jesus realized that they were about to come and take him by force to make him king, he withdrew again to the mountain by himself.

[16] When evening came, his disciples went down to the sea, [17] got into a boat, and started across the sea to Capernaum. It was now dark, and Jesus had not yet come to them. [18] The sea became rough because a strong wind was blowing. [19] When they had rowed about three or four miles, they saw Jesus walking on the sea and coming near the boat, and they were terrified. [20] But he said to them, "It is I; do not be afraid." [21] Then they wanted to take him into the boat, and immediately the boat reached the land toward which they were going.

Primary Hymns and Songs for the Day

"Now Thank We All Our God" (John) (O)
B638, C715, E396 or 397, EL839 or 840, F525, L533 or L534,
N419, P555, UM102 (PD), VU236 (Fr.), W560
H-3   Hbl-78; Chr-140; Desc-81; Org-98
S-1   #252-254. Various treatments

"Jesus, the Very Thought of Thee" (Eph)
B225, C102, E642, EL754, F465, L316, N507, P310, UM175 (PD)
H-3   Hbl-52; Chr-90; Desc-92; Org-131
S-1   #291-292. Descant and harmonization

"Jesus Loves Me" (Eph)
B344 (PD), C113, EL595 (PD), F226, N327, P304, UM191,
VU365
H-3   Chr-117

"Break Thou the Bread of Life" (John, Communion) (C)
B263, C321, EL515, F30, L235, N321, P329, UM599 (PD),
VU501
H-3   Chr-44; Org-15

Additional Hymn Suggestions

"We Utter Our Cry" (2 Sam)
B631, UM439
"What Does the Lord Require" (2 Sam)
C659, E605, P405, UM441, W624
"To God Be the Glory" (Eph)
B153, C39, F365, N14, R68, UM99; V-8 p. 5 Vocal Solo
"O Love, How Deep" (Eph)
E448/E449, EL322, L88, N209, P83, UM267 (PD), VU348
"Pues si vivimos" ("When We Are Living") (Eph)
C536, EL639, N499, P400, UM356, VU581
"Where Cross the Crowded Ways of Life" (John)
C665, E609, EL719, F665, L429, N543, P408, UM427 (PD),
VU681
"My Hope Is Built" (John)
B406, C537, EL596, F92, L293/L294, N368, P379, UM368 (PD)
"Jesus, Lover of My Soul" (John)
B180, C542, E699, F222, N546, P303, UM479 (PD), VU669
"Jesus, Savior, Pilot Me" (John)
EL755, L334, N441, UM509 (PD), VU637
"How Firm a Foundation" (John)
B338, C618, E636, EL796, F32, L507, N407, P361, UM529
(PD), VU660, W585
"Jesus, Priceless Treasure" (John)
E701, EL775, F277, L457, N480, P365, UM532 (PD), VU667,
and VU668 (Fr.)
"Be Still, My Soul" (John)
C566, F77, N488, UM534, VU652
"Deck Thyself, My Soul, with Gladness" (John, Communion)
E339, EL488/EL489, L224, P506, UM612 (PD), VU463
"I Come with Joy" (John, Communion)
B371, C420, E304, EL482, P607, R195, UM617, W726
"You Satisfy the Hungry Heart" (John, Communion)
C429, EL484, P521, UM629, R217, VU478, W736
"O Food to Pilgrims Given" (John, Communion)
E308/E309, L222, UM631
"Blessed Quietness" (John)
F145, C267, N284, S2142, SF2142
"Come Away with Me" (John)
S2202, SF2202

"You Are Mine" (John)
EL581, S2218, SF2218
"O Spirit of the Living God" (Eph) (C)
N263, UM539

Additional Contemporary Suggestions

"If It Had Not Been for the Lord" (Pss)
S2053, SF2053
"Spirit Song" (Eph)
C352, R248, SP134, UM347
"Celebrate Love" (Eph)
S2073, SF2073
"Lord, Be Glorified" (Eph)
B457, EL744, S2150, SF2150, R172, SP196
"Be Glorified" (Eph)
M13
"No Greater Love" (Eph)
M25
"I Could Sing of Your Love Forever" (Eph)
M63; V-3 p. 22 Vocal Solo
"He Is Able" (Eph, John)
M37
"In Christ Alone" (John)
M138
"Amen, Amen" (John)
N161, P299, S2072
"Eat This Bread" (John)
C414, EL472, N788, R228, UM628, VU466, W734

Vocal Solos

"Wondrous Love" (Eph)
V-6   p. 47
"Give Me Jesus" (Eph)
V-8   p. 256

Anthems

"Panis Angelicus" (John)
Eric William Barnum; Pavane HL 08301799
SATB *a cappella*

"Lonely the Boat" (John)
arr. William Rose; Abingdon Press 06874995199
SATB with piano

Other Suggestions

Visuals:
O   Bath towel, sword
P   Broken bread, fear, rescue, rejoicing
E   Kneeling in prayer, globe, flags, missions, love
G   Dried fish, 5 loaves, 12 baskets, boat, storm, Jesus walking
Call to Worship: EL406, S2118, SF2118, W473. "Holy Spirit, Come to Us" (Pss)
Scripture Response: C659, E605, P405, UM441, W624, stanza 2. "What Does the Lord Require?" (2 Sam)
Alternate Lessons: 2 Kgs 4:42-44; Ps 145:10-18 (*See page 3.*)

2 Samuel 11:26–12:13a

[26] When the wife of Uriah heard that her husband was dead, she made lamentation for him. [27] When the mourning was over, David sent and brought her to his house, and she became his wife, and bore him a son.

But the thing that David had done displeased the LORD, [1] and the LORD sent Nathan to David. He came to him, and said to him, "There were two men in a certain city, the one rich and the other poor. [2] The rich man had very many flocks and herds; [3] but the poor man had nothing but one little ewe lamb, which he had bought. He brought it up, and it grew up with him and with his children; it used to eat of his meager fare, and drink from his cup, and lie in his bosom, and it was like a daughter to him. [4] Now there came a traveler to the rich man, and he was loath to take one of his own flock or herd to prepare for the wayfarer who had come to him, but he took the poor man's lamb, and prepared that for the guest who had come to him." [5] Then David's anger was greatly kindled against the man. He said to Nathan, "As the LORD lives, the man who has done this deserves to die; [6] he shall restore the lamb fourfold, because he did this thing, and because he had no pity."

[7] Nathan said to David, "You are the man! Thus says the LORD, the God of Israel: I anointed you king over Israel, and I rescued you from the hand of Saul; [8] I gave you your master's house, and your master's wives into your bosom, and gave you the house of Israel and of Judah; and if that had been too little, I would have added as much more. [9] Why have you despised the word of the LORD, to do what is evil in his sight? You have struck down Uriah the Hittite with the sword, and have taken his wife to be your wife, and have killed him with the sword of the Ammonites. [10] Now therefore the sword shall never depart from your house, for you have despised me, and have taken the wife of Uriah the Hittite to be your wife. [11] Thus says the LORD: I will raise up trouble against you from within your own house; and I will take your wives before your eyes, and give them to your neighbor, and he shall lie with your wives in the sight of this very sun. [12] For you did it secretly; but I will do this thing before all Israel, and before the sun." [13a] David said to Nathan, "I have sinned against the LORD."

Psalm 51:1-12

[1] Have mercy on me, O God, according to your steadfast love; according to your abundant mercy blot out my transgressions. [2] Wash me thoroughly from my iniquity, and cleanse me from my sin. [3] For I know my transgressions, and my sin is ever before me. [4] Against you, you alone, have I sinned, and done what is evil in your sight, so that you are justified in your sentence and blameless when you pass judgment. [5] Indeed, I was born guilty, a sinner when my mother conceived me. [6] You desire truth in the inward being; therefore teach me wisdom in my secret heart. [7] Purge me with hyssop, and I shall be clean; wash me, and I shall be whiter than snow. [8] Let me hear joy and gladness; let the bones that you have crushed rejoice. [9] Hide your face from my sins, and blot out all my iniquities. [10] Create in me a clean heart, O God, and put a new and right spirit within me. [11] Do not cast me away from your presence, and do not take your holy spirit from me. [12] Restore to me the joy of your salvation, and sustain in me a willing spirit.

Ephesians 4:1-16

[1] I therefore, the prisoner in the Lord, beg you to lead a life worthy of the calling to which you have been called, [2] with all humility and gentleness, with patience, bearing with one another in love, [3] making every effort to maintain the unity of the Spirit in the bond of peace. [4] There is one body and one Spirit, just as you were called to the one hope of your calling, [5] one Lord, one faith, one baptism, [6] one God and Father of all, who is above all and through all and in all.

[7] But each of us was given grace according to the measure of Christ's gift. [8] Therefore it is said, "When he ascended on high he made captivity itself a captive; he gave gifts to his people." [9] (When it says, "He ascended," what does it mean but that he had also descended into the lower parts of the earth? [10] He who descended is the same one who ascended far above all the heavens, so that he might fill all things.) [11] The gifts he gave were that some would be apostles, some prophets, some evangelists, some pastors and teachers, [12] to equip the saints for the work of ministry, for building up the body of Christ, [13] until all of us come to the unity of the faith and of the knowledge of the Son of God, to maturity, to the measure of the full stature of Christ. [14] We must no longer be children, tossed to and fro and blown about by every wind of doctrine, by people's trickery, by their craftiness in deceitful scheming. [15] But speaking the truth in love, we must grow up in every way into him who is the head, into Christ, [16] from whom the whole body, joined and knit together by every ligament with which it is equipped, as each part is working properly, promotes the body's growth in building itself up in love.

John 6:24-35

[24] So when the crowd saw that neither Jesus nor his disciples were there, they themselves got into the boats and went to Capernaum looking for Jesus.

[25] When they found him on the other side of the sea, they said to him, "Rabbi, when did you come here?" [26] Jesus answered them, "Very truly, I tell you, you are looking for me, not because you saw signs, but because you ate your fill of the loaves. [27] Do not work for the food that perishes, but for the food that endures for eternal life, which the Son of Man will give you. For it is on him that God the Father has set his seal." [28] Then they said to him, "What must we do to perform the works of God?" [29] Jesus answered them, "This is the work of God, that you believe in him whom he has sent." [30] So they said to him, "What sign are you going to give us then, so that we may see it and believe you? What work are you performing? [31] Our ancestors ate the manna in the wilderness; as it is written, 'He gave them bread from heaven to eat.' "

[32] Then Jesus said to them, "Very truly, I tell you, it was not Moses who gave you the bread from heaven, but it is my Father who gives you the true bread from heaven. [33] For the bread of God is that which comes down from heaven and gives life to the world." [34] They said to him, "Sir, give us this bread always."

[35] Jesus said to them, "I am the bread of life. Whoever comes to me will never be hungry, and whoever believes in me will never be thirsty."

Primary Hymns and Songs for the Day
"The Church's One Foundation" (Eph) (O)
    B350, C272, E525, EL654, F547, L369, N386, P442, UM545
    (PD) and UM 546, VU332 (Fr.)
    H-3   Hbl-94; Chr-180; Desc-16; Org-9
    S-1   #25-26. Descant and harmonization
"Depth of Mercy" (2 Sam, Pss)
    B306, UM355
    H-3   Chr-63, 100
    S-1   #53. Descant
"Eat This Bread" (John, Communion)
    C414, EL472, N788, R228, UM628, VU466, W734
"You Satisfy the Hungry Heart" (John)
    C429, EL484, P521, UM629, R217, VU478, W736
    S-1   #144. Four-part setting of refrain
"Fill My Cup, Lord" (John, Communion) (C)
    C351, F481, UM641
    S-2   #62. Stanzas for soloist

Additional Hymn Suggestions
"Make Me a Captive, Lord" (2 Sam) (O)
    B278, P378, UM421
"We Utter Our Cry" (2 Sam)
    B631, UM439
"What Does the Lord Require" (2 Sam)
    C659, E605, P405, UM441, W624
"Just as I Am, Without One Plea" (2 Sam, Pss)
    B303/B307, C339, E693, EL592, F417, L296, N207, P370, R140,
    UM357 (PD), VU508
"O For a Heart to Praise My God" (Pss)
    F357, UM417 (PD), W591
"God Hath Spoken by the Prophets" (Eph)
    L238, UM108, W516
"Awake, O Sleeper" (Eph)
    E547, EL452, UM551, VU566, W586
"Forward Through the Ages" (Eph)
    N355, UM555 (PD)
"How Shall They Hear the Word of God" (Eph)
    UM649, W629
"I Sing a Song of the Saints of God" (Eph)
    E293, N712, P364, UM712 (PD)
"Together We Serve" (Eph)
    S2175, SF2175
"We Are God's People" (Eph)
    B383, F546, S2220, SF2220
"We Are One in Christ Jesus" (Eph)
    C493, EL643, S2229, SF2229
"Praise and Thanksgiving Be to God" (Eph, Baptism)
    EL458, L191, UM604, VU441
"One Bread, One Body" (Eph, Communion)
    C393, EL496, UM620, VU467
"Come, Share the Lord" (Eph, Communion)
    C408, S2269, SF2269, VU469
"Guide Me, O Thou Great Jehovah" (John)
    B56, C622, E690, EL618, F608, L343, N18/N19, P281, UM127
    (PD), VU651 (Fr.)
"Bread of the World" (John, Communion)
    C387, E301, N346, P502, UM624, VU461
"O Food to Pilgrims Given" (John, Communion)
    E308/E309, L222, UM631

"Gather Us In" (John, Communion)
    C284, EL532, S2236, SF2236, W665

Additional Contemporary Suggestions
"Change My Heart, O God" (2 Sam, Pss)
    EL801, R143, SP195, S2152, SF2152
"Give Me a Clean Heart" (2 Sam, Pss)
    C515, N188, S2133, SF2133
"The Power of Your Love" (Pss)
    M26
"Purify My Heart" (Pss)
    R187, M90
"Above All" (Eph)
    M77; V-3 p. 17 Vocal Solo
"Forever" (Eph)
    M68
"Make Us One" (Eph)
    S2224, SF2224, SP137
"They'll Know We Are Christians" (Eph)
    C494, S2223, SF2223
"Bind Us Together" (Eph)
    R292, S2226, SF2226, SP140
"Halle, Halle, Halleluja" (John)
    C41, EL172, N236, R139, S2026, SF2026, VU958
"Jesus, Name Above All Names" (John)
    R26, S2071, SF2071, SP76
"Holy and Anointed One" (John)
    M32
"You Who Are Thirsty" (John, Communion)
    S2132, SF2132, SP219

Vocal Solos
"A Contrite Heart" (Pss)
V-4   p. 10
"Life Indeed" (John, Communion)
V-8   p. 271

Anthems
"Kyrie" (2 Sam)
Mark Burrows; Abingdon Press 0687330394
SATB with piano

"O Sacrum Convivium" (Luke)
James Biery; Morningstar MSM60-8311
SATB *a cappella*

Other Suggestions
Visuals:
    O   Lamb, sword
    P   Water, hyssop, snow, rejoicing, heart, baptism
    E   Unity, no. 1, baptism, gifts, building, Christ, ministry,
         binding
    G   Boat, seal, bread, feeding, pitcher, flowing water
Call to Prayer: EL538, S2157, SF2157, W561. "Come and Fill Our
    Hearts" (Pss)
Prayer: UM353, UM366, UM456, or UM535 (2 Sam, Pss)
Prayer: C98. "Our Union with Christ" (John)
Alternate Lessons: Exod 16:2-4, 9-15; Ps 78:23-29 (*See page 3.*)

2 Samuel 18:5-9, 15, 31-33

[5] The king ordered Joab and Abishai and Ittai, saying, "Deal gently for my sake with the young man Absalom." And all the people heard when the king gave orders to all the commanders concerning Absalom.

[6] So the army went out into the field against Israel; and the battle was fought in the forest of Ephraim. [7] The men of Israel were defeated there by the servants of David, and the slaughter there was great on that day, twenty thousand men. [8] The battle spread over the face of all the country; and the forest claimed more victims that day than the sword.

[9] Absalom happened to meet the servants of David. Absalom was riding on his mule, and the mule went under the thick branches of a great oak. His head caught fast in the oak, and he was left hanging between heaven and earth, while the mule that was under him went on. . . .

[15] And ten young men, Joab's armor-bearers, surrounded Absalom and struck him, and killed him. . . .

[31] Then the Cushite came; and the Cushite said, "Good tidings for my lord the king! For the LORD has vindicated you this day, delivering you from the power of all who rose up against you." [32] The king said to the Cushite, "Is it well with the young man Absalom?" The Cushite answered, "May the enemies of my lord the king, and all who rise up to do you harm, be like that young man."

[33] The king was deeply moved, and went up to the chamber over the gate, and wept; and as he went, he said, "O my son Absalom, my son, my son Absalom! Would I had died instead of you, O Absalom, my son, my son!"

Psalm 130

[1] Out of the depths I cry to you, O LORD. [2] Lord, hear my voice! Let your ears be attentive to the voice of my supplications! [3] If you, O LORD, should mark iniquities, Lord, who could stand? [4] But there is forgiveness with you, so that you may be revered. [5] I wait for the LORD, my soul waits, and in his word I hope; [6] my soul waits for the Lord more than those who watch for the morning, more than those who watch for the morning. [7] O Israel, hope in the LORD! For with the LORD there is steadfast love, and with him is great power to redeem. [8] It is he who will redeem Israel from all its iniquities.

Ephesians 4:25–5:2

[25] So then, putting away falsehood, let all of us speak the truth to our neighbors, for we are members of one another. [26] Be angry but do not sin; do not let the sun go down on your anger, [27] and do not make room for the devil. [28] Thieves must give up stealing; rather let them labor and work honestly with their own hands, so as to have something to share with the needy. [29] Let no evil talk come out of your mouths, but only what is useful for building up, as there is need, so that your words may give grace to those who hear. [30] And do not grieve the Holy Spirit of God, with which you were marked with a seal for the day of redemption. [31] Put away from you all bitterness and wrath and anger and wrangling and slander, together with all malice, [32] and be kind to one another, tender-hearted, forgiving one another, as God in Christ has forgiven you.

[1] Therefore be imitators of God, as beloved children, [2] and live in love, as Christ loved us and gave himself up for us, a fragrant offering and sacrifice to God.

John 6:35, 41-51

[35] Jesus said to them, "I am the bread of life. Whoever comes to me will never be hungry, and whoever believes in me will never be thirsty." . . .

[41] Then the Jews began to complain about him because he said, "I am the bread that came down from heaven." [42] They were saying, "Is not this Jesus, the son of Joseph, whose father and mother we know? How can he now say, 'I have come down from heaven'?" [43] Jesus answered them, "Do not complain among yourselves. [44] No one can come to me unless drawn by the Father who sent me; and I will raise that person up on the last day. [45] It is written in the prophets, 'And they shall all be taught by God.' Everyone who has heard and learned from the Father comes to me. [46] Not that anyone has seen the Father except the one who is from God; he has seen the Father. [47] Very truly, I tell you, whoever believes has eternal life. [48] I am the bread of life. [49] Your ancestors ate the manna in the wilderness, and they died. [50] This is the bread that comes down from heaven, so that one may eat of it and not die. [51] I am the living bread that came down from heaven. Whoever eats of this bread will live forever; and the bread that I will give for the life of the world is my flesh."

Primary Hymns and Songs for the Day

"Hope of the World" (Eph, John) (O)
    E472, L493, P360, VU215, W565
        H-3   Chr-100
        S-1   #343. Descant
        S-2   #189. Introduction
    C538, UM178
        H-3   Chr-100
        S-1   #343. Descant
        S-2   #189. Introduction
    N46
"The Lord's My Shepherd, I'll Not Want" (2 Sam)
    C79, EL778, F40/F42, L451, N479, P170, UM136, VU748
        H-3   Chr-75, 188
"Life-Giving Bread" (John, Communion)
    S2261, SF2261
"Precious Lord, Take My Hand" (2 Sam, Pss) (C)
    B456, C628, EL773, F611, N472, P404, UM474, VU670
        H-3   Chr-164; Org-116

Additional Hymn Suggestions

"Out of the Depths I Cry to You" (2 Sam, Pss)
    EL600, L295, N483, P240, UM515
"Be Still, My Soul" (2 Sam, Pss)
    C566, F77, N488, UM534, VU652
"Abide with Me" (2 Sam, Pss)
    B63, C636, E662, EL629, F500, L272, N99, P543, UM700 (PD),
    VU436
"Out of the Depths" (2 Sam, Pss)
    C510, N554, S2136, SF2136, VU611
"Take My Life, and Let It Be" (Eph)
    B277/B283, C609, E707, EL583/EL685, L406, P391, R133,
    N448, UM399 (PD), VU506
"O Master, Let Me Walk with Thee" (Eph)
    B279, C602, E659/E660, EL818, F442, L492, N503, P357,
    UM430 (PD), VU560
"Let There Be Peace on Earth" (Eph)
    C677, F681, UM431
"This Is the Spirit's Entry Now" (Eph)
    EL448, L195, UM608, VU451, W722
"Woke Up This Morning" (Eph)
    C623, N85, S2082, SF2082
"Healer of Our Every Ill" (Eph)
    C506, EL612, S2213, SF2213, VU619
"Guide Me, O Thou Great Jehovah" (John)
    B56, C622, E690, EL618, F608, L343, N18/N19, P281, UM127
    (PD), VU651 (Fr.)
"The Lily of the Valley" (John)
    B189, S2062, SF2062
"Bread of the World" (John, Communion)
    C387, E301, N346, P502, UM624, VU461
"You Satisfy the Hungry Heart" (John, Communion)
    C429, EL484, P521, UM629, R217, VU478, W736
"Become to Us the Living Bread" (John, Communion)
    C423, P500, UM630
"O Food to Pilgrims Given" (John, Communion)
    E308/E309, L222, UM631
"The Bread of Life for All Is Broken" (John, Communion)
    E342, N333, UM633

"You Who Are Thirsty" (John, Communion)
    S2132, SF2132, SP219
"Gather Us In" (John, Communion)
    C284, EL532, S2236, SF2236, W665

Additional Contemporary Suggestions

"Hungry" ("Falling on My Knees") (Pss, John)
    M155
"Holy, Holy" (Eph)
    B254, F149, P140, R206, S2039, SP141
"O How He Loves You and Me!" (Eph)
    B146, F622, R27, S2108, SF2108, SP113
"I've Got Peace Like a River" (Eph)
    B418, C530, N478, P368, S2145, VU577
"To Know You More" (Eph)
    S2161, SF2161
"In the Secret" ("I Want to Know You") (Eph)
    M38; V-3 p. 36 Vocal Solo
"Halle, Halle, Halleluja" (John)
    C41, EL172, N236, R139, S2026, SF2026, VU958
"Father, I Adore You" (John)
    B256, F414, S2038, SF2038, SP194
"Jesus, Name Above All Names" (John)
    R26, S2071, SF2071, SP76
"Light of the World" (John)
    S2204
"Eat This Bread" (John, Communion)
    C414, EL472, N788, R228, UM628, VU466, W734
"Take Our Bread" (John, Communion)
    C413, UM640
"Fill My Cup, Lord" (John, Communion)
    C351, F481, UM641

Vocal Solos

"Out of the Depths I Cry to Thee" (Pss)
V-9   p. 16
"Christ Living Within You" (Eph)
V-8   p. 177

Anthems

"Let the Peace of Christ Rule in Your Hearts" (Eph)
Craig Courtney; Brookfield Press 08744177
SATB with keyboard

"Bread of the World in Mercy Broken" (John)
Robert Edward Smith; GIA Publications G-3916
SATB *a cappella*

Other Suggestions

Visuals:
    O   Tree limb, man weeping
    P   Waiting for dawn, forgiveness, praying hands, weeping
    E   Setting sun, children, offering, portrait of Christ
    G   Bread, love feast, Communion, anointing with oil
Prayer: UM461 or UM656 (2 Sam)
Prayer: C468, UM481. "The Prayer of Saint Francis" (Eph)
Alternate Lessons: 1 Kgs 10:4-8; Ps 34:1-8 (*See page 3.*)

1 Kings 2:10-12; 3:3-14

[10] Then David slept with his ancestors, and was buried in the city of David. [11] The time that David reigned over Israel was forty years; he reigned seven years in Hebron, and thirty-three years in Jerusalem. [12] So Solomon sat on the throne of his father David; and his kingdom was firmly established. . . .

[3] Solomon loved the LORD, walking in the statutes of his father David; only, he sacrificed and offered incense at the high places. [4] The king went to Gibeon to sacrifice there, for that was the principal high place; Solomon used to offer a thousand burnt offerings on that altar. [5] At Gibeon the LORD appeared to Solomon in a dream by night; and God said, "Ask what I should give you." [6] And Solomon said, "You have shown great and steadfast love to your servant my father David, because he walked before you in faithfulness, in righteousness, and in uprightness of heart toward you; and you have kept for him this great and steadfast love, and have given him a son to sit on his throne today. [7] And now, O LORD my God, you have made your servant king in place of my father David, although I am only a little child; I do not know how to go out or come in. [8] And your servant is in the midst of the people whom you have chosen, a great people, so numerous they cannot be numbered or counted. [9] Give your servant therefore an understanding mind to govern your people, able to discern between good and evil; for who can govern this your great people?"

[10] It pleased the Lord that Solomon had asked this. [11] God said to him, "Because you have asked this, and have not asked for yourself long life or riches, or for the life of your enemies, but have asked for yourself understanding to discern what is right, [12] I now do according to your word. Indeed I give you a wise and discerning mind; no one like you has been before you and no one like you shall arise after you. [13] I give you also what you have not asked, both riches and honor all your life; no other king shall compare with you. [14] If you will walk in my ways, keeping my statutes and my commandments, as your father David walked, then I will lengthen your life."

Psalm 111

[1] Praise the LORD! I will give thanks to the LORD with my whole heart, in the company of the upright, in the congregation. [2] Great are the works of the LORD, studied by all who delight in them. [3] Full of honor and majesty is his work, and his righteousness endures forever. [4] He has gained renown by his wonderful deeds; the LORD is gracious and merciful. [5] He provides food for those who fear him; he is ever mindful of his covenant. [6] He has shown his people the power of his works, in giving them the heritage of the nations. [7] The works of his hands are faithful and just; all his precepts are trustworthy. [8] They are established forever and ever, to be performed with faithfulness and uprightness. [9] He sent redemption to his people; he has commanded his covenant forever. Holy and awesome is his name. [10] The fear of the LORD is the beginning of wisdom; all those who practice it have a good understanding. His praise endures forever.

Ephesians 5:15-20

[15] Be careful then how you live, not as unwise people but as wise, [16] making the most of the time, because the days are evil. [17] So do not be foolish, but understand what the will of the Lord is. [18] Do not get drunk with wine, for that is debauchery; but be filled with the Spirit, [19] as you sing psalms and hymns and spiritual songs among yourselves, singing and making melody to the Lord in your hearts, [20] giving thanks to God the Father at all times and for everything in the name of our Lord Jesus Christ.

John 6:51-58

[51] "I am the living bread that came down from heaven. Whoever eats of this bread will live forever; and the bread that I will give for the life of the world is my flesh."

[52] The Jews then disputed among themselves, saying, "How can this man give us his flesh to eat?" [53] So Jesus said to them, "Very truly, I tell you, unless you eat the flesh of the Son of Man and drink his blood, you have no life in you. [54] Those who eat my flesh and drink my blood have eternal life, and I will raise them up on the last day; [55] for my flesh is true food and my blood is true drink. [56] Those who eat my flesh and drink my blood abide in me, and I in them. [57] Just as the living Father sent me, and I live because of the Father, so whoever eats me will live because of me. [58] This is the bread that came down from heaven, not like that which your ancestors ate, and they died. But the one who eats this bread will live forever."

Primary Hymns and Songs for the Day

"I'll Praise My Maker While I've Breath" (Pss, Eph) (O)
    B35, C20, E429 (PD), P253, UM60, VU867
        H-3   Chr-109; Org-105
        S-2   #141. Harmonization

"Spirit of God, Descend Upon My Heart" (Eph)
    B245, C265, EL800, F147, L486, N290, P326, UM500 (PD),
    VU378
        H-3   Chr-175; Desc-77; Org-94
        S-2   #125-128. Various treatments

"In Remembrance of Me" (John, Communion)
    B365, C403, S2254

"Bread of the World" (John, Communion) (C)
    C387, E301, N346, P502, UM624, VU461

Additional Hymn Suggestions

"Close to Thee" (1 Kgs)
    B464, F405, UM407 (PD)

"Dear Lord, Lead Me Day by Day" (1 Kgs)
    B459, UM411, VU568

"What Does the Lord Require" (1 Kgs)
    C659, E605, P405, UM441, W624

"Be Thou My Vision" (1 Kgs)
    B60, C595, E488, EL793, F468, N451, P339, R151, UM451,
    VU642

"Great Is Thy Faithfulness" (1 Kgs, Pss) (O)
    B54, C86, EL733, F98, N423, P276, R249, UM140, VU288

"O Master, Let Me Walk with Thee" (1 Kgs, Pss)
    B279, C602, E659/E660, EL818, F442, L492, N503, P357,
    UM430 (PD), VU560

"O Worship the King" (Pss, Eph)
    B16, C17, E388, EL842 (PD), F336, L548, N26, P476, UM73
    (PD), VU235

"Praise the Source of Faith and Learning" (Pss, Eph)
    N411, S2004, SF2004

"O Holy Spirit, Root of Life" (Pss, Eph)
    C251, EL399, N57, S2121, SF2121, VU379

"In the Lord I'll Be Ever Thankful" (Pss, Eph)
    S2195, SF2195

"When We Are Called to Sing Your Praise" (Eph)
    S2216, SF2216

"In the Singing" (Eph, Communion)
    EL466, S2255, SF2255

"When in Our Music God Is Glorified" (Eph)
    B435, C7, E420, EL850/EL851, L555, N561, P264, R62, UM68,
    VU533, W549

"Take Time to Be Holy" (Eph)
    B446, C572, F457, UM395 (PD), VU672

"Filled with the Spirit's Power" (Eph)
    L160, N266, UM537, VU194

"O Spirit of the Living God" (Eph)
    N263, UM539

"Come, My Way, My Truth, My Life" (John)
    E487, EL816, L513, N331, UM164 (PD), VU628, W569

"God the Sculptor of the Mountains" (John)
    EL736, S2060, SF2060

"The Lily of the Valley" (John)
    B189, S2062, SF2062

"Become to Us the Living Bread" (John, Communion)
    C423, P500, UM630

"O Food to Pilgrims Given" (John, Communion)
    E308/E309, L222, UM631

Additional Contemporary Suggestions

"There Is None Like You" (1 Kgs)
    M104

"How Great Are You, Lord" (Pss)
    M103

"Thank You, Lord" (Pss)
    C531, UM84

"Ah, Lord God" (Pss)
    R254, SP2

"Great Is the Lord Almighty!" (Pss)
    SP58

"Great Are You, Lord" (Pss)
    R69, SP102

"Awesome God" (Pss)
    R245, S2040, SF2040, SP11

"Great Is the Lord" (Pss)
    B12, R22, S2022, SF2022, SP30

"Give Thanks" (Eph)
    C528, R266, S2036, SF2036, SP170

"Someone Asked the Question" (Eph)
    N523, S2144

"Shine, Jesus, Shine" (Eph)
    B579, EL671, R247, S2173, SF2173, SP142

"Father, I Adore You" (John)
    B256, F414, S2038, SF2038, SP194

"Enough" (John)
    M160

"Here Is Bread, Here Is Wine" (John, Communion)
    EL483, S2266, SF2266

Vocal Solos

"Be Thou My Vision" (1 Kgs)
V-6   p. 13

"Thanks to God" (Pss)
V-8   p. 296

Anthems

"Sing for Joy" (Eph)
Allen Pote; Choristers Guild CGA161
SATB with piano, opt. instruments

"The Bread That I Will Give" (John)
James Biery; GIA Publications G-5935
SATB *a cappella*

Other Suggestions

Visuals:
    O   Crown, scepter, royal robe, people of wisdom
    P   Images of creation, feasting, heart, humble praise
    E   Singing, instruments, hymnal, worship/revelry
    G   Communion broken bread, chalice, crucifix
Reading: C219. "Christ Present in Worship" (John)
Prayers: C698 and UM586 (1 Kgs, Eph)
Response: C531, UM84. "Thank You, Lord" (Pss)
Alternate Lessons: Prov 9:1-6; Ps 34:9-14 (*See page 3.*)

1 Kings 8:(1, 6, 10-11) 22-30, 41-43

[1] Then Solomon assembled the elders of Israel and all the heads of the tribes, the leaders of the ancestral houses of the Israelites, before King Solomon in Jerusalem, to bring up the ark of the covenant of the LORD out of the city of David, which is Zion. . . .

[6] Then the priests brought the ark of the covenant of the LORD to its place, in the inner sanctuary of the house, in the most holy place, underneath the wings of the cherubim.

[10] And when the priests came out of the holy place, a cloud filled the house of the LORD, [11] so that the priests could not stand to minister because of the cloud; for the glory of the LORD filled the house of the LORD. . . .

[22] Then Solomon stood before the altar of the LORD in the presence of all the assembly of Israel, and spread out his hands to heaven. [23] He said, "O LORD, God of Israel, there is no God like you in heaven above or on earth beneath, keeping covenant and steadfast love for your servants who walk before you with all their heart, [24] the covenant that you kept for your servant my father David as you declared to him; you promised with your mouth and have this day fulfilled with your hand. [25] Therefore, O LORD, God of Israel, keep for your servant my father David that which you promised him, saying, 'There shall never fail you a successor before me to sit on the throne of Israel, if only your children look to their way, to walk before me as you have walked before me.' [26] Therefore, O God of Israel, let your word be confirmed, which you promised to your servant my father David.

[27] "But will God indeed dwell on the earth? Even heaven and the highest heaven cannot contain you, much less this house that I have built! [28] Regard your servant's prayer and his plea, O LORD my God, heeding the cry and the prayer that your servant prays to you today; [29] that your eyes may be open night and day toward this house, the place of which you said, 'My name shall be there,' that you may heed the prayer that your servant prays toward this place. [30] Hear the plea of your servant and of your people Israel when they pray toward this place; O hear in heaven your dwelling place; heed and forgive. . . .

[41] "Likewise when a foreigner, who is not of your people Israel, comes from a distant land because of your name [42]—for they shall hear of your great name, your mighty hand, and your outstretched arm—when a foreigner comes and prays toward this house, [43] then hear in heaven your dwelling place, and do according to all that the foreigner calls to you, so that all the peoples of the earth may know your name and fear you, as do your people Israel, and so that they may know that your name has been invoked on this house that I have built."

Psalm 84

[1] How lovely is your dwelling place, O LORD of hosts!
[2] My soul longs, indeed it faints for the courts of the LORD; my heart and my flesh sing for joy to the living God. [3] Even the sparrow finds a home, and the swallow a nest for herself, where she may lay her young, at your altars, O LORD of hosts, my King and my God. [4] Happy are those who live in your house, ever singing your praise. [5] Happy are those whose strength is in you, in whose heart are the highways to Zion. [6] As they go through the valley of Baca they make it a place of springs; the early rain also covers it with pools. [7] They go from strength to strength; the God of gods will be seen in Zion. [8] O LORD God of hosts, hear my prayer; give ear, O God of Jacob! [9] Behold our shield, O God; look on the face of your anointed. [10] For a day in your courts is better than a thousand elsewhere. I would rather be a doorkeeper in the house of my God than live in the tents of wickedness. [11] For the LORD God is a sun and shield; he bestows favor and honor. No good thing does the LORD withhold from those who walk uprightly. [12] O LORD of hosts, happy is everyone who trusts in you.

Ephesians 6:10-20

[10] Finally, be strong in the Lord and in the strength of his power. [11] Put on the whole armor of God, so that you may be able to stand against the wiles of the devil. [12] For our struggle is not against enemies of blood and flesh, but against the rulers, against the authorities, against the cosmic powers of this present darkness, against the spiritual forces of evil in the heavenly places. [13] Therefore take up the whole armor of God, so that you may be able to withstand on that evil day, and having done everything, to stand firm. [14] Stand therefore, and fasten the belt of truth around your waist, and put on the breastplate of righteousness. [15] As shoes for your feet put on whatever will make you ready to proclaim the gospel of peace. [16] With all of these, take the shield of faith, with which you will be able to quench all the flaming arrows of the evil one. [17] Take the helmet of salvation, and the sword of the Spirit, which is the word of God.

[18] Pray in the Spirit at all times in every prayer and supplication. To that end keep alert and always persevere in supplication for all the saints. [19] Pray also for me, so that when I speak, a message may be given to me to make known with boldness the mystery of the gospel, [20] for which I am an ambassador in chains. Pray that I may declare it boldly, as I must speak.

John 6:56-69

[56] "Those who eat my flesh and drink my blood abide in me, and I in them. [57] Just as the living Father sent me, and I live because of the Father, so whoever eats me will live because of me. [58] This is the bread that came down from heaven, not like that which your ancestors ate, and they died. But the one who eats this bread will live forever." [59] He said these things while he was teaching in the synagogue at Capernaum.

[60] When many of his disciples heard it, they said, "This teaching is difficult; who can accept it?" [61] But Jesus, being aware that his disciples were complaining about it, said to them, "Does this offend you? [62] Then what if you were to see the Son of Man ascending to where he was before? [63] It is the spirit that gives life; the flesh is useless. The words that I have spoken to you are spirit and life. [64] But among you there are some who do not believe." For Jesus knew from the first who were the ones that did not believe, and who was the one that would betray him. [65] And he said, "For this reason I have told you that no one can come to me unless it is granted by the Father."

[66] Because of this many of his disciples turned back and no longer went about with him. [67] So Jesus asked the twelve, "Do you also wish to go away?" [68] Simon Peter answered him, "Lord, to whom can we go? You have the words of eternal life. [69] We have come to believe and know that you are the Holy One of God."

Primary Hymns and Songs for the Day

"Stand Up, Stand Up for Jesus" (Eph) (O)
B485/B487, C613, E561, F616, L389, UM514 (PD)
H-3   Chr-177; Org-177
S-2   #192-94. Various treatments

"How Lovely, Lord, How Lovely" (Pss)
C285, P207, S2042, VU801
H-3   Hbl-70; Chr-103, 174; Desc-76; Org-90

"Wonderful Words of Life" (John)
B261, C323, F29, N319, UM600 (PD)
H-3   Chr-221; Org-186

"Hope of the World" (Eph, John) (C)
E472, L493, P360, VU215, W565
H-3   Chr-100
S-1   #343. Descant
S-2   #189. Introduction
C538, UM178
H-3   Chr-100
S-1   #343. Descant
S-2   #189. Introduction
N46

Additional Hymn Suggestions

"Let All the World in Every Corner Sing" (1 Kgs)
B28, E402, P468, UM93, W536

"O God in Heaven" (1 Kgs)
EL748, N279, UM119

"Standing on the Promises" (Eph)
B335, C552, F69, UM374 (PD)

"O God of Every Nation" (Eph)
C680, E607, EL713, L416, P289, UM435, VU677, W650

"Onward, Christian Soldiers" (Eph)
B493, E562, F617, L509, UM575 (PD)

"Lead On, O King Eternal" (Eph) (O)
B621, C632, E555, EL805 F595, L495, N573, P447/P448, R298, UM580

"Come Away with Me" (Eph)
S2202, SF2202

"Soldiers of Christ, Arise" (Eph)
E548, UM513

"Go Forth for God" (Eph) (C)
E347, R291, UM670, VU418

"Blessed Assurance" (John)
B334, C543, EL638, F67, N473, P341, UM369 (PD), VU337

"'Tis so Sweet to Trust in Jesus" (John)
B411, F91, UM462 (PD)

"Blessed Jesus, at Thy Word" (John)
E440, EL520, N74, P454, R93, UM596 (PD), VU500

"O Word of God Incarnate" (John)
C322, E632, EL514, L231, N315, P327, R97, UM598 (PD), VU499

"Become to Us the Living Bread" (John, Communion)
C423, P500, UM630

"In Remembrance of Me" (John, Communion)
B365, C403, S2254

"Broken for Me" (John, Communion)
S2263, SF2263

"Time Now to Gather" (John, Communion)
S2265, SF2265

Additional Contemporary Suggestions

"Holy Ground" (1 Kgs)
B224, C112, S2272, SF2272, SP86

"Awesome in this Place" (1 Kgs)
M36

"As the Deer" (Pss)
R9, S2025, SF2025, SP200, VU766

"Better Is One Day" (Pss)
M60

"Breathe" (Pss, John)
M61, V-3 p. 42 Vocal Solo

"You Are My All in All" (Pss, Eph)
SP220

"The Battle Belongs to the Lord" (Eph)
R244, SP158

"You Are My Hiding Place" (Eph)
C554, S2055, SF2055

"We Want to See Jesus Lifted High" (Eph)
M67

"Shout to the North" (Eph)
M99

"Father, I Adore You" (John)
B256, F414, S2038, SF2038, SP194

"Jesus, Lover of My Soul" (John)
M72

"Enough" (John)
M160

"Eat This Bread" (John, Communion)
C414, EL472, N788, R228, UM628, VU466, W734

Vocal Solos

"Lord, Listen to Your Children" (1 Kgs, Eph)
V-8   p. 168

"Ivory Palaces" (Pss)
V-8   p. 136

"Joy" (Pss)
V-3   p. 94

Anthems

"How Lovely" (Pss)
Mark Burrows; Abingdon 068704427X
SATB with piano

"Give Me Jesus" (John)
Arr. Jonathan Rodgers; Walton HL 08501655
SATB *a cappella*

Other Suggestions

Visuals:
O   Praying hands, temple (church), hand, outstretched arm
P   Churches, sparrows/nest, rain, water pooling, door
E   Armor, praying hands, people in prayer
G   Bread/wine/Communion, line drawn, question mark

Prayer: C524, UM423. "The Restless Heart" (Pss)

Response: C305, S2193, SF2193, VU400. "Lord, Listen to Your Children Praying" (Pss, Eph)

Scripture Response: B261, C323, F29, N319, UM600 (PD), stanza 1. "Wonderful Words of Life" (John)

Alternate Lessons: Josh 24:1-2a, 14-18; Ps 34:15-22 (*See page 3.*)

INDEX OF SCRIPTURES REFERENCED

WORSHIP PLANNING SHEET 1

Date: _____ Color: _____

Preacher: _____

Liturgist: _____

Selected Scripture: _____

Selected Hymns	No.	Placement

Psalter #_____

Keyboard Selections

Title	Composer	Placement

Anthems

Title	Choir	Composer	Placement

Vocal Solos

Title	Singer	Composer	Placement

Other Ideas:

Acolytes: _____

Head Usher: _____

Altar Guild Contact: _____

Other Participants:

_____

_____

WORSHIP PLANNING SHEET 1

WORSHIP PLANNING SHEET 2

Date: _____ Sunday: _____ Color: _____

Preacher: _____

Liturgist: _____

Opening Voluntary   Composer

_____

Hymn   Tune Name   No.

_____

Opening Prayer: _____

Prayer for Illumination: _____

First Lesson: _____

Psalter: _____

Second Lesson: _____

Gospel Lesson: _____

Hymn   Tune Name   No.

_____

Response to the Word: _____

Prayers of the People: _____

Offertory   Composer

_____

Communion Setting: _____

Communion Hymns   Tune Name   No.

_____

_____

_____

Closing Hymn   Tune Name   No.

_____

Benediction: _____

Closing Voluntary   Composer

_____

CONTEMPORARY WORSHIP PLANNING SHEET

Because of the diversity in orders of worship, you will want to adjust this planning sheet to meet the needs of your worship planning team. A common order used would consist of three to four opening praise choruses and lively hymns, a time of informal prayers of the congregation along with songs of prayer, reading of the primary scripture for the day, a drama or video to illustrate the day's theme, a message from the preacher, a testimony on the theme for the day (if a drama or video was not presented earlier), followed by closing songs appropriate to the mood of the service and the message. Any offering would usually be taken early in the service, and Holy Communion would normally take place following the message. Special music (solos, duets, instrumental music) can be used wherever it best expresses the theme of the service.

Date: _____ Sunday: _____

Thematic Emphasis or Topic: _____

Color: _____ Visual Focus: _____

Opening Songs:

_____

_____

Prayer Songs:

_____

Scripture Selection(s):

_____

Drama or Video: _____

Message Title: _____

Testimony: _____

Special Music:

_____

Closing Songs:

_____

Preacher: _____ Music Leader: _____

Worship Facilitator: _____ Prayer Leader: _____

NOTES

NOTES

NOTES

NOTES